Zarathustra's Secret

Zarathustra's Secret

THE INTERIOR LIFE OF
FRIEDRICH NIETZSCHE

Joachim Köhler

TRANSLATED BY RONALD TAYLOR

Yale University Press
New Haven and London

For information about this and other Yale University Press publications, please contact:
U.S. Office: sales.press@yale.edu   yalebooks.com
Europe Office: sales@yaleup.co.uk   www.yaleup.co.uk

Set in Adobe Garamond by Fakenham Photosetting, Norfolk
Printed in Great Britain by St Edmundsbury Press

ISBN 0–300–09278–4

Library of Congress Control Number: 2002101100

A catalogue record for this book is available from the British Library.

10   9   8   7   6   5   4   3   2   1

Contents

Illustrations

Foreword to the English Edition

Fourteen years ago, at the time I was writing the original German version of *Zarathustra's Secret* (*Zarathustras Geheimnis*), there was no secret to unravel. For almost a century scholars had devoted their attention to Nietzsche with ever-growing intensity. Everything to be known about him was believed to be known. His philosophy seemed to have been explained, and biographies had already been written – not a difficult task, since he had been an indefatigable autobiographer and letter-writer since childhood, recording every thought that occurred to him and everything that befell him. Or almost everything.

In addition to the huge amount of material contained in his works themselves there was the information assiduously compiled by his sister, Elisabeth Förster-Nietzsche, after his death. Thanks to the wealth of impressions and reminiscences she amassed, more became known about Nietzsche's life than about that of any other philosopher. Not only his world-shattering ideas but also the heroic nature of his reclusive life, as Elisabeth described it, became a revolutionary moment in the history of European culture.

But alas, it soon emerged that the sister-cum-scribe was a far from reliable witness. In her efforts to portray her brother as a paradigm of ascetic genius, she forged letters, destroyed documents and decked out the blind spots in his life with the products of her imagination. When, during her own lifetime, her fraudulent activities came to light, a de-mythologisation of the official Nietzsche image set in, and the icon she had created – which resembled not so much a human being as the larger-than-life marble bust of him that she had erected in the Nietzsche Archive – faded away. In its place came 'Nietzsche the timorous eagle', as a popular biography dubbed him – an anaemic, pallid intellectual, whose sickness made him shun human society, drove him to seek lonely solace in Mediterranean climes and finally led to his confinement in a mental institution.

Nietzsche's philosophy stood in stark contrast to the pitiable nature of his life, a philosophy which, from the very beginning, preached values that one seeks in vain to find in his life. He extolled the life-force that he called the 'Will to Power', and idolised the heroes and gods of Greek antiquity, captivated by their beauty and their cruelty. He was driven not by feelings of common humanity but by the will to overcome all things human, if necessary by force. A new ideal confronted him – the ideal of the *Übermensch*, the Superman, a throbbing creature of health and pulsating *joie de vivre*, a creature for whom he yearned as the lover yearns for his distant beloved.

Nietzsche's passion for this masculine idol became the core of his thought. Classical Greece, with its ideal of bravery in battle, its worship of physical beauty and the mysteries of its cult of sexuality, became the model for his own life. As this contradicted everything that had hitherto been understood by the term philosophy, there developed a specific science of Nietzsche interpretation. His works required elucidation, and whole generations of academics set about interpreting and reinterpreting them. There have been thousands of attempts to make his works intelligible and libraries are filled with all manner of studies that set out to explain the meaning of his message.

But rather than supplementing earlier works, each new study claimed to take the place of its predecessors. Each fresh reading spelt the death of all previous explanations. Successive ages brought a succession of new images. The Wilhelmine Nietzsche publicised by Elisabeth was followed by Nietzsche the philosopher of life, and the Nietzsche of the First World War gave way to Nietzsche the National Socialist. There followed Nietzsche the existentialist, Nietzsche the humanist, then Nietzsche the structuralist and Nietzsche the postmodernist. The French Nietzsche had little in common with the German Nietzsche, and both would have found it difficult to recognise the Italian Nietzsche. That these accounts could not all have been true at one and the same time was a problem that did not seem to occur to anyone. After all, had not Nietzsche himself said that there was no such thing as truth but merely constantly shifting perspectives and interpretations?

At the same time he also said that every philosophy was only the expression of the life that had brought it into being. Concealed behind the intellectual contexts of an age are biological and biographical contexts. What might appear to be a logical sequence of thought processes turns out in reality to be a set of subconscious urges and instincts. It is not the mind that philosophises but the body, above all its secret sexuality, especially if that sexuality is denied its natural outlet. Thus every philosophy expresses precisely what its author represses – his unconscious motives, his secret desires and vices. In a word, his real self. Our task is simply to remove his mask.

Throughout his life Nietzsche maintained that he himself always wore a mask – different disguises for different occasions. He called himself 'The Great Incognito', a man in whom sinister forces were lurking in the background and who hid himself from the prying eyes of others. He constantly claimed that he had a secret that distinguished him from other men – a mystery to which he only referred in cryptic allusions. Writers agreed that what he had in mind was probably the mysterious god Dionysus and the principle of the Eternal Recurrence.

But this still left the question: what lay behind the mask of Dionysus and the nebulous theory of the Eternal Recurrence? Strangely enough, scholars persisted in maintaining that we were confronting an issue to be dealt with in strict philosophical terms. No attempt was made to apply to Nietzsche himself his postulate that every philosophy concealed within itself the philosopher's own subconscious urges and concerns. Freud, who left no famous figure unanalysed, seemed to give him and his visions a wide berth. No psychologist appears to have noticed that he suffered from nightmares throughout his life, and no one said a word about his sexuality.

So there remained a dichotomy in the making of the modern image of Nietzsche: on the one hand there was the exposition of his philosophy, with all its contradictions; on the other the pursuit of biographical research, with its blind spots. Because the two fields were so far apart, it did not occur to anyone to bring them together. But maybe, buried in his works, there were hints to be found of what had really happened to him during those months when he lived the life of a hermit, cutting himself off from an inquisitive public. What had he suffered from? What desires had he had? Could his real life provide the key to the understanding of his enigmatic philosophy? Time and again he had said that Zarathustra nursed a secret. But the question of what the secret was remained unanswered.

This was the background against which I wrote this book – the first attempt to understand Nietzsche's life and philosophy as a single unity, as he himself had constantly demanded. My story begins, not with the official documentary evidence of his life and career but with the sketches and dreams of his childhood, which had hitherto been ignored. In 1977, in my doctoral thesis, I offered a first interpretation of the many hundred pages of early poems and autobiographical fragments that had survived. In the course of my studies I discovered that all the essential elements of his thoughts and emotions were already present here *in nuce*. Zarathustra was born not in the mountain peaks of Switzerland but in a village parsonage in Saxony. Thanks to the publication of the critical edition of Nietzsche's collected works and letters, which was almost complete by the 1980s, I was able to reconstruct the course of his life in a way not found in the current biographies.

From my reconstruction of this hidden life, there then emerged a radically different picture of his philosophy. A new Nietzsche emerged, causing scholars to rub their eyes in disbelief. Could it be possible after all that Nietzsche had been a human being, a man with a highly active subconscious, as well as unspeakable anxieties and no less inexpressible desires? Not a sexless intellectual with a walrus moustache but a creature of flesh and blood, seething with hidden torments and passionate yearnings? Might he even have secretly cherished a great love? Was he in fact a poet who could only dedicate his immortal odes to the objects of his desires in cryptic form?

In a review of my book in 1989 one critic wrote that there was an unbridgeable gap between *Zarathustra's Secret* and all other books on Nietzsche. Since that time the gap has closed to a certain extent, as biographers have begun to pay greater attention to his childhood and have discovered a succession of new relationships between his life and his works. Nietzsche the man began to emerge, a man with a subconscious. Zarathustra's secret, however, has remained a taboo subject to this day.

Nevertheless the original edition of *Zarathustra's Secret* has been reprinted a number of times and translated into five languages. I am particularly gratified that the English edition is now published, as was my *Nietzsche and Wagner* (1998), by the Yale University Press, since I carried out my early research in the early 1970s at Stanford University and the State University of New York at Stony Brook.

For this English edition I have omitted the second part of the German original, which consisted of a detailed interpretation of *Thus Spake Zarathustra*. The reader who has followed the birth of Nietzsche's philosophy from the spirit of his nightmares and yearnings as related in the first part of the book no longer has any need of this interpretation. Anyone who has glimpsed the hidden depths of Nietzsche's personality will be in a position to grasp his philosophy without my help. That is the sole object of the exercise.

As with my *Nietzsche and Wagner* I am deeply grateful to Ronald Taylor, my translator, and to Robert Baldock, of Yale University Press, without whom this English edition would not have seen the light of day.

Joachim Köhler
Hamburg, Spring 2002

Preface

In an address to the Ansbach Platen Society, Thomas Mann said of the aristocratic nineteenth-century poet August von Platen-Hallermünde: 'It is our great good fortune that advances made over recent years in our knowledge of humankind have enabled us to speak without inhibition about many subjects at the mention of which earlier generations felt obliged to turn away in embarrassment.' The subject in question was Platen's 'homoerotic predisposition', which Mann not only defended against what he called 'ignorance and a no longer appropriate sense of decorum' but even held up as 'a vital reality essential to the poet's very existence'.[1] As late as 1930 it still took the command of a Thomas Mann to break the taboo on the subject of homosexuality, although Platen himself had made no effort to conceal it.

And to show that homosexuality was at the time not merely an embarrassing topic but a characteristic that could be at the centre of a writer's whole life, Mann added a quotation from Friedrich Nietzsche: 'The nature and the intensity of one's sexuality reach to the innermost recesses of one's intellectual being' – though Mann gives no hint as to why it should be Nietzsche, in particular, whom he put forward as an authority on the subject.[2]

Nietzsche's actual words were slightly different. He talks not of 'innermost recesses' of the mind but of the 'heart' of one's being, and treats 'the nature and intensity of a person's sexuality' as a singular, not, like Mann, as a plural. For Nietzsche is talking of his own sexuality, the nature and intensity of which are inextricably linked.[3]

Thomas Mann was not the first to have the courage to draw a parallel between Nietzsche and Platen, romantic troubadour of homosexual love. Nietzsche's one-time friend and fellow-Wagnerian Erwin Rohde, like himself a classical scholar, whom he set among the ranks of the gods in 1889 and with whom he lived in Leipzig, saw his works as related to Platen's through being 'outbursts of a passionate mind ultimately incapable of achieving what it most urgently desired'.[4] This was not the only harsh judgement that Rohde passed on his former fellow-student but it was certainly the most forthright, especially as it was expressed to another mutual friend in confidence. Rohde was well aware of the secret that Nietzsche nurtured, the man who could not, dared not, do what he 'most urgently desired' and lived out his fate in his writings.

ne of Nietzsche's own students was also reminded of Platen. Ludwig von
ffler, who later edited Platen's diaries, had attracted the interest of his
Greek teacher at the University of Basel; Nietzsche invited him to his home,
going so far in his effusiveness as to propose that they go on holiday together
to Italy. 'That insight into Nietzsche's nature', wrote Scheffler in the Vienna
Neue Freie Presse, 'not only gave me an explanation for many of his peculiar-
ities but also helped me to understand his psychological problems. I was
reminded of Platen, being from the outset aware of the similarity in the two
men's personal disposition. In the case of Platen, his memoirs tell all. In the
case of Nietzsche it was his mode of life and my personal experience that
opened my eyes.'[5]

Scheffler's revealing observations did not go unnoticed. When the subject
of Nietzsche cropped up in Sigmund Freud's Wednesday Circle in 1908, one
of those present drew attention to 'the article that had appeared a year or so
earlier in the *Neue Freie Presse*, in which one of Nietzsche's students referred
to his homosexual proclivities'.[6] This was not unfamiliar territory to the
members of the circle, and Freud himself launched into further speculations
on the nature of Nietzsche's sexuality. But nothing more was heard of what
they discussed, and decades passed before Freud referred to the occasion
again, when he wrote to the writer Arnold Zweig to dissuade him from
embarking on a novel about Nietzsche.[7]

In 1917 Wilhelm Stekel, a pupil of Freud, wrote in an article about the
'unconscious homosexual component essential to an understanding of
Nietzsche's love life'.[8] What love life? So little was known about it that people
had concluded that he had none. The various mysterious 'masks of homosexuality' that Stekel identified were ignored. When Günter Schulte took up
the subject in 1982 in the context of Nietzsche's works, it was regarded as little
more than an item of curiosity. 'Nietzsche's philosophy', wrote Schulte,
'showed itself to be that of the repressed femininity of the male.'[9]

Georg Groddeck, physician and psychologist, who, like Nietzsche himself,
had experienced the strict regime of the boarding school of Schulpforta, not
only took over from him the concept of the Id but also came to the important realisation that 'the suppression of the homosexual urge was one of the
foundations of a one-sided, specifically European mode of thought. It was
through Nietzsche also', added Groddeck, 'that I became aware of the consequences of the proscription of male homosexuality in Christian culture.'[10]

Nietzsche overcame this mode of thought and discovered a new world in
the Mediterranean, a world whose discovery made him feel like 'a new
Columbus', uncovering an unknown continent, the body. The old God was
dead. Only the threat of his shadow – Christianity – remained, against which

he had pledged to fight to the death. The name of the new god, the warmth of whose rays he had already begun to feel, was Dionysus, god of liberated sexuality. Time and again, casting himself as the god's disciple, Nietzsche hinted at what stimulated him and filled him with an unquenchable yearning. 'What a strange fate it is', he wrote to his friend, the theologian Franz Overbeck, 'to be forty years old and still carry around in one's head all the most essential things in life, theoretical and practical, as though they were secrets.'[11] Overbeck knew what Nietzsche meant. The word 'secret', combined with 'practical', could mean only one thing. Platen too had once written of a friend that his secret was 'nothing other than that he cannot love a woman but is irresistibly attracted to his own sex'.[12]

Nietzsche was not short of secrets. Posterity turned them into taboos. His syphilis, usually considered to be the product of his encounter with a prostitute in a brothel in Cologne or Leipzig, is equally likely, it is now held, to have been contracted in a male brothel in Genoa. But his sister, followed by an army of worshippers, stubbornly refused to concede the possibility even of a syphilis acquired by 'normal' means.

Then there was the argument about 'purity'. What has philosophy to do with the body? A great deal, replies Nietzsche. A thinker, he once wrote, 'cannot do other than convert his physical condition into the most highly intellectual of forms – this act of transformation *is* philosophy. We philosophers are not at liberty to distinguish between soul and body. We are not thinking frogs.'[13] Nietzsche allowed his body to speak for itself. In his *Thus Spake Zarathustra* he sang of his desires and laid bare his satyr-like personality. 'Brothers,' cries Zarathustra, 'I have stripped myself of my robes. I am not ashamed of my nakedness!'[14] After all, he is the disciple of the God who has no cause to conceal himself but is proud to appear fully unclothed.

As he repeatedly emphasised, Nietzsche favoured this nakedness. Generally he lacked the courage to entrust his orgiastic tendencies to the printed page, but did so in his *Birth of Tragedy*. And when, in 1889, in the wake of his apotheosis, he performed his abandoned Bacchanalian dances for the benefit of Overbeck, his friend recoiled in horror. It is only thanks to the new critical edition of his notes and jottings that we are in a position today to admire the complete Nietzsche in his unfettered reality.

But one must not avert one's gaze from the scene. In a vision of the end of the world, for him a moment of celebration, Nietzsche writes that all those in attendance, good and evil alike, will dance naked as they sip of the cup of knowledge. 'All will rejoice that everything is now clear and visible in its entirety, like a plant in bloom. How joyful I feel! All morality will melt away, all secrets will be revealed.'[15]

The hidden yearning nestling behind Nietzsche's hatred of morality and of secrecy had as its goal the world of handsome, healthy bodies in a reborn antiquity. The motto of this world was: 'Scorn of sex is the cardinal sin against the holy spirit of life.'[16] In Italy he found what he had been looking for. Wandering incognito along the beaches, to be reached only via poste restante, he attached little importance to being seen as the philosopher he was. 'You ask whether I am a philosopher', he wrote to an admirer. 'What does it matter?'[17] He felt flattered when people mistook him for an officer. 'I rely on two weapons', he continued in the same letter, '– sabre and cannon. And perhaps on a third . . .' Nietzsche, the satyr, had no cause to reveal his weakness, let alone fear other people's opinions. 'I love to listen to the roar of a bad reputation', says Zarathustra.[18]

And what has this to do with philosophy? A great deal, according to Nietzsche. 'Every great philosophy', he wrote, 'is the confession of its founder, a kind of secret and involuntary set of personal memoirs.'[19] Only what a man experiences and suffers can be transformed into philosophy. 'Write with your blood', commands Zarathustra.[20] But this is a demand that Nietzsche's followers, right down to the present day, cannot accept. They want to see him as a man on a plane above that of the human, all too human as expressed in his alleged ideal of the 'blond beast', and as conveyed to his contemporaries by his sister Elisabeth. It was she who thought up the plaster bust with its walrus moustache as his trademark. 'It is my aim and my duty', she wrote, filled with the conviction of her global mission, 'to engrave the shining personality of Nietzsche on every heart.'[21] This was the language people liked to hear – a definition, crystal clear, of individuality, of a noble human being as the architect of his own fate. In a word: Nietzsche's Superman.

To achieve this, much evidence had to be destroyed, forged, re-written – and suppressed. In the course of an argument with an ardent Nietzschean Elisabeth once allowed herself to be provoked into hinting at what was at stake. No one could conceive of the love she felt for her brother, she said. 'I smile to myself when I think how easily I could rob people of their illusions.'[22] Nietzsche's friend and amanuensis Heinrich Köselitz, alias Peter Gast, who had his own insights into the situation, branded the domineering Elisabeth a 'dragon' and accused her of 'merely setting out to cause people pain and worry'.[23]

The philosopher Martin Heidegger was another taken in by the image of the incorporeal thinker who expressed the essence of things as he received it directly from the realm of Being itself. Heidegger was under no illusion that sheltering this brilliant philosophical mind was a fragile human body.

'Nietzsche himself was responsible for making himself into an ambivalent character,' wrote Heidegger, 'and in the context of both his own and the present time, he had no alternative. It is our task' – he was addressing students who would shortly be embarking on their military service – ' to see beyond this ambivalence and grasp the unique, definitive and eternally valid truths that we find there.' These are words that might have come from the mouth of Nietzsche's Superman. 'What we must do', Heidegger concludes, 'is turn away from Nietzsche the man and Nietzsche the author, inasmuch as these are fields that lie within a context of human dimensions.'[24]

But even without adopting Heidegger's premises, we can hardly avoid doing just that. Today Nietzsche's so-called 'philosophy', long the private playground of academics, seems abstruse, impenetrable, open to misinterpretation. Concepts such as human breeding, 'Superman' and 'Will to Power' have fallen into disrepute, while the notion of the 'Eternal Recurrence' survives only in doctoral theses. However much effort one devotes to the task, *Thus Spake Zarathustra* remains impenetrable. Scholars have sacrificed its image as a poem and as a pseudo-gospel in order at least to preserve what is left, frantically keeping it alive by all manner of intellectual stratagems.

The Italian editors of the new complete edition of Nietzsche's works, Giorgio Colli and Mazzino Montinari, also found their work a sobering experience. Montinari came to the conclusion that 'Nietzsche is neither poetic genius, philosopher, "moralist" or psychologist. Nietzsche is a sickness, an unsolved problem.'[25] Montinari spent the rest of his life trying to find a solution to the problem. He was struck by the paucity of ideas in Nietzsche's works, going so far as to maintain that there was a gradual dissipation of genuine content as his life progressed. Montinari died with his work unfinished.

Giorgio Colli, Montinari's co-editor, also died before their work was complete. Colli was well aware of the dangers for Nietzsche's philosophy attendant on the publication of all his notes and jottings. 'By laying bare his soul,' he wrote, 'Nietzsche exposes himself to the most vulgar interpretations. It is easy to indulge in confidences with a man who always keeps his front door open.' Colli, who favoured keeping the front door shut, did, however, credit Nietzsche with the 'clear historical vision' that enabled him to see the summit of antiquity in 'the communal ecstasy and mystical experience of Eleusis'. This was why, said Colli, he avoided making public his prescience of the Eternal Recurrence. This intuition referred to sexuality – 'Nietzsche would hardly have had in mind the rotation of crops or the cyclical rhythm of nature.'[26]

Nietzsche's intuitive philosophy cannot be understood apart from his profoundest experience of sexuality. Without this his concepts remain bizarre and empty shells, and *Zarathustra* a book with seven seals. His friends strove in vain to grasp the meaning of his – literally – 'inspired' works and acknowledged with embarrassment the copies that he sent them. They knew him all too well – a person less suitable to be an idol or a leader of men would be hard to imagine.

Erwin Rohde wrote in 1895 that his philosophy was 'nothing other than a brilliant exercise in self-presentation and self-revelation. I utterly deny that anyone can make anything of his writings except Nietzsche himself.' Rohde concedes that these writings are highly remarkable but also totally sterile. He then betrays his friend by abruptly turning to his own views about the secret that lies at the heart of Nietzsche's works. 'Wherever I look, I find these works deeply disturbing', he writes. 'I find myself confronted by the past and its youthful memories and by the dark shadow that it casts over the present autumn of my unproductive life. Everywhere, to my profound agitation and sorrow, there rises up a cloud of darkness and despair, enveloping all N's moods and utterances.'[27]

Anyone who sets out to solve Zarathustra's secret must follow the course of Nietzsche's life, tread the path that he took and not hold back at moments that might seem to call for discretion, albeit a discretion that has outlived its purpose. His indescribable anxieties and equally unspeakable desires have found a mysterious existence in the figure of his Zarathustra – a prisoner who organises his own escape, conquers a new world and shows others the way into it. Hiding behind the elevated biblical diction lies the reality of the physical experience and behind the mask of the prophet 'Prince Free-as-a-Bird' smiles his 'smile of bliss'.

In the final years of his lucid existence Nietzsche strove to convert the experiences of his tortured body into a cogent doctrine. He failed because liberation cannot be reduced to a system. 'This new soul should have sung, not spoken', he once wrote.[28] His massive attempt to create a rival philosophy to Christianity and Platonism lent an aura of violence to his thought – a cynical initiation into the seizure of power, which its intended audience could not fail to understand.

The initial move to present Nietzsche as the 'pure spirit' of a revived Germanic ideal, at a time when he no longer had control of his mind, came from his sister. During his restless wanderings Elisabeth turned the family home in Naumburg into a propaganda centre promoting anti-Semitism and publicising the Germanic colony in Paraguay which she had founded together with Bernhard Förster, a notorious anti-Semite not unknown to the police. After her brother's mental breakdown Elisabeth set out to make herself the custodian of both his body and his works, totally ignoring the existence of her mother – 'a woman of no character', she called her.

In her so-called 'Nietzsche Archive' in Weimar she displayed to awestruck visitors, like a museum exhibit, the living corpse that was her brother. She could do with him whatever she wanted. And what she wanted was fame. Since the onset of his madness there had been an increasing demand for his books. From having been stored for years in the warehouse, 'like so much ballast', as his publisher put it, 'they became so popular that soon not a single copy was left'.[29] In the room in which he lay, Elisabeth set up a shrine with herself as the high priestess of the new cult. Leaving Nietzsche at the centre of the cult, lying on his bed playing with his dolls, she had herself driven through Weimar 'in a coach and four with a liveried servant mounted on the box, wearing a uniform with a five-pointed crown on the buttons'.[30] She also employed 'a cook, a maidservant, a coachman, a private secretary, two gardeners and sometimes up to four editors'.[31]

Such of his works as were published were those that the age demanded – codes for the conduct of affairs in an all-conquering German Empire, bolstered by aggressive, patriotic slogans with which to counter the influence of effete democratic tendencies. Passages from the works of this uncongenial outsider were cobbled together to create a hymn book for the very petit-bourgeois society that he had contemptuously rejected. When war broke out against France, the arch-enemy – whose culture Nietzsche regarded as far superior to that of the 'German blockheads' – Zarathustra was there. His anti-Christian tirade, read but not understood, which preached the liberation of a repressed sexuality, offered consolation to the men in the trenches. In 1917, 40,000 copies of *Thus Spake Zarathustra* were sold; in the autumn of 1918, the year when the abortive revolution that Elisabeth called 'the revolt of the mob' broke out, 25,000 copies were sold in the space of a mere four weeks.[32] A Nietzsche Prize was founded, the first winner of which was Thomas Mann, for his *Observations of a Non-Political Man*.

Hitler knew he was indebted to Elisabeth Nietzsche and her entourage of rabid nationalists. In 1934 he paid three visits to the 'Nietzsche Archive' in Weimar and declared it to be a 'centre of National-Socialist ideology'.[33] Then he bestowed on Nietzsche what Elisabeth considered the greatest of all honours – a copy of his *Zarathustra* was laid alongside *Mein Kampf* and Rosenberg's *Myth of the Twentieth Century* in the crypt of the Tannenberg monument to Hindenburg, who had granted Elisabeth an annual pension for services to the nation, to be paid to the end of her life.[34]

In the year of Hitler's seizure of power the Nietzsche cult was at its height. The intellectual elite of Europe flocked to Weimar. Even a man such as the Swiss diplomat Carl J. Burckhardt, later a commissioner of the League of Nations and president of the Red Cross, called to take a cup of tea with the

86-year-old Elisabeth, who told him: 'My brother was the herald of the great age in which we are now living.' The 'delicate, yet demonic little creature, with a heart as hard as a diamond', as Burckhardt later wrote, also left no doubt as to who was responsible for her worldwide fame:

'My brother, now living in the realms of the blessed, knows how his poor little sister has fought a lonely battle and suffered for him, and he is helping me ...' This she said with simpering mien, surrounded by a retinue of ladies-in-waiting and archive officials, murmuring softly as they worshipped the vigorous, sharp-witted little pygmy queen from another realm ... On the walls hung giant photographs, suffocating in their clinical brutality, of the paralysed philosopher lying in his living grave, staring unseeingly into the distance. There was also a huge bust of him (five times life-size) standing in the room, with a picture of Hitler in front of it.

In his journey through Germany in 1933 Burckhardt found nothing so lacking in what he called 'any sense of reality. Rarely have I seen in the world a place that exuded such a terrifying mixture of the grandiose and the grotesque, pale decadence and dubious claims to immortality, as in this house in Weimar, which harbours the secret of this powerful, unfathomable, ultimately dangerous thinker, the poisonous influence that emanates from his agony and the preservation of the memory of his philosophy.'[35]

When I was young, I encountered a dangerous divinity, and I would not like to tell any living mortal of the mysterious events, good and bad, which traced a path at that time across the surface of my soul. So I learned at an early age how to hold my peace, as well as that one needs to learn how to talk in order to keep truly silent. A man with backgrounds also has need of foregrounds, whether for others or for himself. And a man has need of foregrounds in order to escape from himself and in order to make it possible for others to live alongside him.

Friedrich Nietzsche

I   *A Plant from the Graveyard*

A LOYAL MINISTER OF THE CROWN

'How can we set about painting a picture of the life and character of a person we have come to know?' pondered the eighteen-year-old Friedrich Nietzsche in September 1863, as he began writing his autobiography *My Life*.[1] Obviously he had come to know himself – but he was in two minds as to how to depict his subject. Probably, he might have thought, in much the same way as one would portray a scene from nature. Nietzsche was not a painter but he was well aware that the most characteristic physical features are not always those that immediately strike one's attention – one must look more closely in order to grasp the 'organic nature' of, say, a landscape. 'It is in the world of plants that we find the most detailed characteristics for a comparative study of nature.' Nietzsche as a plant? But this was indeed the image with which the schoolboy opened his story: 'As a plant I was born close to the graveyard; as a human being I was born in a rectory.'

The seventeenth-century rectory stood in the village of Röcken, on the road between Leipzig and Weissenfels. The approaching traveller saw it as an attractive building surrounded by poplars, elms and willow hedgerows, 'and the only things visible above the treetops from a distance were the chimney-stacks and the medieval church tower'.[2] The spacious house stood beside the church 'in the shadow of three fine spreading acacias' with the churchyard in between, 'full of crosses and fallen gravestones'.[3]

The fifteenth of October 1844, the date of Nietzsche's birth, enjoyed the personal blessing of His Royal Majesty. For on that same day forty-nine years earlier, as though by higher ordinance, fell the birthday of King Friedrich Wilhelm IV of Prussia, who had entrusted the rural parish of Röcken to one

Carl Ludwig Nietzsche. In gratitude Carl Ludwig's son was baptised with the king's name.

But this was not a good omen for little Friedrich Wilhelm Nietzsche. His royal namesake was a failure because he had been unable to realise his dream of a Germano-Christian monarchy for a petit-bourgeois population. Later, like Ludwig II of Bavaria, he became insane. This bound him all the more tightly to the Nietzsches. Pastor Nietzsche was also to lose his reason. The softening of the brain from which he suffered, wrote his son, had symptoms 'uncommonly similar to those of the sickness endured by our late Majesty'.[4]

The first signs of Carl Ludwig's affliction occurred in 1848, the year of revolutions. On hearing that the king had bowed his head in respect before the bodies of the revolutionaries killed in the fighting, Pastor Nietzsche 'burst into tears and rushed out of the house, returning only after several hours'.[5] He had identified himself with his monarch. When, forty years later, his son followed the same path to insanity, he too assumed his hapless namesake's identity. 'In the end,' he declared to his doctors, 'I was Friedrich Wilhelm IV.'[6]

In the first instance, however, Friedrich Nietzsche was the scion of a Protestant rectory and, in his own puzzling words, 'a plant ... close to the graveyard'. This dark little patch of ground, visible from the rectory window, was part of his father's responsibility. Here he buried his parishioners, here he himself was buried and here, in 1850, his youngest son Joseph was also laid to rest. Friedrich described his father as 'kind, delicate and sickly, one destined to spend only a short time on this earth, rather a memory of life than a life itself'.[7] A melancholy picture.

When Carl Ludwig was born in 1813, his father, Friedrich August Ludwig, a respected elder of the Church, was fifty-seven. At his death, his son was twelve. He was brought up by his mother and his two elder sisters in the image of his father, a scholar who had been awarded an honorary doctorate for his theological writings. For his delicate son he represented an unattainable ideal.

Carl Ludwig Nietzsche had a tall physique, with a slightly deformed hip, which disqualified him from military service. There was a shortage of church livings at the time, so after completing his theological studies, he first took a post as tutor to the family of an army officer and was then entrusted with the education of the four Saxon princesses at the ducal court of Altenburg. Having grown up surrounded by women, he must have felt very much at home there – albeit a rather more elegant home than his own. But the dream job soon came to its predictable end – the girls became young ladies and all but one of them married. In compensation the king, who as Crown Prince had already come to appreciate the young man's abilities, appointed him to the benefice of Röcken, with responsibility for two other neighbouring villages.

The sensitive tutor, now in his late twenties and accustomed to elegant court life, did not find his new surroundings congenial. Described by his son as 'the image of a country parson',[8] he withdrew to his study or took to improvising at the piano. This ability had already made an impression on the young princesses. But now his audience consisted merely of his mother and her sisters – a poor substitute.

He isolated himself as far as possible from the female regimen in the rectory and would sit absent-mindedly for hours in his study, absorbed in his books, as his widow recalled. Perhaps he was hoping that the king would offer him preferment so that he could escape from this rustic life of peasants and farm animals. Erdmuthe, his mother, controlled the affairs of the rectory and his half-sister Auguste ran the household, while Rosalie, his nervous and highly-strung sister, read aloud from the newspapers and concerned herself with spiritual matters. The doctor's trap was often to be seen standing outside the rectory. But the pastor set no store by conventional medicine. With the disease that afflicted him it would in any case have been of little use.

His family urged him to get married. A pastor needed a wife, they told him, a woman who could both help in the kitchen and encourage him to turn his mind to higher things. The hours he spent poring over his books had left his mind in a state of utter confusion. It was an appeal that was later made to Friedrich also. If the female side of the family consisted only of old spinsters, they said, then at least the one man present should be at pains to see that the line of the Nietzsches did not die out. But it did.

'I was born on 15 October 1844 on the battlefield of Lützen. The first name I heard was that of Gustavus Adolphus', wrote Friedrich Nietzsche.[9] What he meant was that the Gustavus Adolphus Association, a charitable body named after the king of Sweden, which collected money for communities in need, was frequently mentioned in the rectory. As for the Battle of Lützen, in which the Swedish king fell, Nietzsche explained that the battlefield lay half-an-hour away from his birthplace. The military history of the area filled him with pride. Napoleon had defeated the Prusso-Russian army at Grossgörschen before himself suffering a heavy defeat at the Battle of Leipzig, the so-called 'Battle of the Nations'. The surrounding fields, in other words, were drenched in blood.

CINDERELLA AND THE PRINCE

Near the little hamlet of Pobles there is a hill from which one can look out over all three battlefields. On this hill stood what looked like a farmstead, with a bakery, cow-sheds and barns. Here lived Pastor Nietzsche's colleague David Ernst Oehler with his wife Wilhelmine, daughter of the local lord of the manor. It was assumed that her hand in marriage had only been given to the linen weaver's son because she was blind in one eye and lame. The prominently situated vicarage offered ample room for their eleven children, who had the deepest respect for their parents. Their mother was said to be 'like a powder keg, ready to explode at any moment', while their father was subject to 'sudden fits of rage'.[10]

At the time the well-bred Nietzsches arrived in Röcken, there were in the Oehler family four daughters. Adele, Sidonie and Cäcilie were waiting to be married off. Since no suitors had presented themselves, they set out in their mother's coach to find some. But blush, curtsy and waltz as they might, they always returned empty-handed. The youngest daughter, Franziska, sat at home, waiting anxiously for the latest items of gossip from the world of high society. Her turn had not yet come. Besides that, she was prettier than the other three.

But Fränzchen, as they called her, soon protested at being made to play the part of Cinderella. 'One Sunday', she recounted, 'a group of young friends had arranged an excursion to a beautiful park which was new to me as well. As they brought out the horses and got the carriage ready, I begged my mother to allow me to go with them. "Why shouldn't you?" replied my mother. "Let's go and ask Adele." But Adele turned down the idea. "Is it not enough for you to have three grown-up daughters?" she said to my mother. "Does the child have to come along as well?" '[11]

When the news reached Pobles that a new young pastor had arrived in Röcken, the three sisters sensed their opportunity. Rosy prospects opened up before them. Talk was of a splendid young man, a cultured bachelor who had been one of the king's favourites and a tutor to the royal princesses. And above all – something that set their earnest middle-class hearts beating even faster – he was a superb pianist!

After having paid his initial respects to his colleague in Pobles, the pastor of Röcken was disposed to pay a series of further visits, on one occasion accompanied by the three young ladies of his household. The house on the hill was gleaming in the summer sunshine as the carriage bearing the 'intended' drew up. There were compliments and curtsies, a clattering of parasols and a rustling of skirts and petticoats. It was hardly possible to exclude Fränzchen from the proceedings, though she would certainly have been told not to open her mouth.

Then came the pièce de résistance. 'After a period of pleasant conversation over coffee, the pastor, who was known to be an excellent pianist, was persuaded to improvise at the keyboard, which on this day he did with particular brilliance.' As Carl Ludwig proceeded with his impassioned playing and made his choice – that, after all, was the purpose of the visit – the girls gazed on him tenderly and apprehensively. They were taken above all by the fine quality of the black clothes he was wearing, 'a quality surely to be found only on those who move in court circles'. The upper classes had come to join the lower classes and all was sweetness and harmony – until, leaving the piano, the pastor asked the youngest daughter to show him the orchard, leaving Adele, Sidonie and Cäcilie to look at one another and draw their conclusions.

The two were alone in the garden. The elegantly dressed young pastor offered Fränzchen his arm as they strolled along the paths by the side of the flower beds, gazing out across the fields steeped in history. Then he paused, looked at her like an affectionate uncle and asked her whether she would pick him a posy. They stopped again at the herb garden and he begged her to cut him a sprig of dill, because he was so fond of its scent. Bending down, Franziska did as he asked and held the dill out to him. He brought it to his nose – and his decision was made. Later he told her mother in confidence that the young woman bore a close resemblance to Princess Elisabeth, his former pupil.

Events moved swiftly. The following Sunday Carl Ludwig's maidservant arrived with a letter for Franziska's father, requesting an immediate reply. Oehler had no objection to the speed with which things were moving and was pleased to give his consent to the match without further ado. The three elder sisters were taken aback and left twiddling their thumbs. Fränzchen too felt anxious. When, as usual, her mother went to say goodnight to her, she ventured to say that the only 'mistake' about the planned match was that she was too young. Tactfully, she refrained from saying that the pastor might have been too old.

The wedding took place on 10 October 1843, Carl Ludwig's thirtieth birthday. It was to be a grand occasion, so the reception was held in the Nietzsches' rectory. Just as the bridegroom was about to express his thanks to the assembled guests, his seventeen-year-old bride moved towards him. Because there was not enough room for her, he made to open one of the folding doors, whereupon the lower half of the door fell off its hinges. When Franziska looked back on this moment, she interpreted it as a bad omen. Maybe the bridegroom's clumsiness was to be put down to his anxiety about how to 'open the door' for his young bride. In her letters she thanks all those who 'helped to make it such a joyful occasion for us', but something must have embarrassed her, for she confessed that if anyone looked at her, 'she could not help blushing'.

On another occasion he played a childish prank on her. They had just returned from visiting friends and were taking off their clothes, when he picked up her hat and coat and put them on. Following his lead, she donned his top hat. She found that it looked 'charming' – it would certainly have pleased her son Friedrich, who enjoyed disguises, which, according to a friend, he used as 'masks behind which to conceal secrets that he would never reveal'.[12]

Franziska had a good deal of ground to make up. There were dangerous gaps in her knowledge. On their journey to spend their honeymoon with Carl Ludwig's relatives she failed, to his great amusement, to understand who was meant by 'brother'. What brother? She did not realise that the coachman was also referred to as 'brother'. But nor could the clever young pastor have known why his wife was so taken aback by the word. For he had not been the first to woo the pretty young Fränzchen. A theological student, 'madly in love with her' and younger than Carl Ludwig, had anticipated him – and he was the brother of one of her friends.

Franziska Nietzsche's reminiscences, written during her widowhood, end with her honeymoon. There was not a great deal of pleasure to follow. She was pitched from childhood into marriage, as her nephew put it.[13] And what marriage meant was made abundantly clear to her by the three female residents of the Röcken rectory. The straitjacket in which she was confined released its grip only slowly, as one member of the Nietzsche family after another passed away – her husband in 1849, her little son the following year, her sister-in-law Auguste in 1855, the next year her mother-in-law, and in 1867 her other sister-in-law Rosalie. The only ones left were her elder son and her daughter Elisabeth.

The sick-bay that was the Röcken rectory stood under the regimen of the pious women of the house, all of them older, wiser, more genteel than Fränzchen, the girl from the village, who came last but one in the hierarchy, superior only to Mine, the maidservant. No great displays of affection passed between them, partly, no doubt, because of the envy the women felt for the healthy young newcomer with her new-found husband, by whom she found herself pregnant three months after the wedding.

Nor could her husband do anything to change the pecking order. He had already pledged his loyalty – after all, his women-folk had given up their town life for his benefit. When arguments developed between them and his wife, he left the room and sulked, seeking refuge in his books for hours on end, recalling happier times in the past. He does not seem to have noticed how she suffered.

THE LITTLE FRIEND

A year and five days after the wedding a son was born. There was an air of jubilation in the village, for it was the king's birthday. At the christening Carl Ludwig launched into a strange monologue. 'O blessed month of October,' he began, 'the month in which in previous years all the most important events in my life have occurred' – his own birth apparently shared pride of place with his wedding – 'what a wonderful, glorious moment it is for me to baptise my own little son! O blissful time, O blessed sacrament, O divine mystery beyond the mind of man, blessed be the name of the Lord!'[14] Even the pastor's superior, who was also present, found this pompous verbiage too much to take. The child at the centre of attention was also to become a master of the declamatory manner, with 'O noontide of life! O festive moment! O summer garden!' and other florid apostrophes.[15]

Soon five women were to descend on the little boy. Fritz, as he was known, allowed himself to be spoilt and pampered. But he spoke not a word. When he was still silent after three years, they called in the doctor. Stop treating him like a prince, came the advice, then he will talk as he wishes. Maybe Fritz refused to talk because his mother too had never been allowed to open her mouth.

Soon afterwards, according to his sister, he was talking 'fluently and with the utmost clarity'.[16] At four he was beginning to read and write. His sister's claim that their father had devoted himself to his son's development is pure fantasy. 'Father spent very little time on Fritz's education', was their mother's version, 'because he was always engrossed in his books.' When, to the boy's delight, he was allowed into his father's room, his father called him 'his little friend', which does not suggest any great warmth. Carl Ludwig was preoccupied with his own concerns. And there were signs of the sickness that was to come.

He wrote away for a selection of homeopathic medicines that constituted the 'Hahnemann Method'. But his fits and attacks did not respond to natural cures either. Back at the time when he had been entering his son's name in the baptismal register he had suffered a black-out, and the quotation from the Bible he had intended as a motto does not exist. Fritz too did not seem to be developing normally. If he was prevented from doing something, he would throw a tantrum and go and sit in a corner. Sometimes he would throw himself full-length on the floor in rage. Was he too subject to fits?

In 1848 things took a serious turn. Some insidious force seized hold of the pastor, as though, like Hamlet's father, poison had been poured into his ear. One side of his face became paralysed, he began to stutter and time and again he would sink into complete mental lethargy. Desperately he tried to fight against his total disintegration, anxious to continue preaching and hold confirmation classes. At the age of fourteen Fritz called his father's illness 'the earliest event that has stayed in my conscious memory'.[17]

It was known in the family that Carl Ludwig was prone to fits that caused him to lose consciousness and slump down in his chair with wide-open eyes. His son was to witness such incidents for himself. Soon afterwards he lost the power to speak coherently, leaving his wife to try and make sense of his babbling. Then he ceased to recognise his surroundings and became blind. When, after suffering for a whole year, he finally died, part of his brain was revealed by an autopsy to have decayed. When it was his son's turn, there was to be no such post-mortem examination.

When rumours began to circulate about the cause of the pastor's death, it was agreed that the story should be that he had fallen down the stairs and struck his head. Fritz, who could still recall his father's illness and rapid deterioration in detail years later, knew better. He called it 'softening of the brain'.[18]

When the pastor died, Fritz was four years old. Never did he forget the family's helplessness, his father's lingering death, the ineffectual prayers and the ominous pomp that accompanied his burial. He later recalled that his father had had to endure 'excruciating pains' and that his screams could be heard in the street below.

A spell hung over the rectory in the shade of the three acacia trees. When they told the boy that his father was now in Heaven, he might have begun to think that he too would soon have to make the same journey. In the year before the onset of his own dementia he was still to be found writing of 'the terrible legacy passed down by my father', i.e. 'the predestination to meet with an early death'.[19]

Carl Ludwig Nietzsche died at the age of thirty-six, his son at fifty-five. Franziska, for ever in the shadow of the Nietzsche clan, died of cancer of the womb in 1897, aged seventy-one. Elisabeth survived them all, living to present Adolf Hitler with her brother's walking stick.

THE BRINGER OF DEATH

It was an age that clamoured for ghosts and spirits. At night the phantom of revolution, too frightful to contemplate, haunted people's houses. Hypnotism and spiritualism were in vogue, and many dabbled in the occult. The leading German visionary of the time was the novelist Justinus Kerner, who had a fantastic success with works investigating the world of apparitions, somnambulism and other manifestations of the supernatural. Many a brave citizen broke out in a cold sweat at the prospect of the invasion of his well-ordered existence by strange forces from the world of mystery and magic.

Fritz too felt the attraction of these forces. Between the ages of twelve and fifteen, according to his sister, he read the works by Kerner that were in the rectory library at Pobles. Kerner was also a cleric, a man in whose mind ghosts and the Holy Ghost existed side by side. People who held such superstitions in the mid-nineteenth century were by no means dismissed as mad. Rather, the man who saw ghosts – and Nietzsche saw them – felt himself to be one of a chosen few, a medium who could transmit experiences of the supernatural. Freud later demonstrated that ghosts symbolise a fear of overwhelming patriarchal power. Nietzsche had sensed this half a century earlier.

It was a winter's night in 1850. The rectory, its incumbent in the bosom of his Creator, stood cold and silent. For six months Carl Ludwig's death had been eating into his son's consciousness: 'I dreamt I heard the sound of a mighty organ playing at a funeral in the church. Then a grave suddenly rose up before my eyes and my father stepped out of it. He hurried into the church, then returned bearing a child in his arms. The grave opened, my father entered it and it closed behind him. At once the organ stopped playing and I awoke.'[20]

Nietzsche wrote this nine years after the event but it is as though it had just happened. A second, later version is slightly different: 'It was as though I could hear the murmuring sound of the organ in a nearby church. In my surprise I opened the window which looked out towards the church and the graveyard. My father's grave opened, a figure in white emerged and disappeared into the church. The dark, mysterious tones of the organ rumbled on. Then the figure in white reappeared carrying something under its arm that I could not distinguish. The grave rose, the figure vanished and the organ ceased. Then I awoke.'[21]

The author relates what he remembers. 'It was as though ...' he says. The organ is playing in the church. He is 'surprised' as he goes to the window, as if he had been awakened from sleep. And where everything is usually still and motionless, except when the wind rustles the branches or brushes the ribbons round the wreaths, something stirs. The grave at which he had once wept is opening and out steps a figure he has never before seen. Can this be? Maybe Friedrich had discovered among Grandfather Oehler's books on the occult the story of 'the white lady of Orlamünde', as told by the mystic and spiritualist Jung-Stilling. The creature from the underworld, dangling before his eyes like a puppet, also appears to have arms, for it is carrying something out of the church. Then the whole sequence is reversed – the ghost fades, the grave closes and the sounds of the organ die away.

To the five-year-old dreamer it was all real. He had heard with his own ears and seen with his own eyes what had been happening. And had he not opened the window himself? Yet his account leaves out the most important detail – the fright that the experience had given him. It was not when the organ stopped that he had woken up but when the feeling of fright came over him, a fright he could not bear. A brief pattern of images, like a film-strip, had made him aware of feelings he had suppressed since his father's death – loneliness, a pining for his dearly loved father and at the same time a profound fear of him. Fritz, the eldest male in the family, was his successor; his little brother did not yet come into the reckoning, even though, to Fritz's chagrin, he took up much of their mother's attention. After his dream Fritz was left with the terrifying feeling that his dead father had returned, with the power, like the Erl King in Goethe's poem, to carry away with him whoever he desired. A ghostly bringer of death: 'The day following this dream little Joseph suddenly became ill. He suffered violent convulsions and died a few hours later.'[22]

Carl Ludwig lay in an unquiet grave. It needed only a few chords on the organ for it to open. In 1886 Nietzsche wrote to Franz Overbeck that he had sold his books and used the proceeds to erect a large marble headstone on his father's grave in Röcken.[23] No headstone would have been too large for Nietzsche, the visionary.

A similar experience had befallen another German poet and novelist in the previous century. In 1788 Friedrich de la Motte Fouqué, author of tales of knights and fairies, witnessed the return of his mother as a ghost. According to his biographer Arno Schmidt, Fouqué dreamed that he had crept back to where the body of his mother was lying, and that the figure suddenly sat up and made as if to grab him. Trying to escape, he picked up the first object that came to hand and threw it at the figure. It was a little box that his mother had given him shortly before her death. Horrified by what he had done, he woke from his dream. It was as though he had sacrificed his mother's gift in return for being left in peace.[24]

The graveyard in Röcken remained the focus of Nietzsche's fantasies. In his characteristically paradoxical manner he once wrote: 'How vividly I see the graveyard before me!' Alongside stood the mortuary, a source of 'magical attraction' with its 'catafalques and black flowers', and the 'gloomy sacristy'. Here his father had made ready for Sunday worship. Here too, on a side wall, was a stone engraving which always sent a shudder down his spine: 'It was a well-executed sculpture, over life-size, of St George. His noble features, his terrible weapons and the mysterious semi-darkness always made me look upon him in awe. Once upon a time, according to legend, his eyes glistened with a frightening intensity, filling all who saw him with fear and trembling.'[25]

Did Nietzsche become aware of the saint only after he had embarked on his search for his vanished father? Perhaps the stone guest in the sacristy was not really dead. When his moment came, he would strike fear and terror into his adversaries, fixing them with his penetrating glare and threatening them with his merciless weapons. Small wonder that Fritz was afraid of him. At the same time St George was said to have rescued mankind from the dragon – a figure fierce and threatening, yet also noble and sublime. The prototype of the Superman.

Following Carl Ludwig's death, his re-emergence from the grave and the loss of little Joseph, Fritz had one further test to undergo. The 'plant from the graveyard' had to be moved. The family had to vacate the rectory for the new pastor, leaving the orchard and the flower garden, with its arbours and benches. There were to be no more strolls among the willows that grew by the banks of the ponds, where Fritz would sit and watch the fish frolicking to and fro. Even the acacias were no longer theirs.

The night before they were due to leave, Fritz could not sleep. The moon and the twinkling stars brightened the sky. At half past midnight something made him get up and go down the stairs into the yard. Was he hoping to meet a phantom figure for the last time? Nothing stirred. Only the subdued glow of the lantern lit up the windows of the downstairs rooms. 'Never had my future seemed so uncertain and so dismal as at this moment', he later wrote. 'When dawn came, the horses were harnessed and we drove away through the morning mist, bidding our beloved home a tearful farewell.'[26]

2   *Life as a Nightmare*

Friedrich's fate was written in the stars. He was destined to become 'the little pastor',[1] forced by the widows of his forbears to carry the burden they had laid on his shoulders. He had in any case no other option. In his dreams he imagined a second, 'higher' reality that governed the course of his life. It was not a question of believing that it was so – he knew that it was so. Later he wrote: 'In the age of crude, primitive cultures men believed they experienced a second real world, a world in which lie the origins of metaphysics, and probably also of a belief in God. The dead live on, for they appear to the living in dreams.'[2] Nietzsche the philosopher realised that it was a case of what he called in an aphorism 'the misunderstanding of dreams', for in a child's formative development the only thing that matters is what he sees. Fritz carried his secret metaphysical knowledge with him into the exile that now awaited him.

In the spring of 1850 a sad little band of mourners arrived in the nearby cathedral town of Naumburg, some fifteen miles south of Röcken – two widows, two elderly spinsters, two fatherless children and a maidservant. They unloaded their few chattels in a house belonging to a rail haulage contractor called Carl Gotthelf Otto. Grandmother moved into the parlour at the front of the house, where she received visitors. Her two grandchildren were also allowed to enter the room, but only at mealtimes. When they were also permitted to visit her in the early evening, as the light began to fade, it was regarded as a special treat.[3]

The children and their mother were given the poky little rooms at the back. 'It was terrible for us to have to live in a town after having lived for so long in the country', wrote the fourteen-year-old Fritz.[4] On the occasions when they and their mother managed to get away from the gloomy streets, they felt 'like birds that had escaped from their cage' and they longed for times when they could spend their holidays with relatives in the country.

At twenty-five Franziska was still an attractive woman. She had large brown eyes, which sent her son into raptures, and straight black hair, which contrasted with her pale features. Her movements were described as 'graceful', while her nephew admired her 'buxom figure'. In short, a desirable widow, who wore her black dress like a noblewoman. The three Nietzsche women, to whom mourning had become second nature, had ensured that Franziska too should continue to wear black. She was totally dependent on them, and knew it, for her annual widow's pension amounted to a mere forty-six talers. (For comparison a few years earlier Wagner had earned 1,500 talers a year as Kapellmeister at the Saxon court in Dresden.) Her situation improved when the princesses in Altenburg contributed towards the children's education but it was to be many years before she had enough money to live an independent life.

'A child of the countryside,' wrote her biographer, 'now she does not even have a garden but spends half the day sitting by herself in her back room.'[5] But what offended her most was to be treated by her relatives as though she were merely a visitor in their house. The only course left to her was to make her children and herself into a unit on its own. They read together, wrote poetry together, made music together and prayed together to the memory of their revered paterfamilias. Franziska's marriage may not have been made in heaven but in retrospect it seemed to her like the garden of paradise, in which she tended the two fragile little plants her husband had bequeathed to her. Defensive and withdrawn, as befitted a widow, the lady in black protected them with a wall of coolness and badinage.

Her inner life was no concern of others. 'Given to outbursts of self-recrimination and self-inflicted suffering,' wrote her nephew, 'characteristics that she passed on to her son, she lived in an almost mystical atmosphere, like a nun, devoting her life to the memory of her husband.'[6] On the day in 1889 when she took her deranged son to the asylum in Jena, she asked not to be woken by a knock at the door the next morning 'because she would be in private communion with her God'.[7]

Immersed in the values of the spiritual life, Franziska seems to have created her own private world of religiosity, compared with which the strict discipline exercised by her sister-in-laws was the merest pietism. At times she must have looked like a corpse. Once, when the children were allowed to visit the annual art exhibition in the town, they saw a painting of the risen daughter of Jairus, which reminded them of their mother. Jesus had just brought the twelve-year-old girl back from the dead. A mother raised from the dead was the perfect counterpart of her son, in whom a housekeeper at the rectory claimed to recognise the twelve-year-old Jesus in the Temple. A nun and 'the little pastor' – a Biedermeier idyll.

In an age hungry for miracles the precocious young Fritz seemed to be the embodiment of one. Grandfather Oehler claimed to see similarities between him and the young Luther, and when the boy recited prayers, tears came into the eyes of his listeners. Even the animal world appeared to acknowledge his endowments. His sister told how a circus horse called Pylades, trained to trot round the arena and identify the wisest and most industrious of the spectators, stopped in front of her brother and respectfully bowed its head before him three times. 'Cries of delight burst out all around, and Mine, our maid-servant, shouted at the top of her voice.'[8] Elisabeth does not say what Mine shouted but right down to the years of his madness Fritz remembered the honour the horse had bestowed on him.

Franziska mustered her weapons for the domestic trial of strength. She only needed to reactivate the qualities she had inherited. She learned how to keep the children under control and how to intimidate the others in the household with sudden outbursts of rage. Above all she learned how to economise, saving money not on books but on food. Gruel was their staple diet, with a little meat. Fritz was to shudder when he thought back to those dumplings and stodgy soups. There had been no place for medicines since Carl Ludwig's death. The treatment for the boy's maladies, often caused by the poor light and the damp and cold conditions in which they lived, consisted of compresses and cold affusions. Throughout his life he was to torment himself by dousing his body with cold water – it was, after all, what his mother had always prescribed.

The two children had a spartan upbringing. As Elisabeth flatteringly chose to put it: 'We were never subject to the enervating influence of blind maternal affection.'[9] Severity was a virtue that was highly prized at the time. Orders were carried out to the letter. Often a stern look sufficed: Franziska could show both approval and disapproval – more often the latter – with a mere glance. The children showed her total respect, not least because, like God Himself, she reprimanded lesser misdemeanours on the spot. If, on occasion, she displayed tenderness towards them, Fritz was effusive in his gratitude. On the other hand, he was always prepared to accept punishment for a minor transgression. The hardest thing to bear, however, was when she made fun of him. 'What torture it is for a child', he lamented years later, 'always to find that his ideas of right and wrong are the opposite of his mother's and to be mocked and despised for what he most values!'[10]

He was an adult when he wrote these words but they were the product of his childhood. As Pastor Nietzsche had drilled his princesses, so now his widow was drilling her prince. The whole day was given over to learning – no sooner had Fritz returned home from school than he was made to continue his education at his mother's side. She acquired a piano, and after she had taken lessons from a cantor, mother and son played duets in their back room. The scores they played from had probably belonged to the pastor. Zarathustra was later to talk of education by means of 'meagre rations and harsh blows',[11] which turns a man into a puppet and keeps him under control by invoking the fear of the devil. Such a man, says Zarathustra, has nothing to lose – not even his life.

The way the widow treated her children was entirely in keeping with the spirit of the age. Every boy was expected to become a cadet, every girl a future mother of cadets, or of civil servants, or of pastors. The phrase 'heedless of the consequences' was making the rounds. 'In everyday life,' wrote Nietzsche's sister proudly, 'no heed was paid to individual wishes',[12] and Fritz himself became an accomplished practitioner of the art of self-denial. In order to demonstrate to his schoolmates that the days of iron discipline were not yet over, he would put lighted matches on the palm of his hand, or burn himself with sealing wax.

In later life he looked back in horror on the demands his mother had made on him. The tirades of hate that he launched against her in the final year of his sanity are his answer to the abuse he suffered at her hands during his years in Naumburg. 'What a poisonous atmosphere I had to breathe when I was a boy!' he wrote. 'Was there ever a time when the Germans were more dull-witted, more afraid and more obsequious than during the years I was a child?'[13]

But a child was precisely what he was not supposed to be. The compulsion to change his and Elisabeth's nature, born of a fear of what the outside world would think and carried through with remorseless rigour, produced not natural children but fawning servants and a kind of Prussian elite. One of his names for the horrors of day-to-day life was 'Naumburg virtue' – virtue, because the family belonged to the class of 'good people'. And what made these people good? The answer was aggressive and scornful: 'They are utterly incapable', he said, 'of behaving other than by pretence – pretence of innocence, pretence of profundity, pretence of honesty and fidelity, pretence of virtuousness.'[14] Naumburg, in other words, was a lie.

His childhood life he described as 'more burdensome and more oppressive than was befitting to one of my age'.[15] His sister wrote: 'We were unbelievably well-behaved – real model children.'[16] As to what is known as maternal love, Fritz laboured from the beginning under a certain resignation, which he expressed in one of his earliest poems, dedicated to his mother:

> I love you so much that I should like to smother you in my embrace.
> But perhaps I should not, for fear it would not make you happy.[17]

His yearning for tenderness remained unrequited. All mention of the body was taboo, on the one hand out of respect for tradition, on the other out of a sense of modesty. His spinster aunts took him to task and toughened him with cold douches, doing their best to make the boy forget that he was to become a man with sexual instincts. They regarded men as a threat, and were determined to see that he behaved himself.

In *Ecce homo*, his final autobiographical fragment, Nietzsche sums up the tragic effect of his time in Naumburg on his sexual development: 'Although I have no pleasant memories of my childhood and youth, it would be mistaken to adduce so-called moral reasons ... Ignorance of physical facts and that accursed "idealism" – that is the real tragedy of my life. I attribute to this "idealism" all my mistakes, all the false directions followed by my instincts.'[18]

Nietzsche put 'idealism' in inverted commas. Of course it was not for the sake of some idea that he was kept in childlike innocence. His aunts treated him as sexless out of fear of their own sexuality, suppressing any thoughts of physical desire, even if it were only a wish to feel the warmth of a little human affection. They forced him to repress his needs until those needs found violent expression. The ultimate tragedy was 'the way he was made to feel contempt for the demands of the flesh, even to turn away from the very discovery of the flesh'.[19] The time was to come when he would set out to discover this *terra incognita*. But until that point, the 'accursed' idealism prevailed. Fritz, the 'little pastor', who would soon have to play the part of a child prodigy also, was under permanent stress. When signs of a gifted intellect began to appear at school, the course of his life was fixed. At twenty-four he occupied a university chair. The historian Jacob Burckhardt, an academic colleague, saw the disaster that lay ahead: 'Because he was already an infant prodigy at Schulpforta, he was expected to accomplish ever more prodigious achievements. As a result he was put under unnatural stress and the roots of his health were permanently damaged.'[20]

Again one is reminded of the image of the plant. Burckhardt's diagnosis was uncannily accurate. Launched under the most propitious circumstances, Nietzsche's career followed a biblical course and found a biblical end. Having suffered his loneliness on the Mount of Olives, 'subjected to a protracted crucifixion at the hands of German doctors', he descended into Hell, rose to Heaven from the gutter of a street in Turin and came to sit on his sister's right hand in a villa in Weimar, available for consultation by appointment only.[21]

THE MASKS OF THE DEMON

To offset the pressure brought to bear on him by the pious ladies of the household, Fritz set up a cult of his father. As with his stern mother, but independent of her, the distant paradise in Röcken became the centre of his spiritual life, a place in which women had no part to play. He confided his nostalgic secrets to the pages of his diary, sometimes in verse, sometimes in prose. Passionately he abandoned himself to the 'sweet sorrow' that he felt at the thought of the childhood that was now lost.[22] His father, he knew, was not in Heaven but on the distant blessed isles of his native land.

Forced to conceal his true feelings, Fritz developed into an Orphean figure who presented himself at the gates of the underworld bearing a 'golden lyre'.[23] He did not do so in vain. His beloved father let himself be conjured up in a variety of guises – as a god or a king, or as a duke or a forester. Shortly before the onset of his insanity Friedrich was to tell the world what he owed to Pastor Nietzsche, who had by then been dead almost forty years: 'I consider it a great privilege to have had such a father – indeed, I sometimes think that that explains all the other privileges I have enjoyed.'[24]

One such privilege was granted to him shortly after leaving the rectory. He was in Naumburg, in their house in the Neugasse, 'when I suddenly heard my father's warning voice'. His father's voice? Was it perhaps a ghost? Or might it have been, as he once wrote, that 'the father had returned in the form of the son, who was, so to speak, carrying on his father's life after his premature death'?[25] But why should that have been the reason why his father's voice lived on in him?

In 1878 Nietzsche was pondering this question, wondering who could have whispered these mystifying words in his ear as he lay sleeping. He found an answer in antiquity, namely in the figure of the 'demon, the warning voice of my father'.[26] Socrates heard just such an inner voice that told him which path to follow. 'From my youth,' said Socrates, 'I have been conscious of an inner voice that persistently urges me to refrain from some act which I was contemplating.' It is the voice we call conscience. Everyone who has experienced a strict upbringing comes to find that conscience relieves one of the burden of choice. Because it tyrannises the ego, Freud called it the superego. And here lay concealed, according to Nietzsche, what was at the heart of Socrates' *dae-monion* – the warning voice of his dead father. Nietzsche really had heard this voice. In 1888 he dismissed the thought of his demon as a hallucination caused by an ear infection. Once his sickness held him in its grip, the judgement of the avenging demon had become a reality, no less frightening than the ghost in the graveyard. The 'plant from the graveyard' knew what was going on.

Fritz was also different to other children in the games he played. Deprived of the rural paradise he had been forced to leave behind, he wanted somehow to preserve its memory. So he simply built a model of it. At the centre of his imaginary world of tin soldiers and other ornamental figures stood 'King Squirrel', a china figure three-and-a-half centimetres high on whose head, as befitted his regal status, Fritz had set a tiny crown of pearls. King Squirrel reigned over a well-organised household, and between 1853 and 1855 the children's room in the Neugasse was dominated by the ruler with the bushy tail. Friedrich's friends, Wilhelm and Gustav – all the favourite Prussian names in one room – must have been astonished to find that their nine-year-old leader was still playing with dolls.

He was deadly earnest about the king. Acting as His Majesty's Master of Ceremonies, he would carry out his ruler's instructions to the letter. 'All the buildings my brother made were dedicated to King Squirrel', wrote his sister.[27] Seized with an urge to plan and build things, like Ludwig II of Bavaria, he designed a picture gallery, which he decked out with exhibits of his own choice – among them, we can be sure, a picture of the raising of Jairus' daughter. Then he built an ancient monastery, which may well have resembled a certain sacristy of recent memory, with an old-fashioned lamp hanging from the ceiling that cast a mysterious red light over the room below. The king's retinue were accommodated in various side rooms, while a red carpet covered the steps that led up to the throne on which His Majesty sat.

'I do not recollect', wrote Elisabeth Nietzsche later, 'how this little squirrel came to be vested with regal powers.'[28] But Nietzsche knew. In 1862 he noted in his diary, to jog his memory: 'Squirrel, earliest memory of fable.' Fables were a popular, because harmless, way of educating children. Fritz might well have come across La Fontaine's story of the fox and the squirrel through his father, who had perhaps translated it in the lessons with his princesses. Whatever the case, it matched the boy's mood in the period following his father's death.

In La Fontaine's fable the wicked fox is trying to intimidate the innocent little squirrel during a storm:

You will not escape your fate, said Reynard,
Your coffin awaits you, however high you climb.
It is no good covering your head with your tail,
For when you reach the top of the tree, death will be waiting for you.
So what is left of your wit?
You always used to boast that you wanted to be close to the lightning.

The story has a happy ending for the squirrel – the storm abates and the fox is caught by the gamekeeper. But the pastor becomes a victim of the wicked fox's prediction. His coffin awaits him. His son is impressed by the image of the danger that looms in getting too close to the flash of lightning. 'The realm of the clouds is too close', he writes. 'I am waiting for the first shaft of lightning.'[29]

André Gide described La Fontaine as expressing in light, playful terms the frightening truths that Nietzsche pronounces in passionate rhetoric. In 1854 the young Fritz brings the role of his dead father to an end with all the impetuous eloquence that a ten-year-old boy can muster. In his dramatic sketch *The Office of the King*, he has the ruler deposed. The king, naturally, had already had the opportunity to present the heir apparent to his soldiers as the man who would eventually govern in his place. He must have sensed what was to come – he is driven out of the country by the revolution and his son proclaims himself king in his stead. But the jubilation does not last. Disguised as a poor beggar, the king returns from exile 'to see how his kingdom is faring'.[30]

Friedrich, who decades later still delighted in playfully calling himself 'Prince Squirrel', saw himself as his father's successor. But unfortunately there was a possibility that the rightful incumbent of the throne might return at any moment. A few years after his initial sketch Nietzsche returned to his dramatic fragment and developed it further. The orphaned hero is adopted by a nobleman. Revolution breaks out afresh, and the rebels take up arms, killing most of the king's supporters, driving the rest out of the country and razing their houses to the ground. This was not exactly what had happened in the revolution of 1848 but it may well have been how it appeared to the fevered imagination of the ailing pastor in Röcken. The uprising is a serious blow to the nobleman: 'He would himself have fought in the ranks of the king's army, had he not been too weak to do so.'[31]

Maybe the sick pastor had made a similar remark when he returned from his excursion into the realm of despair. He had to watch with his own eyes as the rejoicing crowds surged through the village, their banners waving in the wind. Now at last the curse was to be lifted from him. Hardly has the mob captured the nobleman than his son appears as his saviour – 'a vigorous young man, several military decorations on his breast and with the fire of joy flashing from his eyes'.[32]

By the time he had finished writing down his bold revision of history to accommodate the redemption of the deposed 'King Squirrel', Friedrich had long since abandoned his world of toy soldiers and china figures. Real war was now the object of his enthusiasm. Since 1854 he and his two friends had been re-enacting the battles of the Crimean War. Now, as a young cadet, he was about to set out on what he anticipated would be a brilliant military career.

THE STORY OF THE DIRTY MOUSE

The Crimean War turned Fritz into a poet. Sevastopol, at that moment under siege, replaced the sleepy little backwater of Naumburg as the centre of his world. Details of the battles were recorded and little home-made bombs exploded. For all his highly developed intelligence Fritz still appeared to be suffering from the characteristic problems of childhood. As if he could still sense the gardens of his early years behind the discipline of his compulsory daily lessons, he obstinately retained what had been the privilege of those days – not to place any restrictions on the exercise of his bodily functions, particularly those over which the dark veil of night could be drawn.

His obstinacy demanded its price. A boy who, at his age, still wetted and soiled his bed could be sure he would have to answer to his mother and face the mockery of his sister. But Fritz made it serve his own purposes. Adelbert Oehler remembered how the children were taught by their mother to write little poems and find rhymes for particular words. Fritz's first efforts took himself, the future prophet of the mountain regions, as their subject:

High upon a mountain peak,
There's the solitude I seek.

Then came near-nonsense doggerel that showed the other side of his nature:

Shame on you,
The things you do.
Dirty too:
What can make you new?[33]

Fritz showed himself to be a skilled rhymester, an ability he retained throughout his adult life. With his mother he would set out to find as many words as possible that rhymed with a word she gave him, whereby his imagination led him into areas that would otherwise have never entered the conversation. He would imagine all kinds of animals crawling in and out of his bed, and describe the experience in a series of nonsense verses, which hovered on the brink of propriety, complete with titillating allusions that the family found highly amusing.

On the surface his rhymes seemed harmless enough, but his puns and plays on words often contained an embarrassing hidden agenda:

On the mountain side there lies a mess,
A heap of horrid mouse's cess
The cess then falls upon my head
And strikes me there and then stone-dead.[34]

The nightmare in which he imagines a furry beast waiting to fall on him like an executioner was a regular occurrence. It was followed by another horrible vision – an avalanche had buried him as he slept. From his nightmare he awoke to find that he had soiled his bed. It was not me, he protested to his mother – it was the mouse. The nightmare was behind him but its physical consequences still confronted him.

A memory of these childhood visions returned in 1887, a year before he lost his sanity. He pondered, in a paradoxical formulation, 'how one could spoil someone's pleasure in an enjoyable vice'. His answer – 'One must mix the vice with . . .'.[35] It was a painful experience he had already had in 1854, when he summed up his fear of dirtying his bed yet again in another of his childhood rhymes:

When I go to rest,
I put it to the test:
If there is no dirt,
There will be no hurt.[36]

WOTAN'S WILD HUNT

No sooner did his mother put out the light in the evening than Fritz's room filled with terrifying visions. In his dreams the visions became reality. He felt that the Christian God was powerless against these invaders, in league, as He evidently was, with the spectre of his father. He had to find other, more powerful gods, like those in Germanic legends – fierce, warlike heroes who struck fear into the hearts of their enemies. Just as in Röcken he had built little chapels, and later a mystic sacristy for his 'King Squirrel', so now he had to erect altars to his new divinities.

Elisabeth was present at one of these cultic ceremonies. 'We happened to hear that the nearby hill called the Kirchberg had originally been a place of sacrifice, so we collected stones and fragments of bone and built an altar round which we erected a pile of bones and wood, then set fire to it. When our goodly pastor, attracted by the strange smell, came to see what we were doing, he found us striding solemnly round the altar with burning torches held aloft, chanting a kind of hymn to the words "Wotan, hear us!" '[37]

Wotan, god of thunder and lightning, was the right antidote for Fritz to counter the evil spirits that came to him in the night. Had his beloved father not vanished in a storm? Had not dark clouds collected in the sky as he lay dying? It was a moment Fritz would never forget. 'Shafts of lightning pierced the sky, wreaking destruction on the earth.'[38] Having disappeared behind the clouds, his father now returned in the form of the god of thunder. 'See ye not my thunderbolts?' he rants to the children who have invoked him: 'Hear ye not my winds?'[39] Wotan knows full well why his son has summoned him. The boy needs help, needs to be rescued from the terrible attacks to which he was being subjected. And the only rescue could come in the form of a storm, a sudden, deafening explosion. The hymn the children had sung on the Kirchberg was Friedrich's cry for help, and an eagle that soared through the air above them had uttered the name of the god in its screeching tones:

Who can rescue us?
Who can we call upon in our moment of need?
Help us, O Wotan,
Help us in our struggle
Against the evil powers
Of the night.

Maybe Friedrich had invoked the wrong god. But Röcken was the focal point of his emotional life and the storm-like disaster lit up the whole scene. A sweet scent wafted towards him from his childhood, 'bringing tears to his eyes', as Zarathustra was to say.[40] But that scene had also been the source of the fear that had gripped him when he saw the figure in white rise up from the grave.

Antiquity too has many such stories to tell, as he may well have known. Dead heroes long to return to the land of the living, like Heracles' companion who appeared before the Argonauts as one sent by Persephone from the underworld, and who cast wistful glances towards the warriors. Standing on his grave mound, he finally plunged back into the world of darkness. Even Odysseus has to witness how the dead thirst after the glowing blood of life, and Fritz and his sister played at re-living Odysseus' adventures – the bold young hero in search of distant Attica.

There was something irresistible about Fritz's obsession with his rural childhood. In 1858, shortly before being driven into exile a second time, on this occasion from Naumburg to the boarding-school of Schulpforta, he recalled his poem 'The Transience of Happiness', in which he had described his predicament in allegorical terms. It told of 'a wanderer slumbering among the ruins of Carthage. The dream-god was made to display before him the one-time glories of the city. Then the fates intervened, and he awoke.'[41]

The vision of a flourishing city later razed to the ground seemed to offer a perfect image of Fritz's short-lived happiness in Röcken. He re-lived in his dream the years spent in a paradise suddenly and brutally destroyed. In his autobiographical sketch 'From My Life' he wrote: 'Up to this time joy and happiness had always shone upon us. Then came a ravaging storm.'[42] The wanderer could be grateful to the god for awakening him from his terrifying experience.

There was no guarantee that he would do so, however. Much vanishes in the night. Moreover the poem in question, to be found among Nietzsche's childhood jottings, ends far less optimistically than he remembered. The wanderer is visiting the ruins of classical antiquity (is there a hint here of Chateaubriand's epic, *René*?), having been carried there on the back of a mighty eagle. His goal is Nineveh. Casting himself as a well-informed, independent traveller, Fritz is well aware of what will await him at the famous site. He begins to dig and only a few feet down finds a collection of sculptures. But the discovery does not make him happy, and as the sun goes down, he is overcome with weariness and disillusion. Lowering his care-worn head, he falls into the pit that he has just dug – digs his own grave, in other words.[43] His voyage of discovery to find his lost father ends with him falling to his death, as though, like his little brother, he were being irresistibly drawn to join his father in the grave.

The way back is steep. In the autumn of 1859, almost fifteen, Friedrich was looking forward to the holidays, now finally able to turn his back on that intellectual sweat-shop Schulpforta. The night before he departed, he had a shattering dream about what 'going home' meant for him, for 'home' was not Naumburg. In his dream, as he wrote it down, he and a friend left a 'gloomy' town together, which, 'for all its bustling atmosphere made an unpleasant impression on me'. The sun had just set. Behind them shone its last golden rays, before them lay the ever-darkening landscape. Sweet memories come into his mind as he reflects on the life he has left behind, spread out like a peaceful rustic scene.

The idyll comes to an abrupt end. A piercing scream is heard from a nearby mental asylum. Clasping each other's hand tightly, the two friends feel as though an evil spirit has brushed their faces with its horrid wings. In Fritz's interpretation – my father suddenly falls ill, screams like a madman, sending shivers down my spine. What had started as an unruffled rural scene reminiscent of the novels of Jean Paul turns into one of E. T. A. Hoffmann's sinister and disturbing tales.

An enchanted forest rises up before them, and as midnight approaches, they realise they have lost their way. The clouds take on menacing forms and the moon disappears. They sense that something mysterious is about to happen. 'Then we caught sight of a dark figure,' wrote Fritz, ' who looked like a gamekeeper.' A special kind of gamekeeper. 'His wild, glowering features, together with the dog barking fiercely at his side, made us prepare for the worst.' What sort of person disguises himself in a black cloak? Had Fritz read in Grimms' fairy tales the story of the 'Wild Huntsman', who assumed the guise of Wotan, god of thunder, after he had abandoned the service of mankind? Or is it the pastor in his black cassock? 'Finally we reached a valley,' Fritz continued, 'surrounded by wild undergrowth. Suddenly our companion took a whistle from his pocket and blew a shrill tone. At once the forest came to life, torches were to be seen here and there and we were surrounded by men in masks. I was in a daze and did not know what was happening to me.'[44]

Did he really not know? He was experiencing anew the whole trauma of Röcken. The peace and quiet of the scene had first been shattered by the 'piercing scream' from the asylum; now the sound of the sinister stranger's whistle brought the night's events to their consummation – in the tree-lined graveyard, where veiled figures disguised in black robes stood around him in a circle while others approached an open grave. He fainted but he survived the experience. 'When I woke up,' he recorded, 'I was still surrounded by those frightening images but soon a more cheerful mood began to come over me – I was still in school at Pforta, it was my last morning, and in two hours I would be back in Naumburg.'

WHEN SLEEP BEGETS MONSTERS

Fritz survived his nightmare unscathed. It had found its natural point of repose – his evening stroll through the fourteen years of his life had brought him back to the graveyard at Röcken, where his father was just being buried. What he had been unable to come to terms with at that time also caused him to lose consciousness when the events were repeated in his dream. When his Zarathustra later declared that 'there can only be resurrections where there have been graves', he could draw on the experience of his childhood.[45]

An indefatigable chronicler of the stream of day-to-day events, young Fritz particularly enjoyed writing down his dreams. Might they one day come true? he wondered. Besides that, there is pleasure to be had from recording dangers that one has managed to escape: one can later embellish them and add poetic imagery to what were merely dry diary entries. And they will always serve as auguries of what is to come. As he had known in advance of the death of little Joseph, so he also foresaw the passing of his grandfather David Oehler. He was later to say that he spent almost every night in the company of the deceased. But his pride in anticipating the future was outweighed by his fear. As though he had not suffered enough under the strict discipline imposed on him during the day, the ghostly figures conjured up by his imagination pestered him throughout the night. The visions of a highly-strung child? But for him there was nothing fictitious about them. Even after he had woken, the horrible apparitions continued to haunt him. The very thought of them, as his Zarathustra later observed, was enough to set his heart thumping.[46]

Nightmares have little in common with the weird apparitions invoked by Justinus Kerner, which are harmless by comparison, restricting themselves to spiritualist phenomena such as knocking and wailing. The monsters created by nightmares know no limits. Inducing fear and terror is for them a triviality – what counts is the real physical threat they pose. And precisely because of their realness nightmares continue to be taboo subjects. A person who suffers from them does not willingly talk about them. They are a denial of the image of man as proud master of his own fate; they reduce him to a piteous creature of shivering flesh. Reality is for him not merely that which he can see with his own eyes and grasp with his own hands – it is also the ghostly figure that stretches out its hand towards him and fixes him with its own eyes. It has escaped attention till now that Nietzsche was later to investigate these experiences in *Thus Spake Zarathustra*.

Indeed, many of the cases described by investigators into nightmares read like excerpts from Nietzsche's work. There are, for example, American psychoanalysts who maintain that a man who suffers from nightmares 'is unable to bring his ghosts under control'.[47] One describes the horror-trips as 'long, vivid, frightening dreams which awaken the sleeper and are usually clearly recalled'.[48] Nightmares occur mostly in the second half of the night. The dreamer's whole being is gripped by a sense of panic – physical agitation and the events of the dream exacerbate each other until the tension, embodied in the fearful image, finally becomes unbearable. The dreamer awakes with a loud cry, and the ghost, which had a filled the room a moment ago, vanishes.

In the nineteenth century the causes of such dreams were held to lie in breathing problems or indigestion. Nietzsche, an unshakeable materialist, also believed this. But the American psychologist Ernest Hartmann found it impossible to establish a link between the two phenomena. According to Hartmann's interpretation, nightmares occur at a phase in the dream that seems to be reserved for experiences of early childhood. The vision represents merely the repetition of a traumatic experience that the sleeper had in the first years of his life.

If, for instance, a child loses one dear to him or has to suffer the transference of his mother's attention to a newly born brother or sister, there may be a sudden shock of deprivation, which is so unbearable that the child excludes the experience from its consciousness. If in later life a similar situation of extreme helplessness occurs, the experience is recalled from its exclusion and the sequence is repeated in the new context. No one can help the victim because his helplessness has become the subject of his dream. Release comes only when he wakes up.

Nightmares are more common than generally thought. According to Hartmann, five per cent of American adults suffer recurrent attacks. He characterises those affected as highly sensitive, artistically gifted and given to grandiose conceptions of themselves. Sexually many describe themselves as a combination of masculine and feminine. And because they cannot distinguish as clearly as others between dreaming and waking, or imagination and reality, they also experience parapsychological phenomena such as clairvoyance and déjà vu. They also have an unhappy proclivity to mental illness.

Fear, especially in a dream, releases creativity. In a monograph called *Ephialtes, A Pathological – Mythological Treatise on the Nightmare in Classical Antiquity* (1900), Wilhelm Heinrich Roscher, a fellow-student of Nietzsche in Leipzig, maintained that 'the extraordinary vividness of nightmare visions often surpasses by far that which is experienced in a waking state'.[49] Nietzsche, who suffered from nightmares throughout his life and exploited them in his works, saw in them the forces that perpetually threatened his life. Masked and otherwise disguised, these forces constantly assumed new forms that nevertheless always continued to menace and frighten him. His secret suffering remained hidden, as did, therefore, his attempts to overcome it.

Roscher described nightmares as spectacular nocturnal events, which frequently begin with a feeling of suffocation. Visions of snakes and toads appear, which quickly cease to be visions but, in repulsive reality, make to throttle the dreamer. On other occasions an ugly dwarf-like being with sub-human features might appear before his bed, sometimes transforming itself into a ghoulish animal half-dog, half-ape. Some with a particularly vivid imagination also say that it has the skin of a mole.

The dwarf's favoured position is squatting on the victim's chest. Sometimes the dreamer is made to carry the creature on his shoulders up a steep hill, over a yawning chasm, while it gets heavier and heavier at every step. Roscher also observes that dwarfs have particularly large genitalia.[50] Resistance is pointless and will be met, as Ludwig Laistner puts it in his book on the Sphinx, with 'mocking laughter'.[51] Touch one of its limbs, and one's arm will be paralysed; try to scream, and one will be struck dumb. If one collapses under the hideous burden, one will be jolted into a feeling of being buffeted by violent winds or driven mad by a deafening crashing and rumbling. On waking with a scream, the victim will be left feeling that he has narrowly escaped from a situation of mortal danger. Some even think that the end of the world is at hand, with the trumpets about to sound on the Day of Judgement.

Apparitions can also imitate voices. At one moment they emit obscene, pulsating groans, at the next whimpers of pain and delight or, according to Laistner, a 'hoarse, agonising grunt which pierces the victim to the quick and reminds him of the groans uttered by his father as he lay dying'.[52] Nor do they shrink from the basest of tricks. In order to disguise their scabrous intentions, they sometimes pretend to talk like a child, speaking in short, stuttering phrases.

Ernest Jones, pupil of Freud, found in the nightmare a prime example of the psychoanalyst's field of activity, claiming it to be the product of a repressed sexuality. A nightmare, according to Jones, culminates in feelings of sexual desire against which the dreamer struggles in vain. 'The latent content of a Nightmare', wrote Jones, 'consists of a representation of a normal act of sexual intercourse, particularly in the form characteristic for women; the pressure on the breast, the self-surrender portrayed by the feeling of paralysis, and the genital secretion directly indicate its sexual nature, and the other symptoms, the palpitation, sweating, sense of suffocation, etc., are merely exaggerations of manifestations commonly experienced in some degree during coitus when fear is present.'[53]

Why are the nightmare figures in this pleasant activity so repulsive? Because, according to Jones, 'the representation of the underlying wish is not permitted in its naked form, so that the dream is a compromise of the wish on the one hand, and on the other of the intense fear belonging to the inhi-bition'. Desire meets with resistance, and since, as the ironic saying has it, 'if it's not possible, it's not permissible', this resistance transforms the secret object of desire into a revolting, ever-growing dwarf-like monster. Mounting desire turns into a quivering, uncontrollable sense of terror and the cry of ecstasy sounds like a cry of death. The victim who experiences this loses his senses, but not before they have had their fill.

The patients on whom Ernest Hartmann carried out his experiments exhibited no such symptoms. In his view, sex does not play a dominant role in nightmares. That waking from a nightmare is linked with an orgasm – which Roscher also accepts – is for him untrue. 'The lack of sexual themes in the nightmares, the lack of pronounced sex difference in the nightmares, and the lack of difference in relating to male and female interviewers', wrote Hartmann, 'suggest that nightmares may have their origin in early childhood experiences and involve early primitive fears, vulnerabilities, and boundary problems from a time before definite sexual identity was formed.'[54]

At the same time Hartmann was aware of a related problem that occupied the minds of American psychoanalysts. The 'ego-boundaries [of nightmare sufferers] can be considered thin', wrote Hartmann, 'in that these people allow sexual and aggressive material to enter into consciousness more than most of us.' Maybe access to such material was forbidden in earlier and more prudish ages, so that it could only emerge under the cover of darkness. At all events it was not the only threat confronting nightmare sufferers in earlier times, lurking behind dwarfs, serpents and moles.

Nietzsche endured all the variations on this theme, playing out his sexual and aggressive fantasies in his dreams. His regular encounters with these nocturnal monsters remained agonising mysteries. He was perpetually turning them over in his mind, wrote Lou Salomé: any solution he might be offered brought him 'visible relief'.[55] He had been plagued by visions even before he learned to write. And long after he had laid down his pen and exchanged the life of an intellectual vagabond for the place of honour in his sister's museum-cum-asylum in Weimar, his 'blood-chilling cries of agony and despair, which pierced the silence of the night like the howls uttered by a mortally wounded animal', left no doubt that he was far from bringing his internal demons under control.[56]

Long before Freud Nietzsche knew the hidden meaning of nightmares. To believe, he wrote in his thirties, that it is possible to destroy one's sensual nature, is to deceive oneself. 'For a man's sensuality lives on, like a hideous vampire, tormenting him in all manner of repulsive guises.'[57]

3 *The Pangs of Adolescence*

THE SICKLY CADET

'On a grassy slope at the side of the road, as it meandered its quiet way from Naumburg', noted the writer Ludwig Bechstein on his journey through the romantic countryside of Thuringia, 'stands the famous school of Pforta, seat of learning for the sons of princes and the intellectual elite ... a former Cistercian monastery, now a boarding-school, in which the country's youth is instructed in the manifold arts of virtuous living'.[1]

Nietzsche's biographers painted the same picture of the school as Nietzsche himself. 'Pforta had a great deal in common with a Prussian military academy', wrote Curt Paul Janz,[2] while Werner Ross described it as a place 'in which firm discipline was exercised, comparable to that of a strict monastic order'.[3] Looking back, Nietzsche, who had been granted a free place in 1858 on the basis of having been deprived of paternal guidance, wrote: 'What such exclusive schools actually do is to enforce a brutal regime aimed at producing as quickly as possible a large number of young men trained to be of use – more accurately, misuse – to the state.'[4]

Life followed a strict routine, as it had at home. The boys were woken at four. Anyone who was still not up by five was punished. Prayers were at half-past five, with a reading from the Bible. Breakfast, consisting of warm milk and bread rolls, followed quickly and lessons began at six. Lunch was at midday. 'On Mondays there was soup, beef, vegetables and fruit; on Tuesdays, soup, beef, vegetables and butter; on Wednesdays, soup, beef, vegetables and fruit; on Thursdays beef and vegetables, grilled kidney and salad; on Friday, soup, pork and vegetables. In addition each boy was given a twelfth of a loaf of bread at each meal.' Such was Nietzsche's account of the week's menu.[5]

After lunch the boys had to walk in the garden until half-past one – anyone found going to his dormitory earlier than this was punished. From two to four there were more lessons, then a short break, followed by tests. The hours between five and seven were given over to revision. Then came supper. Lights out was at nine.

Fritz reacted to this regime by having nightmares and falling ill. In conformity with the spartan ideal pupils were expected to keep quiet about their various aches and pains. Later he made no bones about drawing attention to one ailment or another, but in the rigorous routine of Pforta complaining about pain and discomfort was frowned upon, and only in exceptional cases was a pupil granted a sick note. A boy was expected to feel himself a man and behave accordingly.

Nevertheless the school's health register does contain an alarming list of complaints suffered by its alumnus Master Friedrich Nietzsche – rheumatism, catarrh, rheumatic pains in the head and neck, headache, diarrhoea, congestions, all entered time and again in the school records. Dr August Zimmermann, the school doctor, breaks off this melancholy catalogue of recurrent medical conditions in order to offer a biographical explanation. 'Nietzsche', he writes, 'is a well-built, stocky young man with a strikingly unblinking gaze, shortsighted and frequently plagued with pains in varying parts of his head. His father died of softening of the brain while still young, having been conceived when his parents were at an advanced age. The son, in turn, was conceived at a time when his father was already ill. As yet there are no adverse symptoms but it is necessary to have regard to these circumstances of his earlier life.'[6]

A man with a medical history, in other words – a pupil about whom his masters conversed in whispers. Dr Zimmermann, the man responsible for collecting this information, will not have derived much enjoyment from his dealings with his patient. Nietzsche once called him, within ear-shot, 'an old windbag'.[7] The doctor inflicted various 'remedies' on him, usually to no avail – mustard poultices, cupping, leeches and the particularly painful cantharides. The rheumatism, catarrh and congestions only worsened.

In January 1861 he referred to 'constant headaches', which even impaired his powers of perception. 'I never really become fully conscious', he complained: 'everything around me seems to be like a dream'.[8] He added defiantly that under no circumstances would he expose himself to the dishonour of being confined to the sick bay. The rigours of life in Naumburg stood him in good stead. Nevertheless a few days later we find him writing to his mother that besides himself there were eight others in the sick bay. The last thing he wanted was for her to think that he was the only one in the school to be unwell.

It was not only his headaches that became chronic – the circumstances that provoked them also tended to recur. Gritting his teeth as he fought to overcome his homesickness, he was left with the rectory in Pobles as the sole remaining outpost of the paradise he had once enjoyed. Here he spent his summer holidays, forgetting for a few weeks what school had done to him. He was allowed access to his grandfather's library with its collection of works on the occult, and at other times he would retire to the cottage in the garden with his new biography of Platen.

In 1859 Grandfather Oehler celebrated his seventieth birthday. His grandson had composed a special poem for the occasion, a poem unmistakably autobiographical in tone:

O place that hath always vouchsafed me
A fresh glimmer of the homestead
That I had lost,
Thou art special to me,
Helping me to preserve
The faithful memories of childhood
That would otherwise have faded away,
And to satisfy my craving
For the home I once called my own.[9]

Ten years had elapsed since the tragedy in Röcken that he now recalled in a spirit half naïve, half sentimental. Nothing had been forgotten.

In the night before he recited his nostalgic lines to the assembled company, he had had a dream. The rectory in Pobles was lying in ruins, with his grandmother sitting alone among the broken timbers.[10] Waking from his dream, he rushed out into the garden and paced to and fro until dawn. According to his sister Elisabeth, their mother, who was herself highly superstitious, forbade them to tell the dream to anyone. But it was of no avail. Six months later Grandfather Oehler, hitherto hale and hearty, was dead. Shortly afterwards the family left the rectory with its historical views and private memories. Fritz, the boy whose dreams came true, was once more the loser. In 1875 he made a note in his diary, recalling Pobles 'as I wept over my lost childhood'.[11]

As to Schulpforta, he later wrote that it had only given him 'a substitute for an education at the hands of a father'. What he received he judged by what he had lost. At all events a strict routine and an ethos of military discipline were no way to deal with him. He had already had enough of this at the hands of his mother. Soon, he went on, he would escape the fetters of laws and conventions and cultivate his 'private tastes and ambitions'. In sum: 'I would live in a secret cult of certain mysterious arts.'[12]

He had wrapped himself in a cocoon. His motives were nobody's business. While on the surface he appeared to submit to the school's strict disciplinary code and act the part of the ambitious scholar, his real self wrote poems which he could not discuss with others. He composed verses and music because he needed a safety valve. And by an irony of fate it was in Pforta, of all places, that he met with success. The age needed geniuses. His teachers saw themselves as talent spotters. And here was a boy whose talent was worth cultivating.

THE KISS OF THE MOON BOY

In June 1862 he wrote to his mother with some exciting news. He had been chosen to recite one of his poems at the school's annual speech day. 'I recited my poem "The Death of Ermanaric" ', he told her, and that he had been awarded the highest mark in the class. Unfortunately, he went on, he could not send it to her because it was too long to copy out. He had good reason for not showing it to her, for it concealed a secret that was no business of hers.

Nietzsche's poem was his third attempt at a literary work on the subject of Ermanaric, king of the Goths. A year earlier one of his teachers had drawn the figure to his attention, and in July 1861 he made a sketch of Ermanaric's life and death on the basis of books he found in the school library at Pforta: 'Swanhilda is betrothed to Ermanaric. The king's evil adviser is Bicci, who points out to Swanhilda that Randwer, the king's son, would make a more suitable husband for her than the ageing Ermanaric. The proposal delights the young couple. But Bicci betrays their secret to the king, who thereupon orders Randwer to be hanged and Swanhilda trampled to death by horses.'[13]

It was just the type of story to appeal to the young Nietzsche. First the young prince cuckolds his old father with the young queen, then the king kills both of them. Honour is done. Let the cruel tyrant Ermanaric see how he can appease his conscience. In his poem Fritz subjects the king to the torments of hell.

In September of the same year, gripped by the subject anew, he composed what he called a 'symphonic poem – starting in a sombre, heroic mood and ending in total silence, in death, awaiting salvation'.[14] After completing the poem in the spring of the following year, he went back to the music in September and added a further poem in October. In November he worked on design sketches, and in December he wrote a lengthy essay on Ermanaric, which made a great impression at the school. Is this boy not a born scholar? they asked. And in 1865 we find our amateur composer planning an opera on the subject. All together he spent four years, on and off, on the Ermanaric project. The story, which bears an unmistakable and hardly coincidental resemblance to Wagner's *Tristan and Isolde*, was one that forced itself on his attention time and again. But he never succeeded in completing it.

In Nietzsche's sketches for an Ermanaric drama the woman has no part to play. Her only role is as the catalyst that brings about the tragic confrontation of father and son. By the time that the two suffering heroes, both tormented by pangs of conscience, finally encounter each other in Nietzsche's poem 'The Death of Ermanaric', Swanhilda has long been trampled to death. Without her the father would not have become a murderer, or the son a traitor. Nietzsche does not actually say as much but it is an obvious conclusion to draw. Without the woman the two men would have got on tolerably well with each other. From this point of view the title of Nietzsche's poem is a misnomer. Instead of the Schillerian 'Death of Ermanaric' it should be the Wagnerian 'Ermanaric and Randwer'. Nietzsche had known Wagner's drama of love and death since 1861. The poem he recited to the audience at Pforta described a *Liebestod* of father and son. Was the audience listening?

In a storm-battered forest, a scene reminiscent of Wagner's opera on incest *The Valkyrie*, Ermanaric curses his fate. First he is cuckolded, then made a murderer, and finally his castle is burned down – shades of 1848. The moon looks down on him mockingly, then vanishes behind the clouds. At the end a ghost appears to the terrified king – the familiar situation in reverse. Half-crazed and showering curses on himself, he watches as the pallid figure of his son advances towards him. In his paranoia the king cries out:

His is the form that rises up before me!
It swells and grows, threatening to suffocate me,
Threatening to pierce me with its stare!
What have I done to thee, O bloodstained figure?
Why doth thy glistening eye cast its savage gaze upon me?

Fritz responded in the same vein. Since those distant days in Röcken he had been tormented by the memory of that ghostly vision in the graveyard. Now the threat of suffocation is added to the nightmare. Let his father suffer – it will not be for long!

In 1888 Nietzsche was to invoke a god of a tormented conscience to whom his victim makes his whimpering plea:

Why, never tiring of tormenting humankind,
Dost thou fix me with thy cruel, glinting eyes?
Thou smotherest me, persecutest me,
Thou God! Thou Hangman!

In 1862 the victim of this attack had been Ermanaric, with his ghostly son, never tired of torturing his father, as the hangman. As the father shudders and trembles, the son approaches him menacingly:

He crept up to the old man,
Then fell to the ground, sobbing gently.
Rooted to the spot, the king fixed him with his eye
And moaned in fear: 'O image of hell!
Thou hast the features of the son I lost!'[15]

A piercing eye seems to have been a characteristic of the Nietzsche clan. This time, however, the eye sees not a phantom pretending to be reality but reality itself. The son, having escaped the clutches of his would-be murderers, casts himself down at his father's feet and begs for forgiveness, as though it were he who had instigated the murder. The father prostrates himself before his son. As Tristan and Isolde become one in their night of love, so in Nietzsche's poem the father is united with his prodigal son:

The old man begins to waver, his eye becomes cloudy,
He grasps his son's hand and holds it tight
And covers his face with kisses
Until the spirit of life finally leaves him.
They sink to the ground in each other's arms.
The youth shudders and smiles in his fright
And death creeps slowly over his body
As he sobs and moans.
One last kiss, and he too breathed his last,
Leaving them surrounded by a deathly silence.[16]

The erotic, morbid father fixation of a seventeen-year-old schoolboy. Two lovers, each a ghost to the other, finally embraced in death. By dying together they are both purged of their sins, freed from their unendurable guilt. The rest is silence. The gulf that had separated father from son has vanished.

Six months later it was to open up again. This time the guiding force was not Wagner but the patriotic Hungarian poet Sandor Petöfi. Fritz first came upon Petőfi's emotional lyrics of love and war in 1862, and at once set them to music, discovering in the process how close they were to his Ermanaric drama. Petőfi, a freedom fighter who died on the battlefield, was an idol in Germany in the later nineteenth century. Many were the young men who dreamed of giving their lives for freedom and fatherland. Petőfi's collection of poems 'The Night and the Moon' had appeared in German translation in 1860 and stirred Nietzsche's emotions. Here, with its imagery of love and nature, of visions rising from the grave, of yearning and of bitter-sweet reunion, was something from the world of Ermanaric.

In October 1862 Nietzsche wrote a romantic heroic poem in the spirit of Petőfi, beginning: 'A song sent flaming into the night'. It was a song for Ermanaric to sing. As he awaits his death, according to the legend, his adversaries plot to seize his throne. All I want, he says, is 'to send my song out into the night', then they can lay me in the grave. His song is his confession of guilt and describes the terrible deed that weighs on his conscience. If any man learns of this deed and its frightening consequences, his heart will turn to ice:

> It is pale murder that has wounded my heart,
> Broken open the shrine of my grave,
> Thrown away the key so that I cannot find it,
> While all the time the dead peer in at me,
> Peer at my face.
> Never will they leave me in peace.[17]

Ermanaric is a murderer, but his crime rebounded on him. His own heart was mortally wounded, while those whom he had killed returned as ghosts, rising from his tomb to stare at him. Under the accusing eyes of his victims he struggles with his conscience, and from his apparently hopeless fight emerges a vision of ultimate salvation:

> Until the moon, pale boy, awakes
> Whom the pale dead love to kiss ...
> Now am I like the dearly beloved dead
> And have also chosen a dear one to love:
> The pallid moon.
> Dost not ask why?
> At night we wander among the graves.
>
> Kiss me, beloved moon, O pallid youth,
> Then I must fight on helplessly alone.

There is still time for us to dream.
The dead still hover above the grave
And have joined the happy throng
Dancing away my pain,
My endless pain, in the light of the stars.

It is the same scene as in 'The Death of Ermanaric'. The king, longing for death, is confronted by his ashen son who has escaped his own death only in order to die in the company of his father. With a little help from Petöfi, Ermanaric emerges as a forerunner of Gustav von Aschenbach in Thomas Mann's *Death in Venice*, playing and dancing with the pallid youth, the moon, even demanding a kiss. Who would deny the right of the guilt-laden king to lighten his load a little with the help of innocence and beauty? In any case it all takes place in the timeless hours after midnight when only ghosts are around and when mysterious beings are seen and heard. An hour for plants from the graveyard. Yet after the moon's embrace and the dance of death Aschenbach has to die:

There is a story, old and grim,
How the moon creeps over the earth,
Gliding over the woods and the mountains,
And leaving a dew of burning tears
On a cold and silent corpse.
With pallid cheeks
It gazes and gazes,
Creeping and weeping so loud, so loud . . .

TEMPTATIONS

youth = man

There was no shortage of pallid youths in Schulpforta. Tired of the company of women, Fritz welcomed the change. As far as affairs of heart and soul were concerned, his two Naumburg friends, sons of Appeal Court judges, who had been more or less conveyed into his care under an agreement between their parents, hardly counted. News of what they did one day found its way back to his family the next. Not that they got up to much. They did, however, found a society for the advancement of knowledge, which they called 'Germania' and in which they urged each other to write poetry and compose music. But there was no chance that Fritz would get up to any tricks with them. When he finally found a new friend at school, he proved to be equally unadventurous. This was also a pastor's son, a boy called Paul Deussen.

Fritz craved for more – not necessarily for high jinks but for a friend, a boyhood hero for whom he would be prepared to lay down his life. His dormitory offered him a wide choice. But only when he became a senior did he begin to play closer attention to his fellow pupils. The boys were divided into seniors and juniors, a system that ensured that they kept an eye on each other. Ludwig Bechstein described it as 'an institutionalised tyranny that turned the younger boys into the slaves of the older'.[18]

This was not Nietzsche's way, however. The paternal concern that he missed in his masters he transferred to his young charges. If fate denied him the friend he was hoping for, then perhaps he could forge one himself. A classmate recorded that he was especially kind towards a 'junior', a curly-haired boy called Siegfried Bormann, 'to whom he devoted the most meticulous care and attention, almost making the others feel jealous'.[19] He even wrote a birthday ode for Bormann in February 1861 but it has not survived.

In the summer of 1859, after having been in Pforta for some three months, Fritz made his first attempt at a novel. Its central theme was to be that of friendship, and the fact that it was intended to run to twenty chapters indicates the value the young writer attached to this ideal. Only three chapters, however, were ever written – the real world intervened. The surviving fragment is called 'Capri and Heligoland' – a daring title, inasmuch as Fritz had never set foot on either of the two islands at this time. The names are not significant in a geographical sense, however – rather, they reflect a topography of the soul. Heligoland stands for the gloomy, provincial Naumburg, where his aunts were busy with their sewing and their crochet work, while jabbering away to one another without pause. Capri, on the other hand, is the island of secret brotherhood, of adventure, of beauty and all the other things unknown in Naumburg; the island beyond the grasp of the north wind and the frigidity of the soul.

Nietzsche had perhaps come across the name of the legendary island in Platen, whose works he first read in the summer of 1859. Platen had visited Capri in October 1827 and written a number of poems inspired by the island. These verses and notes may have been the inspiration for the novel the boy planned. Platen wandered through the ruins of the Villa of Tiberius as Nietzsche would one day return to the debris of his own past. Platen also embarked on a boat trip round Capri, as Fritz, dreaming of the distant Mediterranean, sails round the barren rock in the North Sea.

He travels under a pseudonym, calling himself, with characteristic modesty, Graf von Adelsberg. As he returns to his island villa, Adelsberg is filled with grief. Who would relish the prospect of returning to Heligoland? 'I have lived there far too short a time to feel a yearning like that for my homeland', says the 'Count', as though Fritz were talking about Naumburg. He longs for southern climes.

There also happen to be two Italians on the boat to Heligoland. One is Fiorillo, a tall, striking figure. More interesting, however, is Fiorillo's companion, Baron Clementi. With blond locks, like young Siegfried, as agile as a lizard, he wears a 'sardonic, sensual expression, his delicate, gold-rimmed spectacles intensifying his piercing gaze'. The man from Heligoland seems confused. What lies behind the Italian's suggestive smirk? He asks 'not to be tempted at such a sad moment'.[20]

The temptation is not all that serious. Adelsberg invites the two Italians to make a trip round the island – there is still plenty of time before he needs to go home. Then a melancholy thought enters his mind. 'O Capri,' he muses, 'the golden age of my youth I spent in your hills. How restful a time it was when I searched for sea shells on your shores and hearkened to the sad melodies that came to me across the water. Then the thought of one of my former playfellows came to me, a friend with whom I used to clamber over the ancient remains and revel in the ruins of the past.'

Fritz's favourite subject again. Hardly had he invoked these memories than a storm blows up. Happy recollections give way to worries and anxieties. The little boat is tossed to and fro by the waves and danger threatens. Clementi seems unmoved, assuming the role not only of the hero of the moment but also of the friend in the story. Facing the raging hurricane, he challenges the elements in the rhetoric of Heine's North Sea poems. 'Suddenly a shaft of lightning lit up the sea, followed by a crash of thunder, and the boat and its passengers were buried beneath the waves. Then an impenetrable darkness settled over the scene.'[21]

Once again disaster has repeated itself. He who returns to the past perishes in the past – unless a friend dies at the same time, in which case there will be a promise of joyful resurrection. The three men are miraculously rescued and their shared ordeal cements their friendship. Now 'Count Adelsberg' can risk telling Clementi, the little satyr, his deepest secret: 'I will show you my souvenir of my friend, which is likewise to be found with him . . .' – a stilted way of simply saying that a friend left on Capri had given him a souvenir and had kept the pendant for himself. Each of the two brothers holds something also in the possession of the other. He who seeks shall find.

For a boy who had grown up in a household of women this was a vital discovery. 'He drew out a little board on which were delicately and carefully sketched the outlines of the island of Capri, signed with a large C. As soon as

Clementi saw it, he showed signs of great agitation, his hands began to tremble and his eyes glistened ...' Full of excitement, he takes out his own pendant, which is equally finely and beautifully drawn. A textual variant makes the situation explicit: 'My friend must have a similar keepsake of his own. If he has, I shall know that he has retained his love for me.' And indeed, he had preserved the pendant. It was 'small' and 'lovely'.

Unfortunately Nietzsche did not reveal how he intended to develop the story. The recognition scene perhaps said all that there was to be said. The psychiatrist Georg Groddeck, who was himself a pupil at Schulpforta twenty years later, made a similar observation: 'To be sure, I was well aware that intimate relationships developed between boys in the school – "queenies" we used to call them – but it would never have occurred to me that actual sexual practices would take place.'[22]

LORD OF THE VICES

When he was seventeen, Fritz had a momentous experience. Lord Byron entered his life – the grandiose, exotic, ambiguous figure who set out to savour the extravagances of the wild side of life and who died a hero's death on the battlefield at a mere thirty-six. For a boy like Nietzsche, subjected to the rigorous discipline of a boarding-school, Byron was an ideal role model, as much for his romantic lifestyle as for the passion of his literary works and his political *engagement.* Moreover he was a man of masks and disguises, behind which lurked a sense of fear and terror. Fritz saw his own reflection in Byron's magic mirror – the image of a hero who, in the throes of death, becomes a god, while the jaws of hell open up below him.

Byron's poem *The Giaour*, published in 1813, was one of a series of Eastern tales. Tragedy hangs over the hero's life – he has committed murder. Driven out of his mind by pangs of conscience, he takes refuge in a monastery, there to lead a harsh life of penance away from others. The monks sense a tormented soul whose features cannot conceal that he is haunted and cruelly persecuted by a ghostly vision:

> But when the anthem shakes the choir,
> And kneel the monks, his steps retire;
> By yonder lone and wavering torch
> His aspect glares within the porch ...
> Lo! – mark ye, as the harmony
> Peals louder praises to the sky,

That livid cheek, that stony air
Of mix'd defiance and despair!

How could Fritz fail to recognise the Giaour as the double of the figure in the graveyard? And how reassuring that he was not the only one to suffer such a fate, while at the same time finding his unapproachable, solitary existence approved. Here was proof that a man could be a monster revelling in all forbidden passions – like Byron – and yet die a hero's death for Greece and its immortal ideal of beauty. What joys of expectation for the boy confined within Pforta's monastery walls!

In his *Ecce homo* Nietzsche maintained that by the age of thirteen he had been mature enough to grasp the meaning of Byron's egocentric drama *Manfred* and had identified in himself all the perils awaiting the hero. In a condescending tone worthy of Zarathustra himself, he informs his readers that to those who 'in the presence of Manfred utter the name of Faust, he deigns to give but a single glance' – presumably a glance of scorn.[23] For Faust, the weakling, allows himself to be redeemed by the principle of the Eternal Feminine, whereas Manfred, the superman, seeks death in an Alpine abyss.

Nietzsche does not conceal in *Ecce homo* that he had once made a gesture of homage to Byron in the form of an unfortunate orchestral *Manfred Overture*, the like of which, said the conductor Hans von Bülow, he had never seen, describing it as 'the rape of Euterpe' – an attack on a defenceless muse.[24] In 1888 Nietzsche could afford to smile, for what the cuckolded Bülow was hinting at in his drastic imagery only drew him closer to the real content of his work. Violent sexuality lived out on the literary page, of which Bülow waxes so scornful, was Byron's characteristic subject. Nietzsche knew what he owed to the great poet, whom he described as 'one of those ambivalent men of the moment, sensuous and inspired, yet childlike, their soul concealing a wound, often seeking through their works to avenge the memory of an earlier indignity, often at pains to ward off a spirit of loathing, the ever-recurring spectre of a lost faith'.[25]

In other words, a man like himself. But within the venerable walls of Schulpforta he would never have found such a one. The character of Euphorion in Goethe's *Faust* is a memorial to Byron but this would be no reason to make the wild Englishman part of the school curriculum. He was simply too eccentric, too licentious – too English. But this made him all the more attractive to Fritz. The school had enough plaster busts of the great and the good to last him a lifetime. The 1860s were a time of war, the German Empire was being forged in blood and iron and schools were required to instruct the future elite of the country in the proper military ideals. Byron offered a different kind of role model. He was not only a poetic genius but also a freedom fighter, who, heedless of danger, had made his way to the native land of Homer in order to help liberate it from the Ottoman yoke. His role was soon over. In 1824 he died of a mixture of fever and boredom. The perversions that punctuated his life, from incest and paedophilia to sado-masochism and the pleasures of the transvestite, did nothing to shake his great reputation. Rather, already during his lifetime they helped to create that demonic aura about whose origin people were reluctant to enquire.

Letting his hair grow long in the manner of a Greek partisan, our young hero was introduced to the poetry of Byron, no doubt with the best of inten-tions, by one of his teachers. The keen pupil included Byron's works, in the original English, in the list of presents he wanted for Christmas, explaining artlessly: 'I shall be starting to learn English in the New Year, and the works of my favourite English poet will be a great stimulus for me.'[26] He adopted his idol's sentiments and ideas, and in his school journal *Germania* he wrote a formal disquisition on Byron's dramatic poems. Later he took up in a poem called 'The Daughters of the Desert' the names of the sphinx-like prostitutes Suleika (from *The Bride of Abydos)* and Dudu (from *Don Juan*), and pursued the careers of Byron's heroes to the point of longing for death. An entry in his diary describing a nightmare he had in 1864 even ends with a concealed quote from *Manfred.*

Today Byron's perversions are well known – in Nietzsche's day one had to go through his works with a fine-toothed comb in order to prise them out. A note made by Nietzsche in 1881 shows that he was far from being the blue-eyed innocent in his approach to the Dionysian English romantic. He expa-tiates with relish on the revulsion aroused by the thought of 'masses of blood, filthy intestines, these sucking, pumping monsters' and quotes as his auth-ority Byron, said to have disliked watching women eating – to which Nietzsche adds that 'women do not like hearing about the digestive process' (because of its unpleasant associations). He portrays Byron as an aesthete who is repelled by the 'natural functions' of women.[27] A spiritual affinity.

Other works of Byron also seemed to read like anticipations of Nietzsche's secret spiritual life. In *Cain*, for instance, Byron displays sympathy for the murderous brother. In *Childe Harold's Pilgrimage* the hero, exhausted by his sexual excesses, leaves his homeland for the south. Among the perversions and torments in *Don Juan* the seducer disguises himself as a woman in order to infiltrate a harem. In *Lara* the heroine's page turns out to be a woman in breeches. And the sinister figure of the Giaour, like Manfred – who as early as 1861 was described as a 'Superman'[28] – comes to experience the ecstasy of hell.

Nietzsche, the impressionable schoolboy, paid his tribute to Byron and his outrageous conceits in his fragmentary story 'Euphorion', in which he set out to demonstrate to a fellow-pupil called Raimund Granier the depths of depravity he had in him. From Fritz's accompanying letter Granier could easily see that the young Byronist had fallen in love with him. Feeling himself ignored, Fritz had sent Granier his 'Euphorion' as a gesture of pique. It was a huge project that lasted a year or more, as revealed in a cryptic diary note for the spring of 1861: 'Convent. Euphorion. Mary as nun. University.'[29]

In Goethe's *Faust* the Byronic figure of Euphorion, son of Faust and Helena, symbolised the ultimate incompatibility of the Nordic and the classical worlds. If Nietzsche's ultra-prudish sister Elisabeth had come across her brother's sally into the world of pornography, not even the one completed chapter of the work would have survived. Granier, however, kept it, and it was published in the complete edition of Nietzsche's works, there described as a 'youthful indiscretion'.

Reminiscent of the tales of E. T. A. Hoffmann, it was in fact something quite different. Behind the persona of a light-hearted student Fritz conceals genuine anxieties. The last sentence reads: 'Euphorion leaned back and groaned, for his spine was being eaten away.'[30] It was not meant as a joke. Weary of his licentious mode of life, Nietzsche's hero is beginning to suffer the consequences. Schoolboys of Fritz's age were told that masturbation caused softening of the spine and brain, leading to madness and an early death. At the beginning of the twentieth century the pioneering sexologist Magnus Hirschfeld declared masturbation to be harmless, and expressly stated that it could not possibly lead to brain damage. The country must have heaved a collective sigh of relief.

Had Fritz been told that there could be a link between this dreaded disease and the popular adolescent pastime, he would have felt sick in the pit of his stomach. For this was the diagnosis of the condition that had led to his father's death. They had cut open his skull and discovered the terrible truth. So Fritz had to conclude that onanism was a fatal condition, or at least responsible for melancholia and mental derangement.

The well-known physician Christoph Wilhelm Hufeland, professor of pathology at the University of Berlin, had investigated the subject of masturbation in his famous book *Macrobiotics, Or The Art of Prolonging Life*, published in 1796, and described it as a practice that would undoubtedly shorten a man's life: 'Nature has a terrible prospect in store for such a sinner. He is like a faded rose, a withered tree, a walking corpse. All the fire of his life will be extinguished by this silent vice, which leads to enervation, listlessness, anaemia, decay of the body and depression of the mind.'[31]

It is a judgement that could have been delivered with Euphorion in mind. Had Fritz come across a learned textbook that stated bluntly: 'Onanism leads to madness'? Or had he discovered in an authoritative encyclopedia the categorical assertion, stated as an empirical fact: 'Masturbation leads to pederasty'? Who can be surprised that in the face of such prognoses Euphorion had lost all sense of pleasure in life? He feels like weeping, then dying. His sickness will ensure that his wish is fulfilled. And as though he had just finished performing the shameful act, he says: 'I am exhausted and my hand is trembling . . .'[32]

At last, it seems, Euphorion has realised the truth of his situation. 'I feel that I have cast off my disguises and now fully understand myself', he says. So he has finally abandoned the mask which he had donned to hide his real lack of character from the world. Now the horrible facts are on the table. But he has one remaining wish – 'to find the head of my Doppelgänger and dissect his brain, or my own curly-haired head'. A memory of the cruel beast of prey at his brother's grave? Of the trauma of the autopsy performed on his father? A horror film produced and directed by himself? Fritz has his own answer:

> Opposite my house lives a nun whom I visit from time to time in order to share and enjoy her piety. I know her well, from head to toe – better than I know myself. She used to be a nun, slight and slender, while I was a doctor and soon succeeded in making her fat. Her brother lived with her in short-lived wedlock; he was too fat for me, too healthy, and him I made thin – as thin as a corpse. He is sure to die in the next few days, which will suit me admirably, because I shall then be able to dissect him. But before that I intend to write my autobiography, for apart from the fact that it is interesting, it is also highly instructive towards making young men old – an accomplishment of which I am a past master.[33]

Evidently Euphorion's sinning is not confined to one sex: he makes a nun pregnant but also seduces her brother into masturbating, with the familiar fatal consequences. But this is all to the good, because it enables him to bring his third vice to bear, namely playing with a sharp knife, with which he can cut the brother open. Before this he intends to write a manual on how to defile oneself, probably including illustrations of an explicit, pornographic nature. Regrettably the book never materialised. It would have thrown fresh light on our image of Nietzsche.

In his accompanying letter to the utterly confused Granier, Nietzsche calls his emotional outburst 'disgusting', adding that it is his intention to abandon the whole project after having written the first chapter. 'I am sending you the monstrous manuscript to be used on the . . .'[34] He leaves the sentence unfinished. Did Granier, 'the distant lover', grasp what the master was telling him to do?

Three years later Granier wrote a letter to Nietzsche. 'You will recall a man' he told his pornographic mentor, 'who had believed he was loved but now realised that he was being laughed at.'[35]

THE EYE OF THE GOD

In 1862 Nietzsche's young friend and admirer Paul Deussen had good cause to feel jealous. A pretty young boy at Pforta by the name of Guido Meyer, artistic, sensual and lascivious by nature, elbowed his friend Friedrich aside. To make matters worse, Deussen acquired the mocking reputation of being 'petit bourgeois', which made him watch his rival all the more closely.

Deussen was forced to admit that as well as being 'handsome, kind by nature and witty', young Meyer was 'an excellent caricaturist' – that is to say, he drew clever cartoons that made fun of 'petit bourgeois' pupils like Deussen. The worst thing of all, according to Deussen, whose anger persisted for decades afterwards, was that Meyer had deliberately tried to inveigle Nietzsche into his orbit.[36]

In March 1863, to Deussen's heartfelt relief, the nightmare passed when Meyer, who was perpetually at odds with his teachers and with school regulations, was expelled. In a letter to his mother Nietzsche wrote that his friend 'had always been held in high esteem by those who had come to know him more intimately, and that his expulsion was a source of great sorrow to him'. The immediate cause was a drunken orgy, which had been accompanied by certain 'aggravating circumstances'. The day Meyer left, Nietzsche told his mother, was 'the saddest day he had known at the school'. For Deussen, on the other hand, it must certainly have been one of the happiest. Hypocritically he wrote: 'Nietzsche and I accompanied Meyer to the school gates and watched him walk away, only turning back after he was lost to view.'[37]

It must have tugged at Nietzsche's conscience that he had allowed his young friend to leave in a display of such apparent indifference. Should friends not die together? Ought he not to have left his educational prison arm-in-arm with his young admirer? In his imagination he followed Guido a few weeks later when, with a fellow-pupil, he spent the evening in the bar at the local railway station. According to the school's punishment record he drank four glasses of beer in the course of an hour. The episode had a happier ending for Nietzsche than the events surrounding Meyer – he was only made to forfeit his position as head boy and given a severe talking-to by his mother.

Nietzsche developed a striking attraction at this time to classical erotic verse. He made a number of translations from Sappho, who 'trembles' at the sight of her lesbian lover, and from the paedophilic Anacreon, who is 'driven mad' by his Cleobulos. This poetry had a stimulating effect on him. He wrote a love poem of his own, in which Cupid puts words into his mouth that he would never have uttered on a formal occasion in Pforta. It was a poem that sounded as though it had been written by the new Anacreon in memory of his departed Guido.

As a motto for his poem Nietzsche chose a line from Sappho: 'Eros shatters my mind once again. A storm in the mountains descends upon the oak trees.' This is the storm wind that blew away the dust that had settled on his schoolboy soul:

> Still in the distance, yet I already feel
> How the bold power of thy spirit,
> How thy words, quickly vanishing,
> Sweep me up with them like a storm wind.

Nietzsche sings a hymn in praise of the distant beloved, even the memory of whose brilliant eloquence can still make him tremble. Having once had thoughts of divine love in his mind, he is now plagued by doubts about earthly love. Desire haunts his thoughts but they lead nowhere. Only the dream is left:

> Why should I stay silent
> When I gaze into the depths of thine eyes
> And when thy smile spreads over me
> Like the morning dew.

All doubts have now passed – the poet is playing his favourite game with flashing eyes whose glances say more than words. And as the eyes inflame, it is no longer a mere mortal who stands before him but a Greek god:

> There thou standest, leaning gently backwards,
> Prepared to confront the storm.
> Thou watchest it with eagle eye –
> The flames rise, then die down.
> Thy movements are not hasty,
> For thou seekest firm ground.
> So light and charming is thy greeting,
> As though thou wast only floating past.

The poet's language has become gentle. The loved one, a marble Dionysus, stands 'leaning gently backwards', and when he follows his tracks, as the son follows the tracks of his father, or as Alcibiades follows Socrates, then he will 'float past', confident of victory and bestowing a 'light and charming' greeting. But one severe glance suffices to nip any display of passion in the bud. He stands gazing at the poet – the man who calms the storm, a Greek from the *fin de siècle*, god as giver of love. Overwhelmed, Fritz lays the whole universe at his feet:

> O would that the shining light of Heaven
> Would be shed on thee alone,
> So that in the glorious dance of spring
> Fresh blossoms would continue to spring forth from thee!
> Would that I could see these blossoms,
> Watch them flourish in my care,
> Then peace would hover above me
> And my glowing heart find rest![38]

Would that that which flows from the naked body in its gently inclined posture – so sighs the poet – would blossom under his gentle care until the blinding light of Heaven spreads over his glistening marble skin! Come, O thou herald of spring! Nietzsche does not say this in so many words but it seems to be the only meaning we can take from these lines. Only after 'the dance of spring' is over will his passion be quelled – and that, alas, only in his imagination, for the object of his desire was soon to vanish beyond his ken.

Six years later, in 1869, the memory of his lost schoolmate came back to him. Recently appointed a university professor, he wrote to Paul Deussen about his close relationship to Wagner, adding in a postscript, as though the thought had suddenly occurred to him: 'Where is our old companion Meyer? Give him my best wishes and ask him to let me have the poems I wrote during my school years – if he still has them.'[39]

Deussen did in fact meet his former rival again. Describing him as 'a second Euphorion', he wrote: 'Seldom have I seen a man whose heart was so torn asunder. He had been buffeted by all manner of cruel acts of providence and was both physically and psychologically sick, at odds with God, the world and himself.'[40] It was a savage triumph for the once-scorned Deussen – and not his last. When, recently promoted to a professorship, he visited Nietzsche in September 1887 in his Swiss retreat of Sils-Maria, he in his turn found him alarmingly changed, unkempt and slovenly, surrounded by books, 'egg-shells, manuscripts, toiletries and other domestic equipment, all higgledy-piggledy. There was no longer any sign of the proud bearing, the athletic gait and the fluent speech of earlier times. Only with effort, leaning to one side, did he manage to move, and he often expressed himself hesitantly and clumsily.'[41]

REHEARSAL FOR REVOLT

By 1862, at the latest, Nietzsche knew that his life had somehow taken a wrong turn. He was weighed down by the past, his teaching sapped his energies, and what was expected of him ran contrary to his own hopes. His yearning was for a different world. But he was fettered to reality, like Prometheus.

In his mind he had already once taken steps to free himself from his shackles. In a letter written in April to his *Germania* friends in Naumburg he blamed 'the illusion of a supernatural world' for conveying a false conception of reality, claiming that only through a series of doubts and struggles could he work himself free and could mankind become 'truly masculine'.[42] So let us shed this metaphysical ballast that keeps us in a state of self-induced slavery, he went on – from now on earth shall be our heaven! Such thoughts were not unknown at the time but by sending his challenge to the *Germania*, Nietzsche was making it clear that he was serious.

In truth he had no other option. The ambiguous nature of his existence was making him ill, his forbidden desires lay heavily on his conscience and his excessive hours of study were undermining his health. At thirteen, in the earliest of his philosophical games, he had made God the 'father of evil'; now, at seventeen, he declared man to be the architect of his own fortune. In his first philosophical essay 'Fate and History' he shows himself thoroughly convinced that he needed to liberate himself from both these forces in order to discover his own true nature. As he could scarcely write about himself and his own problems, he spoke of 'mankind' and 'being'.

His metaphysical vision was as follows: the universe is like a giant clock, its hand moving across the clock face from one hour to the next. When the hand reaches twelve, it starts its circuit anew. The clock is history, the face represents events, and the whole of existence is a senseless circular motion that drags people along in its wake. In the centre stands he, Nietzsche. But what makes him so sluggish and prevents his ideas from 'soaring upwards into the sky'? He is only one of many, he concedes, who are conditioned by their 'physical and mental constitution, the character and class of their parents, their everyday circumstances, even the monotony of their home. We are influenced without having the strength to counteract this influence, without recognising that we are in fact being influenced. It is a painful feeling – that against our will the seeds of future confusion and uncertainty have been sown in our souls.'[43]

And who, or what, is to blame? Answer: the fatalistic legacy of his father, source of the weakness of his brain and spine, together with the meanness of his years in the oppressive piety of his youth in Naumburg. I became sick and was so cunningly manipulated that I did not even feel the need to resist. But I have now put an end to all that. Awake, Friedrich! 'As soon as it becomes possible for a strong will to overturn the whole past history of the world, we would enter the independent realm of the gods, and the history of the world would then become for us a dreamlike state of rapture.'

The man who can free himself from all dependence, continued the young philosopher, must be a god. And how does one become a god? By rebellion, by breaking the spell of the past that persistently haunts one like a bad dream. But some time a man will appear and put an end to the whole masquerade, restoring everything to normal. Then the dream will pass 'and man will recover his bearings, like a child who leaves behind the world of make-believe, or who wakes with the dawn and blithely wipes all memory of his terrible dreams from his mind'. For the time being the revolt that is to restore the paradise of childhood has to be confined to paper, and tensions resolved on the written page. Pforta did not provide for rebellions of any kind – but the use of pen and ink was keenly encouraged.

The summer of 1864 – Nietzsche was twenty years of age – was oppressively hot in Naumburg. Sitting in his dressing-gown at a large table laden with books, drenched in sweat and sipping hot water to refresh himself, he finds himself being ogled from a distance by what he described as 'the benign spectre of my examination'. For he was preparing for his Abitur. The noise of the fair outside disturbs his concentration. He decides to try and compose a few bars, takes out a sheet of manuscript paper and sits down at the piano. Nothing comes. 'I first tried it in notes', he wrote in resignation, 'but it didn't work.' There he sat, first summoned by the muse, then cruelly spurned by her. He feels a tension rise within him that he would dearly release with his pen but an obstacle bars his way – what he really wants is something one does not talk about. So he makes a second attempt, 'in verse – not in rhyme but in quiet, measured rhythms'. Gradually he realises that his emotions call for a different tempo. 'So give me another sheet of paper, quickly, and ink, and a pen to scribble with!'[44]

Rapid writing, he says in a poem of 1871, jolts him into action so that 'the ink flows and words spring from the point of his pen'.[45] But it is not always a pleasurable experience. In a letter written at the time of the annual Naumburg fair he curses the ink and the pen: 'Can I not write something without the words becoming sullied and horrible?'[46] It is as though the ink were flowing of its own accord, forming words that merged into blots over which he had no control. 'You know my mania for tidiness', he adds. But on this torrid summer's day, sitting in his room, he has no fear that the devil will make blots on his paper. Today he is going to take things into his own hands.

'A balmy summer evening: daylight is pale and fading. Children's voices in the streets, music and noise in the distance. The fair is here – people are dancing, coloured lanterns are glowing, the wild animals are growling, the sound of rifle shots is heard and the rhythmic banging of the drum, deafening.'[47] The impressionistic sounds of the scene fill his mind. Is he not like one of those wild animals in their cage? Singing is heard from afar, the lanterns flicker. Gradually he is becoming irritated. A feeling of agitation comes over him that is 'hotter than the light, darker than the falling dusk, livelier than the distant voices, bringing a tremble to my heart and resounding like a great bell being rung in a storm'.

The rhythm so long desired is now pulsating insistently through his veins, like the menacing bell that had tolled at his father's funeral. Slowly he feels the situation becoming intolerable. 'I shall summon up a mighty storm!' he cries, like a shaman. 'Do not ringing bells attract the lightning?' In fact they should protect against it, but in Nietzsche's highly personal mythology thunderbolts from heaven coincide with the tolling of the funeral bell. The moment has returned – Carthage awaits its destruction: 'Lo! The first flash strikes the centre of my heart and a long grey cloud rises upwards. The thunder rumbles and a voice rings out: "Thou art purged!"'

Purged of what? Of ink stains? Of forbidden desires to be a beast of prey? Or relieved from the stress of his examinations? Three times he is struck by lightning in the course of the evening. Each time he quivers in delight, summoning up the god of thunder as he had once done as a boy on the Triebel Kirchberg: 'Pierce my heart! Storm and wind! Thunder and lightning! Pierce me to the quick!' His cry is heard, and a voice rings out: ' "Thou art made new!" '

The sultry conditions that hung over Naumburg that July evening culminated in a storm that 'purged' the atmosphere. When the storm had passed, Fritz cried: 'All hail to thee, soothing, comforting rain!' In the end – the text leaves no doubt – his frustrated body feels as redeemed as the nature that surrounds him.

4 *The Knight, Death and the Dominatrix*

On 4 September 1864 Nietzsche arrived back in Naumburg with his Abitur certificate in his pocket and stayed for two weeks. Not until 13 May 1890 did he return to live permanently in Naumburg again. In the intervening period he lodged in rented rooms and boarding-houses, first as a student and a university professor, then as a 'wanderer' – as he described himself – and itinerant writer. When he packed his bags at the end of September 1864 to leave for Bonn, he seemed to have an inkling of what was to come:

Once more, before I leave
And direct my gaze to the future,
I raise my hands to thee in my loneliness,
Upwards to thee to whom I flee,
And to whom in all solemnity
I erected altars,
So that at all times
His voice would call me back.

He would never forget him, this 'unknown god' of Röcken. It was to him that he built his altars, him to whose voice he hearkened. And when he moved on from one place to the next, because he felt stifled by his surroundings, that god would always be there for him to flee to:

I am his, and I feel the snares
That hold me down in the struggle

And, should I wish to flee,
Yet bind me in his service.

I want to know thee, O unknown power,
That thrusts its hand into my soul,
Raging through my life like a storm,
O unfathomable One, my kinsman!
I want to know thee and serve thee.[1]

Not everybody has a demon as a relative. Nietzsche offers him his services but
is forced to admit that he has no choice. For if he turns away, something drags
him down. If he resists, the demon will use force – an unknown power with
direct access to his soul. The day after his twentieth birthday Friedrich
Wilhelm Nietzsche arrived by steamboat in Bonn and enrolled at the university – called the Friedrich Wilhelm University, after its royal founder – as a
student of theology.

Although his mother had urged him to move in with the worthy Deussen,
he took a room for himself with a balcony, three large windows 'and a sofa',
as he told her, in a fine house situated on the corner of two busy streets.
'Everything is very elegant and very tidy.'[2] He was not a man to do things by
halves. He also rented an upright piano for three talers a month. And as fate
would have it, nearby was Beethoven's birthplace.

At the end of October occurred a particularly important event, the most
important in his luxurious life so far – he joined a student duelling society
called 'Franconia'. 'We wear white caps with a golden band', he tells his
mother, going on to sing the praises of his 'coffee pot', which provided him
with 'an excellent cup of coffee every morning'. At the same time he asks his
mother to send him, as a matter of urgency, the 'Certificate of Indigence' that
would entitle him to a grant of thirty talers a month. Later this allowance
increased to forty talers but by the end of the semester he had still run up a
number of debts. He was evidently going to live on a grand scale.[3]

A somewhat reluctant student, the freshman wrote home well before
Christmas – to allow for delays in the post – with a list of the presents he
would like. First and foremost was Schumann's music to Byron's *Manfred*. He
had already made a pilgrimage to Schumann's grave in Bonn and laid a
wreath there, although such an act was hardly in keeping with what would be
expected of a man who, for a while, put the emblem of the 'Franconia' on his
letters to his mother. A group photograph of the young bloods shows them
sporting incipient moustaches and wearing long sabres, their caps pulled
down over their foreheads at a provocative angle. On the right stands an

inebriated worthy with a bottle in his hand, while Fritz himself sits in the middle on a little barrel with 'F' chalked on it. His hair is long and thick, as befits a genius, and it is combed straight back behind his ears. An ironical smile flickers on his upper lip.

He was not displeased to be spending New Year's Eve without his comrades. The piano score of *Manfred* stood open on the music stand of the rented piano. His worship of Byron was spoilt, however, by aching gums and the pain from a hollow tooth. He drank punch to deaden the pain, then, becoming drowsy, lay down on the sofa. All was still. A pale lamp was shining and sometimes the coal crackled in the stove. A time to dream. His thoughts wandered from Naumburg to Pforta, then back to his room. But such trips down memory lane invariably ended at his birthplace. Röcken, it seemed, was everywhere. 'But what do I see on my bed? Someone is lying there. He groans softly – he is in the throes of death!'[4]

In his farewell poem to Naumburg he had called out to the voice. Now he hears it again. He is transported back to the bedroom where, lying on the bed, moaning and gasping, he finds his father at death's door. Clouds hover above the bed, whispering shadows of which he tries to make sense. For, as he later wrote, the figure in his bed, praising or cursing the old year, averting his gaze or hoping for a last-minute miracle, is he himself, bearing the thoughts that flashed through his mind before he fell asleep.

His nightmare is governed by fear. A ghost is lying on his bed. Once again he sees the situation as real – he is lying on the sofa, his father lies dying in his bed. He proves he is there by uttering a terrible scream. 'I heard the death rattle of the old year. It sounded like a sigh. Suddenly everything became bright. The walls of the room fell away and the ceiling was borne aloft. I looked towards the bed. It was empty.'

Then came an explosion and the vision passed. Relieved, Friedrich looks round the room. He is in Bonn, and the bells are about to ring in the New Year. Outside it is noisy – inside he sits and records his vision. Dipping his pen into the ink for the last time, he invokes an angelic voice that will proclaim the joyful message of his redemption: 'O ye fools and slaves of time, which exists nowhere but in your own heads . . . When ye are ready, the fruit will drop – not sooner!'

The message comes from the mouth of Manfred, who, pursued by the ghosts of his past, bursts out in Act Two of Byron's drama with the lament: 'We are all fools of time and terror.' No longer, Friedrich swears to himself, will I allow myself to be made a fool of by this phantom from the past. What counts is the future, 'the heroic struggle in which the gods will put us to the test'.

Would this not be the moment to shake off at last the chains that bound him to Röcken, the moment when a new year was beginning and a new period in his life opening up? For an instant he felt as if he had. He recalled the occasion over a dozen years later, in 1877, when he made a cursory note in his diary: 'New Year's Eve: The ghostly sound from my ears disappears.'[5]

A TERRIFYING VOICE

Leipzig, where Nietzsche enrolled as a student of classical philology in 1865, secured his breakthrough. Professor Friedrich Wilhelm Ritschl, who had an eye for his student's potential, took him under his wing and gave him every encouragement. After listening to an address given by Nietzsche to the university's Philological Society, Ritschl declared that he had never known a second-year student of such talent.[6] Nietzsche was over the moon. Like a man possessed, he immersed himself in the Greek classics as though trying to study them all at the same time. Even from his first year we find references in his notebooks to Theognis, Aeschylus, Democritus, the lexicographer Suidas and Diogenes Laertius. With Ritschl's support he also won the Leipzig Philology Prize.

Nietzsche's notebooks also reveal the opposite side of his meteoric rise to prominence, however. He made himself ill by overwork. The consequence of such pressure was, as always, rheumatic pains, migraines and stomach disorders. When Ritschl coaxed the university authorities at Basel into appointing the 24-year-old student to a professorship, he referred in passing to his protégé's state of health. Nietzsche, he said, was 'strong, robust and healthy'.[7] At the time he did not know any better. In the event he was saddling the University of Basel with a prime candidate for early retirement on health grounds. And also, as it transpired, with a believer in ghosts. Nietzsche was to hold his chair for a mere ten years.

There is a mysterious entry at the end of one of Nietzsche's notebooks that somehow escaped the destructive attention of the indefatigable Elisabeth. In contrast to other clear, scholarly notes, it appears, according to the editors of Nietzsche's collected works, to have been written 'in a state of great agitation'.[8] Years later he described what can happen to a man in a state of physical exhaustion, claiming that such conditions provided 'fruitful soil for an experience of what is sudden, terrible and inexplicable'.[9] When one adds to this, as he wrote elsewhere, a decline in physical activity and desire, the way opens up to all manner of mental disorders, such as visual and aural hallucinations.[10] He gave an account of one such happening during his time as a student in Leipzig: 'What I fear', he wrote, 'is not the terrible figure behind my chair but its voice – and not the actual words but the terrifyingly inarticulate and inhuman tone of the spectre. If only it spoke as humans speak!'[11]

Hallucinations and nightmares are not as rare as is sometimes made out. Ingmar Bergman, the Swedish film director, wrote in his autobiography that he was frequently haunted by ghosts, demons and devils 'who spoke with clearly audible voices – not readily intelligible but I could not fail to be aware of them'.[12] Strindberg wrote in a similar vein: 'I often feel that there is someone standing behind my chair.'[13] Thomas Mann, too, had a personal encounter with a spirit during one of his visits to Palestrina between 1895 and 1897. Mann could clearly understand the words the spirit spoke, to the extent – as one can read in his *Doctor Faustus* – of holding a conversation with it. At that time Nietzsche's note had not yet come to light but by the time of *Doctor Faustus* it certainly had.

Aural hallucinations combined with nightmarish features can indeed sometimes occur. What Nietzsche recorded was the product of precise observation. 'If a hallucination is not located in a stable interpersonal world,' wrote the philosopher Maurice Merleau-Ponty, 'it will be because it lacks a certain corporeality, an inner articulation. Every hallucination is in the first instance an hallucination of one's own body ... In their physical experiences sufferers are aware – beside them, under them, in front of them, behind them – of a personal presence.'[14] Only when the nightmare has started does the monster show its hideous face.

The sound of a voice coming from behind him was something Nietzsche had first experienced in the family home in Naumburg, then in Bonn on New Year's Eve. It also recurred during his time in Leipzig. Not even the treacherous way it had crept up on him was new. A poem from his schooldays in Pforta had portrayed Napoleon as the victim of just such a nightmare:

He is tormented in his dream by a vision
That stands menacingly behind his shoulders
And whispers repeatedly in his ear:
'You lie! You lie!' And envelops him in a freezing cloud ...[15]

The voice of conscience, dreamed but experienced as real. The charge it lays against him – Nietzsche will come to identify himself with Napoleon – sends an icy tremor down his spine: You lie! You are guilty! You will face a terrible punishment!

It had been the groaning, inarticulate tone of his dying father's voice that he remembered. His father knew what he wanted to say, his mother had explained, 'but, as is characteristic of those suffering from softening of the brain, he could not form proper sentences and was glad when I could guess what he was trying to say'.[16] What Nietzsche feared, almost twenty years later, was the sound made by that shrouded figure which rose from the grave like a terrible memory from the realm of the unconscious: 'If only it spoke as humans speak', Nietzsche wrote. Was that perhaps the thought that had flashed through Fritz's mind as he watched his father die – had the figure that now stood behind him come to torment his conscience? You have betrayed me, my son – murdered me!

Nietzsche may have written all this down in a state of great agitation but it was not an isolated experience. It is as though he had come to realise at this moment that it was not the vision or the words of the spectre that frightened him but the memory it evoked. The sound of the voice was real, and he knew where it came from.

Confused by what he had discovered in this note of Nietzsche's, one of the editors of his works later approached his sister, then in her eighties, for an explanation. Unable to deny the existence of the jotting, Elisabeth made light of the matter. 'She coolly admitted that her brother had frequently had such visions, both in Leipzig and in Basel. On one occasion, when the body of the recently deceased landlord was still lying in the next room, awaiting burial, the figure appeared wearing a nightshirt and sleeping-cap. "People just laughed and told me to say nothing about it." '[17]

If Elisabeth really did say this, she must have had a definite intention in mind, for she was not a person to reveal more than necessary. In the event she made an impromptu decision to pour scorn on the potentially incriminating passage. The legend of the nightshirt and sleeping-cap never became part of the critical apparatus. The only ghosts in Elisabeth's legends about her brother are the omissions. She was aware that his note was meant seriously but it did not fit into the image she wished to promote.

There had already been an earlier occasion that she wanted to play down and re-interpret for her own purposes. This too had been during Nietzsche's Leipzig period, in August 1866, when Naumburg, where he was spending his summer vacation as usual, was in the grip of a cholera epidemic. The outbreak had already claimed one victim in their house, a comb-maker called Lurgenstein, whose cadaver was still lying in a room on the ground floor. Seventeen years later Nietzsche recalled the moment in a letter: 'One of my most terrifying memories from my student days is that of having spent a night with the corpse of a cholera victim.'[18]

What is so terrifying about the death of someone in the same house? It was something for which one had to be prepared. And after all, Nietzsche was no longer a child. Such thoughts must have gone through Elisabeth's mind when she came across the letter. She immediately changed it. 'One particular night,' she now wrote in her biography, 'which he spent in the same house as a victim of the cholera epidemic, has left a sinister mark on his mind.'[19] 'Terrifying' she turns into 'sinister', adding that the night with the corpse was spent 'under the same roof'. But this was not what her brother had written. And while she was about it, she decided to spin out the story with further ficti-tious details. 'My brother has retained frightening memories of the cholera outbreak', she wrote. 'He told me that he had been twice struck down by the disease and that he had cured himself by constantly drinking draughts of hot water and sweating.'

So that was what had been so 'frightening' about that night! The back-ground to Elisabeth's re-interpretation was completely different. Some years later Nietzsche was taken to the mental asylum in Basel. There he said 'that he had become infected on two occasions'. He was explicitly referring to syphilis. Not at all, said Elisabeth: what he meant was cholera. True, he had written that the family fled to Kösen 'to avoid the cholera in Naumburg, which has already claimed one life in our house'. But there is no mention of infection.

So what really happened when poor Lurgenstein fell victim to the cholera and Nietzsche was immersing himself in Greek philosophy? Or was he per-haps reading Schopenhauer, who claimed that it was most frequently in a state of daydreaming that 'the figures of people who have died but whose bodies are still in the house appear before us'?[20] Was it the body itself that had appeared before him, joked Elisabeth – maybe even taking up a position behind his chair while he was dozing, exhausted, at his desk?

There was to be one more peculiar occasion when the shadow of the poor comb-maker made an appearance. In October 1874 Nietzsche wrote to Wagner that he and his two friends in Basel 'often went on long walks together, during which we could not but feel there was something ridiculous about an isolated trinity like us. As we watched our three shadows growing longer and longer in the setting sun, Gottfried Keller's story *The Three Just Comb-Makers* came to our minds, and we all laughed.'[21] There is little of the ridiculous in Keller's story but the memory of the shadows that had appeared to him in Naumburg might have evinced from Nietzsche a rueful smile.

PHILOSOPHICAL OSMOSIS

October 1865 was a hectic month. All augured well for Nietzsche's career. The house in the Blumengasse, surrounded by gardens, into which he moved stood in a quiet corner of Leipzig, far from the madding crowds. An irritating feature was the bugs. A certain amount of noise also came from a factory manufacturing safes, exceeded only by the commotion made by the children of the Rohn family, who also lived in the house. When it rained and the water dripped from the gutters, the neighbours became ill-humoured and the dank gardens looked grey and lifeless, 'like mummies'.[22]

Although the children 'did quite a lot of shouting', the new tenant wanted to keep on the right side of their father. For Herr Rohn ran a second-hand bookshop. Nietzsche had arrived in advance of his baggage, and when he saw the empty walls of his room, he rushed into the town to find Rohn's shop. Here, while browsing among the contents of the dusty shelves, he heard the voice again. 'One day, while in old Rohn's store,' he wrote, 'I saw this book, took it down and began to turn the pages. Then a demon whispered in my ear: "Take this book home with you." '[23]

There would have been no need of the demon. What the young classics student found as he looked down the chapter headings – 'The Platonic Idea as the Object of Art', 'Acceptance and Denial of the Will to Live', 'Genius' and 'Madness', 'Death' and 'Sexual Love' – was demonic enough. Why wander about in the city when one can pick up and take home in a briefcase what one was looking for? 'When I got home,' he wrote, 'I sat down on the sofa with my newly acquired possession and waited for the spirit of this powerful, mysterious genius to work its miracles on me. I found a mirror in which was reflected in terrifying grandeur the world, life and my own personality.'

Terrifying grandeur – a striking oxymoron. A person who sees himself reflected thus in a mirror soon forgets insect bites and children's screams. Arthur Schopenhauer, the gloomy genius, not only made him aware of the problem that was his life but also provided a solution. 'Here,' said Nietzsche reverently, 'I saw sickness and healing, banishment and sanctuary, hell and heaven.' Two pessimists, it seemed, had achieved a meeting of minds.

Schopenhauer's gospel for outcasts, *The World as Will and Idea,* made a deep impression on the young Nietzsche. He felt himself gripped by 'a desire for self-knowledge, even self-mortification . . . My restless, melancholy diaries of that time, with their pointless self-recriminations, still testify to the change of direction this book brought about in my life.' What these recriminations were, he does not say. There is an almost religious tone in his voice when he talks of 'a desperate upward gaze towards the deification and transformation of the very heart of mankind'. Did he perhaps catch sight of an opportunity to correct a faulty line of development and heroically embrace the decrees of fate? He works off his aggressions on himself, 'including physical torture', he adds, as though, by holding Schopenhauer's book in his hands, he were partaking of forbidden fruit.

The diaries to which he refers have disappeared, and he does not discuss his crisis in his letters. Instead he submits to Ritschl's blandishments, seeks refuge in classical literature, dons the mask of a scholar and carries Schopenhauer in his pocket. 'A sense of nervous excitement came over me', was the way he described his initiation into Schopenhauer's world, 'and who knows how far my folly would have driven me if the discipline of regular study had not drawn me in the opposite direction.' The old discipline of swotting! The would-be academic had his eye on a university career, not on nirvana.

Only once during his early days in Leipzig did he hint at his inner conflict. The crate containing his books has arrived, he writes to the family in Naumburg: some items are missing but in the last resort this does not really matter, for many decisions in life have to be made in the recesses of one's own mind. 'Do you really find it so easy to come to terms with this paradoxical existence, in which nothing is clear except that nothing is clear?' he wrote. The recipients of his letter must have had the same thought, for the writer seems to have forgotten all about them as he continues his interior monologue: 'Has one done enough to satisfy the claims of one's humanity if one satisfies the demands of the circumstances into which we are born? Who tells us to allow ourselves to be governed by circumstance? But if we are not prepared to do this and decide to follow only our own interests, forcing people to accept us as we are – what then?'

The spirit of rebellion that had inspired 'Fate and History', the address he had delivered before the *Germania* at Pforta, is now turned on his mother and sister. What I would really like, he is saying, is to compel you to accept me as I am. What could you do to stop me? Nothing. His family were not the ones in whom to confide his dilemma, as they represented the 'circumstances' into which he had been born and which had determined his life from then on. It would have been like preaching to the deaf. Nobody understood him. They also failed to recognise the hidden suicide threat at the end of his letter. If there is any point in being a Christian, he says to those for whom the question has never arisen, then it can only be that then 'one can cast off one's earthly load without suffering' – the weight of which has become wearisome.[24]

The demon who put such thoughts into his mind was not the one who had whispered to him in Rohn's dusty bookshop but one who forced its way into his soul. He knew who the demon was. The space vacated by his father was now filled by Schopenhauer, hence the title of Nietzsche's essay, published in 1874, 'Schopenhauer as Mentor'. This work, which says very little about his hero, he later describes as 'the most intimate story of my life and my development ... and [which] deals only with me'.[25]

As he sat in his room in the Blumengasse, Nietzsche realised that Schopenhauer was *his* philosopher. 'I understood him as if he had been writing only for me', he said. And if one wished to imagine a context for Schopenhauer's austere monologue, then let it consist of 'the son being taught by his father'.[26] 'He radiates a powerful sense of felicity and well-being which embraces all who hear him, from the moment he opens his mouth. We imbibe his message and are instantly restored to health.'

Having prepared the reader for what is to come, he now reveals what it was that gripped him on his first reading of Schopenhauer: 'I describe nothing but the initial physical impression that Schopenhauer made on me, that magical transference of the inner strength of one natural creature to another that comes from the first contact between the two, however slight.'

Philosophical osmosis. Without further ado the second-year student adopts the philosopher of pessimism. It would have been of no interest to Nietzsche to know that, in contrast to himself, his new blood-brother had a completely uninhibited attitude towards women. Such crudities were of no concern to him. He was happy to have found a demi-god about whom he could talk when he was in reality talking about himself. 'Such lonely figures are just the ones who need love, need companions before whom they can act freely and openly, as before themselves, and whose presence removes any need for reticence or concealment.'[27]

The man who does not dare 'to compel people to accept us as we really are' has to keep a lot to himself and must don a succession of masks. Schopenhauer had no such inhibitions and spoke his mind, never hiding his anger. Nietzsche was quite the reverse, seeking more and more desperately a way of relieving his tension. He cast his idol in the role of the lonely knight in Dürer's engraving *Knight, Death and Devil*. 'I feel very close to this picture,' he said, 'though I cannot explain how.'[28] A copy of the work, framed in mauve velvet, hung on the wall of his room in Basel, the gift of a pious patron. Later his sister quietly removed it.

This 'sinister picture', as Nietzsche called it, appears in his *The Birth of Tragedy*. It portrays 'a sorrowful, lonely figure' who follows with determination the terrible path through life that has been laid out for him, 'undeflected from his purpose by his fearsome companions ... Our Schopenhauer, accompanied by his dog, was just such a knight.'[29]

But this Schopenhauer, accompanied not by a dog but by Dürer's two gruesome companions, was our Nietzsche, sitting bolt upright on his steed, holding the reins tightly in his hand, remote and chaste. Sword and lance are of no avail against the horrible figures that escort him on his journey – he does not see them but only hallucinates them. The figure of death mutters hoarsely to him and points to the empty hourglass, while the devil glares obscenely from behind in the guise of a pig's snout, fingering the knight's buttocks. A castle on a distant hill looks down on the scene, as the figures looked down on the lonely Nietzsche in his room. Dürer's engraving seems to have made a deep impression on him. In letters from Basel he twice refers to having been plagued by a vision of a pig's snout, which he found particularly unpleasant.[30]

TWO YOUNG GODS

Nietzsche first met Erwin Rohde, a native of Hamburg, in Ritschl's seminar for aspiring academics in Leipzig. Both of them joined the Literary and Philological Society – a kind of student *Germania* – and quickly discovered that they had much in common. Like Nietzsche's years in Pforta, Rohde's schooling had been not so much an education as a learning by rote. He had been an enthusiastic student of classics at the University of Bonn and then followed Ritschl to Leipzig. But the binding factor was that Rohde too had lost his heart to Schopenhauer. He was deeply pessimistic about the manipulations of a world governed by the principle of progress and soon found himself sharing Nietzsche's position on vital issues. A formal photograph of the members of the Literary and Philological Society shows them sitting at a table with cravat and tails. Nietzsche holds his head high, his visionary gaze focused on the distance, a priest in a seminary; Rohde, by contrast, elegant, with flashing eyes, his legs stretched out casually under the table, looked more like a superior intellectual in a group of ambitious civil servants. An attraction of opposites.

When Carl von Gersdorff left his friend Nietzsche in June 1866 to join the Prussian army in Spandau, Nietzsche at once made his approaches to Rohde. But first he had to free Rohde from his attachment to one Franz Hüffer, a fat, blond, aggressive pro-Wagnerian who made a comic contrast to the slim and elegant Rohde. Nietzsche, by comparison, seemed perfectly suited to Rohde, and was receptive to his North German sarcasms, his arrogant reserve and the attractive tones of his baritone voice.

Nietzsche felt instinctively – or did he see it in his look? – that beneath the cool exterior of the man from Hamburg there beat a passionate heart. A fire was glowing beneath the ashes. They were both looking for the Greeks – and not only in the pages of the texts in Ritschl's seminar. Nietzsche's biographer

Curt Paul Janz maintained that, for all his reserve, Rohde 'was deep down almost feminine in nature, with a craving for love'.[31] Nietzsche felt the desire to take his new friend under his wing. Rohde needed to be treated gently.

By the summer the two were inseparable. They practised pistol shooting and took riding lessons every afternoon between four and five, as Nietzsche wrote to his family, 'which does us a great deal of good, both during and after. The jolting motion is good for the digestion.'[32] In other words, the extravagant luxury was justified on medical grounds. A fellow-student dubbed them Castor and Pollux, the two Dioscuri. 'Often they went straight from riding to Ritschl's seminar, still in riding kit and carrying their crops', he recorded.[33] Nietzsche changed 'often' to 'invariably'.

The army was held in high esteem at the time, otherwise the two amateur jockeys would probably have been laughed out of court. Instead, as the same fellow-student reported, 'when the couple entered the room, gracefully and glowing with health and intellectual eminence, all the other students looked at them in amazement as though they were two young gods' – though only the intellectual faculty could have been attributed to Nietzsche, who wore spectacles. Rohde was always regarded as the most handsome of all the young men in the class.

Rohde looked back on this idyllic period with a certain nostalgia, 'a time of joy and informality', which brought them untrammelled delight. Later they shared the same lodgings. 'What bliss it is', wrote Rohde, 'to enjoy the friendship of this profound and sensitive man. We spent the entire summer together living as though in a magic circle – not brusquely cutting ourselves off from the outside world yet almost always alone together.'[34] And the spirit, the demon, who had brought them together was Schopenhauer.

Rohde, easily roused by music, had found his ideal partner. But he never deceived himself over who was the driving force behind their relationship, and never forgot the gap that separated a 'creative nature', like Nietzsche's, from his own, that of 'a feeble semi-witch'. 'But my soul opened up', he went on, 'when it heard the magic sounds that you produced on the piano in the twilight of those summer evenings.' For his birthday in 1867 he asked Nietzsche for a copy of his setting of Rückert's poem 'From My Youth' for baritone voice, 'which I shall then be able to sing myself'.[35] A few years later Nietzsche was to undertake the extraordinary task of seeking to derive the secret of Greek antiquity from 'the spirit of music'. In 1879, their friendship by that time over, Rohde still looked back on those glorious days in Leipzig when 'I listened for hours to your improvisations at the keyboard.'

Rohde, the 'semi-witch' was, however, uncertain of how he should respond to Nietzsche's importuning. On the one hand so moved was he by Nietzsche's

'Socrates and Tragedy' that he wrote: 'Your essay pierced me to the quick. What bliss I feel when you take me by the hand and lead me into this world of purple darkness.'[36] But on the other hand Rohde was slow to abandon his aloofness. He retained a life-long passion for Greek antiquity but kept it, as he did his friend, at an 'idealistic' distance.

Only later, apparently, did the two Dioscuri realise what they had meant to each other during their time in Leipzig. Rohde compared the letters that Nietzsche wrote to him after they had parted to the radiance that shone from Wagner's 'Star of Eve'. The 'elemental power' of this aria from *Tannhäuser* had flooded his mind during a mountain walk, said Rohde, as he approached a narrow valley towards evening. Suddenly, from out of an overcast sky, came a 'warm ray of light', which he took to mean that his friend, however far away, was always with him, even as a star that would guide him safely through the valley of the shadow of death.

Time and again Rohde invoked the memory of that intimate relationship and 'those days when we loved each other', which were to come to so unhappy an end. He, Rohde, was the 'receiver', while Nietzsche was the 'giver'. Nietzsche the sensitive companion who could hold him in his thrall by music and his gift of vision, Rohde the seeker after beauty, worn down by the pressure of humdrum reality. 'I am athirst for beauty', he wrote, 'for the guidance of a spirit that will free us from ourselves.'[37] That spirit was soon to appear as his liberator as well as Nietzsche's – Richard Wagner, 'son of the gods', for whom Nietzsche had prepared him, as John the Baptist had prepared the way of the Lord.

Rohde thanked his friend in lavish terms 'for having opened up before me the promised land of pure friendship, a land of which, eager for affection, I had formerly only caught a brief glimpse, like a poor child who peeps into a sumptuous garden'. Two 'strands of harmony' have united to bring them together and to produce 'an even more euphonious sound'. In his lonely sojourn in Kiel Rohde feels like 'an unused piano' waiting to be touched by the hands of a virtuoso.

We have from this time a formal photograph of Nietzsche as a Prussian soldier, bespectacled and with drawn sabre. His glossy hair is combed straight back from his forehead and the ends of his moustache are twisted upwards in a flourish. In contrast to his simple uniform of a foot-soldier is the showy modern table on which he has laid his helmet. Taken in August 1868, the photo shows him as a gunner in the cavalry division of the 4th artillery regiment, stationed in Naumburg. He appears to have had a riding accident, for there are signs of a bandage beneath his jacket. He felt 'like an old woman', he wrote to Rohde, hoping that his friend's good wishes for his recovery 'would settle on his injury during the night time, like an incubus'.

After hearing of the accident, Rohde had urged his friend to have his picture taken – in uniform, before it was too late. Nietzsche did his bidding, albeit only three months later. His gaze, apparently so firmly fixed on the camera, is searching for his friend in the distance. It is a look of enquiry; gentle, almost feminine. The sabre is totally out of place in a pianist's hand. In contrast to the majority of portraits of Nietzsche, here he is looking straight at the observer, whose name is Erwin Rohde. In his accompanying letter he disclaims any apparent militaristic associations: 'Here is a photograph that shows me in somewhat provocative pose. In truth it is improper to flaunt oneself before one's friends with a drawn sabre, especially with such a grim expression on one's face. But why do we let a bad photographer annoy us – why do we allow ourselves to become annoyed that we no longer look fresh and bright like newly washed young girls? And why do we always have to stand there holding a sabre, prepared for any eventuality?'[38]

The physical separation of the two friends was a blow to their friendship. When Nietzsche wrote to Rohde in January 1869 to tell him of his appointment to a professorship in Basel, Rohde replied in a tone of despair: 'This means the end of any long-lasting relationship between us ... Never before have I felt so deeply how the best parts of my life are inseparably linked with my love for you.' So bitter did he feel over Nietzsche's cancellation of a trip they had planned to make together to Paris that he completely forgot to congratulate his friend on his appointment. Only a few days later did he send a letter of congratulation, while continuing to talk of his distress: 'What our life together has meant to me, and would continue to mean to me, is something more easily felt than expressed.'[39] Could Nietzsche have known how things would have worked out if they had embarked on a life together? One could imagine them as an attractive couple strolling through the Jardin du Luxembourg. Dejected, feeling himself degraded, 'a mere shadow of a man', Rohde gave up all thought of Paris. 'I could never have cast off my melancholy', he wrote.

So why did Nietzsche sacrifice a life with his beloved partner to his career? The needs of the two were finely divided. Rohde needed a friend to wrench him out of his inner lethargy and lift him into the world of the intellect and of the 'purest friendship', as he once carefully put it. Nietzsche needed a friend *tout court*. Would he perhaps have found in Rohde the Greek comrade-in-arms and lover he was seeking? Did he perhaps give up too quickly, here as at other times? When he ultimately lost his friend to a woman, he was full of bitter disappointment and wrote as if their love had been nothing but a misunderstanding.

It had certainly not been that. Both men had always been aware of what divided them, and later, after his marriage, Rohde explained it to Nietzsche's friend Franz Overbeck. 'I felt his whole nature to be like a purifying force drawing me and his other friends continually upwards', wrote Rohde. 'If in the last analysis I was unable to assimilate much of his nature, then it was because of the peculiar impermeability of the integument of my character.'[40]

In those days sexually suggestive allusions in translations of literary texts were left in the original, and here Rohde is using a Latin term to help him out of his embarrassment. For what he is saying is: Although I learned a lot from Nietzsche, I did not let him get beneath my skin – it is too hard to penetrate. A strange remark? But Overbeck understood. He was aware of Nietzsche's masks. He was also aware that there was nobody whom Nietzsche had loved more than Erwin Rohde.

For a long while, it seems, the two men hid from themselves the fact that, although they were indeed linked in friendship, each had a different conception of what that meant. In September 1867 Rohde sent Nietzsche a portrait of Schopenhauer, claiming that it was thanks above all to Schopenhauer's philosophy that they saw eye to eye on all fundamental matters. What the pessimistically inclined Rohde took Schopenhauer to stand for was clear: asceticism, renunciation of desire and denial of the Will for Life. This Will, according to Schopenhauer, is responsible for the misery of the whole human race. Behind the smokescreen of appearances – for everything that we call reality is in fact only a series of appearances – stands a mighty monster, the primeval Will, blind, cruel and senseless. Once one realises this, one ceases to will, and the pleasures of willing melt away.

We two, explained Rohde, have not sought the joy of each other's physical presence but have found 'disinterested delight' in each other's company, intellectual pleasure that goes far beyond mere desire. And beauty, in Schopenhauer's teaching, redeems man from his willing. Quite the opposite, Nietzsche would later say. But by that time he had parted company with Rohde.

Nietzsche understood Schopenhauer differently – as a knight who had set out determined to discover the cruel truth, unmoved by the ghostly figures that plagued his existence, and with the courage to proclaim the bitter truth that men must find the strength that is in themselves and in nature in order to bring about destruction – their own destruction. What is all our morality compared with the recognition that the world is merely a product of our imagination? In reality the world does not exist. One cannot see the real driving force, namely the Will, which creates the imagination so that it can yearn for it, absorb it and ultimately destroy it.

Shortly after his first encounter with Schopenhauer Nietzsche himself experienced on a mountain-top the power that both holds the world together and tears it apart. 'Yesterday', he wrote, 'a storm was brewing and I quickly climbed a nearby hill, where I found a hut in which sat a man with his boy. The man was slaughtering two young lambs. The storm was raging, with hail and a gale-force wind, and I felt a sense of elation … What did man and his restless striving mean to me? What is the point of being told to do now this, now that? How different are the lightning, the wind, the hail – all free agents, free of any ethical content! How happy they are, powerful forces, pure Will, unsullied by the intellect!'[41]

During this ceremony of religious worship beneath the flashing lightning and the rolling thunder an animal sacrifice had been offered to the demon. And in the rumbling of the storm Nietzsche had heard a voice which silenced all his petty moral scruples, all the virtue and piety of his years in Naumburg. Thanks to Schopenhauer he had scaled the heights from which 'all earthly veils had fallen away'.[42] But at that moment, alas, he had not yet met Rohde.

In 1869 Nietzsche wrote a letter to his boon companion in which he let all these veils drop. With the photo of Schopenhauer that Rohde had sent him on his desk, he summoned up the courage to tell the undisguised truth, unrestrained by considerations of petit-bourgeois morality. He is a hermit, he began, a man who has penetrated the facade of conventional attachments and has no interest in marriage. But this is not because he is a genius. On the contrary, he has become by a quirk of nature a strange mixture of talents and ambitions.

Put another way: his abilities and his desires are at odds with each other – a witches' cauldron of conflicting tendencies. And for this very reason he knows what a wonderful experience it is to have a real friend. He casts his friend Rohde in the role of Wagner's Tannhäuser, who escapes from the Venusberg and from the clutches of the goddess who had allowed him to share in her 'sweet bliss'. In gratitude for his liberation Nietzsche feels that he must erect an altar to 'the unknown god who created this friend'.[43]

Did Rohde know Nietzsche's poem, written in Pforta, in which he pledged himself to the unknown god as Faust had pledged himself to Mephistopheles? At that time Nietzsche had solemnly dedicated altars to this god; now he set up a new shrine in gratitude for this friend that the storm-god had brought him. What value has happiness in the bosom of one's family, he asks – it is far too commonplace to be of much account. 'But friendships … !'

THE DEMON OF SEXUALITY

The chapter of Schopenhauer's *The World as Will and Idea* in which the mask is lifted from the face of Nietzsche's demon bears the title 'The Metaphysics of Sexual Love'. For Nietzsche, now twenty-one, these were two distinct worlds. The sublime and the erotic under the same roof? Precisely, says Schopenhauer – that is where the mystery lies, and the man who cannot grasp this fact is made to suffer for it, for that spirit of the sublime and the erotic appears before him as 'an evil demon that seeks to confuse and overthrow everything'.[44] This cruel god tyrannises his enemies by causing fear and anxiety. But he can also entice and seduce them like a magician who unites what has been separated and turns hostility into love. His arrows, dipped in sweet, sometimes deadly poison, always find their mark. And this whole pantomime is only there to ensure that 'every Jack finds his Jill'. Schopenhauer describes the situation in these blunt, direct terms, considering his educated readers, like Nietzsche, capable of 'translating their meaning into Aristophanian language'.

This menacing god, whom no one can resist, is the driving force behind sexuality, the function of which is the procreation of the generations to come. Whereas men and women imagine that their choice of partner is an entirely personal matter, in reality they are only fulfilling the Will to Live. It is the demon who is responsible for this self-deception. Those who submit to him he leaves to languish in mutual yearning; those who resist him are at the mercy of his torments 'in the most repulsive of disguises', as Nietzsche once put it.

But the demon does not act at random. He looks out through Jack's eyes in search of the right Jill, for he alone can see at a glance what use she can be to him. If such a point is reached, the seed of a new being is planted – 'a new Platonic idea, as it were'.[45] And so that the race can unfold in all its glory, the demon implants in the lovers a desire for health, strength and beauty, 'hence also for youth'. Weaknesses and shortcomings, on the other hand, together with all deviant features, he roots out. He hates what is ugly and strives towards his ultimate goal – perfection.

This sex demon – calculating, selecting, unifying – is the Genius of the Species: a spirit that intervenes, as Schopenhauer emphasises, in the lives of all who are capable of reproduction, on whom he casts his 'penetrating gaze'. But, driven towards his ideal of ever superior beings and thus of perfect pleasure, he has no heart. As his task is measured in terms of eternity, he cannot afford to take account of transient human values, and morality does not interest him. His aim is reproduction, breeding, and therefore he has to be cruel and wasteful in his dealings with human material and ignore the fate of individuals. This demon, warns Schopenhauer, is for ever prepared to sacrifice human beings without further ado.

Nietzsche was electrified. Here, he wrote, 'I saw a mirror in which were reflected in their full grandeur world, life and my own soul.'[46] The old-fashioned phrase 'own soul' makes it sound as if he wanted to get rid of the profoundly disturbing aspects of this notion. In the past, he went on, there had been 'self-reproaches and desperate appeals for the salvation and reconstitution of the whole essence of humanity'. Demonic pan-sexualism, irreconcilable with his real life – or at least attainable only in dreams – drove him to acts of penance and self-castigation, then to the world of classical antiquity under Ritschl.

And ultimately to the bed of a prostitute? 'Apparently', wrote Janz, 'Nietzsche received medical treatment in Leipzig at this time for syphilis.'[47] Had Schopenhauer's love-demon perhaps released him from his inhibitions and freed him from the self-denying ordinance imposed by the family regime in Naumburg? In January 1890, when his mother took her demented son to the asylum in Jena, he said that in 1866 – his Schopenhauer–Rohde year – he had contracted syphilis. It was even known where – in a brothel.

But we are in the realm of legend. According to Deussen, back in his days in Bonn Nietzsche had visited – or been taken to – a brothel. Had he now returned there, back to the realm of the Mothers in Goethe's *Faust*, as Thomas Mann suggested, clasping Faust's key in his hand? Or had fellow-students made him drunk and taken him to a local establishment? In this case he would have been a bad disciple of his master. For the morality of Schopenhauer's 'metaphysics of sexual love' is clear – intercourse is out. For too long men and women have allowed themselves to be misused as tools of the reproductive process, which has brought them nothing but suffering, and ultimately death. It is time, proclaims Schopenhauer, to break the vicious circle of perpetual propagation. Deny the Will to Live and tear the mask from the demon's face!

Nietzsche tried to mortify his wretched flesh but he had dedicated too many altars to the unknown deity to be able to extricate himself completely from its service. The familiar fetters still held him fast. And now, when, thanks to Schopenhauer, the unknown god stood resplendent before him like a Greek garden-demon, should he simply renounce him? He had already had unhappy experiences in his attempts to oppose the despot who sought to rule his life. But how had he shown his compliance? Had he broken out of his room in Bonn one night in order to do what all Jacks and Jills do? Had he then crept back home in shame, past Rohn's sleeping children, only to discover three weeks later an ulcer that left a tell-tale scar on his *frenulum* for the rest of his life? No one could claim that he had any particular hankering for the female sex, let alone any interest in female sexuality. What if, as Thomas Mann suggested, he had deliberately courted the disease in order to stimulate his genius? But then, he had already been a sick genius for a long time.

For Nietzsche there was only one reason to 'go to women' – to find out whether, in principle, he could serve Schopenhauer's 'genius of the species'. For as he well knew, he did not seek the same goal as that genius. He was not on the look-out for his Jill, nor was he interested in founding a family. He may have been capable of impregnating a woman but he had no wish to do so. He respected women and wooed them on occasion, but he had no desire for them. His demon drove him towards the ideal of Apolline beauty. His mind was set not on procreation but on emotion. When Erwin Rohde, champion of Schopenhauer, came to realise this, he gradually lowered his visor.

THE GODDESS OF SAVAGE NATURE

In the summer vacation of 1871 the two friends were again to be found in each other's company, when the young professor at Basel withdrew to the beauty of the Bernese Oberland in the company of Carl von Gersdorff – 'proud wearer of the Iron Cross', as Nietzsche described him in a letter to Rohde. The village of Gimmelwald offered them 'the blissful loneliness of the mountains', while in the Hotel Schilthorn they enjoyed a warm, elegant hospitality. Nietzsche was working on *The Birth of Tragedy*.

His sister Elisabeth, who was allowed to accompany them, had pleasant memories of their two-week stay. 'Fritz was delighted to see his friend again after an interval of almost five years', she wrote, 'and to feel that they were again as one on all important matters.' Elisabeth was always one for the grandiose claim. She did, however, express her surprise that, 'in spite of feeling so happy the whole time, her brother yet chose to write two poems addressed to Melancholy'.[48]

On a number of occasions Nietzsche had tried to find for Rohde, whom he sorely missed, a post close to Basel. This time he wanted to secure him a professorship in Zurich but was forced to admit that, to his deep sadness, he had again been unsuccessful. In one of his letters to Rohde he asked him to try and find a copy of Dürer's engraving *Melencolia I*. In the same letter he describes himself as 'a creature with broken wings'.[49] The wings of the angel in Dürer's work, however, are not broken but only injured and folded. There she sits, earth-bound, brooding. Her thoughts seem to circle around her like the dividers she holds in her hand. On the wall behind her, as in *Knight, Death and Devil*, is an hourglass, and at her side sits a little Cupid, who appears to be recording on a tablet the thoughts in the angel's mind. Schopenhauer's view that the Cupid represents the Genius of the Species is hard to credit.

During the Christmas vacation of 1863 Nietzsche had found himself in a similar situation. 'A god summoned me, shrouding my thoughts in uncontrollable melancholy', he wrote.[50] Soon his mind cleared and the tension passed, his wings unfolded, Cupid drew fresh arrows from his quiver, and he emerged triumphantly into the light.

In Gimmelwald the mountain scene opened up before the hotel – rocks and glaciers, waterfalls and yawning chasms. And once nature is set free, so Nietzsche's chains also fall away. It was not only the situation with Rohde that made him melancholy – Schopenhauer too intensified his world-weariness. He conceded that suicide was no answer. But what if the denial of the Will was not possible, because the demon had established itself too firmly? That only made the world less bearable and the prospects more dismal. But is that my fault? asks Schopenhauer defiantly. Whoever complains about the 'bleak, melancholy nature' of my philosophy should open his eyes and see whether the world is not in fact so. 'It is not my philosophy that is "hell", but the world. A hotbed of tormented creatures that survive only by consuming each other, where every animal is the living grave of a thousand others and its self-preservation a series of cruel deaths.'[51] Here, in the wildness of the mountains, Nietzsche can see this particularly clearly. One false step, and he will be swallowed up by the abyss. Better to sit quietly in some comfortable place, like Dürer's angel, and ponder the terrifying truth.

According to Schopenhauer the truth is as follows: We men seek tirelessly to satisfy an endless succession of wishes. And when we discover that the satisfaction of each wish in turn does not satisfy us, we still do not realise that we are confronting a bottomless pit but continue to pursue one new desire after another. In human society, as Schopenhauer's disciple well knew, wishes are kept secret and desires only talked about in whispers. But in the freedom of nature everything speaks the one true language of unfulfilled desires. *His* language.

The actual condition of melancholy only arises, however, says Schopenhauer, when we 'experience a wish that has not been fulfilled but which we cannot yet renounce'. We are condemned to bear the burden of one single, great pain. But without this profound melancholy genius cannot survive. Schopenhauer's image for the mood of depression that so often surrounds highly gifted minds is Mont Blanc. The peak of this great giant is generally covered in cloud. But what a moment, especially in early morning, when the veil is lifted!

It must have been after just such a brilliant morning in Gimmelwald, emerging from the despondency of the night, that Nietzsche wrote his first poem to melancholy:

> Do not hold it against me, Melancholy,
> That I make my pen ready to praise thee,
> And that I am not sitting on a fallen tree trunk
> Like a hermit, my knee bent in reverence . . .[52]

Often, he continues, Melancholy has seen him living like a recluse performing penance for his sins. Yet while the vulture circled menacingly above his head, a light suddenly shone into the depths of his being. It is precisely this, says Schopenhauer, that constitutes genius – his inborn melancholy derives from the situation where 'the more penetrating the intellect that illuminates it, the more clearly does the Will to Live perceive the misery of its condition'.[53] But the melancholy classicist, sitting alone and pondering like the angel, has long since found pleasure and contentment among the Alpine peaks:

> Sitting thus, I rejoiced in the vulture's flight
> And in the thunderous roar of the avalanche.
> Thou spakest to me, incapable of deceit,
> But yet, in truth, with a mien of terrifying severity.
>
> Thou harsh goddess of savage nature,
> Thou likest to appear by my side like a lover.
> Thou dost show me the vulture's threatening path
> And the desire of the avalanche to deny me.
> Around me lurk teeth-gnashing, murderous creatures,
> Filled with an agonising lust to claim life.
> Growing temptingly on the unyielding rocks,
> The flower yearns for butterflies.

This was just the kind of nature worship that Schopenhauer had warned against. Optimists, he writes, 'are those who open people's eyes to the beauties of the world in the sunshine, with its mountains, its valleys, its rivers, its plants and its animals. But is the world a peepshow? Of course these things are beautiful *to look at*. But *to be* them is something quite different.

True, replied Nietzsche, but this is precisely what arouses my desire. Nature consists not only of suffering and dying but also of causing suffering and death. And he goes on to revel in Byronic fantasies of savage murder and an agonised yearning for life, with a hidden sexual allusion derived from his biology lessons at Schulpforta. Do not hold it against me, he had begun his poem, that I take pleasure in the horrors you paraded before me. The sole reason for my delight is that I recognise myself in these abominations:

> I am all these things – I shudder at the feeling –
> Enticed butterfly, lonely flower,
> Vulture and the plunging icy waterfall,
> The moaning of the wind – all worship thee,
> Thou wrathful goddess, before whom I bent the knee . . .

And it is why he writes this paean of praise. As he does so, she appears before him, takes his hand and shows him what to write:

> He trembles, he whom thou approachest,
> He twitches, he whose hand thou guidest,
> And trembling I stammer out one song after another,
> And quiver in rhythmic forms.
> The ink flows, sprayed by the pen –
> O Goddess, grant me my freedom!

The heavy, numbing weight that hangs over Dürer's engraving is suddenly lifted in Nietzsche's poem. A frightening face appears as in a nightmare and a ghostly hand stretches out towards him, causing him to tremble and shudder. And suddenly he is free. The tension has gone. Formerly he needed the god of thunder and his booming voice; now, in the Gimmelwald mountains, the god seems to have been transformed into a woman. Was he now really released from the clutches of a goddess who made him melancholy, a harsh, evil figure who was threatening to treat him with the strictness with which his mother used to deal with him? The answer lies in his second poem to melancholy, which he entitled 'After a Storm at Night':

> Today thou art shrouded in mist
> Swirling outside my window.

The fluttering snowflakes are blown gruesomely to and fro,
The overflowing streams send out their gruesome tone . . .

Snow in July? With the goddess everything is possible. Torment must continue. After the experience of profound suffering, Nietzsche wrote to Rohde, 'there remains a mysterious urge – to be whipped and tortured by the forces of passion must carry within itself a superior form of desire'.[54] The previous night he had felt this desire. The goddess descended on him in the thunder:

In the flashing lightning,
In the crashing of the thunder,
In the mists of the valley, O magician,
Thou wast preparing a poisoned chalice!

The potion comes from Wagner's *Tristan.* Isolde longs for death because Tristan can never be hers. But instead of a poisoned cup she is given a love potion, which leads to her death only after an experience of intense passion. Like the unsuspecting Tristan, Nietzsche, who knows full well what awaits him, is lost the moment he takes the first draught. He knows the ingredients of this aphrodisiac – 'that terrible mixture of lust and cruelty which was always for me "the witch's potion" '.[55]

The concoction which he first tasted in Gimmelwald – in a dream, in reality or in a realm between the two – goes today by the name of sadomasochism. Leopold von Sacher-Masoch's cult work, *Venus in Furs*, had been published in Leipzig in 1870. 'Everyone knows and feels', wrote Sacher-Masoch, 'how closely lust and cruelty are related.'[56] Nietzsche clothed this axiom in poetic form:

At midnight I shuddered to hear
The mingled lust and pain in thy moaning voice.

He had often trembled at the sound of midnight voices. This time what he heard was not quiet whispers but orgasmic moaning, pleasure in pain. Was it a dream or was he awake? A year later he wrote in his diary during a stay in the mountains: 'Confused night, with violent dreams.' 'Thou stoodst before me in my lonely bed', he says to the goddess Venus – the bed of one condemned to lie alone. Only when the storm breaks and blinding shafts of lightning pierce the blackness of his hotel room is the prospect of liberation in sight.

Sacher-Masoch's Venus likes to announce her arrival with an instrument of torture, even if it be only a whip, with which she knocks on her victim's window. 'Do you still not know me?' she asks mockingly. 'Yes, I am cruel.' Or in Nietzsche's poem:

I am the great, ever-present Amazon,
No longer like a woman or with the gentleness of a dove,
But fighting as a man with scorn and hatred,
Both victor and tiger!

The warlike woman who appears before the bed of the melancholy Nietzsche is the sister of Sacher-Masoch's Venus in Furs. Her creator calls her 'the personification of nature, with all the cruelty of nature'. When men kneel in fear and trembling before her, she feels a divine power within her.[57] What Nietzsche finds so attractive about his nature-goddess is apparently her masculinity, her capacity for hatred and scorn. Sacher-Masoch defined sadism as a combination of 'uncontrolled disdain and diabolical, mocking laughter'.[58] This, Nietzsche insists, can never be feminine. 'I am a woman of stone, your ideal', says Venus. 'Kneel and worship me.'[59] Her humble servant 'squirmed like a worm', while the goddess herself 'took a diabolical delight in crushing the worm under her foot'.[60]

Sacher-Masoch's Venus struck Nietzsche in a sensitive spot. Where women were concerned he was woefully ignorant. Indeed, hitherto his knowledge had been almost entirely based on his experience in the family household in Naumburg. Now this maternal gentleness gave way to the image of the tiger, the predator with flashing green eyes. When he wrote of the 'glib, feline cunning of women' and of 'the sharp claw concealed in a velvet glove', he was not thinking of his mother or his sister.[61] From his mother he attracted nothing more than the occasional glance of disapproval. Charging women with an 'inconstancy of desires', he derived his intimate knowledge of the female sex from hearsay only. The dangerous predator he called 'Woman' is a precise reflection of Sacher-Masoch's Venus. When he heard a powerful contralto voice in an operatic role, the Gimmelwald goddess came to his mind – 'a woman, capable of dominating men because, over and above considerations of sex, women have taken over the best qualities in men and made them their own ideal'.[62]

In which case why not take a man from the beginning? 'It is strange', says an old woman in Nietzsche's *Zarathustra*, 'how little Zarathustra knows about women.'[63] What he does say about them, and what, to the old woman's surprise, is true, comes mostly from Sacher-Masoch. 'Everything about Woman is a riddle', claims Zarathustra. Sacher-Masoch, reflecting on 'the riddles of human existence', concludes that 'the greatest of these riddles is Woman'.[64]

But not only is she herself a riddle, she also poses new riddles of her own, 'which he cannot solve'. But Zarathustra can. 'There is one answer to every-thing about Woman', he declares, 'and that is pregnancy.'[65] Otherwise there would be no reason why Man should concern himself with this inferior crea-ture, except out of pleasure in taking risks. 'But what then is Woman for Man?' asks Zarathustra. Answer: 'The most dangerous of playthings.' In Sacher-Masoch the Woman says the same to the Man: 'You are my plaything, and I can break you in pieces whenever I like.'[66]

There is always danger present in love. 'Man fears Woman when she loves', claims Zarathustra, feeling himself 'torn apart' by her.[67] Sacher-Masoch sees it the same way: 'Man and Woman are by nature enemies, joined together for a short while in one, only to become subject one to the other in the end.'[68] Nietzsche adds a rider: 'Love – war in the means it employs, mutual hatred of the sexes in its essence.'[69] The old woman fires a parting shot that has remained a piece of typical Nietzsche to the world at large: 'You are going to women? Don't forget your whip!'[70] Sacher-Masoch expresses the same senti-ment: 'Because I discipline my wife with the flail, she worships the ground I walk on. Believe me, that is the way to tame women.'[71]

Nietzsche's use of the word 'go' leaves his famous injunction willy-nilly with the implication of a visit to a prostitute. Who 'goes' to women? Venus' victim too, behind whom lurks the figure of Sacher-Masoch himself, con-fesses at the end: 'Would that I had flogged her!' If only he had understood that, 'as created by nature and trained by man, woman is man's enemy and can only be either his slave or his ruler.' To which he added, emphatically: 'But never his partner!'[72] Zarathustra comes to the same devastating conclu-sion: 'Women are not yet capable of friendship: they are like cats, or birds – or at the best, cows.'[73]

While he was in Gimmelwald Nietzsche worked on his first book, *The Birth of Tragedy from the Spirit of Music* and on the essay 'The Contest between Homer and Hesiod'. In his preliminary notes he wrote that 'the Greek temperament encompassed all manifestations of the terrible, from a tigerish passion for destruction to the unnatural urges released when men are charged with the education of youths.'[74]

In the Homer essay he becomes even more explicit. 'The Greeks,' he writes, 'the most humane race in ancient times, had a strain of cruelty run-ning through them, a tiger-like joy in destruction.' It follows, he went on, that in time of war such men were capable of the most extreme brutality, 'and regarded it as imperative to give their feelings of hate full rein. In such moments all their pent-up feelings were released – the tiger in them sprang out, the ecstasy of cruelty burning in his terrifying eyes.'[75] It is as though

Nietzsche had been an eyewitness to the scene, so passionate and spontaneous is his description. His image of Greece had a dangerous influence on young people at this time, as did that of the cruel Venus, which contributed its own share to that image.

Sacher-Masoch's cruelly sensual Greek hero is called Alexis Papadopolis. The moment he appears, the lioness relaxes her claws. Her trainer reveals himself to be an arrogant despot who exerts power purely through the strength of his personality – not to mention the 'icy, tigerish look in his eyes'.[76] Everything about him speaks of the divine – 'his athletic limbs, his black curls, his handsome features'.[77] A strange thought occurs to one of his male admirers (for his devotees are not all female): 'If his hips were less well-developed, one might take him for a woman in disguise.'[78] And why not? Alexis liked dressing as a woman – his provocative dress made one think of an overweening courtesan. With his racial hatred and bestial cruelty, he is a transvestite – not always but when the spirit moves him. 'Now I understand male love', wrote Sacher-Masoch, 'and admire Socrates for remaining pure when confronted by the likes of Alcibiades.' As well as his riding boots Alexis wore 'a richly decorated black jacket with an Astrakhan collar, with a red fez on his head'.

The new Alcibiades liked fanciful attire, too. In October 1876 a guest staying at a hotel in Sorrento was struck by the sight of 'a remarkable-looking man' sitting further down the table, dressed in 'an elegant black jacket buttoned to the neck and with a red fez on his massive round head'. Later, added the writer, he learned that the man who had fixed him with his piercing eye was none other than that 'famous scholar who had suffered a nervous breakdown' – Nietzsche. One of the other guests added his own postscript. 'I am prepared to wager', he said, 'that he contracted the disease only in order to get as much peace and quiet as he could, and to make himself as unapproachable as the Shah of Persia.'[79]

5

The Redemption of the Gods

Nietzsche first came across Alcibiades, one of the most fascinating figures in classical antiquity, when he was twelve years old. His class at Schulpforta was studying the biography of the charismatic statesman and general by Cornelius Nepos. Besides this he also found in Plutarch material that enabled him to construct his own, highly idiosyncratic image of the great Athenian hero.

The most striking feature about Alcibiades was his physical beauty, which put all his contemporaries under his spell. Nietzsche described him as 'one of those magical characters, beyond human comprehension, who are destined to captivate and conquer the world', others including Julius Caesar and Leonardo da Vinci – and naturally Nietzsche himself.[1] Plutarch, in his *Life*, writes ecstatically of Alcibiades' perfect body, the ideal model for sculpture, and of the charm and fascination of his personality. Brought up by Pericles and driven by an ambition to surpass the achievements of his peers, he became a pupil of Socrates, who saved his life at the battle of Potidaeia in 432 and was in turn rescued by Alcibiades at the battle of Delium eight years later. He was put in command of an Athenian expeditionary force but changed sides and joined the Spartans, who also admired his courage in battle. After a tempestuous career, which often brought him into conflict with the law, he was ambushed and assassinated. The life of a hero, in short.

In reality, however, this Athenian warrior in shining armour and waving plume was also a woman. He spoke with a lisp, was both seducer and seduced, surrounded himself with pretty boys and even importuned Socrates, the most sought-after preceptor of the city's youth. Emblazoned on the golden shield that he carried into battle was not the customary heraldic device but the figure of Eros, armed with a thunderbolt – the demon who unleashes flashes of lightning. Lusting after women no less than after boys, he had a vision shortly before his death: he dreamed that he was wearing the clothes of his female companion, 'who was putting make-up on his face as though he were a woman'. He died as a woman who fought like a man.

A further classical influence came from Plato's *Symposium*, the young Nietzsche's favourite work of literature. At a feast in the house of Agathon, Phaedrus gives his opinion that there is no greater blessing for a young man who is beginning life than a benevolent lover. Although but a mere handful, such couples would march side by side into battle and conquer the world. Even the gods recognise this, for they sent Achilles and his young lover Patroclus to the 'Isles of the Blest'.

Aristophanes, writer of comedies, who is also among those present in the Socratic dialogue, gives a definition of male love that anticipates Schopenhauer's 'sexual love'. 'When a lover of youth', says Aristophanes, 'meets with his other half, the pair are lost in an ecstasy of love and friendship and intimacy, and grow together to become one.' Diotima of Mantineia, according to Socrates, adds that love 'is not the love of the beautiful but of reproduction and of birth in beauty, because to the mortal creature reproduction in beauty is a kind of eternity and immortality'.

Reproduction without sexual love? Certainly. 'Those who are pregnant in the body only', says Diotima, as quoted in the *Symposium*,

> betake themselves to women and beget children – this is the character of their love ... But souls that are pregnant – for there are certainly men who are more creative in their souls than in their bodies – conceive that which is proper for the soul to conceive or contain. And what are these conceptions? Wisdom and virtue in general. He who in youth has the seed of these implanted in him and is himself inspired will come to maturity and desire to beget and to generate ... He wanders about seeking beauty that he may beget offspring ... At the touch of the beautiful he brings forth that which he had conceived long before, and in company with another beautiful soul tends that which he brings forth. And they are bound by a far nearer tie and have a far closer relationship than those who beget mortal children. For lovers always aspire to higher things, the one becoming two and the two then opening out to embrace beauty in all its forms.[2]

Suddenly this paean of praise of homosexual love is interrupted by the arrival of the inebriated Alcibiades, supported by the flute-girl and some attendants.

Socrates is angered by Alcibiades' behaviour, while admitting that he is in love with him. At the same time Alcibiades, the idol of Athenian youth, has himself fallen in love with the ugly philosopher with the dusty sandals. 'He can hardly keep his hands off me', complains Socrates to Agathon. Something stands in the way of their divine union, however – something for which Socrates is responsible. For a long while, says Alcibiades, he had pursued Socrates, enticing him with all the means at his command. At last he thought he had quarried his prey when he succeeded in sharing Socrates' couch. 'I lay down beneath his cloak and held this divine and truly wonderful man in my arms the entire night.' But when he awoke the next morning, it was as though he had slept by the side of a father or elder brother.

This seemed to Alcibiades to be somehow perverse. Was Socrates, the satyr-like creature, celibate? Xenophon, who knew him, confirmed that he was. 'He not only exercised strict self-control where physical impulses were concerned', wrote Xenophon in his *Memorabilia*, 'but also demanded that absolute restraint be observed in respect of the pleasure to be had with "the Beautiful Ones"'. By 'Beautiful Ones' Xenophon meant youths.

This irritated Schopenhauer. In the appendix to his metaphysics of sexual love he complained of Xenophon's Socrates that 'he talked about pederasty as something irreproachable, even laudable', and further that he concentrated 'so exclusively on love between males that one could conclude that there were no women in the world'. Of course there are, Socrates would rejoin: their purpose is childbearing. He adds, addressing his son: 'I am sure you do not imagine that people beget children out of passion'.

Although setting such a high value on pederasty, the sage himself resisted it. At the time when Nietzsche was studying Xenophon's recollections of Socrates, he wrote to his friend Gersdorff: 'I have *no* intention of marrying ... Increasingly I find myself basing my mode of life on that of the Greek philosophers. At the moment I am reading Xenophon's *Memorabilia* with the utmost personal interest.'[3]

Socrates the enigma – a full-blooded satyr who maintains in Plato's *Symposium* that 'matters of love' were the only things he understood turns out to be an enemy of sexual pleasure. For Alcibiades, his rejected lover, it was incomprehensible. Socrates had turned his back on beauty, offended the divine spirit of love and at the same time shown contempt for the very heart of Greek virtue! Some alien deity must have taken possession of his soul.

A divine spirit, a demon, indeed – but one in reverse. Nietzsche pondered on what could have induced so quintessentially Athenian a figure as Socrates to adopt this profoundly un-Greek stance of abstinence. In Pforta Socrates had been held up as a paragon of Hellenic values, condemned to martyrdom by the Athenians for his devotion to truth. Nietzsche concluded that there were good grounds for condemning him to death, and even that Socrates himself acquiesced in his own sentence, 'fully aware of what he was doing and without any natural fear of death'.[4] But why, in the demon's name, should a man want to die in the shadow of the Acropolis and all those handsome Greek boys? Why first deny love, then drink the cup of hemlock and descend voluntarily to the shadows of Hades?

Nietzsche had an answer. Socrates had become a monster because he suffered from one vital defect. In him resided a demon of negation, like Mephistopheles in Goethe's *Faust*. 'From my childhood onwards', said Socrates, 'I have been aware of a voice within me, which consistently tried to dissuade me from doing what I wanted to do but never persuaded me to do it.'

During his trial, the voice of Socrates' demon remained silent. 'The moment I began to reflect on how I would defend myself before the judges', he said, according to Xenophon, 'my demon opposed me.' Socrates interpreted this as a positive sign, 'because it cannot be right for us to assume that death is something bad. This is proof positive, as far as I am concerned.' Up to that time the Greeks had considered it the worst of all prospects to be cast down into Hades. Socrates went voluntarily, at the behest of his demon, the spirit of negation. It was this, not Plato's rationalistic optimism, that gave Nietzsche the solution to the enigma: 'A clue to understanding the character of Socrates lies in that remarkable phenomenon known as Socrates' inner spirit, or "*daimonion*". In situations where his formidable powers of reasoning began to flag, he regained his stability through the intervention of a divine inner voice. Whenever this daimonion was heard, it was to *dis*suade.'[5]

Nietzsche knew what was at stake – 'aural hallucinations, which have been given a religious interpretation'.[6] He had experienced for himself during his years in Naumburg how the voice of conscience could plague one's consciousness. Schopenhauer had written that Socrates' daimonion, 'that inner voice of warning', merely represented 'a hazy memory' of a real dream experienced via the aural faculty. Nietzsche may have seen it in similar terms. 'Daimonion – warning voice of my father', he once wrote.

The voice makes itself heard when reason begins to waver, as happened to Socrates on that night with Alcibiades. Eros causes people to falter – the daimonion paralyses them. But according to Nietzsche, it was nothing more than a common or garden earache that Socrates' 'abnormal nature' chose to interpret as a threatening voice. Had he previously been 'abnormal'? Or had the voice compelled him to pay heed to it? At all events Nietzsche knew that this defect had penetrated the whole of the Western world. For what was more characteristic of the post-classical world than a progressive denial of the pleasure principle, an ever-growing guilty conscience, coupled with the worship of reason and the unceasing search for truth? Happiness, it was believed from now on, was achieved through virtue, and virtue through knowledge. The man who strays from the path of righteousness will be led back to the proper path by the voice of conscience.

Socrates was the exemplar. There was a wish to imitate him, 'to bring to bear a permanent beam of light to shine into man's dark desires – the light of reason. One must at all costs remain wise, sober and clear-sighted – any concession to the instincts or the unconscious will lead to perdition.'[7] Nietzsche could not but feel himself to be the living contradiction of this maxim. It had underlain his upbringing from Naumburg to Leipzig, the voices of teachers and of ghosts had manipulated him, and at the end came his sickness. Socrates makes one ill. What an absurd thought that 'all our methods of education should from the beginning have had this one ideal before them'![8] Nietzsche knew from his own painful experience that 'to transform human nature through knowledge, this basic belief of all humanistic education, is the fundamental error of rationalism, from Socrates onwards'.[9]

THE ORGIASTIC URGE

The year 1872 saw the publication of Nietzsche's first book, *The Birth of Tragedy from the Spirit of Music*, a frontal attack on Socratic rationalism. An account of the mysterious bond between the gods Dionysus and Apollo and of the destruction of their offspring by Socrates, it caused irreparable damage to Nietzsche's academic reputation. His university colleagues recognised at once that here was a poacher who had set up his traps on sacred soil. Professor Friedrich Ritschl, his one-time supporter, poured scorn on what he called 'a piece of pseudo-aesthetic, unscholarly religious mystification produced by a man suffering from paranoia'.[10] Hermann Usener, professor at the University of Bonn, described the basic theses of the book as 'utter rubbish' and its author's scholarly reputation as 'non-existent'.[11] One of the younger generation of classicists, also an alumnus of Pforta, tore up the work, exclaiming: 'What shame have you brought down on the hallowed name of our school!'[12] Even the historian Jacob Burckhardt, a man of balanced judgement, reacted 'with an uneasy admiration which one immediately feels in fact conceals the expression of a thinly-veiled irony'.[13]

When, years later, Nietzsche looked back on his debut as a writer, he was himself far from enthusiastic. The book was constructed, he said, 'of undigested, exaggerated personal experiences that were virtually incommunicable'.[14] What he meant by 'personal experiences', and what he may have been concealing, can be found in a jotting in which he describes a strange experience. 'Let the flute play to time', he wrote, 'so that the dance becomes ever wilder, ever more hectic. Later comes the time of repose, when all seems to shudder, as after midnight all seems to take on a ghostly aspect. I am myself in time, and time is in me – self-experience, self-orgiasm.'[15]

This is the theme of *The Birth of Tragedy*. Before dealing with the 'orgiastic' moment as a cultural phenomenon, which he claimed to have identified in classical antiquity, Nietzsche had experienced this spell for himself – as a 'lover of enigmas', as he put it, 'the disciple of an as yet unknown god, driven to and fro by strange, as yet unnamed desires'. Later he even described himself as 'a mystical, almost Maenadic spirit', thereby bordering on exhibitionism. For are Maenads not female beings, afflicted, moreover, with the perverse characteristic of tearing their harmless fellow-citizens to pieces? This savage, destructive urge within him, concealed under the mantle of the classical scholar, set out to find 'kindred spirits to tempt along hidden paths and to new places in which to dance'.[16]

One of these paths, taboo for scholars, leads directly to Röcken, birthplace of the little 'plant from the graveyard'. At the very beginning of the book Nietzsche describes the Socratic scholar, his diametrical opposite, who sits contemplating the world, confident in his individuality and in the laws of nature, undisturbed by the storms of life. Schopenhauer's metaphor is that of the boatman who keeps his nerve while the giant waves toss him to and fro. The perfect professor, in fact! It is always day, because the light of reason illuminates the path of reason. All is under control because everything obeys the eternal laws of nature, which are immutable.

There are exceptions, however. In the same passage from Schopenhauer, adds Nietzsche, there is a description of 'the powerful sensation of fear that seizes people when they suddenly lose contact with the identifiable forms of phenomena' – such as when effects appear without causes, or when graves open up and the past emerges, clothed in a white shroud. Nietzsche does not enlarge on the sinister reference. The experience to which Schopenhauer was alluding evidently lay beyond the limits of communicability as far as Nietzsche was concerned. The passage in question occurs in *The World as Will and Idea*, where Schopenhauer discusses 'the indelibly imprinted sensation of terror felt by all men – and perhaps also by the higher animals – when a change takes place with no apparent cause, or if a person who has died were suddenly to reappear'.[17]

Nietzsche knew all about such things – they were part of his 'self-experience'. When confronted with this feeling of terror, man loses confidence in the everyday world; everything goes awry, the times are out of joint, the ground quakes and man loses his bearings. He may return safe and sound from this experience but nothing will be the same as it was before. All earthly happiness, says Schopenhauer, rests on shifting sands.

The second authority to whom Nietzsche turns in *The Birth of Tragedy* is Hamlet. According to Schopenhauer, the Prince of Denmark is a man who has glimpsed the true nature of things. Since that moment he finds the prospect of action repulsive. He takes no more pleasure in life – 'not even in women', Nietzsche adds.[18] He is paralysed, as though he had looked into the eye of the Medusa. He has 'understood' – but in a different way from that conceived by philosophy. It is not reason or the wisdom derived from books in a library that has opened his eyes but the ghost of his father. I was treacherously slain, the ghost says to him; your mother is sleeping with my murderer, and you are his nephew. Life is a murderers' den and the flames of Hell are waiting below. What not even the ghost knows is that his son will die of the same poison.

The passage from terror to the orgiastic is to be found neither in *Hamlet* nor in any textbook on classical antiquity. Yet without such a transition, believed Nietzsche, antiquity cannot be properly understood. This was the discovery of which he was so proud, the discovery he had experienced for himself. His revolutionary adduction of the encounter with ancient mysteries was regarded by the scholarly world as highly offensive. For what is at stake is the release of pent-up tension, liberation from a crippling paralysis – in short, here is a challenge to the whole academic order. At the centre of the conflict lies the phenomenon of the scream – anarchist among the sounds.

The scream destroys the singular reality of knowledge because its function is ambiguous. On the one hand it expresses the torment of death, on the other the joy in rebirth. In the fear of death Nietzsche heard 'the sighing of the newborn creature ... From out of the greatest joy come the screams of terror'.[19] The world begins to produce sounds. And only the initiated know that such is also the case with physical sensations – 'that pain evokes pleasure and that jubilation calls forth sounds of anguish'.[20] Terror turns into delight.

During the time Nietzsche was at work on *The Birth of Tragedy*, Prussia was at war. 'While the sounds of the Battle of Wörth were rumbling out across Europe', he wrote, the central theme of his book was occupying his thoughts.[21] A few weeks later he was to find himself fighting at Metz, still wrestling with the problem of the much vaunted 'serenity' of the Greeks.

He had little opportunity for serenity in his own life. In August 1870 he volunteered as a medical orderly and witnessed for himself the carnage on the battlefield, 'ravished by the fighting, surrounded by bodies, everywhere the stench of corpses'.[22] He was given the job of tending six seriously injured men, all with broken limbs and several wounded in as many as four places, who were lying in a miserable horse truck. Recovering from the effects of dysentery and diphtheria himself, Nietzsche was suffering from a continuous wailing sound in his ears, which persisted for a long while. He had first heard the sound on the battlefield. The change from a scream of pain to a cry of ecstasy was something he experienced in a field hospital in Erlangen. 'We were giving chloroform to a Frenchman whose hand had been shot to pieces, so as to put his arm in plaster', he wrote, 'when he suddenly cried out from under the anaesthetic: "My God, my God – I'm coming!" '[23]

The Dionysian principle, which is linked to violence and death no less than to love and orgasm, is ambiguous. One way it points in the direction of death, the other in the direction of life. The everyday world cannot survive its presence. In its terror, as in its rapture and bliss, there are no longer any individuals, any laws, or consequently any security – no sense of possession and no shared ideals. The ground is constantly shifting beneath our feet – this is dangerous terrain. In Nietzsche's words: 'Under the spell of Dionysus not only is the bond between man and man restored but also alienated nature is reunited with man, her prodigal son ... The slave becomes a free man, and all the rigid and destructive divisions arbitrarily created between men by insecurity or frivolous fashion will be overcome.'[24]

The symbol for this total fusion is music, which evolved from the ambiguous primal scream. Many sounds merge into one, producing a single, composite entity from which melodies and patterns evolve. Music, which seems to emerge from its own being, knows neither physical objects nor concepts – everything is in perpetual motion, never coming to rest. One cannot know what takes place in music but only feel with it, sing along with it, dance to it. 'By singing and dancing man shows himself to belong to a higher order of communality. Having forgotten how to walk and speak, he is about to dance his way into the heavens.' Even the distinction between men and women is removed. Mankind, an androgynous *Gesamtkunstwerk*, takes its place in a harmoniously ordered cosmos.

But it is an image that flatters to deceive. Since the subjective element in the Dionysian revels vanishes to the point of complete self-oblivion, it perishes, strictly speaking, in the creation of this new unity. One reverts to the primeval Will – to use Schopenhauer's language – that is embodied in music and is absorbed into the totality of musical sound. 'Only from out of the spirit of music can we understand what joy there is in the destruction of the individual', wrote Nietzsche.[25] At the same time, however, the ecstasy of union is accompanied by a fear of the loss of the self. This fear, from which mankind awoke with a scream, is to be heard in every note of the music that evolved from that scream. As soon as the whirling Dionysian dance is over, the ghostly stillness of midnight again creeps over the scene.

Is this not, however, the very 'self-experience' and 'orgiastic self' of Friedrich Nietzsche himself, composer and visionary? What has it to do with the gods of antiquity? Nothing, said his academic colleagues. But in *Ecce homo* he maintained: 'I discovered this one and only parallel known to history and was the first to understand the wonderful phenomenon of the Dionysian.'[26]

What did the Greeks believe they were doing when they abandoned themselves to the temptations of the demon? Firstly, they accepted that everything that is born must be prepared to perish. But also, at the very moment of this painful realisation, they understood that they became one, so to speak, with the boundless primeval desire for life. From one moment to the next all the struggles, all the torments of life would be converted into immeasurable delights. Nietzsche had inklings of such a process during his time as a teacher at the *Gymnasium* in Basel, for in the middle of his war diaries there is an entry in which he is reminded, for no apparent reason, of the classes he used to teach there. 'According to what my pupils said,' he wrote, 'Euripides' *Bacchae* made a deep impression and gave them considerable pleasure.'[27]

The young teacher must have been delighted that his students enjoyed this bloodthirsty tragedy. In it Euripides tells how Dionysus has his enemy Pentheus, embodiment of law and order, first dressed as a woman, then torn to pieces by Maenads. The victim's own mother acts as High Priestess at the ceremony and mounts the head of her murdered son on her thyrsus – she too is dazzled by Dionysus. And this had given his boys 'considerable pleasure'! Not repugnance or horror at the victim's screams or the Maenads' frenzied rejoicing but 'considerable pleasure'. This was precisely what Nietzsche looked for as a teacher of classics.

Having bewildered readers of *The Birth of Tragedy* with his revelation of the Dionysian secret of 'the spirit of music', Nietzsche leads them to witness another mystery. Music, intoxicating symbol of the primeval Will, is only one side of tragedy. Not by chance is it soon played down, then forgotten. The other side is represented by the god Apollo. Only together with Apollo can Dionysus beget the offspring born from his spirit in the fifth century before Christ. The new art form was born after the two male gods had merged like father and mother. Out of the love between Dionysus and Apollo originated the Greek tragedy. For Nietzsche this was only a parable – self-experience, real and imagined, in classical garb. Later he regretted this masquerade. He had been in two minds, he admitted, as to whether he should communicate his thoughts or conceal them, and had in consequence stammered out his words 'as though they were in a foreign tongue'. 'It should have expressed itself in song, this "new soul", not in words!'[28]

Not that it had not tried. In the solitude of the mountains around Gimmelwald, as Nietzsche reflected on his *Birth of Tragedy*, the Dionysian spirit of music had taken hold of him, plunged him into a state of confusion and melancholy, then urged him to burst out into song. Beset by ferocious passions and at the mercy of savage avalanches, he had suddenly felt the power of the Will's 'uncontrollable lust for life' coursing through his veins. 'All this is me!' he cried. 'I shudder as I feel it!'[29]

Then, in the middle of this half-terrified, half-ecstatic outpouring, a miracle occurred. The deity appeared in full armour, handsome and cruel, brandishing his weapon like a Greek hero, or a Prussian cavalry officer flourishing his sabre as he galloped to the attack. Or Venus with her whip. It is the moment when the second mystery becomes reality – the musical tension discharges itself into the image, the image into language. The one erupts from the other like lava from a volcano, yet somehow in controlled form, held back in artful verses. In Gimmelwald the rapturous vision drove Nietzsche from a state of inspiration to one of fear and trembling, as one poem after another sprang from his pen. The frenzy of the creative Will had united with the vision of his dream and begotten the poetic word.

It was not only in effusive tones that Nietzsche could describe the poetic process. Put in more prosaic terms: 'When the productive process has been building up for a long while but has been held back by an obstacle, there finally comes a sudden discharge which, stimulated by the Dionysian forces of beauty, finds expression in the form of the beautiful.'[30] This was the climax of Greek culture, and its supreme embodiment was tragedy. The energy of the Dionysian musical stream flows into the transfigured Apolline form and expresses with icy clarity the terrible wisdom of the Dionysian impulse.

The story had had its allegorical beginnings in the mountains, a landscape of rocky crags and yawning chasms where the lonely plant pined for butterflies, and where the inspired poet Archilochus, a spiritual kinsman of Nietzsche, lived out his solitary existence. Far from the humdrum life in the valley below, Archilochus seeks the poet's state of divine ecstasy. We see him, writes Nietzsche, 'deep in slumber, as Euripides describes in the *Bacchae*, reclining in the Alpine meadow in the midday sun'.[31]

The slumber of which Euripides writes is the lull before the storm. The Maenads are resting on the oak leaves. Then, roused by the lowing of the cattle, they turn to give suck to the deer and wolf cubs at their breasts, weave garlands and strike the earth with the thyrsus, causing fresh springs to well up, while nectar drips from the ivy. Such erotic miracles take place only at noon, 'in the holy mountains'. The next moment all hell breaks loose and the Maenads turn into bloodthirsty hyaenas.

With our lyric poet Archilochus, on the other hand, the situation is quite different. Intoxicated by wine, he lies peacefully on the mossy bank. One of his poems begins: 'Inspired by the god Dionysus, I can strike up a fine song, a dithyramb, for wine has pierced my heart like a shaft of lightning.' As he lies there in the midday sun, the god descends: 'Apollo approaches and brushes him with a laurel wreath. Whereupon he becomes gripped by a Dionysian spell under which lyric poems spring from his head, which in their highest manifestations become tragedies and dramatic dithyrambs.'

Famed for his mocking outbursts and his fits of erotic desire, Archilochus now lies meekly at the feet of the god and pours out one paean of praise after another. It is the work of beauty. Gone is all trace of the orgiastic abandon he once loved – all that remains is his creative ecstasy in the presence of the trans-figured deity. No longer is he the wild poet of no fixed abode. Dionysus has entered into him, a lightning flash of wine and the midday sun, and celebrates within him his union with his brother god Apollo. The inner spirit, as Nietzsche pursues his erotic vision, comes together in the act of artistic pro-creation with the primeval Will, which had once divided into the two gods but has now regained its unity with them. The orgiastic experience of the Greeks becomes a cosmic orgasm, and the wild Bacchanal turns into 'a festi-val of cosmic redemption'.

Since his days in Pforta, Nietzsche had identified with the ecstatic poet Archilochus. And he found his Apollo not in Alpine meadows but in Leipzig. Nietzsche lauds his god's beauty, which stimulates not only 'the inner world of the imagination' but also 'that sense of moderation, that freedom from the wilder impulses' which caused Archilochus so much disquiet.[32] Apollo pre-serves a balance. And Nietzsche points specifically to the fine line 'beyond which a vision dare not go, lest it leave a pathological impression'. The god must keep his distance, otherwise the beautiful vision will fade into 'common reality'.

Behind the figure of the god of sublime moderation stands Erwin Rohde, whose praises Nietzsche's *Birth of Tragedy* sings. Even when he is 'angry and displeased, the aura of the beautiful vision still surrounds him' – this, the lan-guage of one in love. From just such a love between rival gods, a love Nietzsche once called 'a bond of brothers' and 'a mysterious state of wedlock', emerged the phenomenon of tragedy, maybe on one of those magical evenings when Nietzsche-Dionysus played his own compositions and Rohde-Apollo sang in his warm, baritone voice.[33]

Plato appears to be firmly convinced that love between men, in this sublime sense, has the power to create a culture. In his *Symposium* the two Dioscuri win every battle, scale the highest peaks of beauty and are in the end sent to take their place on the isles of the blest. Tragedy, for Nietzsche the most glorious of all forms of art, rising in ineffable beauty above the Dionysian abyss, was also born of homosexual love. Below lurk the terrors of night, while high above, the rocky cliff of human destiny is caught by the rays of the rising dawn. Screams are heard from the deep, while the god floats down from on high. Such was the way Nietzsche saw it. Perhaps, he mused in *Ecce homo*, 'there were, in those centuries when the Greek body glistened and the Greek soul overflowed with life, endemic states of rapture in which visions and hallucinations communicated themselves to entire communities, entire religious bodies'.[34] Nobody knows for certain whether there was a kind of Hellenic Lourdes, where the god appeared before the people and delivered them from their physical woes. But Nietzsche knew very well what he had experienced as a child – apparitions about which one can speak only as one initiate to another.

Nietzsche discovered in a painting by Raphael what science and scholarship could only express in stutterings and stammerings. 'The lower half of Raphael's *Transfiguration*,' he wrote, 'with the figure of the boy possessed by evil spirits, the despairing bearers and the anxious, helpless disciples, shows us a vision of eternal suffering . . .'

Nietzsche only knew the huge picture, which hangs in the Vatican, from a reproduction. The boy depicted in the lower half is apparently an epileptic. The Bible says that he is held in the grip of a 'dumb spirit . . . that teareth him, and he foameth and gnasheth with his teeth, and pineth away'. The boy's father holds him erect; his mouth and his eyes are wide open and his arms stretched out. For Nietzsche it was a familiar scene. He later stated that he himself had suffered epileptic fits up to the age of seventeen, during which, as he deliberately pointed out, he had retained consciousness. He apparently had similar attacks in later life also. His sister once told their mother about 'a strange fit of paralysis that befell him for a while'.[35] Old Pastor Nietzsche had suffered in the same way.

Was Fritz, 'the little pastor', the epileptic boy in Raphael's painting? He was gripped by his demon, the 'dumb spirit' that constantly whispered in his ear. He was also tormented, like the boy in the Bible, by visions and hallucinations. But at the same time he was visited by apparitions of the 'unknown god', and longed for the solitude of his fatherless childhood. In 1878 he noted: 'As a child, saw God in His radiance.'[36] This is precisely what is depicted in Raphael's *Transfiguration*: Heaven reveals itself to the boy as he emerges from his suffering. From the depths of pain, writes Nietzsche, 'there arises, like the scent of ambrosia, a new world, the prospect of a radiant life of painlessness and ecstasy, perceived in its shining glory by those who have eyes to see'.

In his painting Raphael has combined two subjects – 'The Transfiguration of Christ' and 'The Healing of the Boy Possessed'. The upper part portrays the Redeemer in a cloud, revealing Himself to the hallucinating crowd – the vision of the disciples of Dionysus, translated to a Christian context. The epileptic boy, healed by the vision of the Redeemer, is the image through which Nietzsche conveys his message that 'the whole world of suffering is necessary in order to urge the individual onwards to the creation of the vision of redemption'.[37]

6   *In Klingsor's Enchanted Garden*

6

THE WAGNERIAN DISCIPLE

Nietzsche must have had a very candid relationship with Sophie Ritschl, Jewish wife of his professor and backer. From a stay in the 'pretentious spa' of Wittekind in July 1868 he wrote her a flirtatious little letter. Shortly after his arrival, he said, the manager of the spa, 'a rogue wearing a pair of opaque blue spectacles', had sent a 'companion' up to his room, apparently assuming that the young visitor had certain sexual needs. 'Emphatically yet politely', he had managed to decline the offer. There were 'a number of strikingly handsome female guests also sitting at his table'. Apparently our jovial young philosopher could permit himself such suggestive remarks to Frau Ritschl. Or did she perhaps already suspect that to him there was nothing suggestive about them?

He goes on to tell her, in the same vein, that he was reading Heine's *Travel Sketches*, which he greatly enjoyed but which at the same time made it difficult to pursue rational lines of thought with the appropriate seriousness of mind. 'Nothing in life is so serious', he added, '– and certainly not scholarship – that we cannot afford to introduce a light-hearted joke from time to time as a diversion.' This was a bold assertion to make to a professor's wife. But why not, she may have responded. After all, the young man was only twenty – though there was a good deal more to him than met the eye. 'And what god can be surprised if we sometimes behave like satyrs? One can hardly disguise the dubious characteristics of a Schopenhauer or a Wagner, for example.'

This is evidently an allusion to an occasion when he played the piano to the Ritschls, who were shocked by his 'predilection for discords'. At the same time he implies to the attentive reader that his scholarly aspect is merely a persona that he has assumed while imitating his two icons. Has he allowed his mask to slip in Frau Ritschl's presence? At all events he makes a prophecy that will be fulfilled many years later. Only then, he tells her, will she see him as he really is: 'One day I shall perhaps find a subject that I can clothe in musical form. Then I shall drool like a baby, and conjure up a series of impressions like a barbarian who falls asleep in front of a Greek bust of Venus' – and wakes up, it seems, as a bearded disciple of Dionysus lying at the feet of a statue of the radiant Apollo.[1]

Sophie Ritschl knew how she could show her gratitude for her favourite's frankness and confidence. By chance she happened to know Wagner's sister, Ottilie. By chance Wagner was staying that November in Leipzig, incognito. Not by chance Nietzsche received an invitation to meet the Master.

Whereupon the misunderstandings began. 'Imagining that a large company would be invited,' Nietzsche wrote to Rohde, 'I decided to wear my best clothes, and was glad that my tailor had promised to have a new set of tails ready for me by the coming Sunday.' A satyr in formal attire. Only yesterday, he went on, Wagner had received a letter from King Ludwig addressed to 'The Great German Composer Richard Wagner'. Nothing could be too fine for such an occasion, Nietzsche said to himself. Anxiously he waited for the delivery of the promised tails.

Towards evening the tailor's runner arrived. Nietzsche tried on the tails and found that they fitted. Unfortunately, however, he did not have the cash available to pay for them. The runner became aggressive. 'I grabbed the clothes,' Nietzsche wrote, 'then the man got hold of them and stopped me from putting them on. First he fought, then I fought. What a scene! Fighting in my underclothes!' In the end the tragic hero lost, the runner grabbed the tails and made off, 'leaving me sitting on the sofa swearing revenge and wondering whether my black jacket would be good enough for Richard Wagner. Outside it was pouring with rain.'[2]

This slapstick performance was a suitable prelude to the evening. The stage was set not for grand opera but for a Saxon one-man show. The great god Wagner was in shirtsleeves, surrounded by a group of friends. After cracking a few jokes in his native dialect and hurling a few insults at the authorities, he embarked on a solo performance of his recently completed *Mastersingers* without the slightest embarrassment, imitating all the main roles – Wagner as the cobbler Hans Sachs, Wagner as the sweet damsel Eva, Wagner as the knight Walther von Stolzing and as Beckmesser, the Jewish caricature.

Then everything changed. He closed the piano and suddenly became serious, launching into a long discourse with the young student in the black jacket about Schopenhauer. 'You have no idea', wrote Nietzsche in his letter to Rohde, 'what a delight it was for me to hear Wagner speak with such warmth and affection about him, how much he owed to him and how he was the only philosopher to recognise the nature of music.' Finally the two men shook hands warmly, Wagner offering Nietzsche an invitation to visit him again. This is the way one makes disciples.

Fate also played its part. On 12 February 1869 Nietzsche was appointed to a professorship in Basel, where he arrived in April. Whitsun found him standing at the door of Wagner's rented villa of Tribschen on the shores of Lake Lucerne. Here the Wagners discovered they could make good use of the young proselyte and soon he became one of the family. As three years earlier with Ritschl, so now the encouragement he received went to his head. His friendship with Rohde became reduced to an exchange of letters. His vocation and his new appointment took precedence.

He put the passing of their friendship into the pages of *The Birth of Tragedy*. 'The decline of Greek tragedy must seem to us to have been brought about by the forceful separation of the two basic artistic impulses', he wrote.[3] At the end of February 1869 the professor designate wrote to his fellow-Dioscurus: 'Dearest Friend: It fills me with a profound dissatisfaction that we cannot live together. We are virtuosi on an instrument that other men cannot and will not listen to but which is for us the source of the greatest enchantment. And now we are poles apart, you in the north, I in the south, and are both unhappy because we miss the harmony of our instruments and long to restore it.'[4]

Erwin and Friedrich, divine brothers in art, from whose harmony springs a quality 'that other men cannot and will not listen to' – cannot, because they are deaf to the sublime art of tragedy; will not, because homosexual relationships make them uneasy. Now, like Penelope on the shore, both sit and shed copious tears of longing for the distant Odysseus. As it happened, Ritschl, otherwise so unemotional, introduced Nietzsche to his colleagues in Basel as an 'Odysseus figure' who, he thought, would prove to be an excellent grammar school teacher. For combined with his university chair was an appointment to teach classics to the senior classes of the local *Gymnasium*.

But the strain was too great for this young Odysseus. University, *Gymnasium*, Wagnerian affairs at Tribschen – it was impossible to keep them all going. Maybe it would have been possible if Rohde had been there to help him but, left to his own resources, Nietzsche could not but neglect first one duty, then another. For example, he had to miss Wagner's birthday in May. 'How dearly would I have loved to be present on this happy day in your lakeside idyll among the mountains', he wrote. 'If only the fetters of my duties here in Basel did not keep me chained to my miserable dog-kennel.'

In Tribschen antiquity was celebrating its rebirth. 'My Dearest Friend,' Nietzsche, blind to reality, wrote ecstatically to Rohde, 'what I have seen and heard there is indescribable. Schopenhauer and Goethe, Aeschylus and Pindar are all alive and flourishing, believe me!'⁵ Alive in Wagner, of all people. True, he was a genius, at that moment still occupied with the music of *The Ring of the Nibelung*, the most monumental work in the whole history of music drama. But he was also a genius of self-promotion, and had time and again compromised human values in his determined pursuit of an unshakeable will to power, subordinating everything, including the principles of common morality, to his megalomaniac artistic conceptions. At the time Nietzsche came to know him, he was at the peak of his creative powers, had witnessed the triumphant performance of one opera after another and callously stolen the wife of one of his greatest friends and admirers.

Cosima von Bülow, daughter of Liszt, was no stranger to a bohemian existence of inspired anarchy. To offset this she developed a severity of character, religious in its intensity, that men came to respect. A gaunt figure, strikingly ugly – her siblings nicknamed her 'Stork' – she dominated her environment, both physically – she was a head taller than Wagner – and intellectually. What attracted her to Wagner was the grandeur of the conflicts that raged within him. At the same time their immoral behaviour profoundly disturbed her Catholic conscience, leading her to constant self-reproaches and self-recriminations. Her adultery caused her no less pain than her husband, and his suffering became her suffering. He haunted her dreams, reducing her to tears and convulsions of remorse. She indulged in a self-chastisement that amounted to sadomasochism, a state of mind she confided to her diary: 'The more I suffer, the greater the lust this agony causes.'⁶

Nietzsche felt drawn to this world. Here was a strict, unapproachable woman with whom he felt an affinity. Her ascetic person was shrouded in a veil of melancholy and ecstatic suffering. In his eyes the embodiment of pure aristocracy, she drew him to herself, conversing with him in a manner no woman had ever done before. From the moment he set eyes on her, he felt himself in the presence of a kindred spirit, and was so flattered that he failed to notice that he was soon to be exploited in the promotion of the Wagnerian cause. When he no longer served the Master's purposes, he would be replaced by another. Did he suffer under the realisation that Cosima was a woman far superior to him in matters of politics and etiquette? Later she was to make fun of his clumsiness, describing him as a man who had a genius for irritating people. Instinctual creature that he was, he sensed her masochistic tendencies. When he deliberately and maliciously set out to arouse her ire, he portrayed her as a whimpering masochist who could never get enough of her god, begging him to pierce her cruelly with his barb. He cast her as Ariadne, the princess before whom Dionysus appeared with the sardonic advice: 'Must we not first hate each other before we can love each other?'[7] The passionate philosopher of eroticism, who played hide-and-seek with his desires, had found a spiritual mate.

In April 1872 Nietzsche was facing a gloomy future. His academic colleagues regarded him with contempt, and because Wagner and Cosima were about to move to Bayreuth, he could no longer go to Tribschen. Despite many humiliations he had endured there, the villa by the lake had offered a compensation for the stress of his life in Basel, an oasis of calm to which he could flee and from which, in turn, he could also flee. 'I spent a few last melancholy days there as though in a landscape of ruins', he wrote to Rohde. To Gersdorff he said that he felt he had been living 'surrounded by wreckage' – as he had in Röcken, then Pobles and in his visions of Carthage and Nineveh.[8] Wagner's bags and crates were packed and he was preparing to leave. It was evening. A last ray of sunlight illuminated the scene one final time, as though to bring peace and reconciliation to it. Then, once again, another relationship came to an end.

Ten years later Nietzsche returned to the house on the lake with hopes of a different nature in his mind. 'For a long time he sat in silence by the lake shore, sunk in recollection. Then, drawing a line with a stick in the sand, he began to talk softly of those days of yore. When he looked up, I saw that his eyes were filled with tears.'[9] His companion, the woman who described this romantic scene, was Lou Salomé. The line he had drawn in the sand had a biblical parallel that escaped her. When the woman taken in adultery was brought before Jesus, 'He wrote with His finger on the ground and said unto them: "He that is without sin among you, let him first cast a stone at her." ' While Lou was sitting beside him, his thoughts were with the distant Cosima.

A master of reinterpretation, Nietzsche did his best to idealise the Tribschen interlude. In *Ecce homo* he is still to be found singing the joys of those perfect, cloudless days of 'the most sublime coincidences and profoundest moments' that he had experienced there, without making explicit who had made them so sublime. And what did he mean by 'sublime coincidence'? At least he came to learn, thanks to Wagner, what men's silk underwear cost. Wagner, an underwear fetishist, had sent him to Basel to buy some fine underclothes. Embarrassed by the request, Nietzsche sought the help of a friend, to whom he confided: 'Once one has chosen a god, one must adorn him!'[10]

The whole Tribschen episode, indeed, was like a farce performed by a cast of first-class actors. But Nietzsche's role was not that of the joker. Because they set out to use, or abuse, him, they underestimated him. Wagner, an effective slanderer, and Cosima, his indefatigable amanuensis, turned a good-humoured farce into a black comedy by upgrading their victim, who up till then had cheerfully played along with the plot, to the status of a tragic figure. It is not the Nietzsche of *Zarathustra* or the mentally unhinged epileptic in Turin who is tragic, or the man who became hopelessly infatuated with Lou Salomé. Only once did Nietzsche cut a tragic figure, and that was when the Wagners deliberately set out to ruin the man whose fate, as the critic and musician with the deepest understanding of their musical world, was inseparably bound up with their own. 'Wagner's music', said Thomas Mann, 'was the great emotional experience of Nietzsche's life.'[11] Or rather, as with Mann himself, the *other* great emotional experience.

Before Wagner converted Nietzsche, Nietzsche had converted himself. As a sixteen-year-old student he had studied *Tristan* in Bülow's piano reduction, but at that time he was more absorbed in his own tragedy on Ermanaric. In 1866 he worked his way through *The Valkyrie* 'with mixed feelings'. Two years later he met Sophie Ritschl, who fired his enthusiasm for Wagner's operas, and soon the great musical sorcerer was to touch every nerve in his body. It had taken a seven-year incubation period and the gracious intervention of a lady of society for Wagner to take control of his life.

Nietzsche's thoughts during this period were centred on two concepts – primeval pain and the salvation of the world. These were not abstract concerns for him – he struggled through the jungle of learning and lay in wait for his moments of ecstasy. If nothing else helped, he turned to music. Tension would slowly rise, storm clouds would gather in the sky, hurricanes would rage, then suddenly the pent-up energy would be discharged and a sense of deliverance and relief would descend, leaving a world of bliss and 'solemn, soothing harmonies'.[12] In the cynical frankness of his later years he put this in different terms: 'What does my body want from music anyway? ... Relief, as though all my animal functions were to be accelerated.'[13] No musician talks like that. But then, by 'music' Nietzsche meant something different.

When he abandoned himself to Wagner, Nietzsche heard what he understood by 'music' and what he wanted from it as though he had composed it himself. He gave it its 'proper interpretation', as he put it. In this music, he went on, 'I imagined I heard the earthquake caused when the primeval life-force, stifled for years, finally exploded.' If Schopenhauer was correct in seeing music as the immediate expression of the Will, and if Nietzsche could trust his inner experience that the Will was conditioned to discharge its energy in explosive form, then this music, the music of *Tristan* and the *Mastersingers*, was the holy temple in which he became united with the Will to form a single entity, a reflection of the world that remains hidden from those who are not initiated into these mysteries. To him, Nietzsche, was granted the power to see, hear and feel this world, feel himself being carried along by a fast-flowing river towards the fulfilment of his highest dreams: 'To begin with, the river flows uneasily, over jagged rocks and stones, drawn in different directions and split apart. Gradually we see its full power united, becoming ever mightier, carrying all before it, its former restlessness giving way to a single powerful swell towards an as yet unknown goal. Finally, in one supreme surge, it suddenly plunges with a cry of demonic bliss into the dark depths of the abyss before it.'[14]

Such was the demonic bliss of which Isolde sings at the end of *Tristan*. But for Nietzsche the transfigured image of his absent friend rose up above the foaming torrent. 'At last we could let ourselves be carried away by the emotional power of this music,' he wrote to Rohde, 'this Schopenhauerean world every corner of which I can see and feel, so that listening to Wagner's music becomes a joyful intuition, a moment of self-discovery.'[15]

It was a remark of literal biographical significance. In *Tristan* he discovered that 'ecstasy of hell', as Thomas Mann called it, which one must be 'sick enough' to enjoy, while experiencing 'frissons of delight'.[16] At a performance in Munich in 1872 that Nietzsche attended in the company of Wagner's friend and patron Malwida von Meysenbug, he shocked the worthy lady by exclaiming: 'This drama about death does not make me sad – on the contrary, I feel happy and liberated!'[17] That was the programme behind his *Birth of Tragedy*. And it was what led him to call *Tristan* 'the *opus metaphysicum* of all art'.[18] In 1888, even once Nietzsche had become a bitter opponent of Wagner and all he stood for, he was still able to say of this music: 'I am still searching for a work that exerts a comparable fascination, a work of such dangerous appeal, of such sweet yet terrifying boundlessness.'[19] To which he added a cryptic rider: 'All the mysteries in the works of Leonardo da Vinci lose their magic at the sound of the opening notes of *Tristan*.'

Wagner had succeeded in doing what Nietzsche had striven his whole life to do – to give expression to what he called the state of 'silent suffering'.[20] In the last year of his lucid existence, long after he had broken with Wagner, he was still to be found hailing him as the 'Orpheus of silent suffering' – Orpheus, because he could make even the stones shed tears, then descended into Hades and was torn to pieces by the Maenads. Wagner gave musical expression to Nietzsche's 'silent suffering', conjuring up sounds 'from the kingdom of oppressed and tortured souls languishing in the underworld'. He had found the magic language to express 'those secret, uncanny midnights of the soul where cause and effect appear to be at odds with each other and where something can spring out of nothing at any moment'.

Nietzsche, the man of enigmas, did not expound what he meant by this, and the only man who would have understood it – Wagner – had died five years earlier. As we have seen, a similar sentiment is expressed at the beginning of *The Birth of Tragedy*, when he talks of the sense of 'fear and trembling' that grips a man when cause and effect are out of joint. Then, as with Hamlet, the times too are out of joint and the past usurps the present.

The phrase 'midnights of the soul' is an allusion to the classical belief that after midnight dreams become true, become reality. Schopenhauer took up the theme in his 'Essay on Ghosts', where he quotes Horace referring to this notion, and compares it to a situation in which 'abnormal circumstances can cause the inner ear to store up all manner of sounds'. On such occasions 'pale spectres may also appear just as one is falling asleep'.

'There is a part of the night', Nietzsche once wrote, 'when time stops.'[21] At such times a strange feeling came over him that the period of time that had just elapsed was either much too short or much too long. In a word: 'Between one and three o'clock in the morning we have no true sense of time.'

But there is another side to the question. Nietzsche had long noticed that Wagner could break the normal sequence of time, could 'compose away' time, so to speak. In the middle of the Prelude to the *Mastersingers*, for instance, there is, said Nietzsche, 'a moment of inexplicable hesitation, a kind of hiatus between cause and effect, a moment that sets us dreaming, almost an apparition'.[22] In a fragment he quotes the scene in Act II of *The Twilight of the Gods* where Hagen sits guarding the palace at just such a terrifying instant when 'something can emerge from nothing'.[23]

Wagner had composed this scene – a sublime coincidence? – in Tribschen at the time of their friendship. Nietzsche would have found Wagner's own comment on the passage less than sublime. The composer played the piece on the piano to his inner circle in Bayreuth, keenly awaiting what impression it would make. 'The effect will be similar', he said, 'to when two strange animals talk to each other. One cannot understand anything but everything is interesting.'[24]

SLANDER

In August 1876 Bayreuth staged the greatest social and cultural event of the year. The host was Richard Wagner. There were dignitaries aplenty, a crowd of European aristocrats, and even monarchs, united in their curiosity to witness Wotan's demise and Wagner's apotheosis. Kaiser Wilhelm I saw the comical side of the occasion, the Brazilian emperor Dom Pedro II held court and the fairy-tale king of Bavaria, who had financed the whole enterprise, appeared quietly at the back. The list of paying guests – the king of Württemberg, the Grand Electors of Sachsen-Weimar and of Schwerin, the Prussian princesses, four Austrian counts, all with their ministers and retinue – knew no end. Decorations, military and civil, were on display by the kilogram and sabres by the dozen, parading in front of the newly built theatre on the so-called Green Hill. Flushed with the success of the occasion, Wagner exclaimed: 'No composer before me has ever been honoured in this way!' He was indeed entitled to regard himself as the Emperor of Music.

The man who had proclaimed the 'rebirth of tragedy' in Bayreuth was not there to witness the event. Scarcely had he arrived in the city than his migraine returned and he fled to the rural peace and quiet of the Bayerischer Wald, to return only a week later. In reality he was no longer needed. The outsider in Tribschen, Wagner had now become the centre of attention, while Nietzsche remained on the sidelines. The hullabaloo irritated him and he was offended by Wagner's lack of interest in him. Nor was his constitution strong enough to endure the long performances in the stuffy Festspielhaus. So what was he doing here? Yet where else should the prophet of the renaissance of classical tragedy be, if not here, on this hallowed spot?

By now Nietzsche knew that he had been wearing a fool's cap. His confusion was made the greater by a grotesque episode. Out for a walk with a friend, he found himself by mistake at the Bayreuth mental asylum, where one of the inmates presented him with a poem called 'Christ as a Butterfly's Proboscis'. Three years earlier he had written to his idol that without him he would be as 'a stillborn creature. I shudder at the thought that you might one day pass me by'.[25] That was just what had happened. The mighty surge of Wagner's music in which Nietzsche had heard an echo of a tragic loneliness – his own tragic loneliness – had ceased to flow. For him, the death of tragedy took place on the stage of the Bayreuth Festspielhaus.

Then a friend unexpectedly appeared from Basel, bringing companionship and consolation, reading aloud to him and tending him like a mother. He was the very opposite of the friends Nietzsche had made under the Wagnerian spell. A loner, a freethinker, a materialist and a Jew, Paul Rée brought him the nectar of the gods in a cultural desert. The two men returned to Basel and remained together until April of the following year. But as ill-fortune would have it – or as Malwida von Meysenbug plotted it – the two friends were destined to meet the Wagners again.

It happened in Sorrento, a popular resort for German visitors to southern Italy. Nietzsche and Rée had taken lodgings in a *pensione* barely five minutes' walk from the Hotel Vittoria, where Wagner and his wife were staying. If it had been Malwida's intention to bring about a reconciliation between Wagner and Nietzsche, Rée's presence quickly disabused her. 'One evening we had a visit from a Dr Rée,' wrote Cosima in her diary, 'whose cool, sardonic manner displeased us and who we find, on closer acquaintance, must be an Israelite.' In 1878 Wagner was to send an extraordinary outburst to his publisher. 'There are bugs and there are lice', he wrote. 'All right – they are there. But they have to be smoked out. People who do not do so are dirty pigs!'[26] The only good Jew, in Wagner's eyes, was one prepared to submit unconditionally to his demands.

This was the last thing Rée was prepared to do. In consequence the Wagners not only despised him for his Semitic origin but also accused him of having incited Nietzsche to turn his back on them. Later it occurred to Rohde also that Nietzsche's rationalism could well have been the result of an infection caught from the Jews. After the publication of Nietzsche's *Human, All Too Human* in 1879 – the title alone made the Wagners turn up their noses – Cosima wrote in her diary: 'Israel was represented by the figure of one Dr Rée – very smooth, very cool, on the surface utterly absorbed in, and a slave to, Nietzsche but in reality leading him up the garden path – a kind of miniature version of the relationship between Judah and Germania.' Here was just one more example of the alleged Jewish world conspiracy of which Wagner was so afraid, aiming, in this case, to undermine the success of his universal *Gesamtkunstwerk*. Several times the Wagners had warned Nietzsche against consorting with Rée, even urging Malwida to avoid him as well. But she had the audacity to defend him. How could she possibly do such a thing?

The rulers of Bayreuth knew how to take their revenge. Nietzsche had his Achilles' heel. So why hold back the truth any longer? Nietzsche, who had insinuated himself into their circle, was far from being the fine gentleman he pretended to be. There were a number of things known about him. Back in 1874 the Master had earnestly besought him to find himself a woman. 'For my part,' he wrote in a threatening tone, 'I never spent my evenings in the company of young men, as you do in Basel.'

What is Wagner suggesting? When he says 'evenings', does he mean 'nights'? The young disciple must have been well aware that the Master was saying, by inference, that *he* spent his nights with women. 'The young gentle-man seems to have a shortage of women', he added slily. You only spend your time with men, Nietzsche, he is saying, because you are lacking female acquaintances. 'Come to us! Here you will find what your heart is missing! But at the onset of winter you already hinted that you had decided to spend the summer vacation on a high, lonely mountain peak. Does that not sound like a carefully worded rejection of an invitation to join us?' Finally, in des-peration: 'In God's name, marry some rich woman! Why does Gersdorff, of all people, have to be a man?' This sounds like a stern warning: Friend, you are forgetting that Gersdorff is not a woman!

Cosima's suspicions had surfaced even earlier. In 1871, when their friend-ship at Tribschen was at its height, she noted that Nietzsche showed a 'dis-turbing reserve' that was 'not quite natural'. Had he something to hide? As she was later made to realise, everybody who avoided Bayreuth had some-thing to hide. And in Nietzsche's case she knew what that something was. In 1877 she poured out her wicked prattle in a letter to Malwida von Meysenbug, whom they wanted to exclude from his company. The good lady herself had been not inactive in the matter, having already confided to the Wagners that the doctor in Sorrento had urged Nietzsche to find himself a wife.

What can this mean? Cosima pondered. Maybe he is not normal. Take his passion for sweetmeats – she knew as well as Malwida that Ludwig II also had a sweet tooth, as a result of which his teeth decayed and fell out. Then there was Nietzsche's 'strange shyness' – this too, as everyone knew, was a charac-teristic of young Ludwig. What causes a grown man to be so shy, when he has no need to be?

Cosima found an answer to her persistent questions. She concluded that, as far as Nietzsche was concerned, 'it was all connected with that subject which we women cannot understand'. It must have concerned men only, and must have been something that gave rise to suspicions and rumours. Nietzsche was to be found in the company of men – almost exclusively so. Wagner probably explained Nietzsche's peculiar habit to the prudish Cosima with exactly these words: a subject that you women cannot understand. This subject, which had a *frisson* of the unusual as well as of the indecent, was utterly abhorrent on moral grounds – except in the case of useful rulers like Ludwig, co-operative stage designers like Joukowsky, or members of the Wagner family itself, like Siegfried.

Cosima knew the remedy for Nietzsche – marriage. The same proposal had been put to King Ludwig, but to no avail. Nietzsche too searched in vain. 'I know of one woman', the spiteful Cosima wrote, 'and with the necessary dowry – but whom would one want to consign to such a fate?' It sounded like leading a lamb to the slaughter.

Cosima's letter to Malwida was a serious attempt, under the pretence of offering sympathy, to ruin Nietzsche's honour. That the repeated efforts of his family in Naumburg had the same effect, out of sheer blindness to the situation, was something only he could sense. But it is hard to defend oneself against importunate actions taken in the name of 'good will'. His mother tried to persuade him in the same way as her mother-in-law in Röcken had once badgered Pastor Nietzsche. 'I cannot help thinking', she wrote to him in a letter, 'that if you were to get married, you would be rid of all your sufferings. Come to your mama – I know the perfect young woman for you, simple and chaste.'[27] His sister also busied herself trying to find a match for the reluctant suitor. 'No doubt marriage is a very desirable state,' he replied to her, 'but as far as I am concerned, it is highly improbable – of that I am absolutely sure ... And do not imagine that I miss anything in my present solitary state.'[28]

Cosima knew that better than Elisabeth. She seemed to be plagued by the thought that here was a man who, disguising his true nature, in reality had only that one unspeakable subject in mind 'which women cannot understand'. Soon Malwida received another letter from Cosima – ostensibly a further discussion of Nietzsche's psychology but in fact a further attack on him. Cosima spoke mysteriously of 'his sinister depths', of which he himself was unaware. 'Whatever he says and writes,' she noted – including what Malwida herself had come to admire – 'is really of scant value.' So how does one explain the discrepancy between his creative urge and the foolish impression he makes? Cosima quotes the dictum of the Marquis de Vauvenargues that all great ideas come from the heart. Indeed Nietzsche's 'great ideas' – she gives an ironic smile as she writes these words – 'certainly do not come from his head. So where do they come from? If only we knew.'[29] This is not the sort of thing one talks about. Malwida would not have needed recourse to Freud to find the answer.

In October 1877 an unexpected opportunity arose for Cosima to follow up her prying correspondence with a decisive frontal attack. Chronically unwell, Nietzsche had found a new physician, a man who claimed to be a passionate Wagnerian. Ten years older than his new patient, Dr Otto Eiser gave Nietzsche a thorough examination extending over several days in order to identify the possible sources of his mysterious illness. Eiser diagnosed 'considerable damage to the retina in both eyes, which is with virtual certainty the cause of his headaches, and to which must be added a general predisposition to irritability'.[30] In his customary open and garrulous manner, Nietzsche wrote to the Wagners that he was facing blindness 'if he did not obey the instructions of all his doctors neither to read nor write for a number of years'.[31] He also recommended them to read an essay on *The Ring of the Nibelung* that Dr Eiser had recently written and which Nietzsche enclosed with his letter.

It was the perfect point of departure. The Wagners were far less interested in Eiser's exegesis than in what he knew about Nietzsche. Hans von Wolzogen, who had replaced Nietzsche as leading propagandist for the Wagnerian cause, wrote to Eiser to thank him for his essay and to enquire after the health of his patient. In return for a gesture from the master and mistress of Bayreuth, Eiser was prepared to break his professional oath and reveal confidential medical information. In letters to Wolzogen, whom he hardly knew, he provided all manner of information about 'our poor friend', making public the details of his condition.

Nietzsche was to suffer another indignity some years later at the hands of Professor Ludwig Binswanger in the mental asylum at Jena, where Binswanger introduced Nietzsche as an 'old soldier' and made him march up and down in front of his students.[32] Eiser, twelve years earlier, had adopted the self-righteous tone of the Good Samaritan. 'The longer I spent in the company of this proud spirit,' he wrote, 'the greater the grief that I felt as I watched the disease spreading from day to day and making his suffering ever more unbearable.'[33]

Enter Wagner. Cleverly he intervened in the correspondence between the two disciples. 'I found it very significant', he wrote to Eiser, imitating the tone of naïve admiration in which the physician addressed the great composer, 'to learn that the most important advice that Nietzsche received from the doctor whom he consulted in Naples some time ago, had been that he should get married.' As though Nietzsche himself had told him! And had he forgotten that three years earlier he had also given Nietzsche the same advice?

For the doctor's benefit Wagner added an empirical observation of his own. 'As I follow the development of N.'s condition,' he wrote to Eiser, 'I find myself reminded of identical and similar experiences I had on other occasions with highly gifted young men. These young men fell victim to similar symptoms, and I was made all too clearly aware that these symptoms were the result of masturbation.'[34]

Wagner's language betrays his purpose. He had his own agenda. For the 'identical and similar experiences' he claims to have had are nothing but allegations, vague assumptions based on vague information. Wagner accused a number of young men of masturbation, among them Karl Ritter, son of one of his rich patrons. But in 1877 Ritter was living as a writer in Italy, and he survived his accuser by eight years.[35] Another young man with great gifts and imputed with similar 'perverse tendencies' was Ludwig II, but he too died years after Wagner. Or was the composer perhaps alluding to Edmund von Hagen, a philosopher at the University of Göttingen, whom Wolzogen described as one of the most brilliant of the Wagnerians and who first showed signs of mental illness in 1878? But Hagen did not die until 1907. Even assuming that Wagner suspected all these hapless young men of secretly indulging in 'unnatural practices', how could he maintain that he was 'all too aware' of what was going on? He intended to sound compassionate. But his real aim was get Eiser to confirm his own layman's diagnosis. What precisely was his diagnosis, however? By their symptoms ye shall know them, he said, those who spill their seed, those incapable of begetting offspring. 'When, on the basis of those experiences, I came to study N. more closely,' continued Wagner, 'all his traits of character and temperament turned my fears into a conviction.'

The Wagners had treated Rée in the same way. One recognises a Jew by his nose. But how does one recognise a pervert? Did Nietzsche have dark rings under his eyes, or stains on his trousers, or trembling hands like Euphorion of sad memory? Certainly not. Whatever physical symptoms came to light as a result of Wagner's 'closer' observations were a consequence of Nietzsche's sickness. But this is not what Wagner meant either. He had mentioned to Eiser 'certain traits of character and temperament'. Eiser knew what Wagner was implying, namely that Nietzsche was queer, gay. In the nineteenth century the word 'masturbation' was often used as a euphemism for pederasty. An adult who masturbated was supposedly unable to make love to a woman. In the end Wagner recommended that Nietzsche should undertake a cold water cure designed to strengthen his nerves and spinal chord. This much, at least, was familiar to Nietzsche, thanks to his mother.

What would be the use of even the subtlest of intrigues if the victim had no inkling of it? In his reply to Wagner's letter Eiser laid all Nietzsche's cards on the table, concluding with the wish to see the question of Nietzsche's masturbation settled as soon as possible because 'it is an important factor for the diagnosis of his condition'. For in order to cure him of this perverse habit, he first has to be found guilty. 'In order to establish the sexual aspects of his case,' writes the doctor, 'the shortest and most appropriate method of procedure is for me to ask him outright.'

In current medical terms this was in fact a progressive proposal. In 1893 Sigmund Freud is still to be found maintaining that 'neurasthenia is a frequent consequence of an abnormal sex life'.[36] Eiser could therefore subject his patient to this humiliating process with an easy conscience and tactfully confine his homosexuality to the clinical confirmation of masturbation. Eiser expected Nietzsche to be grateful. But instead, as the self-important doctor later wrote to one of his colleagues, his response was tantamount to an admission of guilt: 'I am the only one who really knows why Nietzsche turned his back on Wagner, for it was in my own house that it occurred, when, with the best of intentions, I told him about the letter from Wagner. He burst into a fit of rage and was quite beside himself. I cannot bring myself to repeat the words he uttered about Wagner.'[37]

Eiser had shown Nietzsche Wagner's defamatory letter. But whatever was he thinking of? Was he a traitor, constantly changing sides so as to keep his powder dry? How did he defend his breach of confidentiality? Had Nietzsche not every cause to be furious with him? There was no reason why Eiser, to his eternal shame, should have wanted to pass on the contents of the letter. Ought he not to have realised, as a doctor, that the extreme irritability that he himself had diagnosed as characteristic of Nietzsche would erupt and cause a serious breakdown? Nor had Nietzsche been so naïve as not to sense what lay behind Eiser's enquiry about his attitude to masturbation. He knew full well what was at stake, and he exploded.

Only after Wagner's death in 1883, when all the gossip associated with the episode had been deliberately allowed to leak out beyond the confines of the Wagner clan, did Nietzsche tell his friend and disciple Peter Gast what Eiser had really said to him. 'Wagner is full of spiteful tricks', he wrote to Gast. 'But what do you say to the fact that he wrote letters – even to my doctors – in order to convey his conviction that my changes of temperament were the result of unnatural perversions, with allusions to pederasty.'[38]

THE MADNESS OF MITHRAS

As it was only after Wagner's death that Nietzsche raised the subject of the 'mortal insult' to his character, biographers assumed that only now, over five years later, did he learn about it. Rumours had in fact been circulating at the Bayreuth Festival in 1882, and his sister Elisabeth and his friend Lou Salomé both discerned the tone of disapproval with which people talked about the deserter to the Wagnerian cause. As well as his alleged 'perversity' there was Cosima's accusation that he had wormed his way into their confidence like a spy, presumably on behalf of world Jewry, whose attacks Wagner continued to fear. The latest example of Nietzsche's depravity was provided by Lou herself, who made no bones about admitting that he had proposed that they live together in sin. Nietzsche's mother, kept fully informed by Elisabeth, upbraided her son for leaving 'a badge of dishonour on his father's grave'.[39]

What had been unthinkable in 1876, when Wagner denied all knowledge of him, had now happened in 1882 – Nietzsche had become a subject of conversation at Bayreuth. But not in the way he had hoped.

Wagner's diagnosis had reached Nietzsche not in 1883 but back in 1878, via Eiser, who immediately passed it on. There would have been an opportunity to discuss the issue when, on his way from Baden-Baden to Naumburg in April 1878, Nietzsche had to change trains in Frankfurt, where Eiser had his medical practice. Certainly, after his experience of the hydrotherapy to which he had been subjected, Nietzsche would have had plenty to discuss with his doctor, and the doctor with him. After returning to Basel three weeks later, Nietzsche received a letter from Eiser regretting that he had not broken his journey in Frankfurt, as they had agreed he would, and asking why he had not availed himself of the 'humble hospitality' that the Eisers had offered him.[40] Nietzsche did not reply.

The day after the abortive visit he took the train home. The lightning was not followed by thunder. He sent his latest book to Bayreuth, as though nothing were amiss. He held his peace because he had to. He confined his outbreak of rage to Eiser because that is what the logic of denunciation requires – by denying accusations one only gives them publicity. Nietzsche said nothing, although his silence could be misinterpreted. Was this equivalent to resigning himself to the situation? He chose to hold his peace. In a notebook referring to spring and summer 1878 he wrote: 'I have been insulted. Nevertheless I intend to hold back. No vengeance.'[41]

Nietzsche never saw Richard and Cosima Wagner again. In any case, what form could his revenge have taken? Only after Wagner's death did he come to any definite conclusion. What he had endured during the month after Eiser's revelations, he recorded in a notebook, which he headed 'Memorabilia', after Xenophon. Xenophon had recalled in his memoirs the fate of Socrates, who in his view had been unjustly convicted and compelled to commit suicide. Nietzsche also mentions Plato's 'Apologia', a copy of which his publisher Ernst Schmeitzner had sent him in April. Here Socrates talks of the voice of his 'daimonion', which had not dissuaded him from submitting to his death.

Nietzsche too seems to have been preoccupied during this time in Naumburg with the voice of his conscience. 'Daimonion – warning voice of my father', he wrote in his notebook.[42] He wistfully recalls happy days in the past, 'distant sounds of the organ in Pforta and pancakes', but also how, as a boy of seven, he had mourned 'the passing of his youth', and how now, in his mid-thirties, he realised how unnatural his youth had been – 'weighed down by unnatural pressures and oppressive knowledge'. 'Only now am I beginning to discover myself', he writes.

Self-experience, self-abandonment, self-discovery – stages in Nietzsche's initiation. He now sees that his disastrous relationship with Wagner also developed in stages – 'to be seen, to see, to experience, to be joined, to be parted – five steps. But few reach the topmost rung.' The starting point was Leipzig, where he had first 'been seen' by the Master. The next stage, where he actively 'saw', began with his first visit to Tribschen. For a long while, that Whitsun in 1869, he had stood in front of the noble villa, wondering whether he would have the courage to ring the bell. The sound of a piano reached him from the music room. The Master was composing – Nietzsche remembered 'a particularly painful dissonance that kept recurring'.[43] Later he found the same chord in Act III, Scene ii of Wagner's *Siegfried*, where Brünnhilde sings: 'He who has wakened me has wounded me!'[44] Siegfried climbs to a mountain-top and finds a sleeping figure in full armour. As he makes to loosen the breastplate, he discovers that the figure is a woman. He kisses her, and she opens her eyes. It is Brünnhilde, his aunt. Conscious of her vulnerability, she pushes him away with the cry: 'O disgrace! He who has wakened me has wounded me!'

It was a situation that matched that of the wounded Nietzsche. A woman in knight's armour is unmasked and pierced to the quick – as though the musical prelude to Nietzsche's friendship with Wagner had already antici-pated its end. The composer behaved no less brutally than his hero. Nietzsche was unsure how to judge the situation: 'Shameless interference', he noted. 'It may have been compassion – but I would wish for compassion coupled with intelligence.'[45]

Eiser had evidently tried to persuade him that Wagner had acted from purely unselfish motives. In the second volume of *Human, All Too Human* Nietzsche refers to the subject in an almost conciliatory tone: 'A negative fea-ture of Compassion: Compassion is accompanied by an element of imperti-nence. For while on the one hand it genuinely seeks to help, it feels no discomfiture about either how the sickness is to be cured or about the nature and origin of that sickness, but indulges in all manner of quack remedies at the expense of both the health and the reputation of the patient.'[46]

This is mere sophistry. The alternative to compassion *without* intelligence, which he also formulated in his 'Memorabilia', is closer to the truth, namely com-passion as a pretext. He no longer enquires about the possible cause but about the intended effect – 'to spread the most outrageous slanders behind a person's back while hypocritically claiming to act in the name of compassion'.[47] A note written in the summer of 1878 takes a middle position between the two extremes: 'A man who has not experienced how the most despicable slanders and the most spiteful envy can be disguised as compassion, can know nothing of what real malice is.'[48]

The slander was laid at Wagner's door, the spite at Eiser's, Wagner's hench-man. As late as August 1877 we find Nietzsche referring to Eiser as '*my* doctor ... whom I have good reason to trust explicitly'[49] and shortly afterwards he recommended him to Cosima as 'a highly valued friend'.[50] He was soon to find out what Eiser meant in his essay on Wagner's *Ring* by the loyalty of the Nibelungs.

In 1880, replying with bitter irony to Eiser's New Year greetings, Nietzsche wrote: 'There is nobody I trust more implicitly than you.'[51] The philosophi-cal consequences he drew from the episode were, first, 'a deep-seated distrust of all moral acts'; second, the realisation that up to then his instincts had misled him over what constituted people's objective interests, 'which I had always equated with my own'; and finally, a recognition that 'I have never met a man of convictions who did not eventually arouse my irony as a result of these convictions.'

But his irony had become a blunted weapon. Desperately he searched for historical parallels in which to find reflections of his own situation. There is always consolation to be found when others have suffered a like fate. One such victim of human malice was Socrates, whose 'Apologia' he read with avid interest. Another was his former hero Byron. 'Not much strength needed to launch a boat', Nietzsche noted. 'Byron and the attack on him in *The Edinburgh Review*. Slanders followed.'[52]

It was an appropriate comparison. The episode to which Nietzsche refers occurred at the beginning of Byron's career, and could have well brought it to an abrupt end. Even before the devastating review of his *Hours of Idleness* Byron suspected that preparations were being made to mount an attack against him in the pages of *The Edinburgh Review* in an attempt to ruin his reputation. The insults hurled at him led to a nervous breakdown and he even considered taking his own life.

Nietzsche's first book had also been mercilessly slated, and he still bore the scars of his ostracism from academic circles. 'Slanders followed.' What Nietzsche experienced with Wagner, Byron had suffered at the hands of London society. From having been the darling of high society, Byron became the subject of rumours that he was a homosexual and had made his half-sister Augusta pregnant. He had even boasted about such rumours to his closest friends. He was forced to leave the country and spent the last eight years of his life abroad.

Nietzsche's image for Byron's fate is the 'boat that does not take much strength to launch'. In a later aphorism, also in *Human, All Too Human*, he is at pains to prevent any misunderstanding. It was not Wagner's rejection of him that became the source of his genius, he wrote, but his liberation from

1. Friedrich **Nietzsche in** 1894, aged fifty, sitting on the veranda of his family house in Naumburg. His friend Erwin **Rohde, who** visited him at that time, wrote: 'The unhappy man was completely insensitive to the **outside** world. The only people he recognised were his mother and his sister.'

22. 'Lips made for kissing!' was Nietzsche's reaction when a student enthusiastically drew his attention to the putative self-portrait by Hans Holbein in the municipal art gallery in Basel.

him – the liberation of his real self: 'A common mistake among biographers: The ease with which one can push out a boat into the current must not be confused with the strength of the current that bears the boat away.'[53]

The fact that he was now being borne along by his own current was not in itself enough, however. Changing his metaphor, as he wrote in his 'Memorabilia', he needed 'the unguents and medications of *all* classical philosophers' for his salvation.[54] He rejected the notion that his suffering was a punishment or trial through which he would be purged – rather, it was a challenge to put his sickness to use, to engage 'the random forces of life' that make a mockery of the demands of common human morality. Was the guilt-laden Orestes not cleansed of his sin by the grace of the gods? Was there not in antiquity the concept of 'respect for great criminals'? Could a stigma not be turned into a badge of honour? 'If one wishes to possess a real personality of one's own,' he reflected, 'one must not shrink from the fact that one will also cast a shadow.'

Nietzsche tossed the problem to and fro in his mind but could find no solution. Indeed, by constantly brooding on it, he only made his condition worse. Then a radical idea came to him, stimulated by his stay in Sorrento the previous year. At that time, after Wagner and his wife had left, his friendship with them in tatters, he had made a trip with Malwida and Rée to Capri, in spite of the bad weather. The trip left him feeling unwell. Not only that, but on the island they met a group of women, friends of Malwida, who insisted that he improvise for them on the piano. Painful memories returned. His break with Wagner was final but somehow he still hankered after the Master. The three friends also visited the Mithras Grotto, held to be an ancient place of cultic worship but in reality merely a cave. For Nietzsche it was far more, however, and his 'Memorabilia' continually return to the grotto and the sacred rite that he envisaged being performed there.

According to the historian Ferdinand Gregorovius, a relief had been discovered in the cave depicting a sacrifice offered up by the Persian sun god Mithras. Mithras plunges his dagger into the neck of a bull and puts it out of the agony it is suffering from the wounds inflicted by a serpent, a dog and a scorpion. According to the cult, the sacrifice of the bull signifies not death, but redemption and rebirth, as the blood of the bull fertilises the soil.

A second legend, also related by Gregorovius, could well have been of particular interest to Nietzsche. According to this story an inscription had been found in the grotto describing how, in the grip of the demon, the Emperor Tiberius had sacrificed Hypatos, his favourite catamite, to the sun god in this very place. Nietzsche was much exercised by the fate of Hypatos, 'whom Tiberius first showered with gifts, then consigned to Hades'.[55] Gregorovius, a friend of Malwida von Meysenbug, was a trustworthy authority. As late as 1886 Nietzsche is to be found quoting the story as an instance of 'religious cruelty'. 'In ancient times,' he wrote, 'people used to make human sacrifices to their god, maybe even of those whom they loved most deeply, as with the Emperor Tiberius in the Mithras Grotto on the island of Capri, the most terrifying of all Roman anachronisms.'[56] What was anachronistic about it? Had Wagner not just sacrificed him, Nietzsche, no less deliberately and cold-bloodedly?

In Naumburg the parallels began to dawn on him. He was the boy whose sacrifice was the result of a fit of ill temper. But he also saw himself in the wounded bull, who died a lingering death from a poisoned spear while being tormented by repulsive beasts. Creeping away to his cave in Naumburg, he wondered what it is that turns the mighty into murderers. His answer? The joy of destruction, a tyrannical urge to trample all around them into the dust, to put their victims to the sword and to delight in the shedding of blood. Had he not dedicated altars to the god of thunder, who had pierced hearts with his double-edged shaft?

Such desires were not alien to him. He had himself drunk of the witches' potion – in his dreams. But on a sober self-appraisal, he concluded that he was the exact counterpart of the sadist Tiberius. 'Tiberius – Madness of the ability to Act. Antithesis – Madness of the ability to Know.'[57] It was out of madness that Tiberius killed – I torment myself to death for the same reason. My knowledge drives me out of my mind. Why can I not behave like him, rage like him, destroy like him? There is only one route to salvation, the old satyr's path of lascivious thrills: 'Knowledge = paralysis. Action = epilepsy – involuntary. I am as though pierced with the curare-tipped arrow of Understanding: Seeing all.'

Curare resembles the poison of the 'mortal insult'. It paralyses. It also conveys, at least to Nietzsche, a particular power of perception. The proof of this is his 'Memorabilia'. He now knows all but can do nothing. The paralysis that spread its nightmarish tentacles over his body will sooner or later turn into its opposite. This he knows. A scream is heard from the depths of the abyss as the unbearable tension relaxes and dissolves into convulsions of joy. 'Epilepsy – involuntary'. In this state man is capable of anything. The madness of rebirth and of the Bacchanalian intoxication of those who have survived and awoken from the world of darkness – it is the only hope left to the suffering animal. 'Mithras – Hope. Mithras – Madness!' he noted.

Such was the name Nietzsche gave to the grotto on Capri. Of the three designations that Gregorovius mentions, Nietzsche chose 'Mitromania', which he translated as 'Mithras Madness'. The callous god slays the suffering bull:

'Mithras kills the bull, which is still being tortured by the serpent and the scorpion.'

Death, as Nietzsche knew, means relief. Cruelty, the madness of the flashing sword, means liberation. The wisdom of a religious cult as the sadomasochist's secret knowledge. Nietzsche carried the argument further: How would it be if one were to take one's own life in order to be rid of one's incurable agonies, thereby playing the roles of both sacrificer and sacrificed and surviving the madness of this cruelty? Double agony means double ecstasy. Nietzsche planned the drama of his suicide like a theatre director. Scene – the Mithras Grotto on Capri; Time – Dawn; Cast – the Sun God and the Suicide.

'Mitromania', wrote Nietzsche: 'Waiting for the first rays of dawn – glimpse them, then scorn them and put out one's own light.' This is the world of the demon. Nietzsche had dipped his pen in Euphorion's black inkwell. To die while cursing life and revelling in the ecstasy of hell. A Byron of Naumburg, preparing to put an end to that degrading phenomenon called life. How would it be, mused the former disciple of the God of Bayreuth, if one were to make this suicide the starting point of a mystery cult? In one visionary moment the whole ludicrous comedy called life would be wrapped up and discarded – 'life would be re-conceived as a celebration born in Mithromania', as he put it.

He was deadly serious about this. Time and again over the following years he formulated and re-formulated the bloodthirsty concept of a 'sacrificial mankind'.[58] Wagner's *Ring*, too, ends in a gigantic 'Twilight of the Gods' in which deities, heroes and humankind all perish in the flames. Why only on the stage? Nietzsche wondered. If, as he has Tiberius say in one place, life is nothing but a 'long-drawn-out death', why should the mass suicide of all people not provide at least one brief, joyful climactic moment?[59]

7   *A Chapter of Accidents*

One morning in April 1869 a horse-carriage drew up outside the corner house at Weingarten No. 18 in Naumburg. The coachman knew the family well. Over twenty-five years earlier he had taken the Nietzsches to their wedding. Now he had come to collect the widow's son and drive him to the railway station.

The 24-year-old Fritz was well equipped for the long journey to Basel. In order to give him a suitably dignified appearance, his mother and sister had bought him a new set of clothes intended to make him look somewhat older. He shared their taste. 'Only fabrics, cuts and hats such as were found on older gentlemen met with his approval.'[1] His teacher, Professor Friedrich Ritschl, had personally stated that in intellectual terms he had long outstripped his contemporaries, so it was only right and proper that the outside world should be made aware of the fact. Togged up like a bridegroom setting out for his wedding, he boarded his carriage, bound for a distinguished career. His sadness over the tears shed by his mother and sister was relieved only by his sense of pride.

The inhabitants of Basel grew accustomed to seeing the smartly dressed young man walking daily from his rooms to the university lecture hall or to the *Gymnasium* on the cathedral square. A rumour later went the rounds that the Swiss novelist Gottfried Keller had had him in mind when writing his story *Clothes Make the Man*. Indeed, Nietzsche was to the people of Basel a flamboyant figure from another era. In addition to dressing like a man three times his age, he sported a grey top hat, such as only a retired civil servant would dream of wearing. His upright posture formed a contrast to his mincing gait as he hurried along the cobbled streets, his file of notes under his arm and occasionally raising his hat to a passer-by. The most striking feature about him was his moustache, an exuberant growth even by contemporary standards, that he affectionately styled his 'respirator'.[2]

His daily routine ran like clockwork. 'Regularly at about midday,' recalled a local resident, 'a young gentleman, who could only be a German professor, would pass by our window, accompanied by a young lady.' His clothes were immaculately clean and brushed, 'as though they had just been taken out of the box'. Also fresh from the box were his light-coloured trousers, brown jacket and black velvet waistcoat. Before he set out for lunch in the company of his sister, who had joined him in Basel, she ensured that everything was in perfect order. 'From their similar gait, in particular their short steps, one could see that they must be brother and sister.'[3] Both extremely short-sighted, they held on to each other as they walked down the uneven cobbled streets.

Thus elegantly attired, the young newcomer from Naumburg quickly familiarised himself with his new surroundings. His lectures were well received, his colleagues found him an amiable companion, and even the ranks of high society had their attention drawn to him. He was a graceful adjunct to any gathering and willingly accepted invitations to social occasions, where he entertained the company with fanciful stories. He forgot what he had been and became what people wanted him to be, slipping without difficulty into the roles of worthy citizen and society *galant*. On the other hand he could be so droll that he was sometimes taken for a mere youth and dubbed 'the principal clown'. Hidden beneath the dignified garb of the professor, it seemed, lurked a young joker. Some would have dearly adopted him.

For a time, together with two of his friends, he was a member of the 'Tuesday Club', a *conversazione* that met every two weeks for lively discussion. If the weather was fine, they would sit in the garden and drink coffee. Nietzsche brought an air of conviviality to the proceedings and often took a book with him – the stories of Mark Twain, for example, whose comic qualities he particularly enjoyed. They would read on into the evening, for which new kinds of entertainment were planned. They leapt and capered around until well into the night, the new professor from Germany joining in with undisguised enthusiasm.

In his honour the members of the club planned a surprise – a *tableau vivant* from Wagner's *Mastersingers*, performed by two boys and a girl: 'When our guests were assembled,' said the hostess, Ida von Miaskovsky,

I asked Nietzsche to play the Prize Song. Then I opened the door to the adjoining room, in which my husband had set up the tableau. The children had an added charm in that they were all so young. Little Eva, in a light blue smock, was having her foot measured by the three-year-old Hans Sachs, the master cobbler, who was wearing a leather apron and a cap. On an improvised dais stood little Walther von Stolzing in a crimson jerkin trimmed in white lace with white puffs, and with a heavy gold chain round his neck, looking at the pretty scene. They were all enchanted – Nietzsche in particular was deeply moved. He clasped my hands and pressed them over and over again to thank me for the delightful surprise.

His emotion was genuine. The professor was experiencing the childhood he had never had. On occasion he acted himself. A man who is constantly meditating on tragedy, teaches tragedy to his students and has had the meaning of tragedy taught to him at Tribschen, will at some time or other assume the guise of a tragic actor. And when Nietzsche acted, the walls shook. 'Especially powerful and moving', wrote his sister, 'was his interpretation of the figure of Philoctetes' – the hero who is rendered powerless by a bite from a venomous snake and is visited on the lonely island of Lemnos by the pretty boy Neoptolemos, who brings him relief from his suffering. Nietzsche particularly liked declaiming in the original Greek, 'sighing and screaming in such pitiful tones', said Elisabeth, 'that our maid, evidently driven by curiosity, brought us our tea an hour earlier than usual'. 'I wanted to ask her the reason why', Elisabeth went on, but it was not necessary, because the worthy Caroline explained 'with a superior smile: "I saw at once that the Herr Professor was play-acting." '[4]

Nietzsche had little interest in antiquity as an object of study. What mattered was reality. The new Philoctetes, as he called himself several times later, meditated on how to bring about the rebirth of antiquity, first in Basel, then in Germany as a whole. In his early lectures on 'The Future of our Educational Establishments' he had already implied that this was a goal that could not be reached by the conventional paths of education, which offered not inspiration but merely training. What he dreamed of was an Eros as educator, a god who would stimulate students to grow wings. In the summer of 1873 the vision seemed almost within his grasp.

He was staying for a few weeks in the spa of Flims, in the Grisons, with Carl von Gersdorff. They were happy together, went for long mountain walks and enjoyed what Gersdorff called in a letter to Erwin Rohde 'the serenity and clock-like regularity of life'. 'To breathe the best, the most fragrant mountain air,' he went on, 'with swimming every day in the green waters of Lake Cauma, good food and unassuming company, and reading the best and greatest of the world's writers – Wagner, Goethe, Plutarch – all this has had a good effect on Nietzsche's health. You have often been in our thoughts, and we could have wished for nothing more dearly than to have you with us here in the little castle at Flims, twelve minutes away from our *pensione*. You could have completed your work and spent your leisure hours with us.'⁵

It was a programme dictated by Nietzsche – work and leisure, Wagner paramount in the literary hierarchy, with swims in the mountain lake to toughen himself up. Here, on a marble slab projecting above the water, Gersdorff, Nietzsche and a third companion etched the opening words of the first of Nietzsche's *Thoughts Out of Season*, together with its date of publication. 'Afterwards we swam across to a rock in the middle of the lake and scratched our initials on it, clambering around like Wagner's Rhine Maidens.' Then, in time-honoured student fashion, they 'dedicated' the rock by pouring a glass of wine over it.

Then an idea occurred to Nietzsche: Why should they not preserve this Arcadian utopia for ever – nature and man in harmony, friend in company with friend, beauty all around and themselves at the service of the muses? If Rohde could not join them at once, then maybe he would when their plan for a new Greece, a Hellenic Academy, had taken shape.

This was the moment, according to Elisabeth, who joined them towards the end of their stay, when her brother decided to found 'a new place of study and learning'.⁶ The little castle at Flims, which had long been up for sale, was an ideal spot. But it had a drawback – it was haunted by aristocratic spirits. Whether these ghosts were those of the castle's one-time owner Josef von Capol, who was shot in 1621 by the Swiss patriot Jörg Jenatsch, or of his successor Herkules, who died on the battlefield in Belgium, far from his homeland, or even of their widows, is unclear. The fact remained that the charming little building was for sale for a sum equivalent to five times Nietzsche's annual salary. Also preserved in the castle, according to Elisabeth, was a Baroque room panelled in Renaissance style, which was sold to a buyer in Berlin in 1884 for 25,000 marks and later found its way to the Metropolitan Museum of Art in New York. The panelling alone was worth the price.

Something sinister about the castle must have put them off. The eighteenth-century poet Johann Gaudenz von Salis-Seewies was said to have been inspired to write his poem 'The Grave' here, a melancholy work that could have been written by Nietzsche in his schooldays at Schulpforta, and which was set to music by Schubert. Until the middle of the nineteenth century the castle remained in the poet's family, then changed hands several times and served as a rectory after 1948.

It would have taken substantial restoration and development work to turn the place into a classical academy. 'Extensive covered ambulatories would have to be built around the walls,' wrote Elisabeth, 'since the lectures and discussions would mostly take place while walking, not sitting, and the green sward in the centre would be left free for the pentathlon.' The friends envisaged themselves in their tunics at their physical training sessions every morning – Nietzsche as discus thrower, Rohde as wrestler, Gersdorff as marathon runner, Deussen with the javelin and Overbeck in the long jump. The Olympic Games of Flims. The five comrades would form the corpus of a fraternity of teachers and educators. Maybe it would have developed into an elite educational establishment of the kind familiar in present-day Switzerland. But they did not even send out 'the extravagantly worded invitations' that Nietzsche had read out to his sister. The plan was postponed and hopes pinned on Basel.

A DECLARATION OF LOVE

Nietzsche still had good reason to be pleased at the prospect of a career in Basel. His pupils at the *Gymnasium*, according to his sister, 'were greatly attached to him and some of the students at the university had come to Basel expressly because of him. They hung on his every word and were lavish in their displays of affection, while the romantically inclined among them brought flowers to his room.'[7]

Elisabeth misinterpreted these gifts of flowers but what she said was basically true. They loved him. Why should he set up an academy in some mountain village if the students would come to Basel to worship him there? One of them recalled that when *The Birth of Tragedy* appeared, students and pupils alike were caught up in a wave of enthusiasm that swept through the town.[8] When Carl Albrecht Bernoulli was collecting information for his biography of Nietzsche at the beginning of the twentieth century, he interviewed a number of the professor's former students about their experiences. All were agreed, reported Bernoulli, 'that they felt not so much as having sat at the feet of a teacher as having been confronted with a classical ephor in the flesh, who had leapt across the centuries in order to tell them about Homer, Sophocles, Plato and their gods'.[9]

This 'leaping over the centuries' illustrates how Nietzsche conducted his classes. It was as though he had come from another world. Facing his listeners in the gloomy classroom – the shutters were drawn to protect his sensitive eyes – he would teach, not what the curriculum called simply 'classics', but the living spirit of antiquity. His pupils listened in reverence as he wove his spell, talking as though he had witnessed at first hand the mysteries normally confined to the dusty pages of the text books in the library. Sometimes the atmosphere almost became one of religious celebration. Nietzsche would get them to meditate and recall through their own intuition the living presence of the heroes of antiquity, while he himself would bring Alcibiades or Achilles to life, as Faust had summoned up Helena. Only the sound of the bell of the nearby cathedral, chiming the hour, brought him back to reality.

His teaching at the *Gymnasium* gave him great pleasure. He introduced his pupils to the Socratic dialogues in order 'to inculcate philosophy into them',[10] then turned to the eighteenth book of the *Iliad* and Achilles' heart-rending lament for the dead Patrocles, in order to introduce them to the Greek concept of love between friends.

His work at the university, on the other hand, was less satisfying, partly because he had far fewer students. In his first winter term we find him complaining to Ritschl about his 'three stupid young men'.[11] At the beginning of every term he grumbled that his pupils were either too few or too stupid. At the time of the publication of *The Birth of Tragedy*, with the whole of Basel said to be buzzing with the news, he recorded that he had with the utmost difficulty managed to find two men prepared to enrol in a course of his lectures, 'one of whom was studying German, the other, law'. In the *Gymnasium*, by contrast, he had no need to worry about attendances. Here he was a success. The historian Jacob Burckhardt remarked to a colleague that 'the people of Basel would be unlikely to find such a teacher again'.[12] But he said nothing about Nietzsche's university lectures.

The pupils' gratitude was not long in showing itself, and they made no attempt to disguise their affection. Sometimes this took on a somewhat *risqué* form. 'In our class,' wrote one, 'a pupil had gone into the room before the lesson, taken a piece of chalk and drawn a heart on the lid of the teacher's desk, laying two little posies of violets on top of the drawing. When Nietzsche entered the room, he glanced at the present and blushed deeply . . .'[13]

This was the 'bouquet of admiration' that Elisabeth mentioned. The boy who recorded the episode clearly found the gesture unseemly, and went on to say, in extenuation, that the miscreant had later become an excellent schoolmaster himself. But what had the boy wanted to convey by leaving the violets? Hardly that he was in love with his teacher – the drawing was anonymous. Nor was it intended as an expression of gratitude for his teacher's generous heart. Nietzsche, accustomed to derision since his schooldays at Pforta, appears to have grasped its meaning, namely that hearts and violets, conventional symbols of puppy love among children, were out of place in a classroom in which there were only boys and their master. Or were they? Nietzsche saw what was at stake, blushed and without a word hurriedly began the lesson. The eighteen seventeen-year-olds in the class must have drawn their own conclusion.

Though possibly, in this particular case, they may have been mistaken. Nietzsche liked to invite boys he especially liked to his home, where he encouraged them to forget the gulf between pupil and teacher as they sat together in plush armchairs with bright floral patterns of roses and violets. Maybe the drawing had been a way of thanking him for such an invitation.

One of the privileged few to enjoy this hospitality was a certain Louis Kelterborn, who had been raised to 'a state of exaltation' by Nietzsche's teaching.[14] The pupil's initial impression that here was 'one of an inspired few chosen to lead us into the world of Hellenic philosophy and art' became ever stronger as time went on. This was not instruction but initiation. At the same time Nietzsche had to discover which of his pupils were worthy to receive this honour, for the message of antiquity was not for everyone's ears. He therefore set the class an examination aimed not only at testing their linguistic and scholarly ability but also at probing the character of each boy in the round. 'In order to ascertain the individual qualities of each member of the class,' wrote Kelterborn, 'he made us read aloud and translate from Euripides' *Bacchae*, then write an essay on the first impression that a Greek tragedy had made on us.'

Nietzsche still took pleasure in the results of this exercise during his time in the Prussian army the following year. That his students had succeeded in working their way through the murderous frenzy of the Maenads and the androgynous sado-deity exceeded all his expectations. He also wondered whether they had noticed how many parallels could be drawn between their mystagogue and Euripides' Dionysus. 'As a god in human form he came to Thebes and enchanted them all with his feminine attire, the scent of his hair and his dark eyes, which concealed the charms of Aphrodite. But Dionysus, the magician, is locked away because he tempts men to acts of immorality. In return for this he wreaks a cruel vengeance on his enemy by making his mother tear off his head.'

Kelterborn gave a particularly good account of himself in the test, leading his teacher to describe his essay as 'a praiseworthy piece of work which augurs well for the future'.[15] Not long afterwards he received his reward – a personal invitation to visit his teacher at his home.

Nietzsche was the perfect host, displaying great vivacity when pressed to share his opinions. In the summer he cooled his room with ice and offered his guests Kulmbach beer, 'which he drank from a silver goblet'. The elegant good taste that he showed, both in his dress and in his manner, was matched by a natural politeness that bridged any differences of age or social status. It was this attractive, natural kindness that made young Kelterborn feel that 'almost without knowing it, he had been transported into a fuller, richer, higher intellectual realm'.[16]

The effect was intentional. Thanks to his 'Dionysian nature', Nietzsche knew how to capture the loyalty of young men. Like a composer who makes skilful use of moments of silence in his works, he often sat in his darkened room in silence, leaving his guests to feel that they were in the presence of a mystery, which they were being permitted to experience at close quarters. During such periods of silence Kelterborn had an opportunity to observe Nietzsche's 'fascinating features – his eloquent mouth, eloquent even when silent, his rounded chin, his swarthy, healthy complexion, his prominent, well-shaped nose with its distended nostrils'.[17]

Kelterborn had noticed a particular characteristic of Nietzsche, namely that when he became agitated, his nostrils swelled – a peculiarity for which Kelterborn had no explanation. He was also attracted by 'the pleasant way he laughed'. To his guests Nietzsche was no longer the man in the formal top hat but a friend and counsellor, skilled in the art of paying compliments. If one were not careful, one could catch oneself falling in love with him. Kelterborn was not unreceptive to these signals. As time went by, Nietzsche invited him more and more frequently, sometimes even after a chance meeting in the street. If the weather was good enough, he suggested that they might go for walks in the surrounding countryside, in the course of which he would expound his concept of a rebirth of classical antiquity.

On one occasion he gave his favourite pupil a concrete example of what he meant. At the end of 1871, after he had left the *Gymnasium* for the university, Kelterborn read *The Birth of Tragedy*. More precisely, he read it four times in succession, two of them aloud. What an honour, thought the young student, to be able to go through the book page by page with the revered author, having interesting details pointed out to him, together with the tasteful production of the book, in particular the vignette on the title page. This depicts a muscular bearded athlete with broken fetters on his hands and feet, his face turned upward in gratitude and with his right foot planted on an eagle, its neck shot through. Clearly the figure represents Prometheus, his gaze fastened on Hercules, his liberator.

The designer of this little illustration was one Leopold Rau, one of Gersdorff's 'artistic friends', as Nietzsche described them, and the only artist he knew 'in whom the spirit of Greek sculpture lived on'.[18] Apart from the fact that Rau, together with the genre painter Adolf Mosengel, seems to have been the only artist Nietzsche knew personally, his judgement could hardly have been based on Rau's artistic talents. Or could it? When later that year Rau won second prize in a competition for a statue in Vienna, Nietzsche was beside himself with joy, while Gersdorff ran through the streets of Florence in delight, 'almost like a Bacchant'. But the glowing future that Nietzsche predicted for Rau never came to pass. He died in 1882 at the age of thirty-five and is today forgotten.

In the summer of 1875 Nietzsche was having treatment for his stomach pains in a spa in the southern part of the Black Forest, when Louis Kelterborn, in his final year as a student of law, decided to pay him a visit. Kelterborn found himself face to face with a man in pain, 'who at once embarked on a detailed description of his state of health and also of the treatment he was receiving'.[19] They wandered together through the pine forests, and Kelterborn was struck by his former teacher's 'resolute, almost marching gait'. In Basel he had walked quite differently. There was a slight contretemps between the two men when they arrived back at the swimming-bath next to the Kurhaus. Nietzsche urged Kelterborn to take a swim but he declined. Did he sense that Nietzsche not only felt a special affinity to Greek antiquity but was also attracted to the naked human body? He similarly turned down an invitation from Nietzsche to spend the night at the spa, preferring to stay in a village a few kilometres away.

So Kelterborn proved to be another friend whose defences he could not pierce. There was only one means to which he could have recourse, as he had found out earlier with the obstinate Rohde, namely music, in particular playing piano duets. It was an experience the young student described as 'an explosion of my musical soul'.[20] 'As we played together,' he wrote, 'Nietzsche was the image of kindness, patience and at the same time passion and encouragement. We played the Prelude to *Tristan* several times in succession, then the "Ode to Joy" and above all the great *Manfred* music, the passionate intensity of which he conveyed by extraordinarily powerful playing, carrying me away on the swell of his profound emotional response to this music.'

EATING A TOAD

Under Nietzsche's smart and elegant exterior a fire was smouldering. Not only musical passions betrayed the subterranean rumblings of the volcano. One illness followed another, forcing him to curtail radically his 'immensely beneficial' teaching, as Kelterborn described it.[21] First he sprained his ankle, as though suspecting that Basel had been a mistake. Then, following what Kelterborn called his 'patriotic conscience', he joined the army, only to return a few months later seriously ill, which prevented him from resuming his teaching. Following this a further undefined illness resulted in his spending a considerable time recuperating in sunny Lugano.

For Louis Kelterborn this was a disappointment, while the university authorities regarded his frequent absences with growing disapproval. One of the professors called upon to substitute for him, a certain Jacob Mähly, a man sixteen years his senior, openly called Nietzsche's appointment a 'miscalculation' and described with barely disguised jealousy how the younger man 'had been spoilt and pampered by old and young alike as a youthful prodigy'.[22] But in spite of the deficiencies in Nietzsche's knowledge, Mähly was forced to admit that his students loved and revered him. Not that this was a feeling based on academic considerations, he hastened to add – it was simply that they felt Nietzsche shared their youthful enthusiasms and was one of them, not some dry teacher. Emotions took precedence over knowledge.

Mähly, the pedant with the poisonous tongue, was not blind to Nietzsche's vanity and the scrupulous care he devoted to his appearance, designed to impress his students – 'especially his huge moustache, which protected him from any charge of having feminine characteristics about him'.[23] What an insidious remark! Nietzsche minus moustache equals woman. That this was precisely what Mähly meant is made clear by the following sentence, in which he records that 'Nietzsche usually had an attractive scent about him.' He goes on: 'It is said that Nietzsche grew up principally under the influence of women, an influence subsequently apparent in the way he dressed.' At the same time there had been no reports that he had any 'close intellectual relationships with any women in the town'.

Is this an allusion to the rumour that Nietzsche had been cultivating a non-intellectual relationship with a lady living in the Totengasse? For this story too, like many others, was going the rounds. Or was Mähly saying that this effeminate man was content to receive the love and veneration of his unsuspecting pupils? At all events his abnormality appears to have been a regular subject of conversation. There were even whispers that he was threatened by the onset of mental illness, which ran in the family. Mähly's fears were confirmed when he saw Nietzsche a few years later after his return from Italy: 'He was wearing a threadbare coat of indistinguishable hue', wrote Mähly, 'with a shabby travelling-bag slung over his shoulder and held by a tattered strap. From under his hat, dating back to his distant youth, strands of untidy blond hair hung down, and his listless eyes shifted uneasily from one side to the other.'

Confirmation that all was not well with the young professor also came from Ida Rothpletz, a woman from Zurich who first met him casually in

1870, then married his friend Franz Overbeck and came to know him more intimately. 'When I was together with Nietzsche,' she later wrote, 'I had the feeling of being in the company of an enigma. The natural simplicity of a young girl seemed to be offset by a certain formality and solemnity – that is to say, he concealed his own feminine nature behind a mask of belonging to an intellectual elite.' At the time of his *Zarathustra* we also find him hankering for 'girlish' qualities. He had 'an attractive deportment', Fräulein Rothpletz remembered, 'with a trace of the feminine about it'. Wagner made a similar observation, as did Nietzsche's physician Dr Eiser, carried along in Wagner's wake. But, Rothpletz added, almost defiantly, 'I did not want Nietzsche to be anything other than a Greek.'[24]

Often he did not know himself who or what he was. Sometimes a dream would help. Once he dreamed that he had been invited to dinner one evening in Basel. A nubile young lady was seated next to him and it was his responsibility to engage her in conversation – he was regarded at the time as a highly eligible bachelor. He told her he had once dreamt he was a camellia. The young lady found this an entertaining idea – the Herr Professor, a scented camellia! But this was not what the dream meant to him. A camellia is not only a flower but also a *cocotte*, a courtesan – a character familiar from Alexandre Dumas's popular *La Dame aux camélias* and later used by Dostoevsky in *The Idiot*. In Dumas's novel, source of Verdi's opera *La Traviata*, the sick courtesan renounces her love for the sake of her lover's future and dies of tuberculosis and a broken heart. What led Nietzsche to tell his dinner companion this dream? Did he expect her to give it an interesting interpretation? Hardly. Rather, that she should not cherish any expectations as far as he was concerned.

Franz Overbeck, professor of theology, whom Nietzsche came to know in Basel, with whom he lived in the trenches and who brought him back from Turin in 1889, had no illusions about his friend and the attention he attracted. From an early date he found himself with reason to wonder about Nietzsche's honesty and integrity. He could see through the pose of the noble Greek that he affected, as well as that of a promising young academic set on making a name for himself. 'Nietzsche was not, in the true sense of the word, a great man', wrote Overbeck in the context of the Nietzsche cult that sprang up in Germany at the turn of the century. 'Indeed, not even he believed himself to be a genius.'[25]

But what disturbed Overbeck above all was what he called Nietzsche's lofty 'affectation of nobility' – extravagant displays of self-confidence that were in fact expressions of a lack of self-confidence. Nietzsche had profound doubts about himself. And Overbeck points to what may have compelled him to adopt a constantly changing pattern of masks: 'It was in particular the fact that Nietzsche preferred to consort with men that gave him the cachet of being un-masculine.'

Overbeck also declined to shed any light on the 'heartbreaking confessions' that Nietzsche had made in 1873, when they were sitting on the sofa in Overbeck's room. Nietzsche's sole purpose in coming, said Overbeck, 'was to mourn his lack of artistic talent. He did not make things explicit, and in particular spoke without mentioning anyone other than himself.' The poem of Nietzsche's that speaks expressly of a broken heart, however, is a love poem. Another friend, Paul Deussen, whom he had once spurned and often chided, found harsh words to describe him: 'Nietzsche is and always has been a basically unsettled, inconstant personality. It was this inner turmoil that prevented him from finding any long-term satisfaction as a teacher in Basel.' [26]

The garlands of praise with which Basel had crowned him soon withered. He became the subject of gossip. His colleagues poked fun at his high-flown manner and what they regarded as his exaggerated intensity. Why could he not behave naturally, like them, and like other young men? Jacob Burckhardt, never short of spiteful comments on Nietzsche's character and career, was said to have made the vulgar comment: 'Nietzsche cannot even let out a fart like any natural young man.'[27] Nietzsche was deeply wounded by such remarks which, often passed when others were also present, made him feel physically sick. A man who has a double identity is easily hurt.

Julius Piccard, professor of chemistry at the university, described three events that illustrate Nietzsche's deep-seated feeling of insecurity in his early career. Piccard calls him 'a man of outstanding generosity and sensitivity' but at once adds that 'one would have to be blind if one failed to notice that this sensitivity had something unhealthy about it'. Piccard regarded him as a kind of paranoid Don Quixote. One evening, at a gathering in the house of a local councillor, Nietzsche played one of his own compositions, which met with considerable displeasure. When anxiously asked by the composer how the piece had fared, Piccard gave an evasive answer but referred in particular to a section consisting of 'repeated staccato rhythms', which 'struck me and probably other listeners also as somewhat strange'. 'But Piccard,' the composer exclaimed, 'did you not recognise that they were the stars in the sky during a walk at night?' My response to his piece made him very sad, said Piccard, 'and I felt deeply sorry for him'.

On another occasion Nietzsche reacted so violently that Piccard suspected that he was suffering from paranoia. At a meeting of the Academic Society a toast had been proposed by a young man who had the impudence to introduce into his speech, without attribution, the term 'cultural philistine', a phrase coined by Nietzsche. Nietzsche was outraged and stormed out of the room. Piccard went to calm him and found him lying on a sofa, beside himself with rage. 'In the darkness of the room,' wrote Piccard, 'his eyes had an unnatural glow about them. When I tried to pacify him, he stared at me and exclaimed: "Didn't you hear, Piccard, how they were all laughing at me?" ' It was, to be sure, a joke at Nietzsche's expense but a harmless one, compared with what people elsewhere said about him.

A third anecdote also went the rounds in the university. In Lausanne Nietzsche had tried in vain to find the cathedral. When asked why he did not ask one of the passers-by, he confessed that he did not have the nerve to do so. 'If I had,' he confessed to Piccard, 'they would have laughed at me.'[28] People laughed at him anyway.

Nietzsche sensed that he was not being taken seriously. Little pin-pricks began to get bigger. The more aware he became of the ironical glances cast in his direction, the more tense he became. And the more formal his behaviour, the greater the mockery it provoked. His university colleagues were clearly at pains to make out that his illness pre-dated his arrival in Basel. He was already mad when he joined us, they said. Gottfried Keller, who had probably heard about the situation from Basel, received a visit from Nietzsche in Zurich in 1884. 'The man's crazy,' was Keller's verdict.[29]

By a series of remarkable coincidences at key moments in Nietzsche's life the daughter of a patrician Basel family came to learn more from him and about him. In 1889 she was to meet the train that was bringing the mentally sick Nietzsche and his mother to Jena, and was the first to hear how he had broken out into fits of rage against his mother during the journey. A bosom friend of his sister, she was drawn into Elisabeth's unpleasant intrigues against Lou Salomé and had witnessed the two women exchanging slanderous allegations against each other. The ambitious young Nietzsche had met her at a party in the early 1870s, where he found himself seated next to her at table.

Clara Gelzer, née Thurneysen, appears to have gained his confidence, if not his affection. Between courses the man with the fearsome moustache and the gentle eyes began to tell her of a bad dream he had had, a dream that was to repeat itself many times in the future. It haunts his notebooks between 1876 and 1881 but was far too revolting to be told at the dinner-table. The young lady was surprised. Only later was she to realise that in this matter her otherwise so charming and correct companion was not a free agent. The horrible story just had to be told. 'I dreamed the other night', Nietzsche began, 'that my hand was lying on the table in front of me. Suddenly it began to be covered with a glassy, transparent skin. When I looked through it, I could see the bone, the tissue and the tendons. Then, all of a sudden, I saw a toad squatting on the hand, and had an irresistible urge to eat it. Overcoming my repulsion, I swallowed it down.'

What else could the bewildered young lady do but laugh? This was, however, precisely the wrong response. Once again Nietzsche felt himself a butt of ridicule, a joke figure, and felt that his confidence had been abused. 'Do you find that something to laugh at?' he asked, in a deadly serious tone, turning his eyes on her with an expression half quizzical, half sad.[30]

In his notebooks for 1876 we find references to a 'dream of the toad', and in 1881, in a list of further dreams, 'Eats the toad'. In the mid-1880s he shocked a young Englishwoman named Emily Fynn, whom he had met in Sils-Maria and who had shown an interest in marrying him, by taking an enormous toad into her hotel bedroom, wrapped in a bloodstained handkerchief – as a subject for a painting. He seems to have been seized with an overwhelming desire to catch the repulsive creature and deliver it to Miss Fynn personally. For the slimy toad was a symbol of her own repulsiveness, her womanhood, representing everything that makes a woman what she is. He once described Rome in the age of Juvenal as 'a poisonous toad with the eyes of Venus'.[31] What he gave back to Miss Fynn was the offer she had made him – and not only her but also all the others who wanted him and would never have him. Put brutally: Here is your womanhood back! Take this revolting creature away and leave me in peace!

The dream about the toad was to plague him for a long time to come. It suggested to him that he had no choice but to overcome his aversion and get married. It made abundantly clear to him that he was expected, sooner or later, to take a wife. Was this the source of the 'irresistible urge'? Or was it his self-inflicted pain – I must force myself to do what I hate? Or perhaps it was because in fact he lusted after everything that aroused lust – what was slimy, amorphous, bloodstained, everything characteristic of predators and creatures of the dark, everything that reeked of paradise, the long-gone paradise of his childhood? And at the same time there was his 'frightful aversion' to all this. If one could rid the object of this lust of all its repulsive feminine characteristics, and could turn the toad into a prince, all would be solved. But Clara and Emily and all the others were simply toads. It was to take years before he could bite off the head of the slimy creature he had been so unwise to talk about, and finally spit it out. And then, as in all the best fairy tales, he would find a prince in shining armour standing before him.

In Basel this point had not yet been reached – the dream just warned him of what was to come. He had to swallow the toad if he was not to be exposed. The beginning of the dream had made it quite clear – we have seen through your masquerade, your secret vice is there for all to see, your innermost secrets are revealed. The only way out is to marry – that is, to 'swallow' the young lady at your side. What a horrid thought!

Clara Gelzer had come to her own conclusions. When Bernoulli interviewed her for his biography of Nietzsche, she said: 'Nietzsche took the transparency of his hand to represent intense pain and suffering, from which he could only be relieved by swallowing a live toad.'[32]

A COMPANY OF LIARS

Nietzsche knew the threat that hung over him. A man who deceives others must expect to be unmasked himself. And if he wants to survive, he must respect convention, if necessary in the face of his utmost reluctance to do so. It is not truth that is at stake but conformity. Inability to do this is to put one's whole existence at risk. But does not conformity also involve pretence, lying and masquerade? Who could attach any importance to truth? Certainly not Nietzsche himself. He knew too much of what lay hidden below the surface. Later he cunningly revealed what he considered the truth – 'a woman, nothing better'.[33]

Why a woman? And what is so bad about being '*feminini generis*', a phrase he used to characterise the late Wagner? That is easily answered, he replied – because women and truth both have good reason 'not to let their reasons be known'.[34] They have something to hide, something that cannot be expressed or revealed, something that can only make one tremble. Therefore they pretend, dress themselves up, don masks, so as to hide it and make people forget it – forget the fear associated with the toad, that makes him feel ill, the fear like that felt in the presence of the Medusa, who petrified all those who set eyes on her, or like the Orphic goddess Baubo, who brazenly raises her skirts, an act that can in reality arouse merriment only in a deity. Nietzsche knew that there are things that are so ugly that they must be concealed and denied, not only on grounds of good taste but also out of sheer humanity. Truth, for example.

Nietzsche contained his fear by putting pen to paper. In an essay entitled 'On Truth and Lies in an Extra-Moral Sense', published posthumously, he makes an attempt to introduce clarity into the concept of truth. Strictly speaking, he says, there are two kinds of truth. The one is that in which society believes and which it holds dear; those who flout it are ostracised. The other, which causes him nightmares, appears not to exist as far as society is concerned. Nobody talks about it. It has to be kept out of sight.

Nietzsche claims to have finally seen through this society. It consists, he says, of 'deception, flattery, lies, talking behind people's backs, decking oneself with borrowed plumes, perverting reality, conventionality, play-acting, both in public and within one's own four walls . . . regulations and laws'. Such were the conditions to which he was subjected in Basel and which could not but make him feel ill, for 'the philosopher, the proudest of men, has to endure having the eyes of the world fixed on his every thought and action, as though a telescope were trained on him'.[35]

Naturally he knew that he was deceiving himself and merely imagining things. For the human intellect, he maintained, conveys a completely false impression of a person both to himself and to others – indeed, all the impressions it conveys are false. Its task, as conventional wisdom has it, is not to recognise truth but to disguise it. In a world in which everyone is fighting everyone else, lies are more useful than the truth. That society nevertheless sets such store by truth need not contradict this, because society itself decides what constitutes truth. The truth is that which members of society must necessarily believe because that is what guarantees the survival of society. Truth comprises the conditions of existence, and agreement has been reached on what lies are to be counted as true. Society, as defined by Nietzsche, consists of all those who have pledged themselves 'to lie in accordance with a set pattern of conventions'. Those who lie differently will be ostracised. Twice he emphasises in his essay that no one trusts a liar, and that all denounce him.

In so doing they lie and deceive themselves. For they are denied access to real truth and cannot recognise it, since their intellect serves only the interests of self-preservation. Indeed they could not bear the real truth. Not for nothing has nature locked them into a 'false consciousness' and thrown away the key, allowing them only a glimpse outside, sufficient for them to sense 'that mankind rests on a foundation of the ruthless, the covetous, the insatiable and the murderous'.[36]

Clara Gelzer appears to have had such a glimpse, after Nietzsche had shown her where to look. 'He allowed me a glance through a narrow crack into the dark abyss of his soul', she told Bernoulli. Nietzsche's experience was similar. For at the very point in his essay where the crack opens up, he quotes the opening scene of his toad dream: 'What does man really know about himself? If he could but see himself in his entirety, laid out as in an illuminated glass showcase. Does not nature withhold the most important values from him?'

His piercing gaze had already penetrated Euphorion's deepest secrets. Now his dream laid out before him what he had striven to conceal from others, in particular from those unsuspecting guests around the dinner table. As his dream had revealed it to him, so he revealed it to the lady at his side. Could he have failed to feel that the others had fastened their intrusive gaze on him, as on the naked figure in the showcase? Now, as his thoughts on truth and lies gradually coalesced, the proper answer came to him. You meek and feeble Philistines who make fun of me, he says – you are all in the same position as I. You carry around in your minds the knowledge that you cannot endure. But you keep it concealed and take care not to touch it. It is taboo for what you call truth, and has to be kept out of sight, treated as though it did not exist. Do you not understand that you are all liars because you hide the truth and cover up the fact that you are nurturing a beast within you?

For Nietzsche the philosopher this realisation must have come as a crushing blow. If society's truth is only an officially approved lie which is keeping real truth in captivity, knowledge can only be the guardian of those questionable principles that underpin society. The philosopher is not helping to build the temple of truth but is merely adding to the 'graveyard of ideas' in which lie the remains of concepts formerly held to be true. As a professor, Nietzsche arranged and documented the lies of conventionality, juggled with concepts conveying not knowledge but complicity, 'seeking to construct, as it were, an immensely complex cathedral on a flowing river'.[37] It was an image appropriate to his circumstances. He taught in the shadow of Basel Cathedral, under which flows the Rhine. Only he could know the dangerous dungeons and caves upon which was built the fragile edifice of knowledge.

It was Nietzsche's responsibility to supervise the ordering of concepts. Truth is order, and each stone has to rest firmly on the others. Anything built on an uneven surface is in need of support. Nietzsche, guardian of this graveyard in the shadow of the cathedral, had taken up an impregnable position in his bastion. He knew how exposed he and his truth were – 'if he were to escape for just one moment from the prison walls of this faith, his vaunted "self-awareness" would be over once and for all'.[38] It is the famous crack through which the eye looks into the depths and encounters a terrible sight, namely the self, 'as though hanging in a dream from the back of a tiger'.[39] Did this image remind him that he had seen in the wild tigers with fearsome gnashing teeth the figures of Greek warriors, as Sacher-Masoch had seen in Alexis Papadopolis? And now he was dreaming that he was riding on the tiger's back?

The Greeks are not far away, even though he does not mention them by name. The second image of the threat facing him as a philosopher also comes from antiquity. He must arm himself against it, don the warrior's armour, for 'there are terrible forces bearing down upon him which oppose philosophical truth with "truths" of a completely different kind, with divers images on their shields'.[40]

Has he in mind the shield of Athene, depicting the head of Medusa, writhing with snakes? Does he see before him the whole phalanx of heroes, with a multitude of devices on their shields, described in loving detail by Homer, as they advance into battle? Or does he feel the famous shield of Achilles bearing down upon him, with its emblem of Greek heroes in the bloom of youth?

In the end he resigns himself to the situation. He has, after all, acquired sufficient self-discipline in order to protect himself to a certain degree against the injustices inflicted on him by society. Then, as he emphasises, he will be seen, not with a 'twitching human visage but wearing a mask with regular, dignified features'.[41] It was the self-control he had learnt in Pforta, a quality that was necessary when the first hostile reviews of his *Birth of Tragedy* appeared, and was to become all the more important as time went on. Each new publication, he said to Kelterborn, brought with it the risk 'that people will empty their bed-pans over my head'.[42] Or in the language of 'Truth and Lies': 'If a rain cloud bursts in the sky above him, he will just draw his coat more closely round himself and walk on with measured pace.'[43]

With this image he ends his essay, shaking off the raindrops and making the best of a bad job. The rain cloud had been around for a long time. It had once descended on him in the market in Naumburg, at the moment when he was feeling desperately unhappy in a strange town. Born in the country, he had problems in finding his bearings in the dark and narrow streets of the town and in understanding the language of his fellow-pupils, who constantly poked fun at him and his difficulties. His sister Elisabeth remembered an episode from this time:

> The boys' school was in the Topfmarkt, the market not far from where we lived. One day, just after school was over, there came a sudden downpour. We looked towards the Priestergasse to see if our Fritz was coming. The boys were all rushing home as fast as they could. Finally we caught sight of him. He was walking at a leisurely pace, his cap folded underneath his slate and his little handkerchief wrapped round them. Mama waved to him and called out to him to hurry up but the pouring rain prevented us from hearing what he replied. When he finally arrived home, soaked from head to foot, mama scolded him. 'But Mama,' he protested, in all seriousness, 'it's a school rule that we mustn't run when we come out of school but walk home quietly in a well-behaved manner.'

Fritz, the young Stoic, did not need school rules. A boy who can keep his composure when others make fun of him is not likely to run away from a cloudburst. In Basel the young professor was to recall this episode.

'LIPS MADE FOR KISSING!'

In the summer term of 1876 Nietzsche acquired a disciple, a young man prepared to undertake the duties of private secretary – without remuneration, naturally. Heinrich Köselitz, born in Annaberg in the Saxon Erzgebirge, was ten years younger than Nietzsche and had studied at the conservatoire in Leipzig. Carried away by Nietzsche's writings, he hastened to Basel to meet their author. First he listened deferentially to the young philosopher's lectures, then introduced himself, and was rewarded with an invitation to visit him in his lodgings. For his essay 'Richard Wagner in Bayreuth', Nietzsche said, he urgently needed someone to act as his amanuensis, taking dictation and reading aloud – 'which I did almost every day in my first year', wrote the new recruit proudly. He continued to do so, with occasional interruptions, until the time of Nietzsche's mental collapse. Without Köselitz's skill in deciphering his master's handwriting the publication of Nietzsche's collected works would have hardly been feasible.

To symbolise his admission into Nietzsche's world Köselitz was re-christened Peter Gast – a new and permanent 'guest' in his household. Nietzsche once called his Zarathustra 'the guest of guests'.[44] Nietzsche as an open house.

Peter Gast became for Nietzsche what the philosopher was to become – but did not want to become – for Wagner. His need to worship somebody or something knew no bounds. He smothered his new master with incense as Wagner lavished adulation on King Ludwig – except that Wagner knew when he was deliberately weaving a spell. Gast believed that residing in Nietzsche was a god, and he was prepared to do almost anything for him.

In the summer of 1876 a young history student called Ludwig von Scheffler happened to meet the young amanuensis. Gast was then just twenty-two – but he already knew how much he owed his master. Scheffler had come to Basel in order to attend lectures by the great historian Jacob Burckhardt. By chance he found himself in Nietzsche's lecture room, where the subject 'The Life and Teaching of Plato' had been announced. The chairs in the room – which was barely larger than an office – were empty. The only person present was a man leaning against the window-sill and looking down at the river, which had overflowed its banks. Scheffler noticed that the man was wearing the dark habit of a student at the Leipzig conservatoire – a black coat with old-fashioned long tails. When, in response to a light-hearted remark by Scheffler, the man turned round, mildly irritated at being disturbed, Scheffler could not believe his eyes: 'Another Richard Wagner, but younger, in his prime! Not only were his sideburns an exact imitation of the Master's but also his nose, his brow and his chin were as though modelled on the features of the great composer.'[45]

The Wagner double introduced himself and explained that he was one of the professor's followers. Nietzsche would be there at any moment, he added. When he arrived, Scheffler was disappointed – a figure short rather than of medium height, slightly built, his head deeply embedded in his shoulders. The most striking features of his face were his large, bushy moustache and his thick, glistening spectacles – both to the detriment, Scheffler thought, of his 'intellectual mien'.

His dress – light-coloured trousers, short jacket with a fancifully tied cravat round his neck – was self-consciously that of an artist. In a less withdrawn man one would have identified him as a dandy but for that his long hair was too lank and straggly and his complexion too pale. He dragged his feet some-what – fine quality shoes on delicate feet. Once behind the lectern, he took off his glasses, and Scheffler saw his eyes for the first time: 'Dull, short-sighted eyes, unattractive by virtue of one peculiarity – their dark pupils were excep-tionally large, yet larger still were the whites of his eyes. Looked at in profile, this gave him a stern, somewhat agitated look.'[46]

To the accompaniment of the roar of the river outside, Nietzsche began his lecture. His voice was not particularly strong, and his articulation was not of the clearest – rather, gentle and unaffected, 'a voice from the soul', with a melody that had for Scheffler a magical charm. He spoke softly. Indeed, he had no particular need to raise his voice – it was an intimate gathering. The lecture was a monologue in which he discussed the various themes he had conjured up as though he were working out an exercise in counterpoint. At times he spoke more slowly, more hesitantly, as though he were checking what he had just said. At certain points his voice sank to a pianissimo. Finally he reached a powerful finale, to match the roar of the Rhine below. The meagre audience applauded and the lecturer crept softly and silently out of the room.

Nietzsche was not so blind as not to recognise the presence of a new face. And although he had only recently been drawn into Nietzsche's circle, Gast asked Scheffler whether he was likely to come back. When Scheffler said yes, Gast took him into his full confidence, explaining Nietzsche's importance and listing all the great friends he had, from Wagner to Burckhardt. Scheffler realised that a great opportunity was opening up before him, and he grabbed it with both hands. When Nietzsche invited him to take tea with him after one of his lectures, he must have felt like one of the chosen few – a novice on the path that led to the sanctum sanctorum.

Nietzsche lived in an attractive two-storey house outside the Spalentor Gate. Scheffler rang the bell and a young lady, the philosopher's sister

Elisabeth, opened the door, then disappeared. He entered the drawing-room, where Nietzsche and Gast were waiting for him. Everything looked quite different from what he had imagined. They were a group of men but the room had the feel of a lady's boudoir.

Right from the beginning Scheffler felt a warm, friendly atmosphere, and after politely greeting the other two, sat down in one of the large, soft armchairs whose white covers were decorated with a floral pattern reminiscent of the drawing Nietzsche had found on his desk in the *Gymnasium*. Flowers were everywhere – 'in glasses, in pots, on the tables, in the corners, a display of delicate colour that vied with the watercolours on the walls and gave off a gentle fragrance'.[47] As the curtains were always kept drawn, a subdued afternoon light settled on the room – a colourful scene like that of an impressionist painting. Suddenly Scheffler had the feeling 'that he had been invited to the house not of a professor but of a dear female friend'.

The host, whose attractive voice filled the room, served the tea himself 'with a smile that flickered over his expressionless face like a ray of sunlight'. This fixed look was a feature of Nietzsche's appearance that also struck a friend of Gast, who described it as 'almost hard'.[48] Scheffler may well have noticed that Nietzsche had donned a mask but he was too flattered to give the matter much thought. He enjoyed to the hilt the scene that had been prepared for him, although he did observe after a while that there was something forced about the professor's manner.

But Gast took care to ensure that there was no sense of embarrassment. When Nietzsche stopped talking, Gast would immediately intervene, pompously holding forth about the backwardness of musical life in Basel, until his master broke in to ask whether Scheffler might not wish to say something – about the visual arts, for example, or about Burckhardt. Thus encouraged, Scheffler launched into a voluble discourse while Nietzsche, who had taken off his glasses, listened, fixing him with his big, dull eyes. Then, as Scheffler was on the point of talking about himself and his fellow-students, he found himself interrupted and suddenly unable to continue – 'especially as I had already been distracted by a deep sigh that Nietzsche had uttered'.[49]

Nietzsche broke in again. As requested, Scheffler had begun to expound his views on the visual arts and had arrived at the subject of Holbein. Nietzsche and Gast listened attentively, for they were familiar with the sketch that Scheffler now set out to discuss – a chalk drawing with coloured wash and heightened with white, taken at the time to be a self-portrait. Wearing a red beret and with a bow round the neck of his shirt, the figure looks out past the viewer with the passionless gaze characteristic of a sitter. But Scheffler obviously saw more in the picture and, stimulated by Nietzsche's attentive interest, embarked on an ecstatic outburst:

> I strove in vain to find words to describe the magical attraction of the wonderful portrait. There was nothing to be gained from following its features line by line, so to speak, nor could words do justice to its expression of resolute manliness combined with the fresh charm of youth. I could not manage to capture even individual traits of the sketch. Words failed me. I saw the lips before my eyes – full and succulent, yet at the same time confident and determined. Lips that did not call for water yet were made to be enjoyed! 'Lips,' I stammered helplessly, 'made for . . .'[50]

From a quiet corner of the room came a soft voice: '. . . made for kissing!' Scheffler stared at the floor in confusion: 'The voice was Nietzsche's. He delivered the words in a tone that contrasted strangely with their sensual nature. Slumped in his armchair, his arms dangling limply over the sides and with his head drooping forward on to his chest, he seemed more like a figure who had spoken out of a dream than added the final words to my sentence.'

Baffled, Scheffler looked across to Gast. But he too could only smile uncomprehendingly. Only later did Scheffler come to understand that Nietzsche had uttered a confession. The professor with the severe external features had allowed him 'to glimpse his gentle inner nature through a narrow crack, so to speak'. Only the unperceptive reader, he added, would fail to recognise how close Nietzsche's enigmatic psyche came to Michelangelo, or Plato, or Platen. 'How great is the similarity between both men . . .'[51]

Scheffler passed the test. From then on he was allowed to accompany Nietzsche part of the way home after his lectures. Gast stayed in the background. But as Scheffler recalled, Nietzsche talked to him not about Plato but about mountain walks in autumn and holidays in far-off places.

In June 1876 the university had granted Nietzsche a year's sick leave. Malwida von Meysenbug had suggested he go to the Adriatic coast in her company. Having first agreed, however, he had in the meantime lighted on another possibility for spending this year – only he did not know how to tell the young man.

Once, when Scheffler arrived late for a lecture, flushed and out of breath, he saw to his surprise that he and Nietzsche were the only two present. Gast had made his apologies. Nietzsche welcomed him 'with an amiability and cheerfulness that I had never seen in him before', he wrote.[52] With a smile on his face he made his way with a light step to the lectern and proceeded to deliver an introduction to the philosophy of Plato. When he had finished, he drew a deep breath and said, first in Greek, then in German: 'I was searching for myself' – a familiar Greek saying.

The sound of the Rhine was clearly audible in the room as the professor and his solitary student sat there together, deeply moved. Then Nietzsche suddenly got to his feet and announced that today it was his turn to accompany his student on his way home: there was in any case something he wanted to discuss with the caretaker. Indeed, he was interested to see how Scheffler lived – another reason for going with him. When Nietzsche complained about the uneven cobblestones by the bridge, Scheffler offered him his arm. They talked about the sunny weather, and the younger man pointed to the billowing white clouds overhead in the deep blue sky, which reminded him of a painting by Veronese. 'They are always in motion,' said Nietzsche, with a meaningful expression, and looked at his young student. 'He suddenly dropped my arm,' wrote Scheffler, 'then grasped it again with both hands and said: "The vacation will start soon, and I am going away. Will you come with me? Shall we go and watch the clouds go by in Veronese's own land?" '[53]

It was an invitation that came like a bolt from the blue. Scheffler did not know how to take it. For a moment he said nothing, then mumbled some excuse for declining the offer. Later he justified himself by saying that for two people to go on holiday together demanded an 'absolute sympathy' between them. Nietzsche seems to have felt just such a sympathy for his student, so Scheffler's rejection of his invitation can only have come to him like a slap in the face, and for a moment he seemed to lose his composure: 'Nietzsche immediately let go of my arm. I looked across to him and was shocked at the change that had come over him. No longer was he the professor I knew – his face had become a lifeless mask as he stared at me in silence.'[54]

Scheffler thought he was facing 'the agony of a tragic mask, its mouth open as though about to say something'. Then Nietzsche turned away from him, resumed his normal expression and accompanied him to the front door of Scheffler's lodgings, conversing in a forced manner about totally insignificant matters. There the two men took perfunctory leave of each other. It was the end of their relationship. Shortly afterwards Scheffler left Basel with a complicated eye problem, while Nietzsche set out for Bayreuth, where the next disaster was awaiting him.

THE VOICE FROM THE 'BROWN NIGHT'

By the time he arrived in Bayreuth in July 1876, with rehearsals for the first Wagner Festival in full swing, Nietzsche was also in need of consolation on a second count. For a week he had known that he had lost his friend Rohde once and for all. A comrade from Leipzig days, Rohde had become engaged to be married, and the cherished dream that they might live together, go on holiday together, establish a monastic community together, was finally shattered. His suffering, as Overbeck put it, was akin 'to that of a man in love'.[55] By contrast, the news that Overbeck himself had also become engaged made little mark on him.

It must have been a disturbing realisation for Nietzsche during his stay in Bayreuth that all the luminaries of the proposed order of philosophers assembled there in Wagner's honour had the thought of women in their minds. As well as Rohde and Overbeck the love-bug attacked Gersdorff, who had become infatuated with the charming Nerina Finochietta, an Italian countess to whom he had been introduced by Malwida von Meysenbug.

Nietzsche considered accommodating himself to these changed circumstances. Probably through the good offices of the ubiquitous Malwida he met a young lady called Louise Ott, to whom he immediately felt himself attracted, until finding out that she was married and had a young family in Paris. He showed no inclination to take the matter further. After her departure he sent her several letters of a kind hardly calculated to make her husband jealous. 'Let us hold fast to the purity of spirit that has brought us together', he wrote, in a tone more appropriate to a priest. She replied as 'Sister Louise', accepting him as her spiritual brother. It was a role that he evidently relished. 'My brotherly affection for you', he assured her, 'goes so deep that I could love your husband because he is *your* husband. Such is the purity of my thoughts.'[56]

With Erwin Rohde the situation was more complicated. He could not simply turn the clock back. For ten years they had been brothers, exchanging passionate letters and longing for a time when they would be together. Now all this was over. Maybe Nietzsche had come to Bayreuth hoping that the festival would cure him of his despair, as Greek tragedy had healed the suffering satyr. Wagner as divine vision.

But Bayreuth was not the place to lift his spirits. Even the attempt to cure himself through the little episode with Louise Ott, enticed by the prospect of an extra-marital adventure, had gone awry. The very same evening as he received Rohde's news he tried to rid himself of his pain by pouring out his sorrow in a reply. He enclosed with his letter a poem that expresses his emotions better than the diffuse accompanying letter – a poem that tells of the loneliness that now confronts him, and of the suspicion that their love may have been founded on a misunderstanding. 'I hardly know how to express or explain my longing and my unhappiness.'[57]

His longing and his unhappiness were one and the same. And because he felt things differently from his friend – because he himself was different from his friend – that friend could no longer be the object of his all-consuming yearning. So that Rohde would understand, really understand, the nature of the rift between them, Nietzsche sent him this poem – 'a poem about what you have done. I am not a poet but you will understand what I am trying to say.'[58]

The poem was 'The Wanderer'. As he walks through the darkness, the Wanderer is suddenly stopped in his tracks:

> A bird is singing in the night –
> 'O bird, what hast thou done?
> Why dost thou thwart my path and my thoughts
> And fill me with such sweet weariness of soul
> That I must stay my step
> And give ear
> To understand thy sound and thy message?'[59]

Almost reluctantly the Wanderer has stopped to listen to the bird's song, for his instinct was to march onwards unheeding, like the knight in Dürer's engraving. But he cannot. And as he wonders what the bird means – like Wagner's Siegfried, who would dearly understand the song of the woodbird – a sweet melancholy fills his heart. He has fallen in love with the bird's song, perhaps even with the bird itself and its enticing call. Nietzsche frequently associated his friend with a bird, the swan of Lohengrin, but also with a bird that migrated from south to north, for which he set a snare. But it was all a misunderstanding:

> The bird went silent, saying:
> 'No, Wanderer! It was not thee I was addressing
> With those notes!
> I was singing because the night is so beautiful.'[60]

The bird, who also has the power of speech in Wagner's *Siegfried*, sets him free by explaining that it was not for him that its song was meant but that it was singing for its own sake. This is how Nietzsche put it in his letter to Rohde, but it was not what he really meant. In autumn 1884 he replaced this harmless version with what he had actually intended to say – what Rohde had told him:

> 'No, Wanderer, no! It is not thee I am charming
> With the notes of my song –
> It is a woman I am charming from the mountain tops.
> What concern is it of thine?'

It was a rebuff. And Nietzsche made a further change in the later version. The bird asks the Wanderer what it is about his 'flute song' that hurts him. He does not know. Maybe the bird had aroused false expectations. Or perhaps it is not a bird at all but a mischievous flute-player from among the followers of Dionysus, who has lost his way. Nietzsche once called the music of his heart 'the flute of Dionysus'.[61] Could that have been what he heard in the middle of the night? He ended his letter to Rohde with the puzzling words 'Such were the words spoken to me in the night after your letter arrived.' Who had spoken? Whose was the voice that had brought him this sad news? Did he mean it in the figurative sense of an inspiration or was it another of his aural hallucinations? But since when did the voice whisper in verse?

Rohde will have understood. The poem, with its mysterious concluding words, must have reminded him of an earlier letter of Nietzsche's, written in the honeymoon of their friendship, when Nietzsche was in Basel and he, Rohde, was detained in Rome. 'As I read your words,' Nietzsche had written, 'I felt as though I had suddenly awoken to find myself engulfed in a deep brown night and as though there came from the far distance a plaintive sound such as I had not heard for a long while.'

The sound that seemed to lift him into a dream of a higher significance did indeed come 'from the far distance'. In May 1863, while a pupil at Pforta, Nietzsche had written an essay on the character of Cassius in Shakespeare's *Julius Caesar*, in which he dealt with the relationship between the two conspirators Brutus and Cassius. He saw the souls of the two men 'immersed in each other, so to speak', and he shared their pain when they were forced to take leave of each other. He also found in a passage from Goethe's *Italian Journey* that same sentiment of mutual yearning shared by friends forced to part: 'Goethe tells of the strange fascination exerted on him by the singing of the gondoliers in Venice. "The sound of their voices came from afar", wrote Goethe, "– a strange sound like a lamentation without mourning, an extraordinary quality that had the power to reduce one to tears." We have a similar experience when we seem to sense from afar a profound human passion through the fetters by which either strength of human will or force of circumstances has bound it.'[62]

Six years later, in 1869, this notion turned out to have been prophetic. Yoked in a spiritual union, the two friends had to live out their friendship by correspondence, creating the circumstances in which as 'from afar' their compulsive love could convey itself through the written word like a real voice. Lamentation without mourning – a strange sound that can call forth tears.

In the same year as he heard the sound of love in 'the deep brown night', Nietzsche sought to share with Rohde his enthusiasm for Wagner's recent essay on Beethoven. 'Read it', he urged his friend – 'it is a revelation of the world in which we – *we!* shall live in the future.' He had already discovered his own past here.

What Goethe had experienced in Venice, Wagner had also known. In September 1858, lovesick and far from his beloved Mathilde Wesendonk, he was staying in a *palazzo* on the Canal Grande: later he wrote in his 'Beethoven': 'In the deathly silence there arose the mighty sound of a lament from a boat where the gondolier had just awoken from his slumbers. Repeatedly he called out into the night, until from the other end of the canal his call was echoed. After a pause the dialogue was renewed and the voices merged, until finally the sounds from near and far died away and slumber returned.'

This, for Wagner, was the primeval experience of music, where the Will perceives and responds to itself. 'This is the way the yearning youth understands the enticing call of the woodbird', because it is *one* yearning that he hears and that hears itself, and he feels 'that his innermost being is at one with the innermost being of everything he perceives'.[63]

When Nietzsche read this, it must have struck a chord. The sound that he hears from afar is the promise of unity: what Goethe felt and Wagner described became reality in him, Friedrich Nietzsche. From the lines of Rohde's letter he hears the call of the woodbird, the flute-song of Dionysus. Years later he held Rohde's letter in his hand and heard that sound again, though now in a strangely different form, like a foreign tongue that he no longer understood. 'My desire and my pain are different', he wrote to Rohde.

Towards the end of his lucid life Nietzsche himself wrote a poem in which, like a Venetian gondolier, he calls out into the dark brown night and waits for an answer. Written in Turin in 1888, one of his best-known poems, it ends with a question:

Once I stood on the bridge
In the brown night.
A song came from afar,
And drops of gold fell
On to the quivering surface.
Gondolas, lights, music –
Deliriously it was borne out into the twilight . . .

My soul, a stringed instrument,
Invisibly plucked, secretly
Sang its own gondolier's song,

Trembling with shining bliss.
– Was anyone listening?

Three years earlier Nietzsche had had a similar experience on the Rialto Bridge with music 'that moved me to tears'. He had written the poem in secret and it never seems to have left his mind – until that freezing January night in 1889 when Franz Overbeck took his demented friend back by train through the Gotthard Tunnel to Basel. Overbeck was suddenly woken by the sound of his friend singing the words of the gondolier's song 'to an utterly mysterious melody'.[64]

A HIDDEN BURDEN

Disasters are prone to recur. Nightmares constantly return. Once what is dearest has been lost, it is fated to be lost over and over; once exiled from one's homeland, every new homeland becomes a new place of exile. The losses that Nietzsche had sustained, which now included Wagner and Rohde, repeated his first irreplaceable loss – that of his childhood in Röcken. This was followed by his flight from Bonn, the end of the Tribschen idyll and finally his alienation from Basel. 'I am now yours once again', he wrote to Overbeck and his wife in 1879, adding in parentheses: – 'if only it were not in this accursed Basel, about which I have real nightmares'.[65] He was not speaking only metaphorically. For if Elisabeth is to be believed, the ghostly figure from his childhood continued to persecute him. Bernoulli recorded that he went pale when he learned that some of the older local residents still believed that the district was haunted and stubbornly maintained that they had heard the spirit roaring.[66]

The past could not be shaken off. It only seemed to be the past – in reality it always returned, as a ghost or as a dream that in the end makes life intolerable. In 1874 Nietzsche published *On the Uses and Disadvantages of History for Life*. He has a remarkable conception of the nature of the past, talking already in the second paragraph of the book about 'the moment, now here, now gone, previously nothing, subsequently nothing, which yet returns as a ghost to destroy the calm of a later moment'.[67]

It is an extraordinary sentence. Apart from the 'calm' of the moment, by which he must mean the silence of the night, he describes history, a field of activity to which some of the greatest minds of the century devoted their energies, as a phantom whose frightening features cause man to tremble in fear. But was there not general agreement in the age of Burckhardt, Ranke and Mommsen that the past was subject to the authority of human memory, whose evidence is both scientifically demonstrable and plausible? What is stored in human memory, like the knowledge preserved in the archives, is subject to scrutiny. Man controls history in his own interests – without the power of memory it would be long forgotten. This was an item of faith.

Nietzsche challenged this. His experience had been different. The past can govern the present no less than the present can govern the past. A ghost, an intangible reality, itself attains to reality and thereby puts a question mark against human reality. If the present becomes the stage on which the past is played out, where tragedy and human disaster repeatedly recur in a series of ever-changing masks, then death has overcome life, nothingness has conquered humankind.

Nietzsche knew how serious the threat was. The greater the scope permitted to history, the sooner it would become 'the gravedigger of the present', as he put it.[68] Death calls man to his grave, and at some time the earth will become 'a swaying burial mound'.[69] As long as man is unable to free himself from what was, preferring to force everything that is into the shadow of the past, he will remain unable to truly live. Instead he will live out his paltry life in a state of ignorance. More and more of the past will amass around him, gradually turning him into a custodian of death. In Nietzsche's own words: 'Man strives to resist the ever heavier burden of the past, the burden that presses down on him from above or bends him to one side, laying a sinister, invisible weight upon him that hampers his movements.'[70]

It was not only Nietzsche himself – whose stoop under the pressure of this weight seemed to illustrate his proposition – who was threatened by the past but the whole of mankind. And it is science, knowledge, that conjures up the ghostly spirit, feverishly collecting the withered leaves and empty husks of yesteryear and piling them up on the living present. A nightmarish prospect – a slow burial in the midst of corpses and rotting junk. The shadow of death gradually extinguishes the light of day – which was why Nietzsche would soon have to light again the lamp of Diogenes.

Like Hamlet, Nietzsche sees a menacing ghost confronting the human race embodying a revulsion from everything that exists, a revulsion from corpses, from carrion, from nightmares.[71] So, on behalf of mankind, Nietzsche-Hamlet poses the question of whether to be or not to be. Either man allows the non-being of the past to overcome his own living being or he resolves to take up the heroic struggle against the return of death, against the moment that disturbs his peace of mind, against the immense burden of the past that forces him into the abyss.

Nietzsche responds to the challenge by taking up arms. The task is not to forget but to compel, to dominate. History is as wax in our hands once we have learnt to shape it into forms that cause us not to shiver in fear but to tremble with longing and expectation. This is why we need heroes to stamp their authority on the past and re-interpret it as part of their own pre-history. It was a thought that Nietzsche had once turned over in his mind in an essay called 'Fate and History', written when he was only seventeen: 'If it were to become possible, through a powerful exercise of will, to turn the whole past history of the world upside down, mankind itself would join the ranks of the gods, and history would become for us merely a reverie, an unreal dream.'[72]

The man who is incapable of such a reversal, wrote the adolescent Nietzsche, in a menacing tone, will simply be 'wiped out' by history. The others will be triumphant because they are stronger than their enemies – the others being the youthful heroes. With an apocalyptic flourish of Wagnerian brass he summons the young to the fore: 'Set our youth free, and you will have set life itself free. For that power only lay dormant, in prison – it has not died. Ask yourselves!'

Towards the end of his time in Basel defeat seemed to be staring Nietzsche in the face. Having fought bitterly against a past with which he could not come to terms, he became more seriously ill than ever before. It was as though, instead of plaguing him with a series of identifiable symptoms, nature was experimenting with a generalised disease called simply 'sick', a condition that led neither to cure nor to death. Its victim was suffering from a malady neither of the head nor of the stomach: instead his life had become a permanent state of sickness. We can only surmise the extent to which the syphilis he had contracted in his student days exacerbated the dangers inherent in his medical history. At all events the attacks to which he was prone assumed unheard-of proportions and tore at every fibre in his body.

His letters from this period, 1878–9, are a never-ending series of laments. On 19 October 1878 he wrote to his mother in Naumburg: 'I am sitting here, wracked in pain.'[73] Two days later he informed her: 'I have been suffering from headaches for the last nine days without cease.' Two days after that he wrote to a friend: 'Here I am again, after some of the worst weeks I have ever known.' Five days later: 'a terrible Sunday'. On 9 November, again to Naumburg: 'On Sunday I was struck down with a particularly violent fit. This makes ten Sundays in succession.'[74] On 23 November: 'I suffered two fits in one week – the first on Sunday evening and Monday, the second on Thursday evening and Friday.' Finally, a week later: 'Violent attacks over three days.'[75]

He suffered sudden repeated seizures that struck him like bolts of lightning and left him paralysed, his eyes clouded over and his intestines 'literally torn apart'. He compared his pain to 'cruelty inflicted on dumb animals and the first torments of hell',[76] and hinted that he would soon give up his academic post – perhaps the thought of any future post, and perhaps even ... He left the sentence hanging in the air. Looking back on this time later, he said: 'I was longing for death.'[77]

In the autumn of 1878 Ludwig von Scheffler, who had recently gained his doctorate, turned up again in Basel and made his way to Nietzsche's new apartment in Bachlettenstrasse. Two years had elapsed since that scene on the bridge. To Scheffler's astonishment he found that Nietzsche had chosen to live in 'an ugly, run-down district', sparsely inhabited and far from the centre of town.[78] He walked down a lonely country road flanked only by a few houses and with tall, age-old poplar trees on either side, their leaves scattered across the road by the wind. In the distance he caught sight of the long mountain ridges, 'looking like coffins'. He could not find the house, and he had to ask passers-by where the professor lived. Ah yes, came the reply, the hermit, and they directed him to a dilapidated old building that might formerly have belonged to a toll-keeper.

The upper storey was empty – only the ground floor seemed to be occupied. Here Nietzsche lived in a small, modestly furnished room.[79] October was a rainy month, and in November came the first frosts. He had to light his stove but wood was expensive.[80] He breakfasted in bed, then, since there was no one to clear up after him, just left everything where it was. Visitors were not welcome. When he had one of his attacks, he could be certain that nobody in this dreary hole on the outskirts of the town would take the slightest notice. He was like a wounded beast that had sought refuge in no man's land.

Scheffler had no idea of all this. He pulled the bell. A harsh, clanging sound rang out through the house but there was no sound of movement. He rang again, then, impatiently, a third time. Was the house empty? Before leaving, he resolved at least to try and catch a glimpse of the interior of the house. He crept up to one of the downstairs windows and peeped through the curtains. The sight made him recoil in shock: 'There he was, sitting at a kind of improvised desk, with teapots and cooking utensils lying around the little area in which there was room for him to work. An eye-shade was secured round his forehead, covering half his face, while his emaciated form was bent forwards over the table. He was like a man listening in fear and trepidation, anxious to hide.'[81]

Nietzsche was afraid. First the three rings at the door, then the succeeding silence. Was someone trying to climb in through the window? He decided not to go to the door. He no longer existed. Scheffler, the spy, appeared not to have understood what he saw: 'I felt I had to go to him and touch him, even if it meant climbing through the window ... Then I watched his body begin to tremble as he listened for the sound of the unwelcome visitor's footsteps leaving the house.' It was a painfully embarrassing situation.

In June 1879 the Cantonal government of Basel put an end to Nietzsche's agony by acceding to his request to be relieved of his teaching duties. His pension was exactly the same as the salary he had earned when he arrived in the town as a tyro ten years before. He had been semi-healthy at that time, and he had carried out his responsibilities, as far as he could. Now he was finally written off.

Nine years after his death his sister felt moved to set the record straight. A rumour had been circulating that her brother had been sick. She, High Priestess of the Nietzsche cult, was not the only one to find this totally unacceptable. Nietzsche was an intellectual hero. He had preached the Great Health, consequently he himself had possessed that Health. In 1909 Elisabeth wrote a scurrilous letter that shamed both her late brother and the citizens of Basel, whom he was accused of having led by the nose. 'I can well understand the misleading impression that my brother's letters leave on outsiders,' wrote Elisabeth, 'and I have not the slightest intention of explaining to primitive minds the real reasons why he talked so often about his illness. To put it in a nutshell: It was his illness that bought him his personal freedom. It was only as a sick man that he took his leave of Basel, only to a sick man that the town granted a pension.'[82]

Indeed, Nietzsche did want to get some of his own back on the Basel authorities and on their leading dignitary Jacob Burckhardt. In the last letter he ever wrote, dated 6 January 1889, he reacted with a mixture of scorn and indignation to what Burckhardt had said about him. The letter left Burckhardt at a loss for words, and he immediately sought out Nietzsche's friend Overbeck. Thereupon Overbeck took the train to Turin and persuaded his demented friend to travel back with him to Basel on the pretext that a grand reception had been prepared for him there. The last sentence of Nietzsche's letter to Burckhardt reads: 'You may make any use you like of this letter provided it does not lower the esteem in which the authorities in Basel hold me.'

In other words, Nietzsche knew what people said about him. And since he no longer had any need to restrain himself, he made Burckhardt aware of the fact. He was condemned, he wrote, to be the butt of poor jokes 'for the next eternity' and had been striving with might and main to make himself 'the greatest chronicler of the *grande monde*'. With a note of scorn in his voice he tells his former colleague to his face what he has long thought of him. Although Burckhardt had always been hesitant to criticise his works, he said, Burckhardt, as the senior man, 'was entitled to make whatever critical comments he wished', and he, Nietzsche, would welcome such comments, 'albeit without promising to make use of them. We writers are incorrigible.'[83] This was an impertinent remark, and the sensitive Burckhardt must have understood Nietzsche's thrust.

At the end of his letter Nietzsche, the unkempt vagabond who has proclaimed himself a god, issued a direct challenge to the respected historian, who had hardly ever set foot outside his native Basel, to visit him in Turin and share a glass of wine, in 'appropriately shabby attire' – a mischievous dig directed by the man in exile at the venerable man of learning, whose untidy appearance he had always disapproved of back in his days in Basel.

'Even the highly respected Jacob Burckhardt,' he had written then, 'a man of substance, lived in shabby surroundings in the worst of taste, and used to join the philistines in the tavern every evening. Add to this the Swiss people's absurd patriotism – like their cheese, it comes from sheep and has the same jaundiced colour – and there are a lot of reasons why one would almost want to take up the life of a hermit.'[84]

8   *'The Honeymoon of Our Friendship'*

'THE LAD WITH THE WEARY, BURNING EYES'

In the summer of 1877 Nietzsche made his way to the little resort of Rosenlauibad in the Bernese Oberland, there to rid himself once and for all, without the help of a physician but with copious supplies of St Moritz mineral water, from what he called his 'deep-seated neurosis'.[1] Perhaps he also hoped that the mountain air would help him settle two particular problems that had long dogged his path. The one concerned Basel, the prospect of which made him shudder, because it was like living 'in a chrysalis' and had made him 'excessively nervous and melancholic'.[2] The other problem was identified in a letter from Elisabeth. 'I must tell you', she wrote, with their mother's approval, 'that we would all like to see you married.'[3] After all, if Rohde could announce his engagement, why not he?

In the course of the three-hour trek from the station at Meiringen to Rosenlauibad, for which, half-blind as he was, he needed a guide, he had time to ponder the two problems. Decisions had to be made – but what decisions? He would have to give up his professorship without sacrificing his salary, and at the same time assure himself of a decent dowry from the wench of his choice.

From the window of his hotel he enjoyed 'without exaggerating, the most beautiful mountain view' he had ever seen, he wrote to his mother.[4] The fact that he was at the beginning the only permanent resident made him feel lonely – alone with the unavoidable decisions he had to make. But at least there were attractions to console him. Almost every morning, for example, while the rest of the hotel was still asleep, he would make his way up to the Rosenlaui glacier. And the hotel had a piano, where, as an eyewitness reported, he would sit and play 'great polyphonic works of his own inven-tion'[5] as soon as the salon was empty. Many guests, however, were drawn to the salon by the strange sounds they heard and stood silently outside the glass door to listen.

With the exception of Dr Otto Eiser, who claimed to be an admirer of Nietzsche and carried his collected works around with him, he hardly got to know anyone. So lonely and preoccupied was he with his own problems that the worries about Basel and the endless line of possible marriage candidates brought him to a state of nervous exhaustion that prevented him from sleep-ing.

Then something happened to take his mind off his problems. On one of his walks he came across a young lad sitting alone in front of a hut, waiting for his parents, who had gone to bring in the hay. He was sick and therefore unable to go with them. Nietzsche stopped to talk to the boy – one sick and lonely person talking to another – and resolved to return. In the end he walked up to the hut almost every day, taking some sweets with him to give to the boy. He even took a cloth with him, which he dampened in a nearby spring and used to bathe the lad's face. According to the boy's parents, he looked forward the whole day to the visit of 'the kind gentleman'.[6]

Nietzsche could not get the thought of the boy out of his head. 'The blind youngster by the mountain path', he wrote in his notebook, adding a descrip-tion of a romantic scene by the glacier: 'Two boys were sitting beside a bil-berry bush, watching a big green beetle, on whose back a drop of moisture glistened in the sun. It had dropped out of a tree.'[7] Did he see himself as the second boy who had joined in the game? Did he perhaps dream of a secret relationship, known to no one? 'I must have bilberry bushes and pine trees around me and a glacier in front of me', he wrote.[8] In the evening, with the scent of pine needles in the air, he looked across to the grey mountains beyond, capped in snow, the blue sky above them. Now, having at last regained his composure, he realised that what he had experienced was a piece of his own self: 'Forests and mountains are not just real objects but part of our experience and our history, part of our own selves.'[9]

Nietzsche wrote a poem on this self-encounter by the glacier, a poem dedi-cated to summer and the mountains, to the pine forest and the sick boy, and ultimately to himself as he felt overpowered in the lonely landscape by a sudden urge – an urge for love. As he had talked every day with the boy, so he now imagined him in silent communion with the mountains until sud-denly a ray of light illuminates the scene, a ray of light that repeats the same words over and over – 'I love you':

At midday, when
The young summer rises over the mountains,
He speaks,
But we only *see* him speaking . . .
The icy peaks and the pines and the springs
Give him their answer,
But we only *see* their answer . . .

What do they say to each other, the summer and the mountains? We are
not yet told. In the final version of the poem Nietzsche discloses who is talking when summer rises over the mountains – it is 'the lad with the weary,
burning eyes'. His little friend's breath comes in short gasps, as in a fever. For
in the mountains the summer is short, and the sultry midday air soon gives
way to the cool of autumn. Summer, like the boy, will not be here long. But
in the moment when it confronts the icy regions, everything seems to rejoice
and come to life:

The foaming torrent plunges down from the rock
As if in greeting
And stands there like a white column, listening.
And the dark firs look out upon the scene with greater devotion
Than at other times.
And between ice and dead grey rocks
Sudden flashes of light are seen.
Who will explain to you what they mean?

They speak but we do not understand what they are saying. Flashes of light
are seen but we cannot explain them. Yet Nietzsche can. What is happening
here is what came to pass when Apollo touched the inebriated poet
Archilochus and released his poetic gifts. The lonely world suddenly seems to
awake from its dream and welcome man with jubilation like a prodigal son.
Caught up in the web of Dionysian magic, Nietzsche sees the glacier light up
as though touched by the god's laurel wreath – and at the same moment sees
the ice of his soul. As the warmth of summer burns away the ice on the
mountains, so 'the lad with the weary, burning eyes' kindles the eye of the
sick, half-blind Nietzsche.

At the same time it revived the old memory of another meeting which
needed no words to describe it. For had not the same thing happened on his
father's death-bed, when he had been allowed to see his father, embrace him
and look into his eyes for one last time? Eyes that seemed to light up at that

moment as though they were able to see again? The moment of a final farewell to a love that would never end? Such is the meaning of Nietzsche's poem:

> In the eye of a dead man
> Light will return.
> His grieving child embraced him
> And kissed him.
> The light in his eyes said:
> 'I love you . . .'

It was the eye of the dying man that was speaking to him. And the glacier, the forest, the white column of the foaming torrent all have but one thing to say: 'We love you! We love you!' And 'the lad with the weary, burning eyes',

> He kisses them full of sorrow
> And of growing passion
> And does not want to leave . . .

As the summer would dearly stay on the glistening glacier, so Nietzsche-son wants to stay with the dying Nietzsche-father. And the sick boy sitting in front of the mountain hut, who pined ever more passionately for 'the kind gentleman' and would not let him go – he too wants to stay with him. For he can feel that his end is approaching:

> He blows his words like a veil
> In front of his mouth – bad words.
> All around hearkens
> And scarcely breathes:
> Then a shudder runs over the scene like
> A glittering on the mountains,
> Nature all around –
> She ponders and remains silent.

Staying silent with the mouth and speaking with the eyes is the medium of this love. August von Platen once wrote in a poem:

> Thou lovest and stayest silent: Would that I too had kept silent
> And only showered my gazes on thee![10]

Nietzsche has made a decision. He wants to take the child home with him and care for him, for he obviously has not long to live. 'My brother enquired after the nature of the boy's illness', wrote Elisabeth, 'and promised that, if his parents would take him to Basel, he would have him treated at his own expense. And indeed, as soon as he got back to Basel, he made arrangements for the boy to be cared for in a clinic there. But sadly he was informed that in the meantime the child had died. As he neared the end, he had kept repeating: "Soon I shall go to see the kind gentleman." '[11]

The sombre news was not unexpected. While still in Rosenlauibad Nietzsche had written a poem about 'the dying child' who was given whatever he asked for, because he had not long to live. Later, in Basel, he added two final lines to his poem, letting the 'lad with the weary, burning eyes' say:

My greeting is my farewell,
I shall die young.[12]

Nietzsche was shaken by the experience. Two years later, under the heading 'When I wept', he wrote in his notebook 'The Rosenlaui Poem'. He had wept over the boy's death but also over the memory of the magic moment when the lifeless mountains began to glow and when, behind his lonely mask, he began to love. But as the boy died, so did love, and autumn returned to the icy realm of the glacier. A similar miracle had occurred in the drama about Ermanaric that he had written in his youth, when the hero's son Randwer, given up for dead, was restored to his despairing father – they recognise each other, they embrace, they die together. It was the symbolic scene of reconciliation between Nietzsche-father and Nietzsche-son. Now the son has become the father, who through his love for the doomed boy is summoned back to life, to love – for one radiant, eternal moment.

In a sketch for the finale of his *Zarathustra* Nietzsche imagined his experience of the mysteries as grand opera. The hero, surrounded by a crowd hanging on his every word, is like Jesus delivering the Sermon on the Mount. Having proclaimed his message, Zarathustra, 'seizing the decisive moment, asks the assembled throng: "Do ye want all that to recur again?" "Yes!" they cry: He dies of happiness ... a flash of light, a terror, a silence passes like a shadow over their thoughts.'[13]

It must have been the strangest question ever put to a faithful congregation, answered with a reply reminiscent of when an audience in a theatre shouts 'Encore!' after a brilliant performance. The play that the doom-laden preacher has in mind is the whole of life. And on hearing their cry of 'Yes!' he dies in ecstasy. Whereupon a feeling of bliss spreads over the whole assembly, as it had once spread over him and over the glacier – the inspired knowledge that supreme rapture and death are one and the same. And the will to experience this time and time again, to die as they had seen him die, inspires the masses like the coming of the Holy Spirit. In the end Nietzsche rightly rejected this final scene as suffering from too much theatrical illusion and too little reality.

STELLA

Nietzsche's sojourn in the Bernese Oberland was the inspiration for a second poem that also spoke of life and death. Later he added to it a despairing refrain: 'This is autumn – it will break your heart!' The boy by the glacier is dead – autumn, the time of snow and ice, approaches. Back in his schooldays at Pforta he had already experienced attacks of melancholy at the thought of the coming season. He cannot bear the prospect that the sun 'will no longer send out its warm rays' and that in the desolate fields 'hungry birds' are facing the rigours of winter. Joy and suffering are divided by but a thin line, 'and the transition is crushing. Begone! Begone!' Dearly would he love to join the birds migrating to distant lands, following them 'with a heavy heart'. 'Away! Away!' he cries, echoing Gretchen as she awaits her fate in prison in Goethe's *Faust*.[14]
   Melancholy again took hold of him – 'the goddess with leaden wings', as Rohde called her.[15] 'Behold, autumn is creeping up on us, and cruel winter will soon creep up on autumn', wrote the romantic poet Adelbert von Chamisso.[16] For Nietzsche too the harsh season is creeping up:

> It is autumn.
> The sun creeps up the mountain
> Climbing upwards
> And resting at every step.
> The wind plays its song
> On tired, limp strings.
> Hope flees,
> The wind laments its passing.
> O fruit of the tree,
> Thou tremblest, fallest!
> What secret did the night
> Show thee,
> That an icy shudder spread
> Over thy purple cheek?[17]

It is a fruit of autumn with which Nietzsche garlands his melancholy. In Bettina von Armin's *Goethe's Correspondence with a Child* there is a similar encounter between the poet and the falling apple: ' "The ripe fruit falls from the tree and rolls down the hill", said Goethe. An icy shudder ran down my spine . . .'[18] The image of the falling fruit recurs in *Zarathustra* as a metaphor for parting, for farewell, for a loss that can never be replaced and that breaks the heart.

But there is also consolation at hand. From out of the sadness that attends the departure of the sun, the rustling wind and the falling fruit emerges a new voice, and the poet listens to its message that comes as though from the distant 'deep brown night':

I am not beautiful,
Says the star-flower,
But I love mankind,
And I console mankind,
Let them now see flowers,
Bend down to me
And, alas, pick me.
In their eyes shines
The memory of more beautiful ones
And of happiness.
I see it, then die,
Die with no regrets.[19]

The star-flower, the aster, speaks to the camellia, i.e. Friedrich Nietzsche: You are in need of love, and because you do not enjoy the love of more beautiful ones, you also need consolation. I, though not beautiful, can give you both. I will give myself to you, die for you, and because my sacrifice brings a gleam of yearning to your eyes, I offer it gladly. Such might have been the hidden meaning of the words spoken by the voice to the lonely poet. It was a voice he knew well. It was the voice of his friend Paul Rée.

Years later, long after their friendship had crumbled, Nietzsche revealed the identity of the star-flower that had spoken to him. In a letter to his mother he attempted to put in a good word for his one-time confidant Rée and thereby, troubled by a guilty conscience, revealed the truth about the relationship. 'You cannot imagine,' he wrote, 'what consolation Dr Rée brought me over the years – *faute de mieux*, of course . . .'[20]

His mother must have been delighted to read this. I only cultivated Rée's company because there was no one better available, her son was saying. But at the same time he did, as a stop-gap, offer me a kind of consolation of which you cannot conceive. And why should you? But behind his phrase *'faute de mieux'* lay another meaning, one which his mother could not have imagined. It was to be found in Plato's *Symposium*, where the beloved reminds his lover of the concept of beauty and shows him through his love a vision of the highest beauty. Compared with that vision, any individual can only ever be a 'stop-gap', a 'memory of more beautiful ones'. When Nietzsche composed his poem of autumn, he had a longing to be with his friend, who may not have been handsome – 'a beautiful one' – but who could serve to stimulate his memory. In order to conceal the overly explicit reference to flowers – or men – Nietzsche replaced the aster's confession with the philosophically vague phrase 'memory of things more beautiful than I' in the final version of the poem.

Nietzsche had also taken a philosophical memory of Rée to Rosenlauibad. As well as Plato, he was reading Rée's tract 'The Origin of Moral Sentiments', which the author had presented to him with the dedication 'With the most abundant gratitude from the father of this essay to its mother'.[21] The dedicatee wrote to the author from his village that 'he must be the first to read the essay in the shadow of the glacier', adding that 'two or three times a day I find myself longing to have you with me here, for I am totally on my own, and of all the relationships I cultivate, yours is for me the dearest and the most highly cherished'.[22]

For his part, Rée, who could not accept Nietzsche's invitation to join him, grieved that 'you are alone up there among the ice and snow. Dearly would I wend my way to you. If only I had the wings of a dove.'[23] Rée, who had shown his unselfish devotion to Nietzsche on many occasions, knew the value of his friendship with this new Plato, whom he could serve and from whom he could learn, but at the same time a man to whom he could turn for help in overcoming his ineptitude in his dealings with members of the opposite sex. Nietzsche gave him a sense of security – a hero full of self-confidence in which his own passivity could find refuge. The Superman and his 'consort', as Rée was later mockingly called,[24] complemented each other like Plato's two halves.

Rée had arrived in Basel in 1873, bearing on the one hand the stigma of being a Jew, on the other the honour of having been wounded in the Franco-Prussian war. Five years younger than his idol, he had grown up on a country estate in Pommerania and was a committed follower of Schopenhauer. Pessimism and denial of the world were natural concomitants of a life in which an unsatisfied urge, called the Will, groped in vain for the phantoms of the imagination, the Ideas, the Representations. Nietzsche was seen as a beacon of neo-German pessimism, and his recently published book on tragedy a manifesto of satyric neo-Hellenism.

All this had appealed to Rée. For hidden beneath his clerical exterior – which sometimes induced children to kiss his hand in reverence – was a disciple of Dionysus waiting only for his god to take possession of him. 'You could have seen a man,' wrote Rée after having received a letter from Nietzsche, 'leaping up and down in the room like a satyr, waving his arms around like one possessed. This manifestation of joy has two sources, one of which is that I had become extraordinarily attached to you during that time in Basel ... I had a kind of unrequited love for you.'[25]

After Rée had left Basel, without having really come close to Nietzsche, Nietzsche heard from Gersdorff what he had lost through Rée's departure. His old friend quoted a remark of Rée's to the effect that sitting in silence with someone in congenial surroundings is a greater sign of friendship than sitting and talking in the same surroundings. In a poem called 'Among Friends', written several years later, Nietzsche rejoined: 'It is good to sit silently with each other,/ But better to laugh with one other.'[26]

Gersdorff also introduced Rée to his artist friends from Berlin and wrote to Rosenlauibad in his usual gossipy tone: 'Rau has made Rée's acquaintance and is delighted. He finds that Rée has a very fine head.'[27] If one accepts the evidence of his autumn poem, Nietzsche was of a different opinion. Rée wooed him with great tenacity. In February 1876 he confesses to being 'homesick' for him and at the same time to feeling a need to make his views clear: 'Whatever I think and feel, however trivial, I am determined not to conceal anything from you, any more than I would conceal it from myself. I would rather you were aware of what displeased you than that I should hide it from you.'[28]

In response Nietzsche promised his new friend complete openness in personal matters, assuming they got on well together. In this case, he added, Rée must be prepared 'to put down anchor in Basel again for a while'.[29] The image of a ship in harbour recurs later. And Rée's offer to recruit suitable disciples for the master was also to have unforeseen consequences.

In the summer of 1876 the young philosopher Heinrich von Stein joined Nietzsche in Bayreuth. But it was not Stein, later tutor to the young Siegfried Wagner, who changed the course of the Wagner-crazed Nietzsche's life. After having lost Wagner and Cosima, and been left in the lurch by Rohde, what Nietzsche needed was consoling and nursing, and above all someone who could read aloud to him. In contrast to Peter Gast, who tended to cast himself in the role of manservant, Rée, as subtle a thinker as he was a sensitive person, was a well-educated man. Rohde described him as being 'the only man with a living heart among a company of masks'.[30]

Nietzsche showed himself to be an appreciative beneficiary of Rée's self-sacrifice, especially since, as a result, he managed to deprive Wagner, his one-time idol, of one of his faithful subscribers to the Bayreuth Festival. At the festival of 1876 there was for Rée only one Master present – *his* Master. In gratitude Nietzsche stayed with Rée into the following year and they became inseparable companions immersed in shared problems to which they sought shared answers. Moral problems. In *Ecce homo* Nietzsche recalled these weeks in Bayreuth, in the course of which he had begun work on *Human, All Too Human*. One of the forces in the background of this work, he wrote, was 'a profound alienation in the face of everything that surrounded me at that time'.[31] At the same time he developed an intimate relationship with 'the splendid Dr Rée', on whom he showered lavish praise in this book.

The first three weeks of October, after the end of the Bayreuth Festival, found the two men in the little Swiss resort of Bex, in the Rhône Valley, that Nietzsche and Gersdorff had discovered earlier. Here they rented a chalet which belonged to the Hôtel du Crochet. Nietzsche wrote back to his family in Naumburg that they were enjoying 'the most glorious autumn'.[32] In order to protect his eyes, he went out only before dawn and after sundown, spending his days sitting on the balcony with the 'incomparable Rée'. Shortly before they had embarked on their holiday together, Rée had written to Nietzsche to say 'how happy he felt' in having his friendship.[33] And although he had suffered a few minor fits, Nietzsche had been able to tell his family that he had had no major attack for almost two weeks.

Rée's presence had a beneficial effect on Nietzsche, at least as long as they were alone together. When they were about to set out on a journey to see Malwida von Meysenbug in Sorrento, where they had hoped to spend the coming year in their new-found state of happiness, Nietzsche suddenly had an attack of migraine that lasted almost two days. Years later Rée was to recall the mysterious influence that he had on his ailing friend. 'We ought not to have parted', he wrote to him: 'perhaps there was some kind of benevolent magnetism between our two bodies. I must not say more.'[34]

After spending three days in Genoa, where Nietzsche breathed sea air for the first time, they made for the south. Rée did not move from his friend's side. Intruders were turned away and their partnership was resolutely defended by all the means at their command. An aristocratic tourist, one Isabelle von der Pahlen, who had unsuspectingly strolled through Pisa in the bearded professor's company, was made to understand that this was something she should not have done, since it had offended his companion. 'Taking me aside in a state of considerable agitation,' the lady recorded, 'he did not conceal his displeasure that, in spite of his efforts to the contrary, I had had an unsettling, disturbing and therefore malign influence on Nietzsche.'[35]

Rée let it be known that Nietzsche's severe nervous disorder could only be cured by withdrawing from all social contact, Rée himself apparently being the only exception. For the 'incomparable Rée' was jealous. When admirers made to approach his charge, he kept them at arm's length, either on grounds of their being undesirable or by maintaining that the Herr Professor did not want to receive visitors that day. In fact the truth was generally the reverse, Nietzsche being eager to receive visitors. But Rée had staked his claim and was not going to give it up. Their relationship was that of master and servant, and there was no room for a third. Yet throughout the years of their friendship they never addressed each other by the intimate form 'Du'.

If the younger man felt a slight cooling-off in their relationship, or that Nietzsche's letters seemed somewhat less affectionate, he would remind him of their loyalty to each other. On Nietzsche's thirty-third birthday, a year after their stay in Bex, Rée reminded him what they had meant to each other in the past, and what they could mean to each other in the future. In his effort to revive their love he called up the memory of that 'garden of Epicurus' that they had discovered together. And in the middle of his sentimental description of the 'philosophical garden' in which they had sported themselves, he hid a key word which he knew only the recipient would understand. 'During the whole of this time,' he wrote, 'my thoughts have been of those weeks in Bex, and I cannot get them out of my mind. They were, so to speak, the honeymoon of our friendship, and the little chalet, the balcony, the vines and Lesage completed the picture of perfection – even if Stella had not been there . . .'[36]

They are words worth pondering. What was the present Rée had given his friend on his birthday? The ratification of an alliance. His hand on his heart, he declares his loyalty to the bond that joins them, a bond consecrated, as it were, by marriage vows. Was our time in Bex not our honeymoon? Nobody shall loose this bond – I shall remain faithful for all time. For it was no chance bond that linked us together but a sense of perfect completeness. Rée had no need to remind the new Plato what the *Symposium* says about love – that mankind, divided in two, is desperately seeking to come together again, men seeking women but also seeking men. And until the one half of a divided being has found its other half, there will be dissatisfaction and imperfection: 'When a person encounters his own, true other half, a childhood friend or other person, they will be miraculously joined together in love, never to part, even for a moment.'

In Plato's *Symposium* this urge to completeness and perfection is called love. And this, says the one friend to the other, is what our honeymoon has given us and sealed – 'even if Stella had not been there'. Who is Stella? Was he – she? – the third member of the group? What could a third person contribute to the completeness of two marriage partners?

Biographers have racked their brains to discover the identity of this 'star'. Curt Paul Janz, for example, suggests that it is a literary allusion to a character from one of the stories of the romantic novelist E.T.A. Hoffmann, but to which 'remains unclear'.[37] Ernst Pfeiffer, on the other hand, considered that there was no need to identify the figure although he did not present an explanation for this.[38] Then came the theory that Stella was a girl, perhaps the chambermaid who had cleaned their room in the cottage in Bex and, for a consideration, had extended the concept of domestic service to include the two young bachelors' sexual needs. Indeed, had not Nietzsche himself admitted, according to the information made public by the tactless Dr Eiser, that he had enjoyed coitus on a number of occasions on medical advice? There would have been no shortage of opportunities for such pursuits in Italy. So we are invited to see Nietzsche as a man who never let a good opportunity go by, a man who waylaid chambermaids in beds that had not yet been made up.

A colourful but mistaken idea. A fragment of evidence referring to Nietzsche's stay in Genoa has survived, which illustrates his attitude to chambermaids, housemaids and maids in general. An Italian journalist reported, in 1924, having met an elderly cook who was still working in the hotel in Ruta where Nietzsche had stayed, and who remembered the occasion. She was a waitress at the time, young and not unattractive. She knocked on the door of Nietzsche's room. The only response was a grunt – 'he was apparently oblivious to the fact that I was a woman'.[39] To her regret, he apparently had no inclination to avail himself of the services on offer. But she still remembered the episode forty years later.

The Hölderlin scholar Pierre Bertaux was closer to the mark when he pointed out that 'Stella' must not necessarily be thought of as a female personage and that the literary association came not from E.T.A. Hoffmann or Goethe but from one closer at hand – Plato.[40] In his novel *Hyperion* Hölderlin conjures up the figure of Plato when the hero asks: 'Do you know how Plato and his Stella loved each other?' – Stella, be it noted, in the masculine gender. In a letter to his beloved Bellarmin, Hyperion writes of his joy in finding that 'like meets like' but even more of the 'divine experience when a great man raises smaller men to his own eminence'. This is precisely what Plato did, as reported by Diogenes Laertius, by bestowing his love on

'Phaedrus, Alexis, Dion – and Aster'. The star-flower, aster – the star, in Greek *astron*, in Latin *stella*.

Bertaux did not quite solve the problem. According to his interpretation 'Stella' was a boy or a youth who had visited the two friends in their lonely chalet – which, in a little Swiss village where everybody knew everybody else, is barely credible. But it is not necessary to assume that, in the state of idyllic perfection of which Rée writes, a third person was involved. The two men needed only each other. Stella, as a concept, symbolised the female part of their alliance. We belonged together like two Platonic halves, like a married couple, Rée points out, and even if we had not played the Plato-Stella game – 'even if Stella had not been there', as he had written in his letter – we would still be perfect, in a state of completeness that has no need of a third party and that resists all change.

Rée's birthday letter to Nietzsche sounds like an offer – even without 'Stella' we can continue to enjoy our present state of perfection. Nietzsche kept his friend waiting for an answer. Then, a month later, he wrote: 'You have probably spoilt me. But I must assure you that never have I enjoyed so many blessings from a friendship as from that with you in this past year – not to mention all that I have learnt from you.'[41]

The painful distance that Nietzsche had again opened up between them was connected with his quest for beauty. Much as he needed Rée as a source of consolation, he could not reconcile himself to his Jewish appearance. The line 'I am not beautiful' in the Rosenlauibad poem leads to the aster's ultimate self-sacrifice. Constantly searching for perfection, Nietzsche needed change. Even before their friendship finally came to an end, he had written its elegy – an aphorism called 'Friendship of Stars'. In the very first line he laments that the two stars had 'become alienated'. Or, in an image of ships at anchor – 'they are lying in one harbour and under one sun', celebrating together, only to be wrenched apart by the force of their different destinies. For as every ship has its destination, so every star has its orbit. 'Thus', Nietzsche says to Rée bitterly, 'there was a power above us that was leading us to grow apart'.[42]

The anti-Semitic Elisabeth Nietzsche naturally denied that the 'starry friend' was Paul Rée. 'My brother would never have called Rée a star!' she exclaimed angrily. But this was just what Lou Salomé, who knew both men well, did say.[43] One intention on her brother's part even seemed to suggest that Elisabeth was right. He was considering including the aphorism in his work 'Nietzsche contra Wagner'. But this may only have confirmed his penchant for re-dedicating earlier writings and compositions and putting them to new purposes. In the end he abandoned the idea. If he had still been alive, Wagner too would have resented being referred to as a 'star', that much is certain.

The Platonic metaphor of the star was not the only coded reference to the two friends' 'honeymoon' in Bex. Rée had read *Gil Blas* aloud in their chalet, while his friend lay on his bed with eyes closed, listening intently. He absorbed the atmosphere of Lesage's picaresque novel and transformed it in his mind into a dream of the south. 'Why do I feel such a persistent desire to re-read *Gil Blas*?' he wondered, in a jotting recollecting 'this world I adore and which I really only leave for a few months at a time'.[44]

Another adventure story that never failed to appeal to him was *Carmen*, tragedy of jealousy. He sent the piano score of Bizet's opera to his disciple Peter Gast for him to study, adding a comment in the margin: 'The epitome of the south! Our *Gil Blas* world to perfection!'[45] He draws Gast's attention in particular to the seductive aria in the first act in which Carmen entices the stiff, formal Don José into her erotic web. This '*séguedille*', he wrote, embodied all the secrets of his time in Bex:

Left on one's own, one becomes bored;
True delights are for two to share.
So to keep me company
I shall take my lover with me.
But my lover went to Hell!
Yesterday I turned him out of the house!
My poor heart longs for consolation.
Who desires to love me? Him shall I love.
Who desires my soul? It is there for the taking.[46]

Nietzsche never forgot the man who brought him consolation. In his *Genealogy of Morals* – a title that sounds like a variant of Rée's 'Origin of Moral Sentiments' – Rée reappears, showered with all the equivocal epithets characteristic of Nietzsche's style, leaving little doubt as to his role. 'The initial impulse to publish my hypotheses on the origins of morality', wrote Nietzsche, 'came from an essay in which I found for the first time a contrary and perverse set of genealogical hypotheses, of a specifically English kind, which had for me the appeal that all oppositional and antipodal theses have.'[47]

In order to disguise their personal relationship, Nietzsche brought into the limelight Rée's book, in the genesis of which he himself – as 'father', he claimed – had been involved in Sorrento and which appeared long after their visit to Bex. It was, of course, not in the 'Origin of Moral Sentiments' that Nietzsche had come across that 'contrary and perverse' mode of thought but in the discoverer and revealer of this origin himself. And the attraction will hardly have been generated by a work that was a reflection of their joint conversations. No – it came from Rée, only Nietzsche could not say so. The reader, however, can. By substituting the book for its author, Nietzsche's own work has the quality of a belated act of homage from one 'star' to another, a confession in a cryptic form, like 'Stella' in his birthday letter. 'The inspiration', Nietzsche intended to say, 'came from my friend Rée, in whom I encountered a contrary, perverse and specifically English method, which had for me the attraction that everything antipodal has'.

Since Heine's shabby gibes at the expense of Platen in his 'Baths of Lucca', the concept of the 'antipodex', alluding to Platen's homosexuality, had become familiar in German intellectual circles, at least in those where Heine was read. Rée suffered from the condition. In his book *Outsiders* the critic Hans Mayer wrote that the 'self-hatred of the homosexual' corresponds to the 'self-hatred of the Jew'.[48] In Rée's case both were combined in one person. He gave himself religious airs so as not to be recognised as Jewish, and played the aesthete so as not to be taken for an 'antipodex'. He identified himself with other people to the point of self-abnegation, because he wanted to abandon the self with which he could not come to terms.

For a while Nietzsche accepted Rée's renunciation of women. Later Rée tried to create a feminine symbiosis with the young Lou Salomé – after the dominant male, the innocent virgin. A measure of his self-despair occurs in a letter to Lou in which he complains of his 'listlessness'. It is a word, taken by the editor of their correspondence to refer to his 'gambling addiction', that had an unmistakable ring. When Thomas Mann accused his son Klaus of displaying publicly what he himself concealed, he used the same word, 'listlessness'. In his confession to Lou, Rée described his hopeless struggle against what he called 'a superhuman opponent':

> It is not as though listlessness were a congenital condition with me – it was not part of my nature from the beginning ... But I lost the battle against a superior enemy, not because I was weak but because my opponent had superhuman strength ... For months I used to stay awake deliberately the whole night, mostly walking up and down the streets of Berlin, albeit for a different reason from you. I do not think I struggled less determinedly than you, but, incredible as it may sound, my enemy was more terrifying than yours. He utterly routed me, and in the end, exhausted, I gave up the struggle. Now listlessness has become part of my being – in fact it is the key to my being, that is, to what over the past four, five and six years I have increasingly become.[49]

Rée's letter about the 'superhuman opponent' who so completely crushed him was written six years after his stay with Nietzsche in Bex. A late fragment of Nietzsche's reads like an obituary tribute to his defeated friend and to his love for him:

Whither he went? Who knows?
Certain is only that he perished.
A star ceased to shine in the desolation of space;
Space grew desolate . . .[50]

9   *The New Columbus*

When, in 1865, Nietzsche made his first excited encounter with Schopenhauer's *The World as Will and Idea* in Leipzig, the particular chapter that
caused him headaches was entitled 'The Metaphysics of Sexual Love', in
which a spirit that Schopenhauer calls the 'Genius of the Species' ensures that
mankind will fulfil its duty willy-nilly to perpetuate the species. Nietzsche
was already familiar with the tricks this spirit employed but he could not
make peace with this ultimate aim. Seventeen years later, now a 37-year-old
retired professor of classics, he believed he had found the solution to the age-
old problem. In *La gaia scienza*, published in 1882, the opening of the first
aphorism reads as follows: 'Whenever I look, whether with an approving or a
disapproving eye, at what people are doing, I find them all engaged in one
activity, individually and severally, doing what promotes the propagation of
the human race.'[1]

In Schopenhauer's work the Genius of the Species ensures that every Jack finds
his Jill. For Nietzsche it is instinct that guarantees the preservation of the human
race – 'nothing is older, stronger, less controllable than that', he writes. In fact we
could call it 'the very essence of our species and our society'. Men believe that
they know what is in the interest of the preservation of the species, and go on to
divide mankind as a whole into beneficial and pernicious, good and evil.

Nothing is more misguided. 'Even the most pernicious of men may be the
most useful when it comes to the preservation of the species', writes
Nietzsche. 'And tell me, friend, is it in fact possible to act against the interests
of the race? Maybe that which might have harmed the species died out thousands of years ago ...'[2]

So the outsider and the outcast can also set their minds at rest over the possible consequences of what are alleged to have been harmful actions. Like all other actions, they form part of the 'economy of the preservation of the species', which is why, in principle, one can act as one likes and permit oneself to enjoy to the full 'the ultimate liberation and irresponsibility'. One example implicit in Nietzsche's response to Schopenhauer is that of the non-preservation of the species, the disobedience of the genius of the species. For whether this will be of harm or benefit to mankind depends solely on the purpose of life as conceived at the time, a purpose which is, like man himself, subject to constant change. 'And consequently! Consequently! Consequently!' he cried. 'Do ye understand me, O my brothers? Do ye not understand this new law of ebb and flow? Our time, too, will come!'[3]

Elisabeth Nietzsche did not fail to notice that her brother had little inclination to adapt to the demands of the age and its fickle attitudes to sexuality. Cosima Wagner too would have been among those who drew her attention to his 'unnatural reticence'. But Elisabeth was the only one who knew that this was a product of his chastity. She was not interested in what underlay his incantation 'Consequently!' As witnesses of his divine nature she called on his doctors, as well as on his long-time companion Peter Gast and a travel writer called Reinhart von Seydlitz, who had caused a stir with a work called 'When, Why, What and How I Wrote'.

Elisabeth's evidence for the case of Nietzsche the Pure also sounds like an exorcism. 'There were also doctors,' she wrote,

> who sought the cause of his headaches in something quite different, namely in his chastity. They pressed on him the desirability of getting married but for so sensitive a man as my brother, for whom the best part of a marriage was friendship, this would have been an embarrassing reason to get married. To look for sexual intercourse in a different form was repugnant to my brother, of whom his friend Baron von Seydlitz wrote: 'Show me the man who could find fault in him. He was as pure and radiant as the waters of a mountain stream. Indeed, mountain streams would rejoice to be so pure. Chastity and virtue have acquired through him a new and higher meaning.' His friend Peter Gast said that his feelings were as tender as those of the sweetest young maiden.[4]

The rejoicing of a mountain stream. The maiden with the Prussian moustache. In 1880, finally rid of his teaching responsibilities, he was in a position to abandon himself to what he had called 'the ultimate liberation and irresponsibility'. He made for Italy. He had had a taste of the south four years earlier when he visited Sorrento and Capri, and now his friends Gersdorff and Rée opened his eyes to what other delights awaited him there.

But although he found the Mediterranean climate beneficial, from Venice, Genoa, Nice and other places came an alarming stream of complaints about endless fits and depressions. And his constant moving from place to place only made things worse. Was he exaggerating matters in order to justify giving up his teaching? Or did he stay in spite of his illness because Italy had something different to offer him, something less connected with his old Adam than with a new, totally different conception of health?

Or did he stay because the Italians, in particular the young folk, had no objection to an occasional infringement of the dictates of the 'Genius of the Species'? Indeed, here things were permitted – under conditions of the utmost discretion, of course – that were strictly forbidden in Leipzig or Basel, let alone in the prudish world of Naumburg. Here one was not eyed suspiciously and disapprovingly as a sinner, or reduced to a mere exchange of glances because any physical contact would have had dire consequences. Here he was a bird of passage, a stranger just passing through, 'free from all constraints such as those of marriage and position'.[5]

In the work of August von Platen, who had inspired his novella 'Capri', Nietzsche found what he needed to know about the land 'where the lemon trees blossom', in Goethe's famous poem – and not only the lemon trees. In Italy, wrote Platen, 'love between men is so common that even the boldest of demands do not meet with a rejection'.[6] 'When Winckelmann travelled to Italy,' said the critic Hans Mayer, 'he was signalling to his followers that that was where they could find erotic fulfilment.'[7] Throughout the nineteenth century and far into the twentieth the exiles from Sodom sought a new home in the 'warm south'. Nietzsche joined them: 'I flew across the sea to the south', he wrote.[8]

But he found no new home there. He remained the eternal traveller, always on the move, incognito, living out of a suitcase, generally to be reached only by poste restante. 'A wandering fugitive', he called himself.[9] He was also a man obsessed, a man on a quest, who never lost sight of his goal. His constant journeying was interrupted only by an occasional lonely sojourn in the Alpine solitude of Sils-Maria, where he spent much of the summer, presenting to his fellow-guests in the hotel the image of an absent-minded professor and pain-racked prophet, which Elisabeth later made the basis of her portrait of the lonely hero among the snows.

In the mountains too he was an exile, even though Zarathustra called them his home. A bird of passage always dreams of the south. So for eight years he wandered from one place to another – Venice, Stresa, Genoa, the Ligurian coast, Rome, Nice, down to Sicily in the south and finally, shortly before the end, up to Turin in the north, from where he caught a glimpse of the snow-covered Alps in the distance.

But why did this loner, a man fearful of human company, always return to the city? The number of months he spent in the bustling port of Genoa alone add up to years. Evidently he needed a post office and a railway station nearby but at the same time miles of empty beaches or rocky cliffs, away from which he could at any time submerge himself in the noisy anonymity of the city.

This escape from the moral prison of Northern Europe led to his decisive philosophical breakthrough. For a man who did not separate philosophy and life, it represented what he called 'the great release', 'the great convalescence', 'the Great Health'.[10] A chain had snapped, and the spectre of death, which had peered over his shoulder one winter's night in Naumburg years ago, had vanished. His breakout from this prison communicated its joy to his philosophy, and titles such as 'Sunrise' and 'La gaia scienza' testify to the discovery of a new world. A man risen from the dead, bathed in the glow – in the 'sunrise' – of a new happiness, he now knows that his life and his philosophy, the blood pulsing through his body and the blood that flows from his pen, are one.

'I gradually came to realise', he wrote in *Beyond Good and Evil*, 'what all great philosophy had hitherto consisted of – namely, the confessions of its author, a collection of involuntary, unpremeditated memoirs. Thus in every philosophy the author's moral (or immoral) intentions have constituted the real seed from which the whole plant has grown.'[11]

The plant that had been born near the churchyard had been uprooted and transplanted. Its self-liberation from the grave site in the shadow of the church and the family home became its philosophy – the confessions of its creator and a kind of conscious, premeditated autobiography in which not morality but immorality – amorality – showed the way forward.

When in 1886 Nietzsche sent his publisher Ernst Wilhelm Fritzsch a number of new prefaces to his works, sales of which were poor, he promised to provide a self-portrait – the writer who had set out to hold up a mirror to the age would now hold up a mirror to himself. But in the event the confessions that Fritzsch may well have hoped for turned out to deal only with his books. The prefaces made it clear: Not only have I personally experienced what is contained in these pages – I *am* what is contained in these pages. Put it to the test and let the reader follow in my path by following his own path.

The psychological drama of self-liberation with which the first of these prefaces deals had its origins in 1876, the year when Nietzsche broke with Bayreuth, when Rohde became engaged and when Rée introduced him to 'the contrary and perverse mode of thought'. Haunted by the fear of isolation, 'to which any man who sees things in a different light is condemned', he needed for his rehabilitation the reassurance that he was not entirely on his own.[12] He was overcome by 'a magical sensation of affinity and similarity with others in appearance and desire, a relaxation in the confidence of friendship, a shared blindness without suspicion or reservation'. But that, as he now claims, was only ever in the imagination. Those companions with like desires were only invented as 'worthy comrades and spirits with whom one laughs and chats when one feels like laughing and chatting, and whom one sends packing when they become boring – a kind of compensation for a lack of friends'. *Faute de mieux*, in other words.

That such 'free spirits' could really exist, with a real, corporeal presence, is something he is reluctant to doubt. And how do such 'free spirits' emerge? Answer: 'The man who is to achieve maturity and perfection' – here his thoughts go back to that time in Bex – 'must have had his decisive experience in a great liberation. It comes suddenly, like an earthquake. All at once the young soul is shattered, wrenched loose – it does not grasp what is happening. There is an energy and an impulse at work whose orders it is forced to heed; there emerge a will and a desire to flee, anywhere, at any cost, and a powerful, menacing curiosity to explore an undiscovered world surges and sears its way through its veins . . .'

Morality and duty are replaced by 'a thrusting, rebellious desire to take to the open road, and perhaps even by an act of desecration, in retrospect, whereupon the soul would be overcome with a flush of shame at what it had just done but at the same time rejoice that it had done it, an intoxicating feeling of jubilant terror that brings with it the assurance of victory'.[13]

But this release does not direct one straight into paradise. First the young soul must cross the desert, where it 'wanders in pain to and fro, driven by unsatisfied lust'. Finally it is hemmed in on all sides by the suffocating pressure of isolation brought to bear by 'the cruel goddess, *mater saeva cupidinum* – the fearsome goddess of unfulfilled desires'.

After this comes the taming of the predator, the gratification of sinful desires, the conquest of shame, the re-possession of a good conscience – in short, healing and recovery. It is the way out of the wilderness to the fertile oasis, 'that overwhelming, overpowering sense of security and health – the mature freedom of the spirit'. This leads in turn to what Nietzsche called 'the Great Health, man's dangerous prerogative to be allowed to commit himself to the great adventure'. He becomes like a bird that permits itself to be carried where the wind lists, submitting to every temptation and savouring 'the freedom, the vision, the exhilaration and every experience enjoyed by the bird in flight. No longer tied to his desk or confined to his sick-bed, he flies away, onwards and upwards . . .'[14]

In the last step to his ultimate liberation, he is greeted by the arrival of soft, warm breezes. He lies in the sun, basking like a lizard, and gradually the veil of 'the great release' is lifted before his eyes. He is standing on the beach, caressed by the south wind, and sees before him a figure lowering its veil, disrobing. And finally he understands. This pitiful, trivial life, in the interests of its own survival and the preservation of the species, has secretly and impudently arrogated to itself the right to undermine and question all higher and greater values. He himself, in other words, has been systematically oppressed and degraded in the name of its own arbitrary standards. But in the end there is such a thing as a hierarchy of values, and neither the pious folk of Naumburg nor the petit-bourgeois citizens of Basel are entitled to pass judgement on him any longer, the man besotted with beauty, the man with a vision of the future. The great day of reckoning has arrived. 'Such, therefore,' writes Nietzsche, 'is the answer that the free spirit gives to the enigma of self-release and self-liberation.' He concludes by extrapolating from his own individual case: 'As it happened to me, so it must happen to everyone.'[15]

In the remaining works that he sent to Fritzsch his missionary zeal had abated somewhat. In the preface to *Sunrise*, he adds to the metaphor of the bird and the lizard another animal image to describe himself – the mole, reminiscent of Hamlet, who bores and digs and undermines, above all, morality and people's confidence in morality. The 'philosophers' Circe', as he called it, the 'mistress of seduction', has cast a spell over her followers, and it needed the likes of the heroic figure of Nietzsche, who was immune to all kinds of feminism, to put an end to her influence. 'If you wish to reduce it to a formula,' he proudly pronounced, 'then it is this: that what is taking place in us is the *repeal of morality*, its *self-annulment*.' He begs his readers to read him 'slowly, carefully, attentively, with ulterior motives, with doors left open, with delicate fingers and eyes' – the door left open as an escape route, the ulterior motive of a man who lives in hotels.[16]

The last preface is that to *La gaia scienza*. One has to have experienced this book, said its author, in order to understand it. 'It is written in the language of the warm spring wind, the language of gratitude', for the healing process of which it tells came quickly, unexpectedly, providentially. Suddenly, he says, he felt 'a ray of hope, hope for recovery, the intoxication of being restored to health'. His book records 'the joyous feeling of returning strength, of a newly awakened faith in tomorrow or the day after tomorrow, of a sudden premonition of the future, of imminent adventures, of seas made newly accessible'.[17]

And this is supposed to be philosophy? Not precepts, syllogisms and systematic pyramids of concepts, based on an unshakeable foundation of truth, but 'self-liberation', wanton regressions and reversions? This philosophising rests not on dogma but on revelation. Its essence lies not in 'truth' – which according to Nietzsche does not exist – but in action. And action takes the form of the aphorism.

Nietzsche had been thinking in terms of this most concise form of expression since being introduced by Rée to the French moralists of the eighteenth century. Montaigne, La Rochefoucauld, Vauvenargues and La Bruyère were Rée's gods. Masters of the aphorism. Nietzsche dictated several of the earliest sketches for *Human, All Too Human* to Rée. Each of these aphorisms is an act of self-revelation, of self-exposure. Sometimes genial, sometimes mischievous, sometimes openly narrative, sometimes couched in irony – but always focused on the subject in question, master of the situation, not infrequently dismissive and destructive.

The aphorism strips the world of its mask, the body of its clothes. What is left stands there naked and pleads for sympathy, since it has just been deprived of the justification for its existence. All the ideological make-up and moralising frippery that men had invested in decking out their 'will to live', and all the masks behind which they had concealed their true face, fall away. Modern man is an emperor with new clothes. The aphorism is often an agent not of revelation but of gleeful violation – an act of cruel exposure, the destruction of feet of clay, the thrust of the surgeon's knife from which blood drips, revealing unimaginable, terrible truths. The aphorism is not, however, concerned with truth. Only society has need of it; it is an accepted construct of lies and collusion that guarantees its own continued existence.

But society has developed in the wrong direction. What deserves to be preserved has been destroyed by morality. What is different is banished and turned against itself by the exercise of a guilty conscience. The great release is the act of liberation, and the aphorism is its tool. One blow follows another and finally all the so-called truths of society are doomed to a destruction which it is a pleasure to behold. For every act of revelation and destruction has to overcome the opposition of fear and habit, and every victory over the powers of opposition, says Nietzsche, gives pleasure – the rejection of morality gives pleasure, the unmasking of 'good taste' gives pleasure, as does the disclosure of the forces of the antipodal. In short, it is the birth of philosophy from the spirit of inversion.

THE LIZARD ON THE SEASHORE

Genoa, the busy commercial and naval port from where 400 years earlier Christopher Columbus had set sail for Lisbon, from there to cross the Atlantic and discover the New World, now became Nietzsche's headquarters. Here he set out on his own expeditions, exposing himself to all the winds and currents. No obligations, no friends. He went to ground.

It had been Rée who put the idea of opting out into his head – Rée, himself a perpetual wanderer, seeking refuge from time to time with his mother in Stibbe. Without him Nietzsche would never have become a 'Columbus *novus*', prepared to leave the familiar coast behind him in order to seek out new shores. 'No doubt', Rée once wrote to him, 'it is laudable to discover a new continent, a comet or some other feature of our universe, but what do you say to the discovery of a human being?'[18] This, as Rée well knew, was what his master had in mind – to discover humankind, the unknown realms behind the masks. The harshest accusation that Nietzsche had levelled against his education in Naumburg and Pforta was that it encouraged him 'to scorn the body and its demands and to deter him from *discovering* the body'.[19] Only in his role as the 'new Columbus' was he free to see, touch and walk on this new 'golden' territory, as he called it, the body and the self within the body, the true '*terra incognita*'.[20]

When he arrived in Genoa, he wanted from the beginning to remain incognito. He wrote anxiously to his mother to beg her to tell the outside world that he was in San Remo, 'whereas in reality I am in Genoa and intend to stay here. The best proof is that yesterday I changed my quarters for the fourth time. But do not tell a soul.'[21] Four different rooms in a week. Peter Gast, too, was asked to keep the information to himself, since Nietzsche was looking to eke out 'an anonymous existence in the most anonymous garret I can find'. To Overbeck he wrote: 'Help me to keep my secret, and deny that I am living in Genoa.'

As to the nature of his life, he enjoyed the hustle and bustle of the city streets but also the paths over the surrounding hills, which he tramped for hours, discovering among other places the Camposanto di Staglieno, a huge cemetery where he walked up and down the aisles admiring the marble and alabaster kitsch. Later he would bring Rée up here, attracted by the dusty pomp of the sculptures and dedicating a poem to the monument he liked the best – one commemorating 'the little girl stroking the fleece of a lamb'.[22]

This anonymous German spent most of his time, however, on the rocky beach, clambering around for hours on end and, when the warm season arrived, lying in the sun. Like a lizard in swimming trunks. He always attached importance to what to wear when bathing. On one occasion, when he went with Gast to Recoaro, he insisted that his friend should take his swimming costume with him. He would spend hours, even whole days, on the beach – a strange sight, with his trunks and his bushy moustache.

One of his rare guests left a description of the man he found. Looking for the professor, the visitor, accompanied by a friend, had been directed to the beach at Nervi and found himself walking down the avenue of plane trees that led from the Grand Hotel straight to the beach. 'A stretch of sand,' he wrote, 'then a return to the rocky shoreline. We scoured the beach with our eyes but could not see anyone. Then a light breeze picked up, carrying with it a broad-brimmed panama hat, which it deposited on the sand nearby. "It's Nietzsche's", cried Bungert. And sure enough, there he lay, buried in the soft, warm sand behind a rock, a figure larger than life. Our introduction was almost comical. Bungert presented the professor, who appeared to have been daydreaming, with his hat, while Nietzsche got to his feet and smilingly brushed the sand from his body.'[23]

The sand-covered professor re-emerges in *Ecce homo.* In *Sunrise*, where, he recalls, he began his campaign against morality, he visualises himself lying in the sand, 'plump, happy, like a marine animal basking among the rocks. In the end I myself became this animal. Almost every word of that book was conceived among that cluster of rocks near Genoa, where I acquired the art of capturing for a while individual moments which I call divine lizards.'[24] And as he records this memory, a 'soft tremble' ripples over his body: 'Still today, when I chance to pick up this book, almost every sentence puts me in mind of some incomparable experience from the depths of the past, and my whole body quivers with the joy of reminiscence.'

Nietzsche, the lizard, lived for five months on entrails, which were tasty and cheap, and on the small fish doled out by soup kitchens. He froze in unheated attic rooms, one of which took 164 stairs to reach, and did his writing in cafés because there was not enough light in the garret to read and write. In October 1881, now thirty-seven, he described himself as having reached 'rock bottom' in his physical requirements.[25] He agreed the lowest possible rent with his landlords for the most frugal facilities. And all this for living the life of a lizard for a few hours on the seashore? Or for a few lines of poetry in the cemetery? It was like living 'in a dog-kennel', as he later put it.[26] Had he, under the pretext of restoring his health, deliberately set out to ruin it and reduce himself to a level below which there were only wastrels and tramps?

But all this had ceased to count. The man in the panama hat had long since adopted different standards – this Genoese explorer and conqueror of a new world, who for a lifetime spent on the beach and in cemeteries, a life spent jotting down philosophical notes and enjoying the new experience of liberation and emancipation, was prepared to rid himself of everything that had hitherto oppressed him. In his Christmas letter to his mother and sister he hailed Genoa as 'the happiest move I have ever made, in respect both of my health and of my peace of mind'.[27] Having written these lines, probably on some rickety old café table, he returned to his room and retired to bed with a fit that plagued him for the next few days.

A month later, his year-end depression overcome, he cries: 'What a glorious time! How beautiful are the wonders of January!' Spring has begun to return to Liguria and the sun has started to warm the sand. His friend Paul Rée is shortly to arrive, and his thoughts turn to Januarius, patron saint of Naples, whose blood liquefies at regular times each year. Nietzsche, the atheist, sets his poem to the martyred saint at the head of Book Four of *La gaia scienza*:

> Thou who with thy flaming spear
> Hast splintered the ice of my soul,
> Sending it as a torrent that roars towards the ocean
> Of its highest hopes,
> Brighter it becomes, ever more life-giving,
> Free, yet held in a loving grip –
> And so it hails thy miracles,
> O most beautiful Januarius![28]

It is a violent image, recalling the Mithras legend. The saint pierces the poet's icy soul with a burning spear, as St George transfixes the dragon. The mortal blow releases a powerful awakening, the glacier melts and becomes a flood that rushes towards the open sea, to the open horizon. When, in Nietzsche's 'Dionysus Dithyramb', Ariadne cries to her god: 'Pierce me! Pierce me once more!', what we hear is her yearning for the miracle of St Januarius.[29]

Nietzsche knew the legend from the time in Naples when, in 1876, he had adopted the saint as an allegory of his own longings. The story of San Gennaro is still part of the city's history. We read in a modern guide book to the city:

> What is the significance of the miracle of San Gennaro? Male by sex,
> woman by virtue of the blood that flows from him at regular intervals,
> admired for his personification of this miraculous dualism, Gennaro is
> the supreme saint of the androgynous principle . . . By identifying with

him, men transcend their natural limits, outstrip their given social roles and float away in their dreams of the fulfilment of their most passionate desires. They enjoy their two sexes without reservation. On 19 September each year the Neapolitans celebrate the liberating loss of their separate sexual identity and their longing for a world in which there are no differences between the sexes – transsexuality, the uninhibited desire to unite man and woman in one. Posters depicting the saint go up all over the city – a youthful figure, almond-eyed, with a delicate, oval face, leaning on a shepherd's crook. The attractive curves of his hips recall the charms of a Greek shepherd . . . The first *femminiello* in Naples was martyred in the company of two of his friends, one called Festo (Celebration), the other Desiderio (Longing). All three were preparing to celebrate in song and dance the rapturous worship of the saint's blood.[30]

THE ADVENTURES OF PRINCE FREE-AS-A-BIRD

Over the following months and years the man in the panama hat – previously the man of the mountains – came to know the whole Mediterranean coastline around Genoa – Pegli, Nervi and Santa Margherita, Portofino and Zoagli, Rapallo, Ruta and La Spezia. To the locals he was a stranger – a German or a Pole, maybe even an *ufficiale*. To himself he was 'Prince Free-as-a-Bird'.

It was an ambiguous name. He had always felt himself to be a prince since the time of the game of 'King Squirrel' in his boyhood days. Now, living in the city of the great Renaissance *principe* Andrea Doria, he felt confirmed in his princely role. 'Genoa', he wrote to Rée in magisterial tone, 'belongs to me, and I look forward to displaying it for your benefit as did the great Andrea Doria'.[31] The perfect ruler and seafarer – except that all that this itinerant prince from Germany ruled over was the decision of what to do with his time. Otherwise he was as 'free as a bird' – ostracised by society, spurned by the defenders of conventional morality and – since turning his back on Basel – homeless.

To offset this, he lived like a bird on the wing. In the grey mists of Germany his Platonic wings had been clipped – even as a student he had been prevented from launching himself into the ether. Back in 1878 he had encouraged Rée to spend his holidays with him and – to retain the metaphor – perch with him on the same branch: 'Dearest Friend, I imagine us walking together for hours. All we weary birds want to do is to sit together side by side in a tree and chirrup to each other.'[32]

But now in Genoa the sky opened up before him and he began to make his first attempts at flight. He was recovering from his weariness. In the poem called 'Prince Free-as-a-Bird' he allows himself only a brief respite from his hours in flight, after which he must catch up with the other birds. His short rest is on the very same branch where he once imagined himself singing to his friend:

Here I perch on this crooked branch
High above sea and hillside;
A bird invited me to join him here –
I flew after him to find a resting place,
Beating my little wings . . .[33]

This poem, published in May 1882 in a literary journal under a pseudonym, represented only an interim stage in his poetic treatment of the theme. Originally he had planned to begin:

Here I perch on this crooked branch
On this Genoese hillside . . .[34]

Having eliminated the direct reference to the city for the published version, he now dispensed altogether with the local reference in the final version of 1887, with the new title 'In the South':

Here I perch on this crooked branch
And cradle my weariness . . .[35]

So now the story takes place 'in the south'. A bird invites him to rest on its branch. There he sits, merrily beating his still under-developed wings, while the ocean stretches out far below. Gradually the state of oblivion that he had once called 'divine art' creeps over him:

I have forgotten my goal and my port of call,
Forgotten fear and praise and punishment:
Now I fly after any bird . . .[36]

Thus speaks the Prince, who simply flees from the threat of any painful recrimination or any fear of being discovered, and is free to fly after any bird that takes his fancy. This is a remarkably democratic claim for a king's son to make, a man raised on the principle of hierarchy. But this is what Nietzsche meant. In *Sunrise* he describes the joy of being able to 'live like a bird, coming and going at will and with no name on its beak'.[37] Discretion is paramount. No visiting card necessary.

In his 1887 version of the poem Nietzsche altered the whole passage – presumably out of discretion. Now the bird gazes out across the white ocean and the purple sails towards 'distant rocks, fig-trees, towers and harbours', and sighs: 'O innocence of the south, take me to thyself!'[38] The innocent south that will protect the freedom of his life as a bird. In 1882 he had already written:

> I love to soar aloft on my wings
> Following every bird.[39]

Now, according to this final version, he learned 'to soar with the birds'.

Evidently the bird on whose branch he perched at the beginning was no particular creature but one of the anonymous crowd. In any case the prince apparently had his problems with the dialect of the Ligurian fishermen:

> Talking is a difficult business,
> Reason and tongue often trip up.[40]

This is what he originally wrote. But then, regretting his bluntness, he changed it to: 'Reason is a difficult business'. Further changes followed. 'Flight gave me new powers', he now writes. But for what, if not for flying? For following other pursuits, 'like singing and joking'? Whereof one cannot speak, thereof one must sing, as Wittgenstein might have said. To the Nietzsche of 1887, moving inexorably towards his apotheosis, this seemed to require an explanation – a thinker who sings? And why does he concern himself with the birds? Well, he loves them:

> To think alone I call wise,
> But to sing alone – would be stupid!
> So hearken to a song in your praise
> And sit quietly around me in a circle,
> Ye bad little birds!
>
> So young, so faithless, so cunning,
> Ye seem made for love
> And every charming pastime.
> In the north – I confess with hesitation –
> I loved a woman, old enough to make one shudder:
> Her name was 'Truth'. . . .[41]

It is an open-ended confession. In the preface to *La gaia scienza* we are told that truth is in fact a woman, who 'has reasons for not exposing her feminine essence'.[42] Or a toad, which, if the worst came to the worst, one might have to swallow. And he never really loved her, as he claims – or if he did, then solely as a philosopher who was searching for 'her feminine essence', only, in the end, to flee back repelled into the arms of Apollo. No, he is no longer concerned with truth. He even hides the truth about himself, yet constantly has to risk leaving intimations of his meaning, since otherwise he will not be understood. What would the great release and the great liberation be, and what the saint who plunges his spear into the chill of his soul, were it not for his truth? And what would Genoa be without its 'bad little birds' that fly around aimlessly like him, and are 'faithless' like him and 'made for love' like him?

In the mid-1880s, at the same time as Prince Free-as-a-Bird, there was another visitor to Liguria who saw these birds adorning the trees like fruit and lying on sun-drenched rocks like lizards. The French novelist Guy de Maupassant, sailing round the grottos and caves of the Genoese coast, had a revelatory experience in the bay of Portofino. 'Never had I felt such a moment of joy', wrote Maupassant. 'When I looked up from the boat at the rocky coast, I saw groups of naked youths with brown bodies gazing down at this intruder. They were sporting themselves like creatures of the deep, new-born Tritons, playing merrily together and scaling the rocks as though seeking to rest there awhile. Some sat in the cracks between the rocks, others stood on the pinnacles, their delicate brown bodies silhouetted like bronze statuettes against the Italian sky.'

Nietzsche had known the pleasures of life on the beach since his visit to Sorrento. Here he could combine his delight in the physical beauty of young men with his enjoyment of swimming. Not far from where the young Tritons played, sat their admirer watching, a lizard among lizards, a bird among winged denizens of the sea. In one of his 'Poems of Prince Free-as-a-Bird', in which he, the poet, makes fun of writing poetry, he compares his rhymes with arrows, with which he shoots at the elusive little creatures:

My rhymes are like arrows:
What a leaping and trembling and quivering breaks out
When my barb strikes the sensitive parts
Of Lacertian's body![43]

Lacertian, the lizard. In an aphorism Nietzsche uses the reptile with the flexible extremity as an indecent metaphor. 'The lizard', he wrote, 'grows an extra finger when it loses one – but with a man it is different.'[44] Strato of

Sardes, author of a third-century Greek anthology of pederastic literature, calls the penis of his young lover a lizard: 'Agathon's little lizard', he observes, 'used to be like a rosy finger but now he is in possession of a rosy arm.'[45] Nietzsche's real feelings were expressed in the title he planned to give his book: 'We Lizards of Fortune' – with the subtitle: 'Thoughts Expressed In Gratitude'.

In an aphorism from *Human, All Too Human* Nietzsche recounts an event that happened to him in Sorrento when, with a fez on his head and wearing blue sunglasses, he was walking across the beach, breathing in the mixture of salt sea air and rotten fish, charcoal fires and seafarers' sweaty bodies that assaulted his nostrils. Suddenly, out of the blue, he experienced a moment of bliss: 'Almost all circumstances contain a moment of bliss, and good artists know how to "fish it out". So such a moment can emerge even from such boring, dirty, unhealthy conditions as the noisy, greedy, common life found on the beach. In his *Barcarolle* Chopin captured this moment of bliss in music that could induce even the gods to spend long summer evenings lying in a barque.'[46]

So the 'good artist' does not find the moment but 'fishes it out'. It is a metaphor that suits the occasion, for the scene is one of fishermen and sea-farers, and Nietzsche, a born 'fisher of men', casts out his cunningly con-structed rods, hoping for a rich catch impaled on their sharp hooks. Did he long to lie among the fishermen in just such a boat and 'fish out', for one blissful moment, a companion who understood what was needed? There is a textual variant that supports this interpretation: 'Chopin conveyed the bliss of a young sea-god who disguised himself as a fisherman and ...' Here the sentence breaks off.[47] Maybe it could be completed thus: '... and appeared among the noisy, greedy mob on the beach, conveying his bliss in such beau-tiful sounds that even the gods would yearn to spend the long summer evenings lying with him in a boat'.

Did Nietzsche talk with his friend Peter Gast about his attraction to the barcarole, the music of the gondola? In a letter containing some observations on Bizet's *Carmen*, a work that Nietzsche had recently discovered, Gast wrote: 'What you love most dearly seems also to me to express the deepest bliss and happiness – those sounds wafted across from the isles of the blest, the music of the *Barcarolle*.'[48]

Later the same year Nietzsche brought to the attention of the readers of the *Internationale Monatsschrift*, published by Schmeitzner in Chemnitz, what he called a 'nocturnal secret', in poetic form. The poem was based on a personal experience. It starts with the words 'Last night' and ends with the astonishing statement that two men had slept together 'so well, so soundly' in a boat. The boat had a lot to answer for. When, five years later, Nietzsche included the poem in his collection 'Songs of Prince Free-as-a-Bird', he called it 'The Mysterious Barque'.

So what had happened last night? The world was sleeping. But Nietzsche, the lonely wanderer, found no rest – neither through sleep, nor through laudanum, with which he had also evidently experimented. And the surest way to peaceful repose – an easy conscience – was not open to him either. Then he suddenly had an inspiration – or was it the bell tolling?

> In the end I put all thought of sleep
> Out of my mind and ran to the beach.
> There was bright moonlight and the air was mild –
> I came across the man and his barque on the warm sand,
> Both of them sleepy, shepherd and sheep.
> Sleepily the boat pushed out from the shore . . .

So they met on the beach – the sleepless man with the guilty conscience and the man with the boat that waits only to be pushed out into the cool, dark waters. And what is a shepherd doing with a boat? Where is he taking his sheep? Both shepherd and sheep are too weary to answer. In any case the boat has already cast off.

A dreamlike scene in the light of the moon – two men get into a boat in the middle of the night in order to leave the land and row out into the bay where they could only be seen by the 'eye of eternity', as the New Columbus put it.[49] They do not do this in order to cast their nets or to fish or to reach some distant shore – in fact there seems to be no need to do anything:

> Morning came. On the dark depths
> Lay a barque, resting, resting –
> What is happening? – thus the cries went up,
> The cries of almost a hundred: What's there? Blood?
> Nothing was happening! We were asleep, all asleep –
> Ah, how good it was, how good!

So that was what had led them to float out across the water – they just wanted to sleep together. And to those – a hundred can only be the product of his fevered imagination – who stood next morning on the shore and stared, and asked whether there had been 'blood', the two rowers replied that they had just been sleeping – sleeping soundly, in fact. Nothing untoward had happened, no bloody deed – perish the thought!

What really happened, far from land and close to the stars, is described in the third of the four strophes, the one that contains the 'mystery' which the title promises – a description delivered through the eyes of the young professor who appears to have forgotten the young shepherd who will one day come into his own in *Thus Spake Zarathustra*:

> An hour, maybe two,
> Or was it a year? Suddenly
> My mind and my thoughts dissolved
> Into an eternal monotony,
> And a gaping abyss, measureless,
> Opened up – and all came to an end.

Time has ceased, eternity has begun – *intempesta nox*, when at any moment something can arise from nothing. A boundless chasm opens up before him, where everything that was, now seems of no importance – where he loses control of his senses and falls into the embrace of eternal darkness. Goethe, in a dramatic fragment, had described this chasm in an exchange between his eponymous hero Prometheus and the maiden Pandora, a passage which Nietzsche knew and which revealed the secret of man's life and death:

Prometheus:	It is the moment in which everything is fulfilled,
	Everything we have ever yearned for, dreamt of,
	hoped for,
	And feared, Pandora –
	It is Death!
Pandora:	Death?
Prometheus:	When, shaken to the depths of your being,
	You feel everything
	That joy and pain have ever given you …
	And all your senses desert you
	And you feel on the point of falling,
	Sinking,
	And everything around you subsides into darkness,
	While you, in the intensity of your emotion,
	Embrace a world –
	Then man will die.
Pandora (embracing him):	O Father, let us die!
Prometheus:	Not yet.
Pandora:	And after death?

Prometheus:	When everything – desire, and joy, and pain –
	Has become absorbed in a frenzy of delight,
	And is then refreshed in blissful sleep –
	Then you will live again, live your youth again,
	In order to fear, to hope and to desire anew![50]

'CAESAR AMONG THE PIRATES'

In the autumn of 1881, as Nietzsche lived out his lazy days on the seashore of Genoa, waiting expectantly, fortune suddenly smiled on him with a blinding radiance he had never before known. The spot became a holy place. When Rée visited him the following February, Nietzsche immediately took him there – 'the place where in a hundred years time they will erect a little column to commemorate my *Sunrise*.'[51] He was said to have already decided what should be inscribed on the monument: 'Columbus-Nietzsche: 1481–1882. Liberators of the Human Race'.[52]

Something had happened to this latter-day Liberator of the Human Race, which he did not want to talk about. Only his notebooks reveal, albeit in allegorical form, what it might have been. The memory that came to him seems to have been so emotionally charged that he had a spasm on this spot – such, at least, is how a passage in a letter to Rée, deleted in the original and only deducible from the context, has to be interpreted: 'Yesterday I went swimming in the sea at that self-same spot where . . . just think – last summer one of my closest relatives suffered just such a spasm while swimming, and because there was nobody nearby, he drowned.'

'Yesterday', begin letters to Gast on 5 February and to Rée on 21 March. A strange note written in January also opens with this time reference, as though Nietzsche's memory of what he had experienced on this spot was so vivid that it seemed to have happened only the previous day. What he sets out to describe in his lines on January was in reality beyond description – time and again he returned to it, editing and correcting it: 'What befell me yesterday on this spot? Never had I been so happy. The flood of life swept over me as waves of happiness cast their most precious seashell towards me, the purple melancholy. I was ready for anything! What dangers would I not have been prepared to face!'[53]

The ramblings of a man in love. On the crest of the wave of his happiness he is overcome by the melancholy of parting. Mourning follows. He had known this feeling from his boyhood days when he had played in the ruins of Carthage. How short-lived is happiness! Now that parting is especially bitter because it is a purple memory, a sensual memory of something unutterable. The word occurs in the first mention of the experience that he made in his notebook in the autumn of 1881 – and it is one of the earliest occasions when he uses his 'son' Zarathustra as his spokesman: 'Prepared for the utmost. All types of bold men ... An indescribable feeling of sadness that life is just flowing away before us. One day I said to myself: Everything will recur, and this wonderful drop of melancholy in the conqueror's happiness will perhaps be the most beautiful of moments. He said to his disciple: "That is the purple melancholy, the loveliest seashell that you can find on the shore of life – the feeling of imminent parting, the rays of the evening sun." '[54]

The happiness that Nietzsche-Zarathustra felt in the unrestrained company of the heroes on the beach at Genoa was the happiness of the conqueror. A Columbus discovers, an Andrea Doria conquers. But this supreme delight – 'Never have I been so happy' – merges into the purple melancholy of imminent farewell – for ever. What good fortune that a few months earlier the secret of life had been revealed to him by the shore of an Alpine lake. Everything will recur. Zarathustra wants his experience on the beach at Genoa to return, time and again. In a third fragment the theme of recurrence sounds like the refrain of a song: 'You have a feeling that you are about to leave, soon maybe, and the sunset rays of this feeling shine into your happiness ... But know this also – that mortality will continue to sing its short-lived song, and that when a man hears the first strophe, he will almost die of yearning at the thought that all may be gone for ever.'[55]

From these three jottings in his notebook Nietzsche later distilled an aphorism. In it he invokes 'the danger of the happiest of men'. So what is this danger? And who is this 'happiest of men' who would have to be warned of this impending hazard? It is the man, according to the aphorism, who goes through life 'with a strong, bold, daring soul', 'prepared for all contingencies and consumed with a desire to confront undiscovered worlds and oceans, men and gods'. An explorer and conqueror attracted by 'the merry music ... to be heard where brave soldiers and seafarers relax and rest awhile' – because he too wants to pause and repose awhile. And because this is only an interlude between two voyages of discovery, 'tears spring into his eyes and he is overcome by the purple melancholy of the happy man as he experiences to the full the profoundest pleasures of the moment.' 'This was', says Nietzsche, 'the happiness of Homer, the condition of the man who gave the Greeks their gods – nay, who gave himself *his* gods!'

Achilles and Ulysses formed on the model of 'courageous warriors and seafarers'! But Homer's happiness is in reality Nietzsche's happiness, as he will go on to say, which is also why he is familiar with the danger that threatens the man who expresses the pleasure of the moment, i.e. the poet, who turns other men into gods. Hardly has that moment passed than he has to take his leave – he is, after all, in the company of sailors and other short-lived inhabitants of the sea. Idolisation turns to bitterness: 'A man with this happiness of Homer's in his soul is the most long-suffering creature under the sun. This is the price he has to pay for the precious shell ...'

There is a price to pay? Yes, one takes temporary possession of the shell and becomes, as its owner, 'ever more refined, and ultimately too refined, in one's enjoyment of pain'. When that time comes, it only needs 'a small element of displeasure and disgust to ruin Homer's life'.

So disgust is the price that has to be paid by bold men for a brief respite and passing pleasures. The harmlessness of what appears to be a merry party on the beach is only the foreground for innocent readers. In reality what is at stake are powerful emotions that the author cannot control, brief gratification followed by a sense of revulsion that offers a strange contrast to melancholy. Mixed emotions. Elsewhere Nietzsche expresses himself even more clearly. He talks of 'menacing, heart-rending attacks of desire and savage, pent-up surges of emotion ... moments of sudden madness when the lonely man embraces the first man to come his way and treats him as a precious gift from heaven' – the precious shell that has its price – 'only to cast him off an hour later in a gesture of disgust. He feels soiled, degraded, a stranger to himself, a man made sick by his own company.'[56]

Homer's gods, according to Nietzsche, have their origin in adventures on the seashore. His own gods too, perhaps, with Dionysus at their head? 'How many more gods are possible!' he cries in the summer of 1888, six months before his sanity deserted him. 'My mind is still full of the living instinct to create new gods,' he wrote, 'and how different each time is the form in which the divine reveals itself to me.' Some gods, for example, exhibit a quality of recklessness, combined with 'halcyonic propensities'. Two years earlier he had encountered just such a god, most likely on the Italian shore:

I saw him – or at least his eyes – now deep, silent,
Now green, slippery honey-eyes,
His halcyonic smile, as
The blood-soaked sky looked on pitilessly.[57]

Who is he talking about? When words fail, the eye takes on the function of communication. Here the eye is first quiet, like the smooth sea, then deceptive, as slippery as honey. The next item in his notebook is headed 'The god with the orgiastic soul of a woman', the god who comes from across the ocean, Dionysus: 'I saw him, his halcyonic smile, his honey-eyes, now deep-set and hooded, now green and slippery, a shimmering surface – slippery, sleepy, trembling, shuddering, the sea surges up in his eyes.'

Sleepy – like the shepherd on the night shore, and like the boat gliding silently through the water. Dionysus too is lying in a boat, and the water trembles in his eyes, as unpredictable as the Maenad soul of a woman that 'wrenches apart when it loves'. Euripides tells us in the *Bacchae* that Dionysus had the eyes of a woman: 'His glowering eye hides Aphrodite's charm'. At the same time he is cruel, 'thirsting for the blood of the sacrificial beast, lusting after its raw flesh'.[58] The cruelty of a woman.

But the eyes that Nietzsche saw were those of a man. In a homoerotic poem Catullus sings the praises of the young Juventius and his '*melitos oculos*', his 'honey eyes'. Even if he were to kiss them three hundred thousand times, says the poet, he would not have had his fill. Did the 'honey eye' that Nietzsche saw on the beach belong to that 'young Triton, disguised as a sailor', who had been sitting on the sand, smiling quizzically at him like a god and inviting him to join him in the boat to the accompaniment of Chopin's *Barcarolle*? Or was it a different figure, one whom he had encountered not in Genoa but in Nice, not in Ruta but in Rapallo?

At all events it was in the company of seafarers, for Nietzsche's very next jotting refers to 'Caesar among the Pirates'. Plutarch records that Caesar was once captured by pirates. When they intended to ask for a ransom of twenty talents, he laughed in their faces. If they knew who their prisoner was, he told them, they would demand at least fifty talents. While his companions left to collect the money, Caesar lived for over a month with the pirates, joking with them, writing poems which he then read aloud to them, and threatening with a smile to have them all put to the sword. Scarcely had the ransom been paid than he assembled a flotilla of ships and proceeded cruelly and cold-bloodedly to carry out his threat.

It was a story much to Nietzsche's taste. On several occasions he used themes taken from it, such as when he gathered the 'bad birds' around him to hear him sing, or when in the 'Ariadne Dithyramb', the heroine cries to her tormentor: 'Ransom? You demand a ransom? Then demand a large one – my pride demands it!' Then, finally, she asks for only one thing: 'Give me love!' she cries.[59] Concealed within this Ariadne is the new Caesar, who feels insulted when his abductors ask too little for his release and who wants to deliver himself body and soul because he has long been captivated by the 'orgiastic eye' of Dionysus that has him in its sights.

'Caesar among the Pirates' is followed by further headings – 'By the Bridge', 'The Wedding', then suddenly 'Ariadne'. The connection between these headings may well be the chronological sequence of Nietzsche's experiences. First comes his encounter with the seafarers, then the haunting lilt of the gondolier's song, followed by the 'wedding' of Dionysus and Ariadne in the boat, and finally the threnody of the lonely Ariadne, deserted by her lover and waiting to die on the island of Naxos. In the dithyramb she waits for him to torture her and finally confesses that that was in fact all she ever desired – eternal pain and torment.

Nietzsche cast himself in the role of Caesar. Stabbed to death by the traitors' daggers, as Ariadne was pierced by the arrows of her lover, Caesar is the final, perfect form of Nietzsche's 'son' Zarathustra. From the preacher in the wilderness comes the conqueror of the world: 'As Zarathustra regains his strength, Caesar emerges, invincible, gracious.' His chief characteristic – 'the fortune that attends the choice of the eternal moment'.[60] But for Nietzsche, Caesar, spiritual kinsman of Alcibiades, is not only one of the world's great imperial rulers but belongs to the select company of 'enigmatic men predestined to a life of victory and temptation.'[61] In January 1889, by which time he had lost control of his mind, he wrote to Cosima Wagner – whom he addressed as 'Princess Ariadne' – that Caesar had been one of his earlier incarnations before he reached his ultimate goal as 'the victorious Dionysus'.[62]

10   *On the Isles of the Blest*

THE DISCREET DISCIPLE

From 1882 Nietzsche had been wearing a new mask – that of Columbus, discoverer of the New World. He was, after all, a resident of Genoa, a city of *palazzi* that testified to the spoils of conquest. And although he lived a somewhat restricted and rough-and-ready life in his little garret, his mind was always set on making new discoveries. Maybe tomorrow he might be able to give up his poverty-stricken existence and command the waves. Did the city not convey to him the 'boundless, magnificent selfishness' of those who built it? He felt this same self-centredness in his own heart, an insatiable yearning for a full, confident life. Was it not awaiting him round the corner? Everywhere he went he found 'men who knew the sea, the Orient and the spirit of adventure, men who scorned the boredom of convention and the concerns of their neighbours and were willing to exchange the dullness of their unsatisfied, melancholy souls for the fleeting joys of a sunny afternoon'.[1]

The Orient. In the harbour lay the sailing-ships from North Africa and the East. He watches them, smells the exotic air and feels that this Genoa, together with its young Tritons, is the beauty that promises him a greater happiness to come – an African happiness, perhaps, or the happiness of Homer. In March 1883 he began to lay plans. 'Ask my old friend Gersdorff', he wrote to Peter Gast in Venice, 'whether he would like to come with me to Tunis for a few years ... Please keep this plan a secret between you and Gersdorff for the present. There is a painter here who has found in Tunis the promised land – this is what has led me to make this proposal to Gersdorff.'[2]

The worthy Gast, who would gain nothing out of the proposed trip to Africa, must have wondered what led Nietzsche to put forward this secret plan. Since the death of his protégé Leopold Rau, Gersdorff had acted as the patron of a number of young artists of slight means and even slighter talent. He had also tried his own hand at painting, with, according to Gast, no success, and then had suddenly fallen in love with Nietzsche's congenial but far from like-minded follower. Gast was thus the obvious person to convey Nietzsche's travel plan to Gersdorff, even though the latter's advances were not much to his liking.

Gast had already written to Nietzsche in February that Gersdorff was planning 'to make something out of me', adding slily: 'But I will not go on talking about things that properly ought never to be put down in black and white.'[3] Gast put two and two together in an attempt to explain why it should be not him but the homosexual Gersdorff whom Nietzsche had invited to accompany him to Tunis – and that for a period of 'a few years'. Gast concluded that Nietzsche intended to start a new life – and without him. What had gone on in his master's mind?

Since Nietzsche had not officially been on speaking terms with Gersdorff for some time, Gast was made to act as go-between. Gersdorff had learned of Nietzsche's plan 'with the greatest delight', said Gast, and was prepared to accompany him 'for a few months' but not until the autumn. Nietzsche, who wanted to tie his friend down, suggested they leave on 15 September, to which Gersdorff replied – there is a touch of *schadenfreude* about the way Gast reports it – 'Maybe.' The outbreak of war in Tunisia gave Nietzsche the opportunity to call the whole plan off.

Gersdorff showed a far greater loyalty to Gast. In November Nietzsche learned from Rée that Gersdorff was finding life in Leipzig intolerable – 'he is pining for Venice – and for Gast'.[4] Nietzsche passed this news on to his disciple with a sneer. When Gersdorff got married the following year to a German lady who happened to be called Fräulein Nitzsche, Gast went out of his way to remark on her nauseous ugliness.

In February 1882 Paul Rée joined Nietzsche in Genoa, and the two men lay in the sun like sea urchins, watching the lizards in the sand. Gast had difficulty in hiding his jealousy. If he was not going to be allowed to join them, they should at least know that he knew all about them. With feigned servility he urged them to stay in Italy until the beginning of May. They would then be able to witness an eclipse of the sun, he added, 'when the stars will become visible for half-an-hour in the middle of the day'.[5]

Towards the end of February Gast received a typewritten letter from Genoa in which Nietzsche, evidently unsure of himself, sought his support and encouragement. The East had not lost its appeal, and day by day the ships came and went, but he hesitates, holds back. He seems to want to take someone into his confidence – indeed, he needs to do so, and he writes to Gast because he believes Gast knows nothing about the situation.

He starts by flattering him with intimate items of personal information, such as that he and Rée had swum three times in the sea and were planning a flying visit to Monaco the following week before their friend moved back to Rome in the middle of March. Then he asks an unexpected question: 'Have you perchance heard whether the Wagners are back from Palermo or whether they are proposing to spend Easter in Rome?'[6] A meeting with Wagner and Cosima was the last thing he wanted. On no account should they be allowed to thwart his plans. Then he suddenly changes the subject and talks about a performance of Rossini's *The Barber of Seville* he had recently seen. He did not enjoy the music – 'The Seville I love is quite different.' And the association of Seville with Bizet's *Carmen* leads him to conclude with a surprising request: 'Could you not think up some great new diversion for me? I feel like spending a few years on adventurous projects that will give my thoughts a chance to relax and germinate in fresh soil. Your friend, Nietzsche.'

Declining to read between the lines, Gast took the request at its face value, pretending not to know what was at stake. He suggested a trip to the North Pole, then to the Balkans or to China – as if Nietzsche could not read the newspapers for himself – and concluded snidely: 'I am not permitted to mention other than geographical adventures.'[7]

Why not? Because Nietzsche had forbidden him to? Or because one does not mention such things? Gast, the discreet friend and servant, had always known when to hold his peace, even though he was not disinclined to make scornful observations from time to time. Elisabeth Nietzsche, who later refused to have any dealings with him, called him 'crude' and 'a simpleton'.[8] The former might be true – although it casts her brother in a dubious light for having cultivated the company of a 'crude' friend. But the latter is certainly untrue. Gast was intelligent – intelligent enough, at any rate, not to allow himself to be caught up in a private war with Elisabeth, as Overbeck did.

Whereas Nietzsche had hair-raising misconceptions about Gast being 'the new Mozart',[9] Gast had no illusions about 'his' Nietzsche. The opinions he expressed to others contrast vividly with the obsequious letters he wrote to Nietzsche in order to bolster his confidence. On occasion, like Wagner with King Ludwig, he became carried away by his own florid rhetoric. And as he generally concealed his reservations in eulogistic passages, Nietzsche, and his readers with him, failed to notice them. Anything that flattered him he took at face value, and he was quite prepared to allow his young 'maestro' to harvest the crumbs that fell from the great man's table.

Venice was the scene of two revealing episodes in 1885. Gast had been given the task of finding Nietzsche accommodation there for his visit but was uncertain about the location and type of rooms he required. 'Nietzsche found something that I considered *mesquin*,' he wrote, 'and disapproved of what I regarded as not at all bad. In a word, he was unpredictable, everything an illusion, like an intellectual Don Quixote.'[10] So when the knight with the sad countenance arrived, his Sancho Panza had not found any accommodation for him. On his own initiative, and against Gast's advice, he took a room close to the Rialto Bridge.

After a few days, during which he had enjoyed listening to the gondoliers' song 'in the brown night', he suddenly turned up at Gast's lodgings in a state of great agitation. The gondoliers' song was not the only thing he had heard. 'Gast, my friend,' he said, 'I think I'm living in a brothel!' In his eyes it was all Gast's fault, as a result of which the whole farce came to an inglorious end. 'Nietzsche wrote to Förster,' said Gast, 'accusing me of putting him up in a prostitute's house. He was the sort of man who would utter such falsehoods just in order to get his own back.'[11]

Gast gave as good as he got. When later that year Nietzsche asked him for a quotation on 'the urgency of female sexual urges' from August Bebel's book *Women in Past, Present and Future*,[12] Gast did not send him the desired lines but selected different ones: 'It is women in particular who have the greatest inhibitions in expressing their most powerful instincts in a natural manner. This conflict between natural needs and social pressures results in perversities, secret vices and wild excesses.'[13]

Although himself not given to 'secret vices', Gast had, ever since their days in Basel, cherished an attachment to Nietzsche that led him to forgive his master all the indignities he inflicted on him. Sometimes even his female friends would be jealous of his devotion to the philosopher. Once, after receiving a tearful letter from Nietzsche, Gast was overcome by the feeling 'that he must lay his head on his bosom and weep ... Never have I loved anybody as I have loved this man ... I feel it is my most joyous duty to die with him.'[14]

This was in 1879, when Nietzsche was at his nadir. Where Nietzsche was the suffering Master, Gast was John, his favourite disciple. Thirteen years after the Master's death he thought otherwise. The popular image of Nietzsche had been falsified by Elisabeth in the same way as she had doctored *The Will to Power*, which she claimed was a late, unpublished work of her brother's. Moreover she expressly forbade Gast from publishing his dealings with her brother. Gast complied. A letter to a woman friend revealed that there were also other reasons for his silence: 'Whether I shall ever write about Nietzsche, I cannot say. At all events it would reveal something that would surprise people. At one time it was a joyful experience for me to play the role of John, the disciple. I often revel in my memories of him and rejoice at the influence he has had on intelligent minds. But the greatest service I could render this influence is to keep silent.'[15]

AN ALLURING WORLD

While Nietzsche and his bosom friend Rée were gambolling in the sea off Genoa and strolling through the ghostly paths of the cemetery that Maupassant called 'an irresistibly grotesque, monumentally banal place', Rée put another idea in his head. If they could not go to Tunis, why not try Biskra, the oasis in the Algerian Sahara that Nietzsche had mentioned in his diary back in 1880? He had read that here 'every girl in the local tribes lived for a while from prostitution',[16] which was not only not considered immoral but was seen as an act of devotion. Venality, moreover, extended to young boys. The two friends may well have wondered whether they should not continue their Swiss honeymoon in an oasis on the edge of the desert. 'For next year,' wrote Rée to Elisabeth in February, 'I have planned a visit to Biskra with your brother – Algiers, the desert mail, oases, camels and the rest.'[17] The amusing list of attractions was intended to distract attention from his embarrassment, for even the prudish spinster in Naumburg can hardly have failed to know that different customs were observed in Africa from Europe. Three weeks later Nietzsche wrote to Gast that he would very much like to join such a trip. But it was too late. Rée was already on his way to Rome, where another adventure was awaiting him.

It was in Biskra, twelve years later, that André Gide experienced his great moment of liberation. In his novel *The Immoralist* he describes how the handsome Arab boys aroused his latent homosexuality. This revelation also marks the climax of his memoirs published under the title *If It Die*:

> I heard, I saw, I breathed as I had never done before; and as the blended stream of sounds, perfumes and colours flooded my empty heart, I felt it dissolve in passionate gratitude.
>
> 'Take me, take me body and soul,' I cried, sobbing out my worship to some unknown Apollo; 'I am thine – obedient, submissive. Let all within me be light! Light and air! My struggle against thee has been vain. But now I know thee. Thy will be done! I resist no longer. I am in thy hands. Take me!'
>
> And so, my face wet with tears, I entered an enchanting universe full of laughter and strangeness.[18]

The Apollo's name was Ali. Gide emphasised that he only discovered Nietzsche later – his great precursor *in eroticis*, alongside Oscar Wilde, who also had his reasons for longing for the south. Truman Capote once described Gide's behaviour during his later years: 'He was so crusty that at his age he was chasing fifteen-year-old boys up and down the alleyways in Taormina, having them into his bedroom in the afternoon siesta hours. All the kids called him "The Five O'Clock Menace". He was always making dates with them at five o'clock, *à cinq heures*.'[19]

From the 1880s onwards the enchanted world that Gide had written about made its way north. Sicilian boys and youths began to conquer the more prudish parts of Europe, including Germany. They were handsome and well-built, looked at people in a knowing way, and to show their origins they wore vine leaves in their hair and carried a flute in their hand. And they were naked. Disciples of Dionysus with leopard skins draped over their shoulders and ungirt loins. They peopled a Homeric landscape, ephebes with and without togas posed on the beaches, satyrs crowned with garlands of vine leaves danced in front of the ruins of classical temples and a snow-capped volcano, played the tambourine, then withdrew to secluded terraces to delight in their own beauty among the giant urns and the potted palms.

As Dionysus had once come to Greece, so Arcadia now came irresistibly to Germany. Nor was this world expensive. One could buy postcards of the objects of one's love separately or in blocks, quietly putting the more lascivious scenes into a drawer and framing the classical poses. The figures that the descendants of Winckelmann could only dream of as marble statues were suddenly available in photographic clarity and exuberant detail. The rebirth of antiquity from the spirit of photography – to re-phrase the title of Nietzsche's book.

The postcards that were beginning to flood an eager market depicted not gods but real men, more handsome than one was accustomed to find in German lands. Such were the figures that one imagined Praxiteles had taken as the models for his gods. Admirers by the thousand were happy to accept photos that would fit into a waistcoat pocket, for hitherto they had been able to study these statues only in hazy reproductions or in sterile art galleries. These photos, produced by heavy, bulky plate-cameras, had a definition beyond compare. Viewed from all angles, firm, athletic bodies with shimmering bronze skin displayed everything with which the god of beauty had equipped them. Only when they began to display a degree of sexual arousal did the artist carefully remove the offending detail.

For the secret brotherhood of the aesthetics of the male body the ideal had become reality. The fear of being arrested or looked at askance dissipated.

Such postcards were considered entirely proper, morally harmless – simply art. And for some *cognoscenti* the Arcadian pin-ups virtually filtered in to real-life experiences – pleasures not of fauns or men in togas but of fishermen, sailors, beachcombers. Most were in any case children, innocents still living in paradise. For them the photo sessions were one long carnival – and they were paid as well. Willing and wide-eyed, they seemed to enjoy being captured in classical poses at the bidding of the photographer, who invited them to 'watch the birdie' as he released the shutter. He trained them and loved them. They, in turn, let themselves be trained and loved.

The man who made Taormina the Mecca for such cardboard dreams was Wilhelm von Gloeden. His father had been forest ranger to the Grand Duke of Mecklenburg-Schwerin, in one of whose palaces Wilhelm had been born in 1856. After his father's death he was given a strict Protestant upbringing by his mother, made to practise the piano and sent to a *Gymnasium* known for its strict Protestant discipline. At the age of twenty he was forced by the onset of tuberculosis to break off his studies to become a painter, and was not expected to live long. But he also suffered from another affliction – he was homosexual. Had he been caught *in flagrante,* he would have ended his life in jail.

The only possibility of finding relief for his suffering in both these respects was to go to Italy. In 1878 he rode up the hill on a mule to the resort of Taormina and took a room in the Vittoria Hotel. At the suggestion of an artist friend he proceeded to tour the area and quickly found everything that a sick and suffering aesthete from Germany could ever dream of – a favourable climate, the views of Etna, the Greek theatre and the congenial company of uninhibited young men.

The therapy worked. Gloeden lived until 1931. According to his biographer Ulrich Pohlmann, his remarkable recovery was largely due to the fact that in Sicily he found it possible to develop his homosexual tendencies unhindered: 'In the nineteenth century Italy had become the favourite refuge for German homosexuals exiled from their own country. Whereas in Germany homosexual relationships were punishable by sentences of up to five years in jail, in Italy there was no such law forbidding the association of males with each other, and places like the Ligurian coast, Florence, the island of Capri and Taormina developed into popular meeting places for such men.'[20]

They congregated above all in Sicily, described by Pohlmann as 'the island of bliss in the cradle of classical civilisation'.[21] Here, at the legendary end of the world, Gloeden began photographing the young fishers frolicking on the shore near the resort of Naxos Giardini. These naked youths corresponded perfectly to the ideals of classical beauty that he had learnt about at art school

– except that they were not plaster casts. 'These Greek forms fascinated me,' he wrote, 'as did the *teint* of their bronze bodies, and I set about trying to reproduce the life of classical antiquity in my paintings.'[22] For him they were not Italians imitating classical nude poses according to his instructions but the genuine descendants of those Greek colonists of yore – maybe even of those sailors who had anchored their fleet off Naxos when Alcibiades had had to return to Athens. It was not a question of striking poses but of manifesting their natural classical grace.

The young Sicilians with the eyes of women did not, however, merely offer themselves as objects of homosexual interest to Gloeden's gaze, or as subjects for his camera – they also became his pupils, waiting to be brought to maturity from their pristine state of youthful innocence. Maybe it was this pedagogical impulse that enabled this latter-day Plato to satisfy his sexual needs while older citizens gave their passive consent and his young charges actively involved themselves in his activities. There was nothing offensive about this as far as the children were concerned, for 'on these sheltered shores', as Pohlmann put it, 'young adolescents were experiencing, through acts of mutual satisfaction, the fulfilment of their earliest sexual desires'.[23] Gloeden trained a few of them to become photographers and gave others fishing boats to help them earn a living. For his regular models he set up bank accounts into which he paid their royalties.

Gloeden's publications soon found imitators. Publications with names such as 'Freedom', 'One's Own' and 'Beauty' illustrated fantasies with his nudes. Not only did the photos satisfy the lusts of the avaricious eye – they also nurtured hopes for a new Greece, for the sweet fruits of Hesiod's garden of heroes. As more and more cards were sent through the post, so artists and travellers flocked to Taormina. Amongst them were aficionados of the naked body, lovers of things exotic and oriental – Gloeden's own favourite youth was called 'Il Moro'. Others were anxious to help in the resurgence of the values of antiquity, which were waiting here to be savoured in their original setting, with its original stage-props and its original cast of supporting actors. The German weekly *Die Zeit* called this first excursion into sex tourism 'Arcadia in the Shadow of Etna', with Taormina 'A Refuge for Homosexuals'.

Arcadia was also the key word that Thomas Mann associated with the cult of the naked body. Mann discovered in the contemporary paintings of Ludwig von Hoffmann – a kind of Gloeden in oils – 'a great number of beautiful adolescent figures, especially males, that I found enchanting. I much like his style and his conception of Arcadian beauty.'[24]

Taormina, offering a live show for connoisseurs of the naked human body, became a honeypot for *fin de siècle* aesthetes at the turn of the century. Oscar

Wilde came, as did King Edward VII, Gabriele d'Annunzio and the Prussian crown prince August Wilhelm. The poet Stefan George, together with his homoerotic circle, given to northern rather than southern ideals, wrote in praise of Gloeden's beautiful boys. Indeed, the youth of Sicily continue to attract visitors from northern Europe today, as a recent tourist guide, ignorant of Gloeden and the island's tradition in this respect, suggests: 'The boys are handsome, ephebes on the soil of classical antiquity who come together in quiet intensity, in the summer wearing brightly coloured seamen's trousers with shirts open to the waist, in the winter to be enjoyed as photos displayed in the windows of various shops – features like those of a Madonna, a hint of hair on their upper lip, elegiac and never, even when posing naked, obscene.'[25]

'WHERE THE GODS CAST OFF THEIR ROBES IN THE DANCE'

At some time Nietzsche, the frustrated Columbus, must have felt the force of the imperative demand and said to himself: Thither will I go! Everything may oppose it, my friends may leave me in the lurch, money may be short and my health fragile – but still: I will! I have waited long enough, Tunis and Biskra have run into the sand. In the middle of March 1882 he wrote to Peter Gast: 'At the end of the month I shall go to the end of the world – wherever that is. If you knew, you would follow me.'[26]

Gast must have been astonished. Evidently Nietzsche's patience had run out and he was quite serious. Would he really go to the North Pole or to China? Or to wherever else the end of the world might be? But the riddle was easily solved, and not only for Gast, as Nietzsche well knew. For at the end of the world, as the whole of antiquity had known since Homer and Hesiod, lay the isles of the blest, the heroes' paradise. As Hesiod wrote, 'Zeus had given the heroes a place to live at the ends of the world, where they lived free from care on the isles of the blest, surrounded by the raging ocean – happy heroes, whom the fertile earth provides with an abundant, honey-sweet harvest three times a year.'

The utopian dream of a paradise inhabited by a handsome race of people, heroic couples who live on nectar where the wells of pleasure never dry up, was perpetuated in the eighteenth century by the *Sturm und Drang* novelist Wilhelm Heinse. After a stay in Italy Heinse wrote a novel set in the Renaissance called *Ardinghello and the Isles of the Blest*, which culminates in the establishment of a colony of free love. Bliss, for Heinse, meant above all the power of enjoyment, and Nietzsche was also drawn to the place where, as Heinse put it, 'love spreads its wings in purest freedom'.[27] There was no need for him to sail to the end of the world when Sicily was only a day's journey away.

His adventure began at the end of March. But instead of taking one of the regular passenger ships, as he had done for his journey from Genoa to Naples in 1876, he found a berth on an uncomfortable cargo boat that took him non-stop to Sicily. According to Gast, 'by pitching him some fictitious yarn, he had succeeded in persuading the captain of a Sicilian sailing boat to allow him on board'.[28] The world seemed to open up before him, time and space to dissolve into eternity, his Genoese dreams to find fulfilment, as he drifted out into the blue.

It did indeed seem to be 'into the blue'. His friends considered it a crazy idea. For in reality, while proudly claiming that 'with one fell swoop and as the sole passenger on board'[29] he had realised his dream of going south to live out his ideals, Nietzsche was sick, prone to fits and afflicted with an exaggerated sense of cleanliness. Besides that he could not stand the heat, direct sunlight being worst of all. Not for nothing was Sicily considered to be a winter resort. The summer was now approaching, with the threat of the sirocco from Africa. When his friend Overbeck received a card from him posted in Messina, Overbeck replied peevishly: 'Much as I can see the value of spending the summer by the sea, I cannot for the life of me see why you should choose to stay in that treacherous climate.'[30]

Writing to Gast, Nietzsche explained the paradox. 'I have arrived at my "end of the world" where, according to Homer, happiness is to be found.' Strangely enough Homer appeared to be right. 'In fact,' he continued, 'I have never felt so content as over the past week, and my fellow-citizens spoil me in the most affectionate way.'[31] Fellow-citizens? A citizen after barely one week? Did he perhaps plan to stay longer than his original two months – even for ever, in the company of these fellow-citizens? Quite a novelty for Nietzsche. At the beginning of April he wrote a letter to Naumburg containing the mystifying sentence 'The last fit I had was just like being sea-sick' – which he probably was.[32] It was his way of letting his family know that he had gone to ground in an insalubrious place. In his next postcard he told them that he had not gone abroad in order to waste money.[33] His description of his arrival reads like a fairy tale. 'When I awoke,' he wrote, 'I found myself lying in a pretty little bed close to a quiet cathedral square. Palm trees were waving in front of my window.'[34] For the next three weeks his address was Messina, poste restante.

Hardly any other episode in Nietzsche's life has caused such confusion among biographers. All we have in writing is four postcards from Messina, all euphoric in tone. Whom could this notorious loner have wanted to meet at the end of the world? 'Nowhere did he live so anonymously as during this time in Messina', wrote Werner Ross. 'He met nobody, attracted nobody's attention, and we know neither where he lived nor what experiences he had. His references to it read like a dream. Did he sit in his Mediterranean surroundings writing poetry? "Idylls from Messina" was the title he gave to the poems he sent Schmeitzner in May for publication in the latter's new journal *The International Monthly*. But Messina plays no part in these poems, which had already been finished in Genoa.'[35]

Nietzsche's record of his poetic activities in Sicily, intended to inform his friends of what he had been writing, is a fraud. Only one thing links the poems written on the beach or in the cemetery in Genoa with his idyll in Sicily. Maybe his friends suspected what it was – his biographers certainly did not. Why do they persist in dwelling on Messina, a town in which there was not enough to do for three weeks? Merely because he sent and collected his mail from the post office there? It would not have taken him long to discover the places where there were lizards and tritons to be found. The only reference he made to his everyday life in Sicily sounds like a return to his gypsy existence in Genoa. 'Underwear in a terrible state! No need of my two decent shirts any more!' he wrote.

Nietzsche will have wasted no time in making for the classical remains in Taormina. These sites, in particular the Greek theatre, had long made the town the main attraction of this part of the coast. Goethe was here in 1787, pondering his tragedy *Nausikaa*. Nietzsche, who obviously knew Goethe's *Italian Journey*, had earlier proposed to Gast that he set Goethe's drama to music. 'The vision of *Nausikaa* is constantly before my eyes,' he wrote enthusiastically, 'an idyll with dances and all the southern glory of those who live by the sea.'[36] He knew what kind of idyll was awaiting him.

But he committed nothing to paper – no jottings, no diary, although he was otherwise so prodigal with notes and comments for his later biographers. Maybe we are looking in the wrong places. Maybe we need to read his postcards more closely. Take one written to Gast, for example, in which he reveals where his journey will take him. It contains a clear allusion to his aphorism 'The Danger Confronting the Happiest' in *La gaia scienza*. In the aphorism he calls the profoundest pleasure, which is followed by 'purple melancholy', 'the happiness of Homer'. 'It is the condition', the allusion continues, 'of the man who has given the Greeks their gods – nay, has given himself *his* gods!'[37] In addition to the three notes from which the aphorism is assembled, there is an earlier form dating from the autumn of 1881, in which the happiness of which he speaks is still dependent on himself – only in the final version, written at the end of May 1882, does he permit himself to share the happiness of

Homer, the happiness that Nietzsche described in his card to Gast in April from Messina as his own: 'Never, indeed, have I been in such good spirits.'

What was the source of these 'good spirits'? Had he created *his* gods, like Homer, and discovered in company with them his own newly invented antiquity? In 1884 he set out to compose an ode to the enticing, exotic music that he had been unable to get out of his head since those days in Genoa, combining with it the motif of the 'isles of the blest', which on the face of it has nothing to do with the music:

> Everything is now to be granted me:
> The eagle of my hope found
> A pure, new Greece,
> The salvation of my ears and of my senses . . .
>
> O do not delay to direct the ship's desire
> Towards southern shores, the isles of the blest,
> And the frolics of the nymphs.
> No ship ever sought a finer goal.[38]

So the eagle of his hope has found him a newer, purer Greece after the soul, freed by the spear of Januarius, had sought the fulfilment of its highest aspirations. Now, his senses having found renewal, he invites others to follow his example and steer the ship's desire towards the south. That is my – our – goal. That is where I can regain my health.

And indeed, when he visited Overbeck in Basel at the beginning of May, Overbeck was amazed by how well his friend looked. 'It was the first time in many years', he wrote, 'that I had seen Nietzsche several days in succession without our time together being interrupted by a fit or some other complaint on his part. He had a healthy colour and there seemed to me no danger of mental or physical collapse, since he had put on a considerable amount of weight. We spent five days together, talking until midnight. He was livelier than I had ever known him and listened a great deal to music – in a word, we cherished the most confident hopes for the future.'[39]

That his ears also recovered is linked to his earlier discovery of *Carmen* and his memories of happy days with Rée in the Alps. A year before his mental collapse, when his hatred of Wagner, who was long since dead, erupted again, he returned to the subject of Bizet's opera. This music, he wrote, was his 'recovery expressed in notes', a means of escape 'from the cold and clammy north'.[40] And he goes on to describe its 'southern, sultry, torrid sensibility' in terms that would leave a modern listener to *Carmen* dumbfounded.[41]

But he also heard something more. As Wagner's *Tristan* reminded him of the tragedy of his childhood, so the music of *Carmen* brought back his spiritual liberation, from the days of his friendship with Rée to the time of his Sicilian adventure, and opened up a new world beyond the north, beyond the snow and ice: 'The joys of Africa, the fatalistic serenity, with a piercing eye both seductive and terrifying; the erotic melancholy of the Moorish dance; glowing passion, swift and sudden as a dagger; with scents wafted up from the water in the yellow afternoon, causing the heart to take fright, as though it had suddenly recalled the forgotten islands where it once dwelt, where it should have dwelt for ever . . .'[42]

This final admission – which he omitted from the published version of *The Case of Wagner* – sounds like a sigh. In the midst of a rapturous description of *Carmen* he suddenly scents the sea air, his heart takes fright and the memory of a lost paradise returns, and with it a yearning for those isles at the end of the world to which he was fated never to return. In *Also sprach Zarathustra* he raised a monument to their memory, and also to that 'powerful, air-borne yearning' which had once swept him away from the mainland: 'Often it carried me away, onwards and upwards, breaking into my laughter. I flew like an arrow through sun-drenched ecstasy, out into the distant future which no dream had yet seen – flew to the heat of the south, hotter than any artists could have imagined, where the gods cast off their robes in the dance . . .'[43]

This was the paradise that Gloeden dangled before the eyes of those living in the north. In his photographs we see dancing boys, raised by Nietzsche to the heroic status of gods who spurn all clothes and are often said to congregate on the slopes of Monte Ziretto at night to celebrate Bacchanalian rites. 'There all is dance and high spirits, where the gods seek each other, flee from each other, find each other again, hear each other again, belong to each other again, where all time mocks the passing moment.' Thus spake Zarathustra.

Then, for a moment that brings a shudder to the heart, Zarathustra-Nietzsche removes his mask and adds: 'It was there that I came across the word "Superman".'[44] Nietzsche did not forget the dance of the gods. When, in January 1889, his mind finally gave way, the wife of the kiosk owner in Turin in whose house he had found accommodation confessed that she had once gone up to his room and peeked through the keyhole. He was singing, she said, 'and capering around in the nude'.[45]

'The Bird of Prey Masquerading as a Canary'

THE HOLY TRINITY

By visiting the isles of the blest, Nietzsche had satisfied an age-old craving. As in 'Capri and Heligoland', the story he had written in his youth, he was able to wander among the ruins of the past and discover in new friends those qualities to which his own inner self responded. In August 1881, as he confessed to his friend Paul Rée, he had also dreamt of distant shores, casting himself as a new Columbus who 'incomplete and miserable creature that I am', could only rarely catch a glimpse of 'that better land in which whole, perfect personalities roam'.[1] Rée, he knew, would understand the image and his yearning, for in Rée he had found one who completed his own incompleteness, complementing by his youth the older man's Platonic imperfections.

In this letter Nietzsche allows himself to be carried away by his euphoric attachment to his friend and transported back to the days of the ode that he had addressed to the school-friend who had been expelled from Pforta:

> O would that the shining light of Heaven
> Would be shed on you alone.
> So that in the most glorious dance of spring
> Fresh blossoms would constantly spring forth from you!

For Rée, his Stella, he made a slight change to the image of the living garden. 'As I may have already told you a dozen times,' he writes to Rée, 'I should like to create a special sun, given the task of shining solely on you and on the flowers growing in your garden.'

In February the following year they were to be found sharing the sun on a Mediterranean beach. Rée was relaxed, blissful, while Nietzsche was mercifully free at last from fits – 'he looks', said his friend proudly, 'like an adolescent'.[2] When he wrote this, Rée had already left Genoa and embarked on another adventure. Shortly afterwards Nietzsche received disturbing news from Rome – Rée had discovered another young person who, like Heinrich von Stein earlier, would make a suitable disciple for the philosopher. But this time it was not a young man.

The electrifying effect Rée's letter had on Nietzsche can be judged from his reply. Knowing that within a week he would be setting out on his trip to Sicily – planned long beforehand but kept from Rée – he sent his best wishes to 'the Russian lady' in question and confirmed that he had designs 'on this species of creature. Indeed, I shall shortly take on the role of predator.'[3] The metaphor of the hunt referred to his imminent expedition to Sicily, described in the language of an Andrea Doria determined to satisfy his longings – by force, if necessary.

Nietzsche's desires were directed at this time towards like-minded disciples whom he could collect around him like Socrates in Athens, albeit without interruption from his demon. Less to his liking was that Rée was contemplating his friend getting married. 'Marriage is a quite different matter', Nietzsche rejoined. 'The most I could consider would be a marriage that lasted two years'[4] – and then only taking into account the immense task that lay before him. Rée evidently considered it necessary, in the interests of propriety, to legitimise the young lady's status as Nietzsche's disciple by arranging a marriage between them. For the sake of appearances, Nietzsche replies, this could be acceptable – but only for a while.

While Nietzsche was setting out to conquer his promised land, his two disciples, the young man and the young woman, became friends, and Rée made her a proposal of marriage. She flatly refused. She knew what men were like, she said, and her love life was over, 'once and for all'.[5] Lou Salomé, of aristocratic Russian descent, had recently turned twenty-one. In Rome, where she was staying with Malwida von Meysenbug, she continued to wear the black, nun-like habit, buttoned up to the neck, worn by female students in Zurich, and had no intention of permitting any inroads on the freedom she had enjoyed since leaving St Petersburg two years earlier.

The only daughter of a Russian general, Gustav von Salomé – his ancestors were Huguenots who had joined the Prussian army and later found their way to the Russian court – Lou was expected to spend her life in aristocratic circles. A general's daughter offered a good match, and the family counted on her compliance. Her life revolved around her father, in whose presence she always felt happy. Indeed, she appears to have idolised him, eagerly accepting the demonstrations of both his love and his anger. Of her own free will she would beg him to beat her on her bare buttocks, 'imploring him with tears in her eyes to punish her'.[6] But the general, who had already retired from the army, was a loving, not a jealous god, and her close relationship to him influenced her whole life – in contrast to her mother, with whom, she herself admitted, 'she lived in a permanent state of war'.[7]

In 1878, at the age of seventeen, Lou left the family home and threw herself into the arms of another father figure, a charismatic forty-year-old preacher called Hendrik Gillot, who 'awakened her femininity' and adopted her as an acolyte. Unbeknown to her family, little Ljola, as they called her, was transformed into 'an ardent religious fanatic who believed that she had the power to love as St Teresa had loved the Lord Jesus'.[8] But her Messiah was a married man, had two daughters of her own age and pursued a less than holy plan, namely to arouse in her the consciousness of womanhood. They would read together as she sat in rapture on his knee, while he fixed her with a penetrating gaze 'which made her feel totally naked'.[9]

Finally he made to seduce her – the familiar scene in contemporary novels where the lascivious priest, accustomed to the success attendant on his position of authority, seeks to deflower an aristocrat's daughter. 'The youthfulness of my body', wrote Lou later, ' – in the north one develops more slowly – led him to conceal from me at first that he was indulging in the gestures that would lead to a union between us. When, taking me by surprise, he then demanded that I exchange the world of the spirit for the call of the flesh, I could not. The scales fell from my eyes, and what I had formerly worshipped passed out of my life for ever.'[10]

That Lou's passion for Gillot ended so abruptly, and that his amorous fumblings had only served to make the break final, was due less to his clumsiness than to Lou's particular kind of love. She was as much like St Teresa as Gillot was like Jesus Christ. For her he had only taken the place of her father-idol, a relationship that had always had its religious aspect. Gustav von Salomé had been sick for a long time, and his illness cast a shadow over the life of the whole family. His death in February, when the affair between Gillot and Lou was at its height, destroyed the family's sense of security. That at that very moment she was in the process of seeking a new security with a new father figure must have appeared to Lou like a betrayal of God Himself. Gillot's attempt to seduce her, and thereby rid himself of his ersatz father role, was for Lou the culmination of this role. He had tried to play with her the games she had innocently played with her father; but now that she had her father's death on her conscience, she could no longer play those games without a sense of sin. The former intimacy between father and daughter had been re-created in this new relationship as a shock-experience. From then on sex was taboo.

But she continued to be the victim of disastrous sexual encounters. Indeed, she often provoked them herself. Attracted to older, charismatic men, she gave her feminine charms free rein, as she had done with her father, and identified herself to the point of self-destruction with her 'lord and master' of the moment, only to draw back hastily at the moment of truth, when her partner began to 'go too far'. Her devotion to the memory of her father became her vengeance on his successors. She was at her happiest, wrote her biographer, 'when others continued to play the parts that she had allocated to them in her imagination'.[11] Her final desolation was part of that happiness.

In Rome, in the spring of 1882, the curtain rose on a new drama. Rée, too young and too listless for the role of father, was given the part of brother. Lou's favourite brother Eugène, who may have served as the model for the part, had always had 'an air of the mysterious' about him – a 'demonic nature' who had once turned up at a family ball 'dressed as a woman, wearing a wig and a corset and dancing with amorous young officers the whole night long'.[12]

Lou at once recognised Rée's feminine characteristics, and she remained faithful to him for five years in the role of a sister. Since it was improper for a young, single lady to travel without a chaperon, the new brother could take on this role himself. Although he may have felt uncomfortable in this somewhat dubious function, he could not but develop a growing affection for his attractive young charge who was determined not to be a woman, until in the end he fell genuinely in love with her. In this respect too he could have felt that he had found his Platonic counterpart.

Rée's letter to Nietzsche about 'a young Russian lady' was designed to do both his master and Lou a favour. Lou needed a husband for reasons of propriety, and because she was more intelligent than other women, that man had to be equally intelligent. Nietzsche, also for reasons of propriety, needed a wife – Rée was well aware how determinedly both Elisabeth and Malwida had tried to find a suitable match for the confirmed bachelor. That sex would play no part in the relationship was guaranteed from both sides – from Nietzsche's, as Rée was convinced, because of inability, from Lou's, as she had made clear, out of a lack of desire. Instead Rée, who was in love with both of them, would join them to form a trio – a state of true perfection in which any suspicion of indecency was nullified by the presence of a woman in otherwise exclusively male company. This led them to the notion of a 'holy trinity', a spiritual equivalent of the familiar *ménage à trois*.

Lou was anxious to meet him, Rée wrote to Nietzsche, and even suggested she travel via Genoa. But by that time Nietzsche had departed for an unknown destination, leaving the lady highly incensed. When, at the age of seventy, she came to publish her memoirs, she denied the whole episode. Her account of events is, however, prejudiced, because she was concerned to draw a veil over her own part in the affair. It is not true that Rée 'rushed over from Monte Carlo',[13] as she maintained – in fact his plan to visit Malwida there in the middle of March had been known since the beginning of February. Equally untrue is her claim that Nietzsche 'arrived unexpectedly from Messina' and imposed himself on them, making himself the third member of the trio and disturbing the plan that she and Rée had made to establish a brother–sister relationship. When Nietzsche, according to Lou, went so far as to ask Rée 'to act as his advocate in making her a proposal of marriage', she was highly indignant, and the two of them, brother and little sister, supposedly put their minds to how to turn Nietzsche away without offending him.[14]

This may sound plausible but it is not correct. It was Rée who had whetted Nietzsche's appetite, organised the meeting, thought up the marriage plan and even passed on to him the information of how desirous Lou was to meet him. Had he invented Lou's trip to Genoa? No. Nietzsche must have felt that he had been invited, even that his presence was eagerly awaited, especially as he had only recently spent a 'delightful time' with his friend in Genoa.[15] Since Lou certainly knew of Rée's letters, neither Nietzsche's arrival nor the marriage proposal can have come as a surprise – at the most, their timing may have. Nor did Rée have any reason to leave Lou in doubt about his plans – his intentions were honourable, and marriage a formality. Furthermore in the years that followed Lou developed a formidable appetite for educated older men. Why should it have vexed her if a well-known poet and thinker, with an aura of mystery about him, should have chosen to pay her his respects? She had no cause to be dissatisfied with her new acquaintance.

But in fact, writing in the 1930s, Lou had good grounds for wanting to portray Nietzsche as a disruptive influence, for otherwise her 'guilt' for the subsequent complications would have become apparent. She had been long enough under the influence of Sigmund Freud to understand this episode as a recurrence of her experience-pattern. The man who allowed himself to be seen as the 'master', senior in both age and worldly knowledge, seemed an ideal candidate for the position of father – which then led to a repetition of the Gillot episode. Lou began to live the life of the new idol, even to fall in love with him, identifying herself with his thoughts, sensing his emotions, finishing his sentences when he broke off, and driving both him and herself towards the inevitable catastrophe.

The drama began in St Peter's in Rome, where Malwida had sent Nietzsche and where Rée was sitting in a confessional, working on his profane aphorisms, while Lou waited for him. Nietzsche discovered the two of them and greeted Lou with words that would have been better directed to the man in the confessional. 'From what stars have we fallen', he said, 'that we have been brought together in this place?'[16] To Lou such language sounded unnecessarily pompous, whereas it was in reality only a private joke, meant for his 'friend from the stars', as he sometimes called Rée, who really had brought them together. Lou disapproved of this way of describing their first meeting, and later gave her own version of events, claiming that what Nietzsche had actually said was: 'What stars have chanced to bring us here?'[17] This made the encounter sound like a coincidence, which was more to her liking.

The story continues two weeks later in the little lakeside town of Orta, behind which rises a wooded hill some hundred metres high, dedicated to St Francis and known as the Monte Sacro. Here Nietzsche and Lou were alone together. Lou's mother had excused herself, complaining of a headache, and etiquette demanded that Rée accompany her. Nietzsche and 'the young Russian lady' went to visit the votive chapels on the hill.

They were away for a long while. Lou's mother was offended, Rée in a bad mood. He did not like it when young ladies talked with his master alone – that was something that Isabelle von der Pahlen had discovered. Still less did he like it when it was his newly acquired little sister going off on her own with his bosom friend. The brother was in a quandary: instead of being the third member of the trinity, he was facing the prospect of being odd man out.

What had happened on the Monte Sacro? Nietzsche later described it to Lou as 'the most ravishing dream I have ever had'. Lou merely wrote: 'Did I kiss Nietzsche when we were on the Monte Sacro? I no longer remember.'[18]

This is characteristic of her reinterpretations. She knew exactly what had happened, and what tricks she had employed to catch her impressionable companion in her net. In one of his sketches for a spectacular finale for *Thus Spake Zarathustra* a woman appears, announcing 'the coming of the eagle and the serpent'.[19] While the world suddenly seems to stand still, she draws Zarathustra's arm towards her breast, whereupon a loud groan is heard as the abyss disgorges its flames. There is no comparable moment to be found anywhere in his works, nor is he likely to have experienced anything similar again.

The third episode took place a week later in Lucerne, where the hallowed ground of Wagner's Tribschen awakened melancholy memories. Here Nietzsche determined to have a heart-to-heart talk with Lou because, as she later wrote, 'in retrospect Paul Rée's intercession on his behalf in Rome had been inadequate' – and also because he now really wanted to have her, not merely pro forma but in reality.[20] On the Monte Sacro a promise had been made. Now, in Lucerne, it was time for Lou to fulfil that promise. Such were Nietzsche's thoughts. As a suitable background he chose Thorwaldsen's sculpture *The Dying Lion* at the Gletschergarten, in which a spear pierces the animal's back. 'He who has awakened me has wounded me!' cries Brünnhilde to her liberator.

In 1889, shortly after his committal to the mental asylum in Basel, Nietzsche drew the dying lion with charcoal on paper. For when he proposed to Lou in front of Thorwaldsen's figure, she turned him down. With forced jollity he persuaded his two friends to have themselves photographed together with him – not as a 'holy trinity' but as two men under the whip. Jules Bonnet, who took the photo in his studio, can rarely have had such a disastrous group to deal with. Lou recalled that it was Nietzsche who was the driving force behind the whole affair: 'In spite of strong protests from Rée, who had a life-long antipathy to having his features reproduced, Nietzsche jocularly insisted. He also busied himself with the details of the composition of the picture' – including the 'tasteless kitsch of the sprig of lilac attached to the whip', which he had probably taken from her bouquet.

In the summer the whip-wielding Lou appears to have taken the compromising photo, which her biographer Ernst Pfeiffer described as 'grotesque and perverse',[21] to Bayreuth and shown it to a large number of people there, to Nietzsche's fury. After this incident with the photo in Bonnet's studio he had taken Lou to Tribschen, where she noticed that there were tears in his eyes – partly, no doubt, at the thought of the loss of his love for Wagner but also for Lou herself. When composing a poem of welcome for Zarathustra two years later, he remembered the melancholy scene with her on the shore of Lake Lucerne in the shadow of the villa where Wagner and Cosima had once lived:

Here I sat, looking, looking – but into the distance.
My fingers playing with the tattered bouquet,
When a tear dropped from my eye
In shame and curiosity: For whom was it shed?[22]

Maybe he was not certain himself. Was it for Cosima, who might have come into his mind as he drew with a stick in the wet sand? Was it for Lou, who led him by the nose like a schoolmistress? Or was it for his son, Zarathustra, the only one who could rescue him from his dilemma?

Then came the final act of the drama. While Lou, under Malwida's sponsorship, managed to wheedle her way into the Wagner inner circle and captivate the guardians of Bayreuth, Nietzsche sat in the Thuringian spa of

Tautenburg and waited. The local council had approved the erection of two new park benches in his honour, leaving him to provide suitable plaques for them. One was to read 'The Dead Man', the other, 'La gaia scienza'. But the maker of the plaques was taking his time. Meanwhile Nietzsche could do nothing but wait with growing impatience, on the one hand for his plaques, on the other for Lou, whom he hoped to impress with them.

His sister Elisabeth, in Tautenburg to see that the proprieties were observed, was irritated by what was unfolding in Bayreuth. Lou was apparently ingratiating herself with the painter Paul von Joukowsky, designer of the stage sets for *Parsifal*. Elisabeth was unaware that Joukowsky was living with an Italian boy called Pepino. Besides this she seems to have taken every opportunity to vilify her brother in Wagner's and Cosima's presence – without realising that this was no longer necessary.

What soon became clear to her, however, was that this striking 21-year-old woman with a Baltic accent and the remarkable gift of being able to waggle her ears separately, had pushed her into the background, leaving her merely as the spinsterish sister of a sick deserter from the Wagnerian cause. The last straw was when Lou engaged in a brief flirtation in a railway carriage with Elisabeth's future husband, Bernhard Förster. The two rivals came face to face with each other in Jena in the house of Clara Gelzer, Nietzsche's one-time dinner partner in Basel, to whom he had told his dream of eating a toad. When Elisabeth accused Lou of having dragged her brother's reputation through the mire, Lou retorted by referring to his proposal for a *ménage à trois* with Rée – whereupon Elisabeth vomited. Moreover, Lou went on, it was not she who had made advances to the noble philosopher but the other way round – and his intentions had been far from honourable.

The feud cunningly fuelled by Elisabeth did not have the desired effect on Nietzsche. Instead of breaking with Lou, he embarked on an intensive three-week study of the philosophy of the Enlightenment, in which she increasingly assumed the role of interlocutor – 'without interference from troublesome outsiders', she added, with Elisabeth in mind.[23]

Unfortunately Nietzsche too was acting out a role. For three weeks Lou had an opportunity to experience his exceptional power as a teacher, as well as to discover the profound compatibility of their natures – including their shared occult skill in summoning up spirits from the dead – and absorb the essence of his personality. For Nietzsche it brought a miraculous release – 'he suddenly found himself able to converse for ten hours a day'.[24] But whereas Lou was turning herself into the image of her new teacher, he was turning into her old teacher – except that Nietzsche was no Gillot and had had no experience of women, did not sit her on his knee but behaved rather like an embarrassed schoolboy. The power of sexuality, which would have plunged the whole comedy into catastrophe, was not to be aroused.

Lou did her best – not by taking the initiative, as on the Monte Sacro, but by employing subtle psychological means. With the sensitivity of a skilful theatrical producer she penetrated his innermost soul and acted out in her imagination what she discovered there. 'It was inevitable', she wrote in her memoirs, 'that I should be fascinated by those matters that were not so often discussed between him and Rée. They aroused memories that took me back to the most intimate, most unforgettable experiences of my childhood.'[25]

Precisely because their relationship harked back to the old father-daughter constellation, the fascination that she felt forced her to turn away, to renounce him. It was a road that led to taboo. She had what Pfeiffer called a 'burning desire' to discover what thoughts were really on Nietzsche's mind, in particular 'those that impinged on the experiences of her earliest childhood'.[26] And she inevitably found what she was looking for. As she observed in Tautenburg, his search for knowledge was religious in character, because he saw it as 'an attempt to rescue and redeem himself from his agonising condition'. His halo concealed a fear. Lou continued to probe: 'As Christian mysticism, in its moment of highest ecstasy, acquires the quality of a religious sensuality, so ideal love can also revert to the sensual ... Human nature will take its revenge – a painful moment, the moment of false passion, of lost truth, of lost honesty of emotion. Is it this that alienates me from Nietzsche?'[27]

Lou's arguments are dishonest. The standard that she claimed for herself, the 'pure spirit' of her nun-like sexlessness, she sought to impose on everyone else as though it were the natural state of affairs, not an individual reaction to an emotional crisis. It was she who had sought Nietzsche's company, disposed of her rival Elisabeth, left Rée to languish in Stibbe, and finally led Nietzsche to 'those dizzy heights to which one climbs in one's loneliness in order to look into the depths below'.[28] She even expressed surprise if they found themselves in the abyss without noticing it. She was attracted like a timorous child to a secret, forbidden room, where she found what she was searching for.

But in Nietzsche's 'secret room', a 'dungeon of hidden nooks and crannies', as Lou called it, something quite different was lurking.[29] It may well have instilled fear in her, but not the fear of a Gillot-like onslaught on her chastity. Thirty years later, in her book on Freud – not in her memoirs – she revealed what she had discovered in this dungeon, namely a perverse torture chamber. 'To the extent that cruel people are also masochists, the whole situation also has a relevance to the question of bisexuality – a phenomenon of profound significance. The first person with whom I talked about the matter was

23. Nietzsche during his Basel period. He attached great value to sartorial elegance, a trait his friend Franz Overbeck described as 'one of the most dubious signs of his inner weakness'.

47. Portrait of Nietzsche in the last years of his life by the painter and sculptor Curt Stoeving, who also did a bronze bust and bronze relief of him. Nietzsche only lived to see the beginning of his fame.

Nietzsche – himself a sadomasochist. And I remember that afterwards we did not dare to look each other in the eye.'³⁰

Are we to believe that, carried away by his elation at discovering a kindred spirit, Nietzsche removed his mask in her presence? Or did the incorruptible Lou, not ignorant where the ways of men were concerned, tear it from his face? The term bisexual was not in common use at the time. In 1878 Darwin applied it to certain hereditary features of particular animals and plants. The idea that a female soul could inhabit a male body was advanced in the middle of the 1860s by one Karl Heinrich Ulrichs, a man who seems to have had a certain influence on Nietzsche. At the end of the century Freud discussed the whole problem of bisexuality with his close friend Wilhelm Fliess but their disagreement over the subject later caused them to part company.

It was only in the early years of the following century that Freud made an explicit connection between bisexuality and sadomasochism. In her article on 'Psychosexuality' published in 1917, Lou states that Freud was the first to link sadomasochism, with its dual active-passive nature, to the antithesis of male and female combined in bisexuality. The first of Freud's *Three Essays on Sexuality*, published in 1905, was originally to have been called 'Human Bisexuality'. But Lou maintained that a female student from Zurich and a sick ex-professor from Basel had lighted on the idea as early as the summer of 1882. Or was she only hinting at what she had uncovered behind Nietzsche's mask and was now, thanks to Freud, able to explain? Whatever the two discussed during their time in Tautenburg, they felt that they had broken a taboo. Lou was moving in the right direction.

A CRUEL QUIRK OF FATE

Was Nietzsche, lover of the classical ideal of beauty, really in love with Lou Salomé? His jealous sister wrote angrily to her friend Clara that he had fallen for her 'hook, line and sinker'.³¹ The Overbecks discovered a passion in him that they had not known before, and Ida Overbeck herself noted 'a state of ecstatic bliss' that this relationship had brought about in him.³² Peter Gast, for his part, remembered that his master was for a while 'totally bewitched by Lou, and the illusion about her to which he surrendered himself gave rise to the mood in which he wrote his *Zarathustra*'.³³ The madness that had already infected him in Tautenburg and that gradually, over a period of months, ate its way into his body, led his mother to say: 'Either my son will marry the girl, or he will go mad, or he will shoot himself.'³⁴

It did not begin as insanity. After Rée's invitation Nietzsche talked only in general terms about a 'lust for new souls'; and after his return from Sicily his most pressing urge, not by chance, was to get married. For it was not only because of the sirocco, as he had tried to tell his friends, that he had fled from Sicily. Sirocco was for him a broad concept. He called it his great 'enemy, also in the metaphorical sense', a force that invoked a sense of angst and paralysed his thoughts. After the affair with Lou was over and done with, she herself took over the role of this metaphorical enemy. 'I call Lou my sirocco incarnate', he wrote to Rée.[35] There was more to the name sirocco than a hot wind from the Sahara. It was something else that had caused his headaches there.

What had really driven him away from the 'isles of the blest' is intimated in the chapter of *Thus Spake Zarathustra* called 'Of Great Events'. Here the hero is discovered by sailors on an island 'where the smoking mountain stands'. To their amazement they recognise him as Zarathustra, the story goes on, in biblical tones, 'for they had lately seen him'. When he hears this, he considers it must have been his shadow, and concludes: 'I must keep him closer to me, so that he does not ruin my reputation.'[36] Later Zarathustra tells his readers that this shadow is a wanderer who had paid a visit to a brothel somewhere in the Orient.

The only shadow that could have been cast over Nietzsche's Arcadia in Sicily was the fear of being discovered. Hence his tentative enquiry of Gast as to whether Wagner and Cosima were still in Palermo. Nietzsche was anxious to uphold his reputation. The thought that someone might have seen him on his lonely expeditions – especially if they had not been all that lonely – was enough to make him ill. Whether or not he had been recognised, like Zarathustra, and had caused 'great amazement', it was his shadow, his dark, hidden side, that was fated to roam the earth. The moment he had the feeling in Sicily that his anonymity had been betrayed, he packed his bags.

What was more natural than to hasten to join Rée and 'the Russian woman' in Rome, so as to prove to the world by getting married that this shadow was not the real Nietzsche? He arrived in the high spirits of a bridegroom whose wedding bed had already been prepared for him by his best man. After being turned down by Lou, he wrote to Rée: 'I thought you had persuaded her to come to my aid.'[37] But he was beginning to have his doubts. Somehow Rée seemed to have changed. Had his bosom friend now become his rival? But then, it was he who had suggested that Nietzsche should come to Rome. To be on the safe side he made it clear to Lou that he did not see himself as Rée's rival, for it had to be clear to her, as he wrote to Ida Overbeck, that Rée was not part of the competition. He, Nietzsche, could not love a woman, let alone become a worthy husband. And he wanted to remind Rée of the situation: 'Is there any more wonderful form of friendship than that between the two of us, my good Rée?'[38]

The same day he wrote a letter to Lou, which was more explicit. 'Rée', he wrote, with feigned generosity, 'is in every respect a better *friend* than I am or can ever be. Take good heed of this difference!'[39] Four days later we find him elaborating on this little difference to her in confidence: 'I want to explain to you personally about friends in general and in particular about our friend Rée. I know very well what I am saying when I call him a better friend than I am or ever could be.'[40] And to Malwida he confided – inviting her to pass the confidence on – that Rée found the idea of human procreation impossible to bear. 'He cannot bring himself to swell the numbers of the unhappy masses.'[41]

Nietzsche, like Rée, wanted to kill two birds with one stone – to show himself to be a more virile suitor than the listless Rée, and at the same time to avoid giving the embarrassing impression of stealing his friend's girl. 'He was convinced that Rée was not a proper man', wrote Werner Ross, and wanted once and for all to make it clear to himself and the world that he was different – a gentleman of the old school.[42] The idea of marriage, which would remove any fear of being unmasked, led to a desire to make a new beginning. In Lou he found a soul who legitimised, stimulated and entertained him and who was desperately anxious to conceal that side of the female psyche which repelled him. She was not interested in sexual love. In her severe black habit she almost gave the impression of being a young man, with a young man's view of the world, 'fighting her way through life with the weapons a man would use'.[43] The poet Rilke, who later became her lover, called her 'a female youth'.

'The truth is', wrote Nietzsche to Overbeck, 'that in the manner in which I intend to act in this situation, I am utterly dominated by my thoughts, my innermost thoughts. It is a prospect that fills me with the same delight as the memory of my stay in Genoa, when I also lived out my thoughts.'[44]

Such is my intention, says the new Columbus, importuning Lou with the words: 'What I had ceased to believe, namely that I would encounter a friend with whom I could share my ultimate joys and sorrows, now seems possible – a golden glow on the horizon of the life that is left to me.' The new friend is at once subjected to a process of idealisation in which she is made to don the masks of his desires. 'Lou is as sharp-witted as an eagle and as bold as a lion, yet in the last analysis a very child-like creature who may not have long to live.'[45]

A premonition of death completed the vision that returned to haunt him from the time of his own childhood. A poem of Lou's, he wrote excitedly to Gast, 'sounded like a voice I had been waiting to hear since I was a child'. The old song re-awakened him. What he had longed for as a boy now seemed about to be fulfilled, albeit with substantial modifications. For the person he called a 'child-like creature who may not have long to live' was in reality a pert, confident, emancipated young woman who had long been making him dance to her tune.

He sensed as much. Already at the time of his initial infatuation, when he made Rée aware of the real situation and thereby scared Lou off, the fear that he thought had left him since his time in Rome returned. His reputation was again at stake. A *ménage à trois* with an unmarried young woman who was spreading hints of moral depravity ... The immoralist cast one eye in the direction of morality, explaining to Lou that he was one who valued 'the seclusion of life' and sincerely hoped 'that we could avoid becoming the subject of gossip all over Europe'. He would do everything, he said, to avoid this. Marriage would be a first step. At the same time he declares that his days of wandering through Italy are over: 'I shall draw a line under this stage of my past, no longer live in isolation but learn how to be a human being again.'[46]

He also sent the news to his doctor in Frankfurt, Otto Eiser, the man who had leaked the contents of his medical file to Wagner and initiated the scandal that was still going the rounds in Bayreuth. Inspired by the sense of his impending happiness, he described himself as 'fully recovered — is that not strange and incredible?' He also offered to pass over more information, if Eiser was interested.[47] He was not. Moreover Nietzsche was refused a rendezvous with the doctor on the grounds that such a meeting 'would only upset me and provoke further bouts of insomnia and the like'.[48]

It was a prophetic remark. When Nietzsche finally realised that Lou had left him and gone back to Rée, and that the episode in Tautenburg was only the prelude to her final break with him, his suffering returned — his two friends lost with one fell swoop, at odds with his family, vilified by his friends, a social outcast. In November he hurriedly returned to an icy Liguria, despite realising that 'a lonely existence in Genoa brought certain dangers with it'.[49]

Scarcely had he arrived there than his self-torment began. A bad dream threatened to suffocate him. Worst of all, however, were his fears for his reputation. Had Rée already given the game away? What rumours were circulating that summer in Bayreuth, where the festival audience had assembled for *Parsifal?* What had Lou told them? He waxed indignant that Lou 'had blackened his whole character', while his relatives and the people back in Basel were suspecting him of being a man with evil intentions 'who was not above resorting to underhand methods'. He could not banish from his mind all the disparaging accusations that Lou, as he believed, was continuing to spread. 'What a cruel stroke of fate!' he cried.

It was indeed a cruel irony. In order to save his reputation he had fled into the arms of the very woman who was now ruining it, even if predominantly only in his imagination, by propagating allegations that he would have laughed at, had they not made him weep. It had been his final attempt to justify himself before the world. His reward was to find himself haunted by paranoia. Was this his demon taking its revenge? Nietzsche saw red. He threatened a duel with Rée and wrote to Georg Rée calling his brother 'a creeping, slandering and lying creature'. About Lou he wrote that she was 'a thin, dirty, bad-smelling monkey with false breasts'.[50]

The winter of 1882 found Nietzsche shivering in Genoa. Attacks of migraine and rage followed one after the other. Once again he made the familiar self-diagnosis: 'I was made to suffer enduring torments and to be burned to death over a slow flame.'[51]

At that same moment the two terrifying spectres of his sleepless nights, Rée and Lou, were taking rooms in a pension in Berlin – one room each, with a third in which to meet. For Lou her 'little brother' was 'a dark, handsome figure with blue eyes and a soft mouth, seemingly weary of life',[52] exuding an ethereal quality. For him his 'little sister' was the incarnation of his own higher self, the ideal to which, as Nietzsche cuttingly observed, he had made himself 'subservient'.[53] But their symbiosis lasted only as long as it took for the next father figure to appear on the scene.

This was Friedrich Carl Andreas, a scholar fifteen years older than Lou, whose beard and cape gave him the appearance of a monk. With his severe features, and wearing a black cassock, he at once drew her into his orbit and compelled her to follow him. Later she wrote of the 'irresistible power and sense of inevitability' that had seized her and dragged her along with it.[54] It was the same spell as her father had exercised over her.

For this reason the sense of fascination stopped at the waist. She felt no trace of erotic attraction. 'My emotional responses were totally different from those of a woman', she recalled. So deeply ingrained was her fear of father-sex that on one occasion, when Andreas tried to take her while she was asleep, she almost throttled him and was only awakened by his terrified gasps. Chastity was an unshakeable principle of her marriage to him. Before the wedding in June 1887 Rée, now a superfluous presence, left the couple, became a doctor in a poor urban community and some years later threw himself off a mountain in the Engadine. In 1917 Lou found herself wishing that he were still alive. 'Only now', she reminisced, 'can I see properly who he was, caught in the pathological grip that dominated his whole life but which at the time I did not understand.'[55]

Not until years after her sterile marriage to Andreas did Lou experience her sexual dawning – mostly with men considerably younger than herself, who were afterwards tactless enough to describe their encounters, calling her 'passionate, spontaneous, unrestrained'.[56] 'With an expression of blissful happiness on her face she now confessed: "My greatest pleasure in life is to receive a man's sperm!" She had an insatiable appetite.' With her desires awakened only late in life, she wanted to experience her liberation over and over again, riding roughshod over any family relationships or existing love affairs. People described her as 'a vampire and a child at one and the same time'.

A subtle interpretation of Lou's personality was given by the Swedish psychiatrist Poul Bjerre, who introduced her to Freud in 1911. Bjerre was married and fifteen years younger, but from the moment he set eyes on her, as her biographer wrote, he was 'utterly bewitched' by the fifty-year-old Lou:

> She had the ability to immerse herself in the thought processes of other people, especially someone she loved. It was as though her powers of concentration kindled the intellectual fire burning in the mind of her lovers ... She had an unusually strong will, combined with a special pleasure in triumphing over men. She could herself also be aroused but only for short periods and with a strangely cool intensity. She undeniably broke up marriages and destroyed people's lives ... but she could never surrender herself body and soul, even in the most impassioned of embraces, even though she was not herself frigid. She yearned to be freed from her strong personality but never was – in a profound sense Lou represented unredeemed womanhood.[57]

FREUD'S DEFENSIVE BATTLE

When, at the Congress of the International Psychoanalytical Society in Weimar in 1911, Sigmund Freud was introduced to Lou Andreas-Salomé, who had in the meantime become well known for her book on Nietzsche, they both felt the looming presence of Elisabeth, spiteful custodian of the Nietzsche Archive, in the background. But they also realised how dangerously close the philosopher's psychological findings were to those of psychoanalysis – dangerous, because there was a conspiracy of silence about the originator of these discoveries. Freud, presiding over his flock of disciples, had never been quite at his ease in the company of the mad philosopher and destroyer of moral values. Nietzsche's concept of the Superman could be used to bolster the claims of militant neo-Teutonism, while his psychology of 'de-masking' had laid the foundations for the process of the 'unveiling of the soul'.

But Freud did not like having precursors. Fearful of finding too much of himself reflected in Nietzsche's works, he kept postponing the reading of his works, as he himself admitted, until he had finally put them almost entirely out of his mind. As far as the repression of unwelcome thoughts was concerned, Freud would tolerate no other gods but himself.

Almost everything that is today associated with the name of Sigmund Freud can be found in the writings of Friedrich Nietzsche, if only one knows where to look. 'The content of our conscience', wrote Nietzsche, 'is everything that was regularly and unquestioningly demanded of us in the years of our childhood ... The source of conscience is a belief in authority.'[58] Religion, according to Nietzsche, emerged from what Freud was later to call the superego. One acknowledges a certain guilt *vis à vis* one's ancestors, 'which steadily grows in the same measure as these ancestors continue to exist as powerful spirits'.[59] 'Fear of one's ancestors and their power increases in proportion as the power of the race itself increases', until finally these ancestors are transfigured into gods. The collected wisdom of a plant from the graveyard. The observation that psychological illnesses can be caused by a trauma in childhood was made by Nietzsche in 1884 when he referred to the 'wave effect', which can often manifest itself throughout the whole of one's life, having once been triggered by a nervous shock when a child.

Nietzsche was also aware of the distinction between the conscious and the unconscious, between the mask and the urge that the mask conceals. 'The decisive value of an act lies precisely in its non-intentional quality – all that can be seen and known about it only belongs to its surface.'[60] He discovered, too, the power of repression, used by consciousness as a defence mechanism against the force of unconscious tendencies: 'Forgetfulness is no mere passive quality, the product of lassitude, but a positive power of holding back, of inhibiting, a guarantor of the preservation of spiritual order.'[61] One can only understand the artist, the scientist and the priest if one has recognised what urges they have sublimated. Nietzsche even discovered the opposition raised against any kind of psychological investigation. 'Psychoanalysis', he wrote, 'has to struggle with unconscious resistances in the heart of the individual analyst.'[62]

Freud, who only began his work after Nietzsche had bade farewell to the world of sanity and reason, soon found that he had to overcome a certain unconscious resistance to Nietzsche. He had already come across his ideas as a student – a fact he concealed – and in the year of Nietzsche's death he wrote to his friend Wilhelm Fliess that he had acquired copies of the philosopher's works, 'hoping to find in them the words for a number of things that I have been hitherto unable to express. But I have not opened them yet.'[63] Several decades later, in an article on the history of the International Psychoanalytical Society, he explained that he had 'deliberately refrained from the pleasure of reading Nietzsche because I did not want to be hindered in my assessment of psychoanalytical impressions by any expectations from other quarters'. Freud reinterprets his repression as the conscious denial of pleasure. He was prepared, he said, to give up any claim to priority in cases where 'laborious psychoanalytical research can only serve to confirm the philosopher's intuitive insights' but at the same time he disparaged Nietzsche's casual and 'playful' approach, contrasting it with his own meticulous research, systematically and scientifically conducted.[64]

Freud did not extend to others who had drawn on Nietzsche the same tolerance as he allowed himself. When he adopted the concept of the Id, which he had found in an essay by Georg Groddeck, he went out of his way to assert in a footnote that Groddeck must have been following Nietzsche, in whose works he maintains the term is commonly found.[65] Commonly? Hardly. It would be like looking for a needle in a haystack.

It was not only the fear that someone else might steal his thunder that made Freud reluctant to talk about the subject. For their meetings in April and October 1908 Freud's Wednesday Circle had chosen Nietzsche as their subject for discussion. Freud himself categorically stated that 'Nietzsche's ideas had had not the slightest influence on his own work.'[66] Then, after a number of aspects of Nietzsche had been discussed, including his latent sadism, his repressed homosexuality and his father-complex, a certain Paul Federn suddenly leapt to his feet. He said that, 'from a trustworthy source he could report that Nietzsche lived, periodically, the life of a homosexual and that he had contracted his syphilis in a homosexual brothel in Genoa'.[67]

Measured by the veneration in which Nietzsche was held at the time, this came close to blasphemy. So as not to bring down more 'Aryan' hatred on the heads of what were commonly branded the 'Jewish-dominated' Freudians, the subject was quickly brushed under the carpet. Biographers and interpreters maintained a stony silence. They would have been well advised to consult the original sources.

One such was Joseph Paneth, a keen member of the Viennese circle of Nietzsche admirers, in which Jews played a significant role. A natural scientist by training, Paneth made Nietzsche's acquaintance in Nice in December 1883, and the two men kept in touch with each other over the following year. The year after that, by which time Paneth had long returned to Vienna, Nietzsche referred to him as 'one of my greatest worshippers and admirers'.[68] Paneth had offered to provide him with the latest news from Vienna – background information about other devotees and similar items of gossip – which he did with indefatigable zeal. At the same time he reported back to Vienna, hot from the press, what he knew about Nietzsche's activities. He became a lecturer in physiology at the University of Vienna and died of tuberculosis in

1890 at the age of thirty-four. Long after he had been forgotten, his name cropped up in a letter from Freud to the writer Arnold Zweig in 1934, in which he wrote: 'A friend of mine, Dr Paneth, met Nietzsche in the Engadine and told me a great deal about him.' Paneth, it appears, was at pains to arouse Freud's interest in Nietzsche, from whom he had hitherto kept his distance on account of the philosopher's 'aloofness and inaccessibility'.[69]

Paneth appears in a negative light in Freud's *Interpretation of Dreams,* published in 1899, where Freud tells of a dream in which he 'slew P. with a single glance'.[70] Paneth's widow took this as a slander on her late husband's name and would have nothing more to do with Freud. When another follower also withdrew his friendship and support, Freud could not help being reminded of Nietzsche. For in 1912 C. G. Jung surprised his former teacher by sending him a letter in which he declared a formal disagreement with Freud's methods, which led to Jung's break with the Psychoanalytical Society. 'I will leave Zarathustra to speak on my behalf', wrote Jung, who knew exactly where to find his master's Achilles' heel. 'It is a poor compliment to a teacher if one remains nothing but his pupil for the rest of one's life.'[71]

A similar case involving Nietzsche was that of Otto Rank, director of the Psychoanalytical Society's publishing house. In his book *The Trauma of Birth,* published in 1924, Rank not only rejected Freud's dogmas but also cast doubt on his exclusive right to be seen as the father of the new discipline. Nietzsche, said Rank, had already identified the phenomenon of sexual repression, had anticipated Freud's 'neurotic trauma' and given 'a psychological analysis of Socrates of unsurpassed clarity and perception'.[72]

Rank presented Freud on his seventieth birthday with a specially printed edition of Nietzsche's works, causing Freud to complain about the waste of gold used in the lettering. But this did not prevent Rank's eventual expulsion from the Society. 'It was', wrote Paul Roazen, author of a biography of the master, 'as though Rank wanted to say with his present: You accused me of taking ideas from you – now just look what you took from Nietzsche.'[73]

In December 1930 Arnold Zweig hailed the father of psychoanalysis as 'the man who completed Nietzsche'.[74] 'Psychological analysis has overturned all values', he wrote, clearly alluding to Nietzsche's 'revaluation of all values', and Freud has 'traced the concept of the Will to Power back to its origin'. Carried away by his discoveries of the bridges that link Freud to Nietzsche, Zweig encourages Freud to write about these little-known bridges. But Freud has long since burnt them. Somewhat tetchily he also requests Zweig not to publish anything on the subject 'until I am no longer alive'.[75]

Four years later Zweig told Freud that he was planning to write a novel on Nietzsche's madness and asked whether he was willing to help him – in particular he wanted to get into contact with Lou Andreas-Salomé. But as in 1930, Zweig met with a rebuff. 'No letter I received on my seventy-eighth birthday occupied my mind as much as yours', replied Freud, making it clear that he had taken an instinctive dislike to Zweig's proposal and stating some of his reasons. 'Maybe part of my objection,' he concluded, 'lies in the way you wish to portray the relationship between him and me.'[76]

Lou's rejection of Zweig's plan, conveyed in a letter to Freud, has a neurotic shrillness about it. 'The idea of any involvement on my part is totally and utterly unthinkable', she wrote. 'It is a subject I refuse to consider and I reject the idea in horror. How right you are to try and dissuade Zweig from carrying it out.'[77]

But Zweig would not give up. He felt – maybe he even knew – that Freud was more deeply involved in the subject than he was prepared to admit. In July 1934, five years before Freud's death, Zweig finally succeeded in persuading him to admit the truth – the truth being that, as far as the question of Nietzsche was concerned, he had no intention of revealing the truth. 'In front of the entrance to the Nietzsche problem,' wrote Freud to Zweig, 'there stand two sentries barring the way. Firstly, one cannot investigate a person unless one is aware of his sexual constitution, and Nietzsche's is a complete enigma. There is even a legend that he was a passive homosexual and contracted syphilis in a homosexual brothel in Genoa. Is that true? Quién sabe? [*sic*] Secondly, he was suffering from a serious illness which eventually led to his complete paralysis. Everyone has his conflicts. But when one is paralysed, aetiological problems recede into the background. Ought a novelist to be allowed to speculate about the causes of a pathological condition?'[78]

The two sentries are guarding the path that leads to Nietzsche because Freud has put them there. Clearly it is not permissible to fantasise or make amateur diagnoses of the causes of genuine mental illness. But Zweig had no intention of doing such a thing. Freud's first argument sounds as though a doctor would say to a patient: I am afraid I cannot offer any diagnosis because I cannot identify your sickness. Was it not precisely at those points where the defence mechanisms of the unconscious, including his own, tried to prevent him, that Freud's diagnostic work began? That a patient's 'sexual condition' was unclear would only have been a further reason to investigate it. And why did Freud dig up Federn's old assertion of Nietzsche's homosexuality, which he added was 'passive', and call it a 'legend'?

But Freud's letter can be read differently. Perhaps the sentries are there to prevent not the discovery of the truth but its dissemination. They represent the forces of opposition that block the path to the truth – and Freud knew what these forces were. His warning that one cannot investigate a person whose sexual proclivities are unknown is not a confession of ignorance or of helplessness – which is the way it has been read – but an admonition to the outsider: Herr Zweig, because you know nothing about his sexuality, you cannot portray him in a work of fiction. And as a shot across the bows of those steering unwittingly towards a minefield, Freud invokes the syphilis 'legend' – which should be enough to put an enthusiastic novelist off for good.

Yet Zweig, who was never to write his Nietzsche novel, could have been helped by this letter to find the right track to follow. In 1924 Freud turned his attention to the taboo subject of sadomasochism. At the very beginning of his essay 'The Economic Problem of Masochism' he advances the two key concepts that underlie his letter to Zweig. 'One is entitled', he writes, 'to describe the existence of the masochistic urge in man's sexual life as economically enigmatic.'[79] This is precisely what it has in common with Nietzsche's 'sexual proclivities' – they too are enigmatic. Two sentences later Freud states the second of these concepts: 'If pain and absence of desire are no longer warnings but aims in themselves, the pleasure principle is stifled – the sentry who guards our spiritual life is, so to speak, anaesthetised.' As the sentry guards the entrance to Nietzsche's 'enigmatic', i.e. masochistic, sexual constitution, so guarding every man's spiritual life is the pleasure principle.

Freud uses a concept of Nietzsche's to explain why this is so. In every living creature the libido encounters its opponent, the 'death' or 'destructive' urge.[80] In its struggle to render this opponent 'harmless', the libido directs it outwards, turning it into an urge to destruction, a 'Will to Power' – Nietzsche's basic concept here interpreted by Freud as the death urge directed at the outside world. The part of this urge, continues Freud, that directly serves the sexual function is the actual sadism; the other part, bound to the libido, which remains within the organism, becomes 'erogenous masochism'. The Will to Power, which rages inwardly against itself because it is denied expression in the outside world, was one of Nietzsche's fundamental concepts. In his *Genealogy of Morals* he maintains that the origin of the individual's pangs of conscience lies in the fact that 'all the free and natural instincts of the human being have been turned inwards and directed against the human being himself. Hostility, cruelty, pleasure in destruction – when all such instincts are turned inwards and directed against the individual himself, then he will become aware of experiencing a so-called "guilty conscience" '.[81]

Part of the enigma that was Nietzsche also involves the 'legend' of his homosexuality – launched not by Federn but by Freud. Freud knew as well as Federn that Nietzsche was homosexual, yet he chose to state in his letter to Zweig that it was only a legend. If Zweig had been familiar with the minutes of the meetings of the Psychoanalytical Society in Vienna – which, ironically,

Freud handed over to Federn – his veneration of the patriarch of psycho-analysis would have suffered a severe blow. In 1908 he made a few notes on Nietzsche which would have formed the basis of his novel. The two sentries had not yet taken up their posts and Freud was not yet suffering from the pathological fear that his unique position would be challenged.

Speaking to the Wednesday Circle, Freud said that in his autobiographical *Ecce homo* Nietzsche had killed his father a second time, recalling 'echoes from his childhood'. Also, Freud continued, 'in puberty he had carried in his mind a Christ fantasy' and later, as a consequence of his paralysis, had indulged in introspection.[82] Freud then proceeded to offer a solution to the enigma of Nietzsche's life, proving that he had an intimate understanding of his predecessor's life and work that contradicted his alleged ignorance of any such knowledge. Was it because of his own latent homosexuality that he denied any familiarity with the subject outside the privacy of the Circle?

In October 1908 Freud delivered his considered judgement. 'Totally cut off from the world by his illness,' he said,

> Nietzsche directed his attention to the only object of research left to him, one which in any case particularly concerned him as a homosexual, namely his own Ego. With great acumen he began to unravel the layers of his personality one by one, making a series of striking discoveries about himself. But then came his illness. Not content with establishing these relationships, he projected the knowledge he had gained about himself on to the outside world. The educational and pastoral urges implanted in him by the Christ-ideal serve to strengthen his psychological insights ... This extraordinary achievement of identifying his urges through each successive layer of his personality was made possible by the process of disintegration induced by his paralysis.[83]

What Freud had to say about Nietzsche's discovery of the inner self is equally applicable to Freud's own work. Had it not been for his ability to recognise the successive layers of the ego, Freud would never have arrived at the theory of psychoanalysis. The only difference is that Nietzsche's illness led him to project on to others what he had discovered in the depths of his own soul, and to use psychological insights to illuminate the course of human history. How closely Nietzsche's findings were connected with his sexuality is hinted at in Freud's concluding remark that the whole tenor of *Ecce homo* 'calls out for a chapter headed "On My Sexuality". Maybe Nietzsche even wrote such a chapter'.[84]

'¿Quién sabe?' Who knows? Freud had asked. It is at least true that Freud also was accused of applying his psychological discoveries to historical, even teleological complexes. The best-known example of this is his *Totem and Taboo*, in which he portrays the Oedipus complex as a kind of 'big bang' in the evolution of mankind. For Freud, as for the sick philosopher himself, Nietzsche was the new Oedipus. He had slain his father – twice – and through this and a number of other 'monstrous, unnatural acts' solved the riddle of the Sphinx. Nietzsche-Oedipus had looked into the fearful blackness of the abyss in which he saw what his intellectual successor saw – patricide and the 'unnatural atrocities' of prehistoric times.[85] The power that will offer healing from this unbearable prospect, Nietzsche had preached, is art. Only in tragedy can the terrifying Oedipus situation be resolved and the mortal god, the accursed Oedipus – Nietzsche himself, slayer of the god – celebrate his resurrection, when a radiant deity will descend on the pain-racked sufferer and touch him with his magic presence. The fusion of the two gods will bring liberation from guilt. As Freud also knew, the Oedipus complex can only be resolved by a liberated sexuality.

Freud had read his Nietzsche closely. A few years after his address to the Wednesday Circle he invoked in *Totem and Taboo* Nietzsche's tragic Oedipal vision of the god who is redeemed by his suffering. Rejected by the scientific community, Freud's book reads like a psychoanalytical interpretation of Nietzsche's childhood. It begins with his father's death, which the boy feels guilty about because behind his apparent tender affection for his father lurked in fact hostility. The demon who pursued him from then on was in reality his father's avenging ghost. In order to banish his recurrent nightmare and at the same time relieve his guilty conscience, he seeks an animal that can take his father's place and be worshipped in his stead – like a squirrel, for example, that one can make into a king. As Nietzsche re-encountered the horrors of his private drama, first in *Hamlet*, then in Greek tragedy, so Freud rediscovered the neurotic suffering of the young in the adolescence of mankind.

Freud's 'primeval hordes' – which, in the opinion of those who should know, never existed in the form he posited – bear a remarkable resemblance to Nietzsche's chorus of satyrs, which similarly existed only in the imagination of their creator. For Freud these hordes consisted of sons who want to have their mother but cannot, because their father is standing in front of her and lying on her. They love him and hate him at the same time, because he is stronger than they are. But their hatred is also stronger than they, and even than he. So they kill him, devour him and suddenly feel a pain in their stomach – a bad conscience, remorse, guilt. This is what keeps them together. They re-cast the dead father as an immortal god, and in order to appease his lust for vengeance, they renounce the possession of the woman

– or women – for whose sake they had killed him. The taboo incest, in other words.

There was one more benefit of being kept together, which also confirms the resemblance between Freud's 'primeval hordes' and Nietzsche's chorus of satyrs. In Freud's words: 'They thereby preserved the organisation which had made them strong and which rested on homosexual emotions and activities.'[86]

At the end of his essay on the origins of the guilty conscience and the genealogy of morals Freud finally accords his forerunner the honour due to him by quoting at the climax of his argument from *The Birth of Tragedy*, albeit without mentioning the work by name – out of respect for the taboo. There was a moment in the history of the culture of classical Greece, the oldest Greek tragedy, wrote Freud – as though he had just discovered it – which was not merely a theatrical experience but the depiction of a historical event. 'A group of characters, assembled under the same name and wearing the same robes, surrounds a single figure on whose words and actions they all depend – the chorus and the hero, who was originally the one and only character, the character forced to suffer for having shouldered the burden of tragic guilt.'[87]

Then Freud poses the question of all questions, to which he gives his own succinct and, he hopes, convincing reply: 'Why must the tragic hero suffer? And what is meant by his "tragic" guilt? Let us cut the discussion short and offer a speedy answer. He has to suffer because he is the originator, the hero, of that grand primeval tragedy which is here being didactically re-enacted, and the tragic guilt is that which he is forced to bear in order to relieve the chorus of its guilt.'[88]

The 'cutting short' that Freud proposes is his way of forestalling the comments of his listeners, who are already preparing to ask a counter-question: Is this not to be found already in Nietzsche? Not quite in this form, but something similar. In Freud's interpretation, the hero is not only the murderer who has to expiate his crime but also the victim who is slain by the hero. The 'primeval father' and the hero become one. And as at the same time the chorus merges with the hero, so the reconciliation between father and son follows, and the 'primeval hordes', here called the chorus of satyrs, have their guilt lifted from them. By carrying Nietzsche's train of thought further, Freud evolved a special kind of Oedipus complex. When his pupils presented him with a commemorative medallion bearing an effigy of Oedipus solving the riddle of the Sphinx, Freud went pale. The image of Nietzsche-Oedipus would not go away.

Freud, who had repressed the inclinations of his 'primeval hordes' in favour of patriarchal status, could not but have been shocked when Federn opened his eyes to Nietzsche's satyric nature. But he appears to have trusted Federn's source. Did he perhaps know it himself? Did he hear it from Paneth, who had met Nietzsche on the Riviera? When Paneth died in 1890, Federn was only nineteen. Could Paul Rée have tried to get his own back on his faithless friend by spreading stories in Vienna or Berlin? There was no lack of people prepared to listen.

One such was Federn's elder brother Karl, who studied in Vienna, a Nietzschean stronghold, in the 1880s and made a name for himself at the turn of the century through his own work on Nietzsche. It was Karl Federn who in 1903 brought the philosopher to the attention of Isadora Duncan, the dancer who set out to revive the dance of classical antiquity touring the concert halls of Europe dressed in a flowing tunic and sandals and attended by a troupe of Greek youths. Through her attraction to the naked human body she found in Nietzsche a kindred spirit, the spirit of Zarathustra.

'Among the artists and writers who frequented our house', wrote Isadora Duncan in her memoirs, 'was a young man with a high forehead, piercing eyes behind glasses, who decided it was his mission to reveal to me the genius of Nietzsche. Only by Nietzsche, he said, will you come to the full revelation of dancing expression as you seek it. He came each afternoon and read me "Zarathustra" in German, explaining to me all the words and phrases that I could not understand.'[89] Federn had to translate some of the most important passages for her into English, including the 'Dance Song', in which Zarathustra has first to discipline his Cupid before he can sing of love and let Cupid dance with the maidens.

Isadora's enthusiasm for Nietzsche even brought her into conflict with the rulers of Bayreuth. Cosima had invited her to choreograph the Venusberg bacchanal in the 1904 production of *Tannhäuser*. They immediately found that their philosophies were poles apart. 'My soul was like a battlefield', Isadora later wrote in her memoirs, 'where Apollo, Dionysus, Christ, Nietzsche and Richard Wagner disputed the ground.' When she herself wanted to appear scantily dressed on the hallowed boards of the Festspielhaus, the antithesis Nietzsche versus Wagner – that is to say, 'naturalness versus hypocrisy' – reached a climax: 'In the first performance of "Tannhäuser" my transparent tunic, showing every part of my dancing body, had created some stir amidst the pink-covered legs of the Ballet and at the last moment even poor Frau Cosima lost her courage. She sent one of her daughters to my loge, with a long white chemise, which she begged me to wear under the filmy scarf which served me for a costume. But I was adamant. ... So here I was, a perfect pagan to all, fighting the Philistines.'[90]

A victory on points for Zarathustra.

THE ARTIFICIAL PARADISE

Rapallo, the Italian seaport in the province of Genoa, is remembered today as the place where the Russo-German Treaty of 1922 was signed. The name most readily associated with the ratification of that treaty is Walther Rathenau, the German foreign minister. If Nietzsche could have had his way, it would be his name that is linked with the town. For here, in the Albergo della Posta, close to the sea and at the foot of Monte Allegro, where he had shivered in his room in spite of having a stove, and where he had 'never eaten so badly', he wrote the first part of his central work, *Thus Spake Zarathustra*.[91]

The work formed in his mind as he 'wandered through the pine forests and gazed out over the sea', he later wrote. 'Suddenly I pictured in my mind the whole of the first part, above all the figure of Zarathustra himself, as a type – or, more accurately, he *suddenly overcame me*.'[92] The world that he, like Columbus, had set out to discover stretched 'from Portofino to Zoagli', he wrote to Peter Gast in Leipzig, 'and I live in the middle, in Rapallo, but my daily walks take me to the frontiers of my kingdom'.[93] He also paid a daily visit to the little town of Santa Margherita nearby, where, from the beginning of December 1882 to the end of February 1883, he collected his letters from the poste restante.

December found him sitting in the Albergo della Posta taking opium. 'My fits are gnawing away at my constitution', he wrote. 'An agonising self-pity, an agonising sense of disappointment, an agonising feeling of injured pride – how am I to endure it?' Answer: 'This evening I am going to take so much opium that I shall lose my senses.'[94]

This confession comes in the draft of a letter to his ex-friends Lou and Rée. He appears to have made his resolution during lonely walks and while sitting at night in his freezing room. 'Do not worry yourselves too much about these outbursts of paranoia and offended vanity', he went on, describing himself as 'one half-ripe for the mental asylum, left in a total state of confusion by his unbroken loneliness'. That was the way they talked about him – he could just hear them, revelling in their mocking laughter. 'I came to this conclusion – a perfectly rational one, as I see it – after taking a huge dose of opium *out of sheer despair*.'[95]

When, having regained his equanimity, he came to make a fair copy of this letter, he laid the emphasis, not on his 'sheer despair' but on his 'perfectly rational' conclusion, and with this alteration he sent the letter off. Shortly afterwards he wrote again, commenting on his previous missive. 'I am far from being mad,' he assured them, 'nor do I suffer from paranoia. Please do not confuse my powers of reason with the nonsense I wrote in my recent opium letter.'[96] He was prepared to take back the inanities he had written – but not the fact that he was taking opium.

He was using the drug as a threat – a substantial dose not only robs one of one's faculties of reason but has the power to kill. Did he hope to give Lou and Rée a guilty conscience? Maybe he never actually took the drug at all but merely wanted to cast himself as a 'demonic Manfred-figure', as Werner Ross surmised, and to use the letter as a work of fiction.[97] Perhaps the suicide threat was fiction – the opium certainly was not.

When he sat in his little room in Rapallo taking his large dose of opium, he was already well acquainted with the mysteries of mind-extending drugs and heightened awareness. After his riding accident in 1868 he had taken opium every evening,[98] and two years later, after his brief period as a medical orderly during the Franco-Prussian War, he was also given opium and tannin clysters. In 1877 a doctor in Naples had prescribed narceine,[99] a derivate of opium, for his migraine, while in one of his notebooks there is a mention of diacodium,[100] which also contains opium. In his poem 'The Mysterious Barque' he speaks of the 'poppy' that induces a deep sleep, while in another poem, also from the 'Poems of Prince Free-as-a-Bird', he beseeches his fever 'to pour the poison of the poppy into his mind'.[101] After he had become insane, reported his sister, 'he often told our mother secretly that he had taken twenty drops – he did not say of what – whereupon the spirit had borne him away'.[102]

It goes against the grain to believe such claims of Elisabeth but a note from his mother, who copied down his babblings in 1895, seems to confirm it. 'Schoolboys good people', he jabbered, '– loved the officials'. Finally, overheard by the maid Alwine, whom he must have also loved, he said: 'Opium.'[103] It was one of his more pleasant memories.

The effects of taking opium were set out in 1821 by Thomas de Quincey in his *Confessions of an English Opium-Eater*. De Quincey describes the drug as a revelation. Awareness of time and place changes, past becomes present, dreams become real and reality becomes dream-like. The insight that opium offers to man divides history into two halves and not only makes a person 'high' but removes all boundaries, affording a glimpse of eternity.

De Quincey did not take the drug for pleasure – he used it to ease his suffering from acute rheumatic head and facial pains. On one occasion he experienced a religious revelation: '. . . and in an hour, oh! Heavens! what a revulsion! what an upheaving, from its lowest depths, of the inner spirit! What an apocalypse of the world within me! That my pains had vanished, was now a trifle in my eyes: – this negative effect was swallowed up in the immensity of those positive effects which had opened before me – in the abyss of divine enjoyment thus suddenly revealed.'[104]

The artificial paradise could be bought in any chemist's shop. Happiness cost one penny and could be carried in one's waistcoat pocket; portable ecstasies were to be had in pint bottles and peace of mind could even be sent through the post. One difference from today is that it was not dispensed as a 'fix' – nor, despite de Quincey's title, was it eaten, but drunk. Furthermore in de Quincey's day it was not known that it was addictive, although it can have been no secret that an overdose could prove fatal.

Racked with pain and desperate for an experience of ecstasy, Nietzsche knew how much to take. But one day an old Dutchman appeared on the scene, said to have come from Java, and gave him a phial containing an anonymous concoction. The effect was overpowering. 'The liquid appeared to be a fairly strong concentration of alcohol', wrote Elisabeth, 'and gave off an exotic scent. It also had a foreign name, which I have since forgotten – we only ever referred to it as "the Javanese sedative". The Dutchman insisted that one should take only a few drops in a glass of water. I tried it for myself and noticed a certain stimulating effect … Later, in the autumn of 1885, my brother confessed to me that he had once evidently taken a few drops too many, which led him to throw himself to the ground in an uncontrollable fit of laughter.'[105]

The liquid gave the impression of being alcohol because the basic ingredient, as de Quincey wrote, was mixed with alcohol. Paul Lanzky, an eccentric writer and hotelier, was perhaps one who recognised this substance. In December 1884 Lanzky lived with Nietzsche in the 'Pension de Genève' in Nice, where he was of some service to him, engaging him in conversation and reading aloud to him. 'At least Lanzky has some idea who I am', he observed.[106] Lanzky wrote that Nietzsche was constantly pondering the question of whether 'the oasis of Biskra in the Sahara might not be a suitable place for a Zarathustra to live in isolation for ten years'.[107] He had also met the mysterious Dutchman who had given Nietzsche the healing potion.

Lanzky was struck by the amount of alcohol that Nietzsche consumed. He disposed of a bottle of cognac in three days, and Lanzky tried to persuade him to drink less.[108] The philosopher, he recorded, 'disapproved of drugs being used as stimulants, while accepting their use in order to ease pain, whether of a physical or psychological nature'. 'Nietzsche showed me', Lanzky went on, 'a little phial of white powder, about 5cm by 2cm, that he had been given by the Dutchman with the express warning to take just one milligram, on very rare occasions, before going to bed. And Nietzsche must indeed have used the powder very sparingly, for he still had it in his possession in 1885 and 1886.'[109]

But what if Nietzsche had dispensed his own prescription and dissolved the powder in cognac? It has often been surmised that the powder was hashish. But one milligram would have had no effect. Lanzky thought it might have been cocaine, a drug with which Freud was experimenting at that time. Lanzky speculated that the Dutchman gave Nietzsche the drug only because 'he complained that he was frequently unable to sleep for more than an hour at a time, which often led him to consider committing suicide'.[110]

Were drugs the answer to his problem? Whatever drug it was, it made him addicted, the boundless fantasies of unfettered freedom being bought at the cost of the cheapening of 'normal' life, from the oppressive dullness of which one can only take refuge again in an illusory, drug-induced paradise. The man who, like de Quincey, had his supply of dreams in a bottle, became lost to everyday life and had no use for what were commonly regarded as the goals of human existence. For such a man a human being was something that had to be overcome.

In August 1884 Nietzsche received a visitor in his Swiss retreat of Sils-Maria. Resa von Schirnhofer, a student from Zurich, sat waiting for him in his little dining-room. The door of the adjoining room opened and Nietzsche appeared. 'He leaned wearily against the frame of the half-open door with a distraught expression on his pale face', wrote Resa, 'and at once began to tell me how unbearable his pain was. He described to me how, as soon as he closed his eyes, he saw a mass of exotic flowers growing ceaselessly upwards, perpetually changing their forms and colours, the one emerging from the other and each intertwining with the rest. "I can find no peace", he muttered – words I shall never forget.'[111]

Anxiously he then asked her twice whether this condition was a symptom of the onset of madness. Possibly it was. But the image of an exuberant growth of exotic flowers points rather to a psychedelic 'trip', coupled with a fear that this experience of a liberated consciousness would never come to an end. He himself once described it as 'the most elated state of awareness and at the same time an oppressive sensation of lethargy'.[112]

When an attack was over, it was as though nothing had happened. 'He was ready to make conversation or to go for a walk,' wrote Resa, 'and nothing was left to remind one of his previous condition.' He himself told her of his headaches and of the various medications he had tried in order to get rid of them. Indeed, in Rapallo and elsewhere on the Riviera he had written his own prescriptions, which had then been filled by pharmacists on the spot, without any questions being asked. 'That some of these preparations were far from harmless', concluded Resa, 'is something I deduced from the fact that

222 • *Zarathustra's Secret*

Nietzsche expressly told me that he was surprised that he had never been asked whether he was a doctor, and therefore qualified to issue such prescriptions.'[113]

Nietzsche persisted with the drug. In the summer of 1886, while in the Engadine, he took one of the women in the hotel into his confidence. Every morning shortly before five Marie von Bradke watched him 'put up his yellow umbrella and hurry down towards the lake with an uncertain, somewhat affected gait'. While taking a constitutional along the lake shore with her, he let her into his secret. 'He told me of his terrible headaches, and that an acquaintance – from India, I believe – had given him a poison to take, after which he lay on the ground as though dead. He also told me that he had tried other poisons too.'[114]

Poisons? Was he out to shock the aristocratic lady, caught, as she was, between pity and fascination, by giving himself an air of sorcery? Or was he out to explain some of the unusual features about himself that might have struck her attention, such as his physical imperfections and his uneven gait? At all events he succeeded in making clear to her that he came from another world and could not be understood in earthly terms. When in January 1889 he was finally admitted to this other world amid ecstatic dances and dithyrambic hymns, people tried to quieten his euphoria by offering him a series of sedatives. The prescription still exists. It was issued by a pharmacist in Turin and is recorded in the register: 'January 8: *Sciroppo diacodio*', i.e. diacodium, opium syrup.[115]

Zarathustra's Secret

THE FEMALE ELEPHANT

At the end of 1888, sensing his impending mental collapse, which seemed to him to mark the dawn of his conquest of the world, Nietzsche set about writing a final autobiography. He gave it the title *Ecce homo* – the image of the Saviour, despised and rejected, awaiting His crucifixion and His resurrection. After the onset of his syphilis-induced paralysis he even signed a number of his letters 'The Man on the Cross'. Nietzsche is the 'homo' being pointed to by the 'ecce', as John points to the crucified Christ in Matthias Grünewald's Isenheim Altar. But he is not only the martyred Son of God but a god himself, the god Dionysus, to whom that other, smiling John seems to be pointing, the figure with a woman's eyes and outstretched finger painted by Leonardo da Vinci. Nietzsche therefore signed the other half of his letters 'Dionysus'. One who suffers like a god but also experiences pleasure like a god. The final sentence of *Ecce homo* reads: 'Have people understood me? – Dionysus versus the Man on the Cross.'

This Nietzsche no longer wears masks – he *is* them, changing them almost by the hour. Previously he had invented his characters, later he hid behind them, and now, finally, he crept inside them. Could he no longer endure living inside himself? He was not that badly off, sitting in Turin cafés, enjoying ice-cream, nibbling *grissini*, 'digesting like a demi-god' and whiling away his evenings by the bridge over the Po, 'beyond good and evil'.[1] On one occasion he even described his existence as 'the idle life of a god by the banks of the Po'.[2]

In *Ecce homo* Nietzsche lays his cards on the table, displaying them with the triumphant flourish of the man who holds a winning hand. 'My

Zarathustra', he proclaims, 'is the greatest gift mankind has ever received!'[3] Not, of course, that mankind had noticed anything of this gift, or of the new synthesis of the gods now walking the earth unrecognised in mortal form. 'Behold Mankind!' he cries. And: 'Behold the book!' Is there any difference between them? 'This book,' he goes on, 'whose voice will be heard over centuries to come, is not only the noblest book there is – it is also the most profound.' Like a well from which the reader can draw buckets full of gold nuggets. One such nugget: 'The figs are falling from the tree; they are ripe and sweet. And as they fall, their red skin splits. I am as the north wind to ripe figs. These words of wisdom fall at your feet like figs, my friends. Now drink their juice and eat their sweet flesh!'[4] This invitation to savour the figs appears in the chapter 'On the Isles of the Blest' in Nietzsche's *Zarathustra*, where the hero is taught to say not 'God' but 'Superman'.

In *Ecce homo* Nietzsche reveals some details about the 'gift' that he presented to mankind with his *Zarathustra*. 'The basic conception of the work', he writes, 'was laid out in August 1881. If I reckon from that time down to the day when, suddenly and totally unexpectedly, the birth pangs began, in February 1883, that makes for a pregnancy lasting eighteen months. Which makes me the equivalent of a female elephant.'[5]

In fact the gestation period of elephants is somewhat longer. But Nietzsche was not concerned with zoological matters – rather with a religious legend. The Buddha was said to have been conceived by a holy elephant in the seventh heaven, to which Queen Maya had been transported in a dream. One day, after she had returned to earth, a shower of blossoms rained down on her – the music of the spheres rang out and the redeemer of the world was born.

Nietzsche had a similar experience with his son Zarathustra. But the child's delivery took place, not in a shower of blossoms, but, as we have seen, in a frosty winter in Rapallo, when Nietzsche was forced to leave the house and walk off the chill of his unheated quarters. On the paths between Zoagli and Portofino, he wrote, the first part of his *Zarathustra* suddenly appeared to him in his totality – 'more accurately, he *suddenly overcame me*'.[6] It was a moment of inspiration. The hero used him as a gateway through which he and his message would march resolutely and in triumph in order to change the world.

I had no option in the matter, he said resignedly: 'With the slightest trace of superstition left in us, we could hardly ward off the thought that we are merely an incarnation, merely a mouthpiece, merely a medium for overwhelming forces ... One listens, one does not search; one takes, one does not ask who gives ... And the thought flashes through the mind like lightning ... I had no choice. A sense of joy which expressed itself in a sudden flood of tears ... Everything that happens is involuntary, as though in the surge of a sudden sensation of freedom, of total commitment, of power, of heavenliness.'[7]

Thus was *Zarathustra* born, said its author. It was as though he were a second incarnation of St John on Patmos, called to write of his revelation. 'The word revelation', wrote Nietzsche, 'simply describes the facts of the situation.' These facts, however, in August 1881, when Zarathustra was conceived, are by no means so easy to ascertain. For Nietzsche was both father and mother. 'It was an immortal moment when I begat the idea of the Eternal Recurrence', he wrote later, leaving no doubt that it was this very moment of conception in whose eternal memory he wrote the book – or, more accurately, recorded what was dictated to him from on high. 'The basic conception of the book,' he maintained, 'the idea of the Eternal Recurrence, the most emphatic expression of affirmation that can be uttered, is to be traced to August 1881.'[8]

But anyone who expects Nietzsche to follow this bald statement with an ecstatic exposition of the genesis of the work will be disappointed. By 1888 and the time of *Ecce homo* he no longer needed to generate propaganda for his works. He merely notes: 'I was walking that day through the woods by the shore of the lake at Silvaplana, and had stopped in front of an enormous rock-pyramid not far from Surlei. Then the idea came to me.'[9]

A gross understatement. From this day on everything in his life had changed. In the eighteen months that followed he explored the entire range of his emotional experience, from the heights to the depths, always with the thought at the back of his mind that everything would recur in perpetuity. In September 1882 he left his Swiss hermitage of Sils-Maria, with its lake and its rock, and returned to Genoa, where he remained until his trip to 'the isles of the blest'. There is nothing to suggest that he found time there to develop his idea – there were other things to be discovered which had no less radical an effect on his life.

Back in Genoa, he had spent six months agonising over whether or not Lou could help him to extend and expound his ideas. In the event, when he tried, after some hesitation, to explain the notion of the Eternal Recurrence to Lou and Paul Rée, they had laughed at him. Then followed the nightmare of his endless self-torturing, which ended with his departure for Rapallo.

He put up in the Albergo della Posta, 'a fairly old, red-painted house on the hill, decorated with a painted frieze of palmettes'. His room was on the upper floor, reached by a narrow stone staircase – 'a small, poorly furnished room', according to one of his visitors. It had just one window, facing up the hill and away from the sea, which he could hear but not see. Indeed, the sound of the sea, he complained, often made it impossible for him to get to sleep.[10]

In a Christmas letter to his friend Overbeck in Basel he described his state of depression: 'This morsel of life is the toughest I have ever had to chew, and it is still possible that I might choke on it. I have endured the demeaning and painful events of this past summer as though they were attacks of madness.'[11] The only remedy seems to have been drugs. In February he wrote again to Overbeck, telling him that he had taken fifty grams of pure chloral hydrate over the last two months in order to sleep – the same drug through which King Ludwig II sought to escape from the nightmare of everyday reality.[12]

Decades later people in Rapallo still remembered the German lodger, though not a book that had been written there. They did, however, recall other things, about which they preferred to keep silent. An admirer who paid a visit to his miserable room was shocked by the wretched conditions under which he lived – and no less taken aback by the lack of respect that people accorded his memory. 'The present landlord of the Albergo and his staff do not speak well of "Signor Luigi" ', she wrote – 'the "*huomo alla barba*", as they called him. I asked a number of questions in my halting Italian but received little by way of reply – so little. "And there is nothing in particular you remember about him?" I asked. "Ah, Signora . . ." came the response, accompanied by a shrug of the shoulders.'[13]

It was the time in which *Zarathustra* was born, the time when its 'medium' took opium, not as a soporific – for that he had the powerful chloral – but as a means of lifting himself out of the doldrums. He climbed 'the glorious hill that leads up to Zoagli, past the lofty pine trees and looking far out across the sea', but in his imagination he was scaling far greater heights.[14] 'Here and in this instant Man was overcome', runs the ringing phrase in *Ecce homo*, 'and the concept of the Superman became profoundest reality – all that which hitherto made Man great now lies in the infinite distance, far below him.'[15] In one of his notebooks Nietzsche records a characteristic of the Superman which brings an unexpected new dimension to the vision that he had had on the isles of the blest: 'From out of a superabundance of life the Superman combines those visions of the opium-eater, of madness and of the Dionysian dance.'[16]

The sick man who is made 'high' by drugs is visited by his ideal, who is high by virtue of his health. This ideal hovers above him, leaving him, a stooping figure with stick and moustache, to follow in his wake, inspired, effortless. So they hasten together towards the future, the ideal and his pursuer, as Gustav von Aschenbach and the boy Tadzio were to do in Thomas Mann's *Death in Venice* – but lightly and gracefully, for 'Zarathustra is a dancer.'[17]

Nietzsche was often assailed by doubts as to whether he was still in his right mind. In the very first letter announcing Zarathustra's successful birth, his progenitor writes that as a result of this book and the claims it makes, 'the German public will probably rank me among the insane'.[18] Back again in his mood of dark despair, he wrote to Overbeck in March: 'There is no chance that I shall do anything good again. So why do anything? It reminds me of my most recent folly – I mean my *Zarathustra.*' And he added bitterly: 'Do you follow my meaning? I am a miserable writer.'[19]

Cosima Wagner had made a similar observation years earlier, and he had never been able to cast it from his mind. Once he even referred to 'the barrel of a gun ... being a source of relatively pleasant thoughts', for he could not bear 'living this secret life any longer, since all my human relationships derive from one or other of my masks'.[20]

But Zarathustra was more than a mask – he came as a saviour. When Nietzsche was being slowly crushed under the torments of the affair with Lou and Rée, with suicide offering the only escape from his agonies, Zarathustra came to his aid. 'He helped to lift a weight off my mind', he wrote to Gast.[21] 'The burden that lies on me as a consequence of the weather', as he interpreted his condition, 'has been converted into thoughts and feelings that are terrible to bear. And when this burden finally passed from me, after ten days of bright, fresh January weather, my Zarathustra finally emerged.'[22]

This was the physical description of the situation. To Overbeck, the theologian, he described it in the language of resurrection: 'Previously I had been in a veritable abyss of emotions ... but in the meantime I have raised myself up to the heights.'[23] In a letter to Ernst Schmeitzner, his publisher, this renewed confidence takes the form of specific requests concerning the production and appearance of the book: he asks for thicker paper than that used for his earlier works, with a black border enclosing each page of text.[24] Most strikingly of all, he wishes to dispense with his name on the title page, leaving the title itself, *Also sprach Zarathustra*, as prominent as possible, 'in red letters on a pale green background'.[25]

When Peter Gast later held a copy of the finished volume in his hands – the first of four – he did not understand a great deal of what he read. But its style and language struck him as somehow familiar, so he concealed his ignorance in a eulogy to which he added his own note of diffidence. 'It is to be hoped', he wrote, 'that this book will become as widely known as the Bible, with which it shares a canonical status and a succession of commentaries from which this status in part derives.'[26] Nietzsche first accepted the compliments – 'So perhaps I have not lived in vain after all', he responded, in a tone of self-congratulation. Then he became aware that Gast's phrase 'a succession of commentaries' had touched a raw nerve, namely that for all the pious hopes that the book would reach a wide readership, it remained largely impenetrable. The new Bible needed a commentary.

The author hastened to provide the necessary information. At the beginning of April he wrote to Overbeck that, after re-reading his *Sunrise* and *La gaia scienza*, he had made a striking discovery: 'Here I had, in fact, already provided the commentary – before writing the text!'[27] There was scarcely a single line in these earlier works, he explained, that could not be taken as an explanation of *Zarathustra*. When in difficulty, go and read more Nietzsche.

He attempted to shock Malwida von Meysenbug by claiming that the book 'laid down a challenge to all religions' and that it was at one and the same time both a masterstroke and an act of folly on his part to compose the commentaries before the actual text.[28] To Gast he wrote that, 'curious as it sounds', one could even go back as far as his 'Schopenhauer as Mentor', the first of his *Thoughts out of Season*, to find explanations of *Zarathustra*.

By now, at the latest, the truth, which he formulated a year later, must have dawned on him: 'My divine work is mysterious and inaccessible and an incitement to laughter – for everyone.'[29] People did not understand it – did not understand *him*. He had presented mankind with a book conceived in a state of euphoria, written with divine inspiration, and mankind rejected it. Three parts appeared, then Schmeitzner refused to publish any more. The fourth volume was published by Nietzsche at his own expense – a private edition distributed among his baffled friends. The common-sense verdict, by which he set no store, was summarised by Thomas Mann: 'This faceless, insubstantial monster Zarathustra, with the rose garland of laughter on his unrecognisable head, and with his "Be hard!" and his legs of a dancer, is not a creature but mere rhetoric, excited wordplay, the voice of a tortured soul and dubious prophecy, a spectre of helpless *grandezza*, often touching but mostly embarrassing – a non-figure swirling around on the border of ridicule.'[30]

Might Thomas Mann be sketching the portrait not of a fictional character but of its creator, a portrait that he had composed long before? Nietzsche, the masochist, would have recognised himself in this ghostly mirror.

THE VISION BY THE LAKE

In July 1881 Nietzsche arrived in the Engadine from Italy. Here was to be 'the birthplace of my *Zarathustra*', he wrote.[31] His stay began with a series of calamities. First he missed his train connection, thus doubling the length of his journey from Recoaro to St Moritz. Then he took a dislike to the elegant and overpriced resort and considered leaving again – until a young Swiss hotelier, whom he had met on the train, recommended to him the nearby village of Sils-Maria, a quiet spot which was comparatively cheap. Nietzsche's spirits rose. 'The woods, lakes, meadows and paths are just what I wanted,' he exclaimed in joy, 'and all the fifty conditions required for my miserable life seem to be fulfilled here.' Except for one – intentionally so.

Every day the voluntary ascetic appeared in the hotel, where he ate, not at the guest table but alone – 'as usual'.[32] But his sickness persisted. After the first fortnight of his stay he wrote of 'four serious fits, each lasting two or three days',[33] followed by two more over the following nine days. One consolation came in the form of the philosopher Spinoza, who 'astonished and delighted' him and came to share his intimate moments during his walks in the high mountains.[34] So preoccupied was he with Spinoza's ideas that for two weeks he wrote no letters.

In the middle of August the sound of a triumphant fanfare rang out from the Alpine valley. Something extraordinary seemed to have happened to him that put all his previous moments of ecstasy in the shade. Peter Gast, who was sent the news, was accustomed to such outbursts from his master but this time something quite exceptional must have taken place. Nietzsche, moreover, wanted it to be seen in this light. 'Ideas have come over my horizon,' he wrote,

> such as I have never experienced before. But I am not going to utter a word about them, so as not to disturb the unshakeable peace of mind that I am enjoying. I imagine I still have a few years left to live! My friend, sometimes I have the feeling that I live a highly dangerous life, for I am like one of those machines that often explode! The intensity of my emotions makes me shudder, then laugh. More than once I was unable to leave my room, for the ridiculous reason that my eyes were inflamed. And why? Because on my walk the day before I had wept too long – not sentimental tears but tears of jubilation. I burst into song and jabbered a lot of nonsense, filled with a new vision that sets me apart from all other men.[35]

Only in terms of its effect on his eyes and his mood could he describe what had befallen him in the seclusion of the Engadine mountains. Had it been a sudden flash of inspiration brought about by his sickness? Apparently he was himself afraid of going mad, of 'exploding', as he put it. Or had he taken an overdose of his self-prescribed drug? The image of the man who becomes one with nature in the midst of his weeping and rejoicing, his singing and his dancing, had been with him for a long while. The divine vision appears before the drunken satyr in the moment of his most intense suffering. Was some unknown power guiding his hand across the paper, 'as though trying out a new pen?'[36] Had he been touched by the god as, like Archilochus, he merged into the oneness of existence? Did the god enter him in order to make him his mouthpiece, his pen?

By the time he told Gast his secret, two weeks had elapsed. His ecstasy had left him and new fits confined him to his room. But he had recorded on a sheet of paper what had passed through his head: 'Beginning of August 1881 in Sils-Maria, 6,000 feet above sea level, and far higher above all earthly things!'[37] Regarding the experience itself the sheet of paper tells us nothing. The statements refer only to its consequences, both for himself and for others – for repercussions were bound to flow from what had been revealed to him, unforeseeable outcomes for the entire history of mankind. Beneath the title 'The Eternal Recurrence' he listed what man must achieve: 1) The Assimilation of Basic Errors; 2) The Assimilation of the Passions; 3) The Assimilation of Knowledge and the Denial of Knowledge (The Passion for Knowledge).

From this derives the vital realisation that it must be proved that there is 'an absolute excess of desire', 'otherwise we must choose our self-destruction as a means to the destruction of mankind'. The question is: 'Do we *want* to live?' For 'this period of human history will and must repeat itself in perpetuity – this we must leave out of the equation, for it is something over which we have no control'. Nietzsche appears to have given no more thought to the validity of the idea itself – it lay beyond the reach of doubt. What remained was the issue of how to use it. If everything eternally recurs, including man, then nothing is left outside the cycle – everything combines to form an indivisible whole. The man who recognises this will literally 'incorporate' everything, absorbing it into his higher existence. Nothing is excluded, nothing foreign remains – or at most the query as to whether the whole enterprise is worthwhile. This is the decisive question that confronts mankind. Nobody can avoid it. 'What are we going to do with the rest of our lives?' asked Nietzsche, in the royal plural. Answer: 'Teach the doctrine.' In the jottings that follow we find him rehearsing his role as the mentor of mankind: 'The vital question in whatever you want to do is: "Is this something I want to do time and again?" This is where the emphasis lies.'[38]

Nietzsche knew why he had withheld from Gast the idea itself. The supreme vision that had shaken him to the core sounded in the cold light of day like the *idée fixe* of a crank. Gast could judge from the consequences what his master had experienced. In fact was it an idea at all or just a brief glance into the future? Had Nietzsche himself not said that he had 'seen' it? But what had he seen? If, as he was convinced, that visionary moment in Sils-Maria was for ever to return, ever to reappear before him as such, there would be nothing more to see than what lay before him at that moment – the lake, the mountains, the rocky pyramid and their reflection in the water. Repeating the experience would not change the view – it would remain as it was, beautiful or otherwise. So was its return only an idea?

When one surveys Nietzsche's notes that deal with this experience, one continually comes across another image – that of lightning. Inspiration had come to him by the lake 'like a shaft of lightning'. At evensong in Naumburg his heart had been pierced by the lightning thrust of a sword. He was newborn. The lightning at Sils, too, completely changed him: 'If only one moment in the world were to return, said the lightning, then all moments would have to return. I saw absolute necessity as a shield decorated with images.'

Was this the vision that set him apart from all other men? Five years later, in the final stage of his creative life, the same sight reappears in one of his 'Dionysus Dithyrambs'. Fame, says the poet scornfully, is something he can dispense with, because it is fleeting. He is attracted by something higher – eternity, on which he has no need to lavish fine words, like other poets, because it has revealed itself to him in all its naked glory. Others can barely conceive of it – *he* has seen it:

Hush! –
Of grand things – I *see* grand things! –
One should be silent
Or talk in grand terms.
Talk grandly, my enchanted wisdom!

I look upward –
There are the rolling waves of the seas of light.
O night, O silence, O noise as quiet as the grave! . . .

I see a sign –
From the farthest distance
A sparkling constellation
Falls slowly towards me . . .

O highest star of Being!
Tablet of eternal images!

Thou comest to me?
What no man has seen,
Thy silent beauty –
What? It does not flinch from my gaze?
Shield of necessity!
Tablet of eternal images!
O highest star of Being![39]

It is possible to explain Nietzsche's vision of eternity. The shining constellations of stars, whose silent beauty is displayed before his eyes alone, represent, in a setting transferred to the heavens, his longing for distant antiquity. From his lonely eyrie in Sils-Maria he looks out towards the land that glows in the distance – at the moment unattainable but at some time, inevitably, to recur. This land reveals itself to him as Homer describes it in Book 18 of the *Iliad*, and the 'shield of necessity, the tablet of eternal images', is the shield of Achilles. Hephaestos, the divine metalworker, portrayed on it the entire Hellenic cosmos, with the fertile earth, the pounding sea, the heavens and the stars, the sun and the moon and with an idealised picture of the Greeks going about their daily round. Battles raged to and fro, presided over by the eternal gods who direct the affairs of men, alternating with idylls of a pastoral life in which man and nature form a unity. Finally the image of the Eternal Recurrence, the profoundest secret of the Greeks, is revealed in the labyrinthine dance of Ariadne.

Nietzsche knew the cosmic shield, loved it already during his time in Basel. Once, just before the summer vacation, he had asked his pupils at the *Gymnasium* to read the description of Achilles' shield in the *Iliad* and provide a commentary on it.[40] He was curious, as he had been with the *Bacchae*, to hear them discuss their impressions. Such texts were not designed as an official part of the curriculum but as ways of apprehending a higher reality.

The golden shield of Achilles symbolised for Nietzsche his Greek ideal at its purest. My '*ne plus ultra*', he called it.[41] The beautiful and the cruel depicted with equal perfection, the bodies of the youths and maidens swaying gracefully in the dance like the circling stars in the sky, the fertile earth at one with the rhythm of human life – and everything endlessly recurring. The world as the isles of the blest. Standing on the shore of the lake at Silvaplana, fresh from of his sick bed after a fit that had lasted several days – induced, perhaps, by a draught of his private potion – he suddenly found himself confronted by a vision of perfection, his beloved Arcadia, the highest condition to which the world could aspire, an 'eternal necessity'.

And this condition knows that it will not perish but return. It had taken an eternity to create and after a further eternity it would recur, joining in the dance of the stars and the frolicking of the young Greek heroes. 'I have discovered antiquity!' cried Nietzsche. 'They believed in the Eternal Recurrence! That is what believing in mysteries means!'[42]

This is what he may have seen, in a flash of lightning, as he stood by the lake. The euphoria that followed recovery from a fit rendered him receptive to visions which might also have been brought on by drugs. Or by an epileptic fit. Not that Nietzsche was an epileptic, but as a boy he had suffered 'epileptic states without losing consciousness'.[43] Was it such an attack that had befallen him as he stood on the lake shore? As the seizure surged over him in waves, did he catch a glimpse of 'his heavenly star of Being'?

An attack is often preceded by the so-called 'aura', during which the sufferer experiences moments of déjà vu, when he says to himself, 'Everything that now follows, I have already seen, exactly as it happens.'[44] Dostoevsky, who suffered from this condition, described it in detail in *The Idiot*: 'Suddenly, in a state of depression, pain and despair, a sudden flash lights up his thoughts, engaging all his faculties and all his strength. The experiences of life and of consciousness are magnified tenfold in such moments, which last no longer than a flash of lightning. They bring an extraordinary increase in self-awareness and self-confidence. If only one could say clearly and consciously to oneself, at this very moment, in the last split second of consciousness: "For a moment such as this I would fain surrender my entire life!"' Nietzsche seems to have experienced a similar moment at the lake of Silvaplana. He wrote in his notebook: 'The moment when I begat the Eternal Recurrence is immortal. It is for the sake of this moment that I bear the thought of the Recurrence.'[45] At the time he wrote this, Nietzsche knew Dostoevsky only by name. Not until around five years later, in February 1887, did he discover the spiritual bond between them.

Whatever happened to Nietzsche by the lakeside on that August day in 1881 – why was he convinced that his vision had objective validity? He sensed from the beginning that his idea could not be proved but simply had to be believed. But why did one have to believe it? A man who has been vouchsafed a vision in a state of ecstasy can believe throughout his life in what he has seen, can found a religion and beautify the spot where it took place – as did Nietzsche with the rock on the lake shore. There is an unbridgeable gulf, however, between a sudden vision and an idea that has to stand up to scrutiny in the cold light of day. Nietzsche may have seen Achilles' shield but he could not have seen that the secret of the universe lay hidden in the dance that was depicted on it. So where did this conviction spring from?

The answer is quite simple: it was not the recurrence as depicted on the shield that persuaded him but the recurrence of the shield itself. It had penetrated his consciousness long ago but he saw it as though for the first time. It seemed to be not an image preserved in his memory but a vision both unique and familiar from time immemorial. Something that had been forgotten for ages past but that now, like a flash of lightning, reappeared, recognisable down to the last detail. The shield was his guarantor of the recurrence. It was not the first time that foreign influences had unsuspectingly become part of his own make-up. His writings are a cosmos in which a great deal recurs without either his or his contemporaneous readers' knowing. Sometimes he deliberately invoked such recurrences – a process he would have called, quite literally, 'incorporation'.

When he came to look back in 1888 at the second part of his *Zarathustra*, Nietzsche sounded like the founder of a new religion. 'In the summer,' he began, 'having returned to the holy place where the flash of inspiration that kindled the Zarathustra idea had first descended on me, I found the second part of my book.'[46] The name of the hero was evidently as intimately linked with the Zarathustra idea as was the idea with the Zarathustra vision. Had it been this strange Persian saint who showed himself to Nietzsche by the lakeside, when the 'heavenly star of Being' rose in the sky and the world held its breath? Or, as he wrote in *Ecce homo*, was it in Rapallo that he had first ambushed his victim? His notebooks suggest that the hero made his appearance soon after the lakeside episode – possibly even at the same time. The unmistakable voice of Zarathustra is heard immediately after the first mention of the idea of the Eternal Recurrence, and in the same month the prophet's name occurs in connection with the book originally to be given the title *Noon and Eternity*. He was thus already present, even though his progenitor, 'the female elephant', only gave birh to him eighteen months later.

Although it was not until 1888, in 'Fame and Eternity', that he gave poetic expression to his vision by the lake, Nietzsche had been trying to do so since 1882. It took time, and for years he worked away at the task until he finally found a form in which his experience was fit for inclusion in the 'Songs of Prince Free-as-a-Bird' in 1887. Zarathustra too, as is clear from each one of the five different versions of the poem, came to him suddenly, maybe even as a hallucination – but certainly as an enigma. The various poetic fragments show the mysterious encounter taking place in different locations and at different times.

The first version belongs to the late summer of 1882, the time when Nietzsche was overcome by the memory of his Columbus period, which led him to write in Lou Salomé's visitors' book: 'My friend – said Columbus –

Do not put your trust in the Genoese again!'[47] Immediately before these words are to be found four lines of verse in which Zarathustra announces his arrival:

Here I sat, waiting – waiting? But for nothing,
Beyond good and evil, not yearning any more
For the light than for the darkness,
A friend to noon and a friend to eternity.[48]

Originally *Thus Spake Zarathustra*, as conceived in Sils-Maria in August 1881, was to have been called 'Noon and Eternity' – the title he also first gave to Part Four of the completed work. But the poem of 1882, which shows him caught in a state of uncertainty 'beyond good and evil', is entitled 'Portofino'. He could not know that it was to be here, on his walks around Rapallo, that his hero would assail him. But in the summer of 1882 the place was already a memory, a remembrance of his first awakening in Genoa – 'the sea and the hills round Portofino, where the melody of the gulf of Genoa fades away'.[49] Could this be the place where he encountered his 'noontide friend', six months before his vision of the shield in Sils-Maria?

Similarly in the next fragment, written a few months later, he seems to be certain that his hero first appeared to him, not in the Engadine but in Genoa. 'All sea, all noontide, all time without aim', he sings.[50] Nietzsche, the idler, sits on a rock jutting out into the sea, far from any human presence, far from his own past, visible only to 'the eye of eternity – given over to play'.[51] What is he waiting for – if he *is* waiting? Here too he gives no answer.

But shortly afterwards, in the third version, it is revealed. In the midst of self-torturing utterances about madness and about how Lou and Rée were intent on presiding over his demise, the vision of Zarathustra appears and relieves his suffering:

All sea, all noontide, all time without aim,
A child, a toy
And suddenly one becomes two
And Zarathustra passed me by.[52]

A child, a toy? The earliest poems of his boyhood had spoken of a 'jutting rock' where he loved to sit. Had he become a child again in the noonday sun, playing with his toys? Or had he become, as he dreamed away the day, the plaything of a god without noticing it? And what had happened when 'one became two?' It all sounds like Faustian sorcery and black magic. Zarathustra, a Persian magus, a spirit concealed in a bottle? Or was this a child pining for his dead father?

According to his sister Elisabeth, inventor of legends, the figure of Zarathustra had hovered before his eyes since childhood – he had even dreamed about him. Was he dreaming again? Was it perhaps an experience like that of the Eternal Recurrence in Silvaplana? Or, as in front of the rock pyramid, had he remembered something that had made a deep impression on him without realising that it was a memory?

In the autumn of 1884, in the middle of preparatory work on the last part of *Zarathustra*, Nietzsche tried once again to give poetic expression to the experience. The scene is no longer Portofino but a lake, and he is no longer the child round whom the world revolves but a lover moved to tears by his memories:

> Here I sat peering, peering – but into the distance.
> My fingers playing with the flowers in the bouquet
> And when a tear fell from my eye
> Coy yet curious – who was it for?
> There ...[53]

Zarathustra is not mentioned here either. The situation, however, is clear. Together with Lou, Nietzsche is paying a visit to the peninsula where Wagner and Cosima had lived, on the lake of Lucerne, carrying a bunch of lilacs in his hand and drawing a figure with his stick in the sand. He is in despair because Lou has just turned him down, and dispirited because of his break with Wagner. Now, over two years later, he sees the situation in a different light: the tears he had shed over the loss of his two friends were in reality meant for his noontide friend. 'Coy and curious', he looked out over the lake and awaited his arrival. When Nietzsche later lamented the end of yet another friendship, he again summons up his hero – as a magician and 'noontide friend' who had appeared at just the right moment. 'There he stood before me', he wrote, after Heinrich von Stein, a young and eager disciple of Wagner, had finally turned his back on him.

By the time the poem of Zarathustra's appearance was published in 1887, Nietzsche had changed the scene of the action yet again – from Liguria to Lucerne, then to the lake at Silvaplana. The poem is now entitled 'Sils-Maria':

> Here I sat, waiting, waiting – but for nothing,
> Beyond good and evil, relishing now the light,
> Now the shade, all mere play,
> All sea, all noontide, all time without aim.
> There, suddenly, my Friend, one became two –
> And Zarathustra walked past me ...[54]

He shouts the message across to Lou, whom he had warned against his rest-less 'Genoese' nature. 'I did not need you,' he cries, 'for a superior creature came to my aid, a magician!' But where did this creature descend and where did he walk past him? Was it perhaps not a single experience, as in Sils, but one repeated a number of times? Maybe it was again an unheeded memory combining everything that had stirred him most deeply in Portofino, Lucerne and now Sils – a longing for a friend and lover from the world of antiquity. Was Zarathustra a substitute figure for the unattainable star?

Such a peerless 'star-like' friend is described by Hölderlin in his novel *Hyperion* – Alabanda, a savage fighter and passionate lover who lusts after his friend as Achilles lusts after Patroclus. But Hyperion and Alabanda have to part. As they bid each other farewell on the seashore, where Alabanda embarks on a ship, never to return, Hyperion calls after him in despair: 'I stood on the shore, stricken by the agonies of parting, looking silently out to sea, hour after hour. My mind counted the days of my slowly-dying youth and hovered like a dove over what was to come.'[55]

Then Hyperion turns to his long-forgotten lyre and sings his 'Song of Fate', in which the spirits 'wander in the ethereal brightness above, their bliss-ful eyes gazing in eternal clarity' – the stars, the lovers who have been lifted up into the heavens. But while the constellations glitter above us, distant and beyond our reach, the poet faces uncertainty and abandonment:

But it is our lot
    To find no rest,
        Suffering mortals
            Dwindle and fall
                Blindly from one
                    Hour to the next,
                        Like water hurled
                            From rock to rock,
                                For years down into the abyss.[56]

Like Hölderlin's Hyperion, Nietzsche sits by the water's edge, surveying the past and the future, lost to the moment and close in his thoughts to his loved one. In his schooldays at Pforta Hölderlin had been his favourite poet. 'The sublime beauty of the characters in *Hyperion* had a similar effect on me as the breaking waves in a rough sea', he had written in October 1861,[57] twenty years before Sils-Maria, in a 'Letter to My Friend'. He felt intensely the desperate yearning in Hölderlin's novel, an emotion implied rather than openly expressed, a love of hidden beauty. 'Although', the young Nietzsche explained to his friend, 'he was caught up in the glow of this transforming radiance, everything is left unsatisfied and unfulfilled. The figures that the poet conjures up are images that arouse the music of homesickness, embracing us, charming us but also arousing unfulfilled yearnings ... Nowhere does the longing for Greece find expression in purer tones ... These lines spring from the purest and gentlest of spirits, overshadowing even the freshness and formal artistry of Platen.'[58]

In Hölderlin's *Hyperion* Nietzsche found the words for those 'visions and apparitions' of his youth, the 'divine moments' on which he would bestow in his *Zarathustra* 'an evergreen garland of life'.[59] At the age of seventeen he had also found in *Hyperion* what was now revealed to him as though for the first time – namely, that the creatures of his secret desire were like distant stars, circling in their divine orbits. He also became aware that love of these astral bodies found fulfilment only in rare moments, when the stars seemed to descend from heaven, when time stood still and eternity dawned. And finally he discovered the principle that everything returned, the moment of desire no less than the stars that traverse the sky.

All this he read in *Hyperion,* absorbing it and making it part of his own being – then promptly forgetting it until it returned, tangible and visible, as a higher reality, perhaps in a supernatural form to which he refers in a mysterious observation: 'He wanders alone. For his figures surround him, though he only sees them. And if he encounters his like, their spirits embrace and see the same figures through four eyes.'[60]

Was the appearance of Zarathustra just such a recurrence of 'his like'? Would the secret teaching of *Hyperion* return with him – that attempt by Hölderlin to set against the rational philosophical systems of his friends Hegel and Schelling the vision of a kingdom of love? Hölderlin too felt himself to be the founder of a new religion, with *Hyperion* as a new creed, a modern gospel, the manifesto in narrative form of that new religion, in which, he wrote to a friend, he had struck out into '*terra incognita* in the realm of literature'.[61]

For what appears to be a pantheistic passion for nature is in reality an erotic cult of beauty that has grown out of the seed of friendship, drawing the whole world into its aura of bliss. Love of a man for a boy, embodied in Adamas and Hyperion, finds its mature equivalent in love between equals, between the hero Alabanda and the hero Hyperion. When Nietzsche characterised the culture of Greek antiquity as a male culture that presupposed an erotic relationship between men and youths, he summoned Hölderlin as his authority, quoting the line: 'Mortal man gives of his best when loving.'

Awakened by the eye of Alabanda, 'until I felt his eye in mine, blushing as we gazed on each other',[62] Hyperion became a philosopher through the force of his burgeoning love. 'Like the winds that rejoice as they surge through the forests and over the mountains, so our souls felt the urge to leap onwards and upwards.' As they sit together under the shade of the laurel tree, their Plato on their knees, Hyperion suddenly has a vision of a new society. 'Away with the old order!' he cries. 'Make room for a new world!' With these words Hyperion sealed their union. 'Alabanda flew into my arms and embraced me, and his kisses pierced me to the depths of my heart.'[63]

Hyperion's friend also owed his heroic nature to a sudden awakening. He had once met a young man on the seashore who attracted him and whose loving gaze 'melted my hard heart'.[64] Together the two young men set out to enjoy the world and to do battle with it, all their hopes pinned on one another.

Hyperion writes to his soulmate Diotima – the name is taken from Plato's *Symposium* – that Alabanda 'exudes the radiance of a bridegroom, whose every glance heralds the advent of the world that is to come'.[65]

From love spring those 'sidereal worlds of joy' that Zarathustra seeks to disperse over the whole of mankind. Once he had even tried to create a private sun for his stellar friend Rée. Hyperion too feels the urge 'to create a new sun ... with new satellites'.[66] At the same time he knows that the blessed spirits in the heavens are only a metaphor for a higher divinity: 'I once caught a glimpse of it, the only thing that my soul searched for. And that perfection, which exists far above the stars and which we have deferred till the end of time, that also have I seen. Do ye know its name, the name that embraces one and all? Its name is Beauty.'[67]

But it only lights up the earth for a second like a fleeting glance that one can never forget. Such glances are instants of supreme happiness when the present also embraces the past and the future. Compressed in one such moment he experienced 'both the loss of all the golden centuries of the past and the power latent in the strength of heroes'.[68] And as to his love for Diotima: 'What is everything that men have thought and done over the centuries compared with just one moment of love?'[69]

He would give his whole life for one such spell, he continues: 'I would wander among the stars for thousands of years, assume any garb, speak any language, just in order to encounter thee once more.' When Alabanda leaves him to die a hero's death, he assures his mourning friend that he is 'eternal, indestructible, without end'. And his farewell – 'maybe we shall yet see each other again' – echoes that of the dying Diotima to Hyperion: 'We shall surely meet again.'[70]

Hölderlin's metaphysics of friendship, out of which grew Nietzsche's doctrine of the Eternal Recurrence, has a precursor in antiquity, namely Pythagoras. Leaving his native Greece to found in southern Italy a religio-philosophical community centred on himself, Pythagoras was already revered as a god in his lifetime. He is said to have acquired his faith in metempsychosis from Egyptian priests. According to Empedocles he had undergone ten, perhaps even twenty incarnations.

Pythagoras taught his disciples the principle of the immortality of the soul, a doctrine linked with that of the divine nature of the stars. Pythagoras' pupil Alcmaion, for instance, considered the stars to be gods because they had a soul. And these heavenly bodies – sun, moon and stars, the entire firmament – were, according to Aristotle, in perpetual motion. Dominating all, finally, both the earthly and the heavenly realms, was Harmony, Beauty expressible in numbers.

Nietzsche had already studied Pythagoras at the time of his *Birth of Tragedy*, and references to a model 'Pythagorean friendship', in which companions hold all their possessions in common, are frequently to be found in his letters. 'Men like Pythagoras', he once wrote, 'live in their own solar system and regard themselves as superhuman, deserving to be treated with almost religious awe.' The epitome of pride and self-centredness, a lone wolf with a supernatural aspect about him, according to Nietzsche, Pythagoras founded an exclusive community similar to the Order of the Knights Templar, based on the principle that 'man is not the product of his past but of the principle of the Eternal Recurrence'.[71]

It was in connection with Pythagoras that the name Zarathustra, in its Greek form, first appears in Nietzsche's works in 1872. Nietzsche rejected the idea that Greek philosophy had simply been imported from the Orient. Closer to the truth, he maintained, was that the Greeks had imbibed 'living knowledge' from their contact with other peoples. Zoroaster thus stood alongside Heraclitus, forming one of a number of such related pairs of names.[72]

Nietzsche could have given his sage the name Pythagoras. But then he would not have been the 'son' that he had himself begotten and given to the world. There is another reason why he chose the name of the Persian prophet, who otherwise played no part in his works. Zoroaster is an aster, a star. In Friedrich Creuzer's *Symbolism and Mythology of the Ancient Peoples*, a work that Nietzsche consulted, the name is translated as 'golden star'. When the philosopher discovered this, apparently only after he had completed the first part of his *Zarathustra*, he wrote to Gast: 'I am very happy about this coincidence. It could give the impression that the whole conception of my book had its origins in this etymological circumstance.'[73]

The conception of the book – had it not taken place at that moment by the lake in Silvaplana? Zarathustra as a heavenly body visible only to *his* eyes? Later the sage described his name as 'both dear to him and a burden'.[74] Nietzsche was the only one who knew the connection between Zoroaster, the star, and the 'heavenly star of being.' A later note reveals that he saw his hero as a star such as Rée had once been to him: 'Believe me – Zarathustra has died and is no more. A star was extinguished in a desolate room. But its light …'[75]

Towards the end of August 1881, the month of his vision by the lake, the title 'Noontide and Eternity' appears for the first time in Nietzsche's note-book, together with the opening of a narrative: 'Born on Lake Urmi, Zarathustra left his family home in his thirtieth year, and during his ten years of solitude in the mountains composed the Avesta.'[76] Creuzer had written: 'Zoroaster went up into the mountains of Elbruz, where he devoted himself to prayer and meditation.'[77] Nietzsche introduced his new prophet in similar words in *La gaia scienza*, and *Thus Spake Zarathustra* also follows the note of 1881, down to the details of the time sequence.

Another book, Gustave Flaubert's *The Temptation of St Anthony*, recently published, also acted as a godfather to Zarathustra. In one of its most important episodes a group of priests has gathered on a platform high above the dark city to observe the stars. The hero, who has been taken there too by the devil, expresses his doubts that the stars are really gods. 'Indeed they are,' responds the devil, 'for everything around us will perish, while the heavens will remain unchanged for ever.' Whereupon he reveals to his victim where he has taken him: 'You are standing', he says, 'on the holiest spot on earth. This is where Pythagoras and Zarathustra met.'[78]

The story of the man of God who withdraws to the loneliness of a high mountain, where he is driven to the edge of madness by the monstrous visions of his repressed desires, is one of the great spiritual dramas of Western literature. In his *Zarathustra* Nietzsche took over many elements of the legend in the theatrical form already given to them by Flaubert. He does not mention the novel by name until 1885 but he had known the work since his time in Basel. In 1872 a composer had asked him to produce an opera libretto based on Flaubert's *Salammbô*, which so offended the Wagnerian in him that in 1888, in *The Case of Wagner*, he scornfully suggested that Flaubert should have translated his *Madame Bovary* into Phoenician 'and offered it to Wagner, duly mythologised, as a libretto'.[79] This was a dig also at Cosima Wagner, who had waxed indignant when a critic ventured to compare the *Mastersingers* with *Madame Bovary*.

The Temptation of St Anthony was published in 1874, after Flaubert had achieved notoriety through his trial over *Madame Bovary*. The subject had first come into his mind in Genoa, where he saw the painting by Brueghel.

Could Nietzsche also have discovered it there? Wagner began to read Flaubert's novel in Naples in 1880 but quickly laid it aside 'in disgust', wrote Cosima.[80] In this respect, at least, Nietzsche shared the opinion of his one-time idol. The story of a man of God who renounces life for the greater glory of a deity pledged to the denial of the world could not but irritate him. For Nietzsche it was an insult to the world. Flaubert was his complete antithesis – a savage *décadent* who lived out his repressed desires on paper because a hatred of life had taken control of him; an apostle of chastity who in reality knew only 'those of weak will in whom desire has taken the place of will'.[81]

But what disturbed Nietzsche most about Flaubert was that he did not have the courage to do what he wanted to do. He hid behind a mask of 'self-inflicted pain and subtle cruelty'.[82] 'I cannot help laughing at Flaubert,' wrote Nietzsche elsewhere, 'with his affected anger at the way the *bourgeois* disguises himself as one thing or another!'[83] Flaubert himself is forced to do the same, because he does not have the courage to face the truth.

And all this, concludes Nietzsche, rests on the foundation of a secret nihilism. This nihilism arose in the middle of the nineteenth century, when the romantic faith in love and a shining future gave way before an 'urge to nothingness'. With this formulation Nietzsche struck two targets at the same time – 'G. F[laubert] for the French and R. W[agner] for the Germans'.[84]

Nietzsche never acknowledged the extent to which Flaubert's *Temptation of St Anthony* influenced his *Zarathustra*. He did, however, plan to give Part Four the subtitle 'The Temptation of Zarathustra'. And his hero's passage through life is similar to that of St Anthony, albeit in the reverse direction. The masks of his own existence appear before him in the mountains. But the lusts that the saint stifles and ultimately overcomes are those that Zarathustra cultivates. What the one condemns, the other extols. What the Christian blesses, Zarathustra curses. The hermit from the nihilist dream factory confronts Nietzsche's Antichrist. And because he has to reverse the false direction in which things have been moving, he opens his story with the scene that Flaubert put at the end. 'Finally the day breaks,' concludes *The Temptation of St Anthony*, 'and like the curtain being raised in front of the tabernacle, golden clouds roll back in great volutes, leaving behind them a clear sky, with the sun in the centre. And from the radiant ball of the sun shines forth the countenance of Jesus Christ.'

For Zarathustra, on the other hand, the sun remains the sun, his brilliant heavenly fellow-star, with whom he is on intimate terms: 'But finally his heart changed – and one morning he rose with the dawn, confronted the sun and said: "O thou great star! What would thy happiness be, if thou hadst not those on whom thou shineth!"'[85]

THE SHADOW ON THE WALL

Among Nietzsche's jottings after his vision by the lake there occurs a confessional passage reminiscent of his first stay in Naples in 1876, which concludes with the observation: 'The breeding of the Greeks makes the men more beautiful than the women.'[86] This revelation struck him as he was riding in a coach with Malwida von Meysenbug and his friend Paul Rée round the hills of Posillipo, a spot famed for its view of Naples. He made two entries in his notebook: 'How did I hitherto bear to live? – The glow of evening' and: 'Posillipo and all those blind people whose eyes have been opened.'[87] Had his eyes already been opened to the beauty of the Neapolitans, descendants of Greek colonisers? At a key moment in *Zarathustra* the allusion to *Tristan* – 'How did I bear to live?' – reappears – the moment when the liberated Superman stands laughing in front of him.

The historian Ferdinand Gregorovius, friend of Malwida von Meysenbug, had a similar experience in the harbour at Naples:

> The Neapolitans swim like dolphins. Water preserves the human body in its most natural original state. Nakedness flourishes in the warm climate and there are fine opportunities for making sketches of the nude body. The scene is one of stark contrasts. Luxurious coaches drive along the quayside, carrying the most elegant members of high society, and in full gaze of a bejewelled prince or the finest lady from a salon in Paris or London throngs of naked youths leap into the water in blissful innocence. The fisher-boys even run naked up and down the street, greeting strangers with graceful bows and lively gestures ... I used to enjoy looking down from the fourth floor window of my house and tempting them out on to the street with a groat. At a sign from me they would jump into the water, demonstrate their agility, then climb out again, dripping wet, and claim their reward.[88]

Writing to her adopted daughter Olga about the same coach ride, with Vesuvius 'shrouded in majestic storm clouds' and the city 'glowing as if it were built of pure gold', Malwida recalled: 'It was wonderful to see the two friends so intoxicated with the views. I have never seen Nietzsche so lively. He was laughing in sheer delight.'[89]

What Malwida had written in October 1876 came back to Nietzsche in the autumn of 1881. Now that his eyes had been opened to the Eternal Recurrence, the 'heavenly star of being', he also grasped the meaning of that other revelation that the beauty of those naked Italian bodies had afforded him. 'I am not strong enough for the north', he wrote. 'It is an area dominated by morose and affected people who are as perpetually preoccupied with planning for the future as is the beaver in his lodge. I spent my entire youth among these people, and this all came back to me when I saw for the first time the sunset over Naples, with its grey and red clouds in the sky. A shiver of self-pity went through me as I reflected that I was beginning to grow old. Tears filled my eyes, and I felt I had been rescued just in the nick of time.'

In the south there was no need to 'plan for the future'. Only an over-fearful Thomas Mann could utter a cry of despair in Naples in 1896: 'What am I suffering from? From sexuality ... Will it be my downfall? ... How can I free myself from sexuality?'[90] Nietzsche, on the other hand, felt that he had been rescued 'in the nick of time'. And the books that describe his rescue – *Sunrise* and *La gaia scienza* – sing the same praises of the south as Hölderlin's hero. For Hyperion too shuddered and turned his back on the north.

For Nietzsche the north signified a permanently guilty conscience, the scourge of his Protestant upbringing. Did he not feel this frustration with almost every thought, every deed? Had he not been forced, throughout his entire life, to deny first his yearnings, then their fulfilment? He had fled to the south in order to escape from malicious threats and the severity of the law. Here there was nobody to point a finger at him. The people he met had no idea who he was, while from those who knew him and remained in correspondence with him he kept his addresses secret, allowing contacts only via poste restante.

But the source of his guilt complex lay deep in his own being, and God's vengeful voice came from his own ear. When he returned to Genoa from Sils-Maria in October 1881, with the concept of the Eternal Recurrence in his mind, a vague awareness made itself felt that also concealed in his baggage was his worst enemy – his guilt complex. Now that the secret of all existence had been revealed to him – namely that there *is* no secret, no God, no beyond, but only what there is, in eternity – he takes up the struggle against his inner voice. In the same notebook in which he treats of his vision of the Homeric shield, there occurs a reference to 'a pang of conscience ... felt even after an unintended offence'. As an example he quotes his mythological alter ego – Oedipus. The worst thing is 'disgust with oneself'.[91] Conscience stirs up its victim against itself, ruins its joys and not infrequently drives it to death. A man who is disgusted at himself would be advised to hang himself or take an overdose of opium. Or – the most tempting course of action for survival – make to throttle the creature responsible for provoking this disgust.

But this creature is long dead. In the autumn of 1881 references to 'the death of God' become more frequent.[92] Book One of *Thus Spake Zarathustra* is headed 'Obituary on the Death of God'. And the author describes himself as Man without God, 'the loneliest of the lonely', who must now find a friend.[93] He knows, of course, who that friend will be, namely the 'magician' who has taken the place of the dead God. But what does it really mean to declare that God is dead? Did Nietzsche intend to recast in poetic form his atheistic belief that faith in the Christian God had become implausible? If so, then the phrase, as used in common parlance, is singularly inappropriate. For if something is dead, must it not have once lived?

If Nietzsche's 'God is Dead' were merely an ingenious form of packaging for a familiar and somewhat hackneyed shibboleth, one could dismiss it as an absurdity. But it was not. There was nothing metaphorical about the dictum for Nietzsche – for him it was reality. What had taken hold of his mind was not the proposition that there was no God but that there had once been a God who had died, as a man dies. The death of God was a terrifying thought, associated with the smell of a corpse and the sound of men digging a grave. Did Nietzsche know where the idea came from? Probably no more than he knew the origin of 'the passing Zarathustra' or the recurrent 'shield of necessity'. Suddenly, it seems, the idea was there, charged with conviction, demanding to be let out. 'Murder of murders!' he wrote in Genoa. 'We wake as murderers! How can such a man find consolation?'[94]

When they told little Friedrich Nietzsche in the rectory in Röcken that his father was dead, he could find no solace. When one's God dies, there is no replacement, and one's world remains devastated, because everything that reminds one of Him – and everything does remind one of Him – testifies only to His absence. Where God has died, the world seems to have died too.

The loneliest of the lonely, Fritz found himself thrust back into a ghostly, nightmarish landscape where the shadows in the churchyard were whispering to each other about the dead God. When, over thirty years later, he proclaimed with despairing persistence the 'death of God', his shocking utterance was sustained not only by his mourning over the irreparable loss of his father but also by the fear of his father's return. For the dead God *had* returned – first in the graveyard, as a murderous shadow from the tomb, then in the voice of the demon, whose whisperings the boy had feared as he feared death itself. 'The ghostly sounds in my ear' accompanied him as the voice of his own living conscience, making himself and his life an object of disgust to him. Although in Naumburg, as 'the little pastor' and an exemplary pupil, he had managed to a large extent to keep this voice muted – by obeying commandments, one avoids persecution – it must have returned with greater tenacity than ever since his adolescence. As his wistful thoughts would not leave his mind, so the dead God refused to be driven away – a ghost to whom he could close neither his eyes nor his ears. There it sat, in the cavern of his consciousness.

The third part of *La gaia scienza*, in which Zarathustra, albeit incognito, makes his first spectacular appearance in Nietzsche's works, opens with an aphorism, conceived in the autumn of 1881, called 'Fresh Struggles': 'For centuries after the Buddha had died, his shadow was displayed in a cave – a huge, terrifying shadow. God is dead, but man being what he is, there may well be caverns in which His shadow will be displayed for centuries to come. And as for us – we too must conquer His shadow!'[95]

God is dead, Nietzsche is saying – now let us also eradicate all trace of His erstwhile presence. His shadow stretches out from the past and lies across the present, depriving plants of light. Himself a graveyard seedling, Nietzsche knew what that meant. Had he himself not withered and almost died? The agonies of conscience inflicted on him by the bloodsucking Christian faith afflict the whole of Christendom. 'Beware the shadow of God!' he warns – 'some people also call it metaphysics'.[96]

Such was the muffled tone of his paean of victory composed in Genoa and Sils, the long shadow cast by his new sun. But what, he pondered, was the source of the power that the past continued to exercise over him? How could something dead teach him, a living person, how to fear? The 'little pastor' already sensed the answer – it was he who was responsible for this death. Death therefore had the power to pronounce his perpetual guilt. His father was a burden on his conscience, a nightmare he could not shake off. And of all his books he chose *La gaia scienza*, the work that conveyed his greatest hopes for the future, in order to proclaim his lifelong guilt complex, disguising himself as a man driven to madness by his conscience because he could not come to terms with what he had done.

One bright morning – so Nietzsche begins his story – a madman ran across the marketplace carrying a lantern and shouting 'I am looking for God! I am looking for God!'[97] That sounds like Diogenes but in fact it comes directly from Nietzsche's childhood. In Naumburg, with its markets and churches, the painful memory of the loss of his father and his home had returned to haunt him. Here, surrounded by strangers, he was an orphan vainly searching for his father. The madman encountered some who in any case did not believe in God, and had to suffer their jeering. 'Has he lost his way, like a child?' they mock. Or: 'Did He go to sea – or emigrate?' How could they understand what it meant, to lose a God? They had never had one. Or maybe they had, but had forgotten.

The man with the lamp, who was looking in the daylight for what he had lost during the night, jumped up and fixed them with his steely glare. The statue of the knight in the sacristy at Röcken had looked at little Fritz in the same way. And what did the madman shout to the 'normal' citizens? ' "Where has God gone?" he cried. "I will tell you! We have killed Him – you and I! We are all of us His murderers!" '

This murderous deed, which his listeners stubbornly refuse to acknowledge, seems to have unhinged him, for what seemed to lie far back in the distant past – assuming that it ever occurred at all – now confronted him as though it had happened only yesterday. 'Do we still not hear the sound of the gravediggers burying God?' he asks. 'Do we not yet catch a whiff of His putrefying body?'[98]

Apparently someone close to him really has died, for he believes he can smell the cadaver while the gardeners prepare the grave site in front of his window, as he recalled in his childhood reminiscences. Moreover the guilt is his – God is a victim of *his* cruelty. With the bloodthirstiness characteristic of his schoolboy poems, in which wailing monks brandish the heads of decapitated bodies, he leaves his madman to confess that they had left their God 'to bleed to death from the wounds inflicted by their knives ... Who shall wipe the blood clean? Where is the water with which to cleanse ourselves?'[99]

Nietzsche had already described an attack of this kind in his *Sunrise*, where he portrayed the madman 'in the throes of preparing the way for a new philosophy'. He too, 'an epileptic foaming at the mouth', was suffering the pangs of guilt. 'I have killed the law,' he cries, 'and the law is tormenting me as a corpse torments a living body!' But those who hear him do not understand what he is saying and eye him with suspicion. Somehow one cannot blame them. But the time will come when they do understand, he says – it is just that the news of the murder has not yet reached men's ears.[100]

But it has apparently reached his. The demonic voice repeatedly whispered it to him while the world slept and the dead God in his heart awoke. At such times loneliness was at its most intense, and the mocking mask of the universe stared him in the face, an experience his tragic hero Oedipus had also undergone. It was as though the entire world were a void, all fixed relationships out of joint – the message shouted by the madman to the crowds in the marketplace. 'What did we do', he cries, 'when we released the earth from the shackles of the sun? Whither is it going? Whither are *we* going? Away from all suns? Are we not plunging irrevocably to our doom – backwards, sideways, forwards, in all directions? Is there still an above and a below? Are we not wandering through an endless nothingness, gloated over by an oppressive void? Has it not grown colder? Does not night return time and again – more and more night?'[101]

The madman tormented by the prospect of a soulless universe is none other than Zarathustra himself. According to the original version of the text, 'Zarathustra lit a lamp in the brightness of the morning' and went out into the marketplace to proclaim his terrible tidings.[102] In the final version of the book the name of the prophet is withheld, presumably because Nietzsche did not want to burden him with the crime of murder before he made his first appearance. Zarathustra, radiant brother of the sun, could not be allowed to be spattered with somebody else's blood.

But he does owe his eloquence to a particular source. For behind the madman's outburst in the market square lies a key passage from Flaubert's *The Temptation of St Anthony*, a passage that describes a godless eternity, an icy universe in which man is condemned to be tossed wantonly hither and thither. By drawing on Flaubert at this point, Nietzsche is not betraying a paucity of original ideas – the desolate world of his own nightmares and visions was real enough to him. But in Flaubert's tale it is the Devil himself who conjures up a world of godless chaos before the eyes of the trembling saint. Must not God's murderer himself become the Devil, the rival God, the Antichrist that as early as 1883 Nietzsche had told Malwida von Meysenbug he felt himself to be?

In Flaubert the Devil appears in the guise of divine knowledge. 'My kingdom extends to the limits of the universe,' he pronounces, radiant as an archangel and glowing like a sun, 'and my thirst knows no bounds ... I am for ever marching onwards, liberating the spirit, weighing the worlds in my hand without hate, without fear, without compassion, without love, without God. They call me Knowledge.'

To prove what he is saying, he takes his sceptical victim on a tour of the universe, giving detailed commentaries on what they encounter. The Saint quickly recognises that the Devil's voice is echoing his own thoughts, responding to his own recollections, as the two men fly through distant nebulae and the reaches of outer space. 'What is the purpose of all this?' asks the pious passenger. 'There is no purpose!' replies the navigator. For everything is eternal. 'Behold the sun!' he whispers in a voice that seems to come from within. 'Flames dart out from its rim and scatter into sparks that turn into worlds. And beyond the last of these worlds, beyond the bottomless pit in which there is nothing but darkness, other suns are circling, and beyond them yet more, and still more, to infinity ...'

All this is too much for the Saint. 'Stop! Stop!' he cries. 'I am afraid! I am falling into the abyss!' The Devil calms him. 'There is no abyss, no farthest or highest point, no end', he says, reassuringly. Anthony begins to comprehend the truth. 'So all my prayers, all my sighs, all the torments of the flesh and all the fervour of my love were sacrificed to an illusion, words spoken in a void, meaningless ...' He begins to feel dizzy, and he intones a lament like the one uttered by Nietzsche's madman: 'An icy terror holds my soul in its grip, more penetrating than all pain. It is a death deeper than death. I am descending into an unfathomable darkness. It pierces me through and through. The infinity of nothingness shatters my consciousness.'

Nietzsche's madman can deliver the Devil's reply himself: perhaps everything is an illusion, the world in a continuous state of flux – which means that nothing is fixed, and that consequently there is no such thing as truth. The only reality would be illusion. 'Do you know that you can see?' the Devil asks the dumbfounded saint. 'Do you know whether you are alive? Perhaps there is nothing there.'

So impressed was he by this episode from Flaubert's tale that Nietzsche quoted from it not only in Zarathustra's first appearance before *Thus Spake Zarathustra* but also, with a wry smile, in a later preface to *The Birth of Tragedy*, where he wrote: 'What I came to understand at that time was something terrible, something fraught with danger, a diabolical problem with horns – not necessarily a bull as such but certainly a new problem. Today I would describe it as the problem of knowledge itself.'[103] During his flight through the universe St Anthony had had to keep tight hold of the horns of the Devil, repository of knowledge: 'Anthony kept a firm grip on the Devil's horns, as he lay outstretched on the Devil's back.'

The meaningless infinity of the universe, a concept with which science has made us familiar in modern times, was something Nietzsche had experienced in the Oedipal nightmares of his boyhood. He knew that the ultimate consequence of a world without God is unbearable and plunges mankind into the torment of total negation. The name of that consequence is Guilt. The Devil was speaking the truth – there was no way of equivocating over the death of his father, any more than there was over his return from the dead, a ghost with a demonic voice.

Before Zarathustra makes his appearance under his own name in the final aphorism of the fourth book of *La gaia scienza*, and prepares to embark on his 'descent', his creator gently explains to the reader once more what he expected to hear from the demonic voice of the dead God. The title he gives the aphorism is the name of the concept first found in a note made in Sils-Maria: 'A new basic idea – the Eternal Recurrence.'[104] Now he calls it 'the *greatest* basic idea', and it is no longer the vision of a gleaming golden shield but a nightmare. *His* nightmare. Long had he reflected on how to put this virtually inexpressible experience into words and make it intelligible to his readers. Initially he had thought to attribute it to the alchemist Paracelsus and describe it as a miraculous legend. Was it a deception perpetrated by one who wished me ill? wondered the magician. If so, it was the 'wickedest temptation' he had ever had to undergo.[105] Nietzsche chose the name Paracelsus partly because of its mysterious overtones but partly also because, like himself, Paracelsus had once held a professorship in Basel, a post he had had to vacate following a dispute with the city fathers.

On his next attempt to make public his frightening message he sought out a 'friendly foreigner' to whom he planned to convey the joyful aspect of the Recurrence – 'the thought that came to me like a star, which would shine down on you and on everyone'. First the shield of beauty, then the mysterious nocturnal sounds rising from the grave.

When he later came to confide to his friends his concept of the Eternal Recurrence, Nietzsche gave precedence to the nightmare version. He initiated Lou Salomé into the secret 'as though it were something whose realisation was a prospect that filled him with fear and trembling'. He spoke, said Lou, 'in hushed tones, as though he were conveying some terrible message'. To Overbeck, too, he spoke in a whisper, 'as if he were sharing some awesome secret'.[106] Resa von Schirnhofer, the student from Zurich, saw it as a piece of play-acting that bordered on the ludicrous. 'He was about to take his leave,' she recalled, 'but as we stood by the door, a sudden change came over him. His features froze, and shielding his mouth with his hand, glancing from one side to the other as though fearing some frightful catastrophe would ensue if anyone were to hear what he was saying, he whispered his secret in my ear.'[107]

The secret of the Eternal Recurrence. In *La gaia scienza* it is revealed in the same subdued tones with which he told it to his shocked friends. It was the voice of his demon that they heard. What, he asked provocatively, would it be like if others had to experience what I was made to experience? Would they not come to the same conclusions? 'Supposing', he went on, 'a demon were to penetrate your loneliest loneliness, by day or by night, and were to say to you: "The life that you are now living and have lived hitherto you will be made to live again and again, innumerable times. Nothing will be new but all the moments in your life, the greatest and smallest alike, will recur, and in the same order and sequence, with this self-same spider and the self-same moonlight shining between the trees, and this self-same moment, and I myself." '[108]

Nietzsche challenges the reader to imagine a situation – the 'loneliest loneliness' – which only he knows. And he summons up the demonic voice which only he hears. He talks of something the reader himself would never dream of – the spider, for whom he expresses a loathing in his earliest poem, together with the moonlight that had first shone on the vision of his father's ghost, and his father's voice, which had frozen him in his tracks and choked the air in his body. Is this the voice that is telling him that everything will return? The voice that is proclaiming the concept of the Eternal Recurrence, which the listener cannot bear? 'Would you not cast yourself on the ground with a gnashing of teeth and curse the demon that said such a thing?' challenges Nietzsche.

Does this mean that he had deciphered his demon's message? Or had he had the same experience as by the lake at Silvaplana, where he mistook the appearance of a memory for its substance? In one of his jottings Nietzsche wonders whether there is not a knowledge 'of which we are afraid and with which we do not want to be left alone, a knowledge whose insistence makes us tremble and whose whisperings make us blench'.[109] But however hard he tries to convince himself of the contrary, it is not the knowledge of the Recurrence that makes him fearful but the Recurrence of the nightmare, which makes him aware of this knowledge. The nightmare caused him to tremble and blench long before the thought of the Recurrence dawned on him – and without the nightmare even the most delightful vision of the lake would have quickly paled and become an incomprehensible memory.

But the ever-recurring nightmare was like the deep, swelling tones of the organ accompanying a hymn of thanksgiving. The man who feels the weight of the new 'basic idea', which offers him the prospect of an eternally recurring life must also bear for all time the nightmare that oppresses and torments him. In the final aphorism of *La gaia scienza* the demon utters the terrifying truth – the agonising secret of the nightmare's victim tortured by the sounds from the grave by night and the voice of his conscience by day.

But Nietzsche now sets a different course. Columbus makes his appearance, reinforced by both the vision of Zarathustra, the sage, and the moment for which he would gladly surrender his entire life – the moment by the lake. And so he asks tentatively, feeling his way, whether there might be lying latent in his readers an undetected star, a supreme moment, which desires to return. 'Have you perhaps experienced an awe-inspiring moment when you said: "Thou art a God – never did I hear such divine utterances!" '[110]

One instant of happiness, of ecstasy, that one wishes to re-live time and again and for which one is willing to return over and over? Would this not represent a totally new approach to life – to ask anyone and everyone whether they want to have and do something time after time? It would indeed represent the highest significance that a man could bestow on his life. It would be the object of his desires 'to yearn for nothing more than this final, definitive surety and guarantee'.

Nietzsche knew full well whom he was addressing – not the world at large but those capable of enduring moments of greatness and therefore of sustaining great ideas. In the original version of this aphorism from *La gaia scienza* he announced the emergence of this superman. He was a fellow-countryman of Hyperion's: 'Could you become that athlete and hero capable of bearing this burden and carrying it aloft? Imagine the grandeur of the task – and as you do so, you will catch sight of the ideal that confronts the mightiest men of the future! How much would you have to love life and yourself in order to feel this weight not as the heaviest burden but as the greatest bliss?'[111]

The name of this athlete and hero is Zarathustra. In the following aphorism he is granted leave to approach the sun and address it as one star to another. From now on it will be his task, as an athlete and a hero, to bear great loads and learn how duty can become pleasure.

The presence of an ideal towards which the heroic athlete is moving was first described in *La gaia scienza*, then, in 1888, in the confessional tone of *Ecce homo*, combined with the figure of Zarathustra. The aphorism comes in 'Sanctus Januarius', Book Five of *La gaia scienza*, and has the title 'The Great Health'. The reference is to the health-giving power of Italy, which cured his northern ailments and revealed to him, as the new Columbus, 'an undiscovered land whose boundaries no man has yet discovered, so rich in beauty, in the unknown, in the frightening and the divine',[112] that one can but despair of contemporary life and everyday existence.

In *Ecce homo* he also discloses that this 'great health' is the 'physiological pre-condition'[113] of the dancer Zarathustra who had once descended upon him in the course of his walks. He is also the seafarer who has sailed all the coasts of his ideal sea, the man who represents the ideal to which 'the athletic hero and mighty man of the future' aspires. It is, as *Ecce homo* reiterates, 'a wondrous ideal, seductive, irresistible and fraught with danger, the ideal of a human-superhuman sense of well being and generosity, which will often appear to be *in*human'.[114]

Just as Nietzsche had earlier revealed the 'human, all-too-human' nature of a hypocritical society, so now he sees opening up before him the vision of a 'human-superhuman' ideal. But it is a vision that belongs to a creature of flesh and blood – and not merely to one such creature but to all those bronzed, muscular gods whom one follows in order to see the Platonic ideal of beauty made manifest before one's eyes.

In the same year that *Ecce homo* was written, Nietzsche observed that he sought to talk about art 'in the same way as I talk to myself on my wild and lonely wanderings, when I sometimes pluck down a sacrilegious joy and ideal happiness into my life'.[115]

This sounds like a poetic description of an inspiration. But in the original version of the note Nietzsche adopts a much more practical approach. These ideals that he used to follow like a dancer really seem to have existed: 'And how many new ideals are still possible! Here is a little ideal that I catch every five weeks or so on one of my wild and lonely wanderings, in an azure blue moment of sacrilegious joy.' The note is dated Nice, 25 March 1888.

A year later he was in the mental asylum in Jena, spending his time splashing around in the bath and giving the doctors the impression that 'in his youth he must have been an agile dancer ... No sooner had Baron X begun to play his zither than Herr Nietzsche sprang to his feet and danced about tirelessly, until the attendant in charge finally calmed him down and led him away.'[116]

Epilogue to the English Edition

Thus Spake Zarathustra, published between 1883 and 1885 in four successive parts, like a serial novel, is today ranked among the classics of European philosophy. As Nietzsche himself foresaw, numerous university departments and other educational establishments are busily engaged in interpreting it, and anyone who studies the course of Western philosophy is bound to be confronted by it. Nietzsche himself spoke of his unique work in the superlative tones of the megalomaniac, comparing it to the Bible and describing it as a 'fifth Gospel' that marked the zenith of German philosophy and the culmination of the German language. 'The most exalted book ever written', he called it. 'The phenomenon of man, by contrast, lies in unconscionable depths beneath it.'

Modern readers have a similar feeling about the work. Its meaning seems to lie in the distance somewhere far above them, and the binoculars with which they could have deciphered it were not supplied with the text. On the other hand, those who approach it with the tools of methodological philosophy will quickly realise that they are not dealing with logical patterns of thought. Rather, Nietzsche seeks to entice them into a new world of mysteries governed by faith – faith in the divinity of his Superman, faith in the inescapability of the Eternal Recurrence, faith in the Will to Power, justification for all acts of violence. As the son of a pastor, he was not unfamiliar with the preacher's art, and Zarathustra's language – at times anachronistic to the point of the risible and the grotesque – has its origins in the Lutheran Bible.

But the story that Nietzsche tells in his 'fifth Gospel' is his own story. Zarathustra was one of the masks that enabled him to say things about which he would otherwise have had to stay silent. Zarathustra's sermonising soliloquies, bizarre visions and ecstatic odes lead back to their creator. What appear before us are the longings, the nightmare and the visions of Nietzsche himself. Above all, however, we are confronted with the experiences that he underwent as an outsider in the world of common mortals. What happened to Zarathustra is a mirror of Nietzsche's own cryptic autobiography.

Overtaken in his loneliness by his yearning for the godlike Superman, Zarathustra preaches his ideal to the masses. He is greeted, however, not with enthusiasm but with derision and animosity. Withdrawing from public gaze, he gathers a band of disciples around him, like Jesus, and reveals to them the mysteries of his doctrine of redemption. His message is that the world of the future will belong to the naked, masculine figure of the Superman, a blend of Greek hero and Renaissance conqueror – Alcibiades and Andrea Doria in one. Provided he has been bred for the task. For only after they have absorbed the message of his ideal of masculinity can Zarathustra's acolytes set about creating this universal hero. Women will be left with the consolation of the knowledge that they will be permitted to give birth to the Superman.

Indeed, he already exists. Zarathustra discovered him on the 'isles of the blest ... where the gods cast off their robes in the dance'. It was here that he picked up the word 'Superman', here that he chanced upon the beautiful naked bodies after which he lusted. And it was here that he assembled around him not his disciples but his 'children', in whom he found 'the meaning of the world'. For Nietzsche the isles of the blest, which were also to be found depicted on the golden shield of Achilles, lay in Sicily, which was where he saw the Superman. Here life echoed to the sounds of the eternal dance of spring. And the man of the future would share the bliss enjoyed by these young dancers. Such was Zarathustra's most passionate desire.

But alas, he soon had to bid farewell to this neo-classical paradise. Evidently out of fear for his reputation, as Zarathustra hints, Nietzsche left Sicily, only to be seized by unbearable pain and torment. What he loved, he was forced to abandon, and he was left with only the anguish of his yearning. His old trauma returns. A series of horrible nightmares convinces him that the pain and the terror will incessantly return. The law of the Eternal Recurrence, portrayed on Achilles' shield as the dance of the blest, now reveals its other side and appears as a horrible vision, a gruesome scene perpetually repeated. As Zarathustra knows, the past will for ever recur – as a coffin, harbinger of death, as a ghostly sound that whispers terrifying words in his ear, or as a mocking dwarf, bearing the message of the meaninglessness of all existence.

Zarathustra sees this traumatic vision before his eyes. The black snake of the Eternal Recurrence insinuates itself into the mouth of a sleeping shepherd boy, who suffocates in agony in the nightmare of his existence. As a child

Nietzsche used to be called 'the little pastor', the shepherd of his flock. Now he sees himself overtaken by the ghost of his past – but also by his guilty conscience, which sinks its fangs into his throat, for his behaviour is immoral and he has to be brought to justice. He is strangled by the constant fear of being caught, unmasked and punished.

But Zarathustra comes to the little pastor's aid, shouting to him in desperation to bite off the snake's head. The boy does so – and by this single act of strength liberates himself from the spell of his terrifying visions, the grip of his guilty conscience and the inescapable fear of punishment. He kills what had threatened to kill him. And in a flash he sees a New Man before him. Leaping in the air in delight, the shepherd boy dances like a naked god and begins to laugh. 'Nobody on the face of the earth ever laughed as he laughed!' cries his creator. 'I heard laughter that was no human laughter, O my brethren! And now I feel the pangs of a great thirst, a pining that will never leave me.'

It is Zarathustra's thirst and pining for the Superman that will no longer leave him. Ever more frenzied grow his cries, ever more obscene become the metaphors with which he shouts his lusts. 'O my soul,' he thunders in the autobiographical ode 'On the Great Yearning' from *Thus Spake Zarathustra*, 'I washed the petty sense of shame and false propriety from you and persuaded you to stand naked before the eyes of the sun.' But here, on the sands of the Mediterranean, Zarathustra's soul is awaiting its divine lover, who will be wafted towards him in a golden barque, surrounded by dancing dolphins. It is the 'Great Redeemer'. Nietzsche calls him Dionysus. But his own soul, weeping as it waits for its lover-god, is called Ariadne. Originally he intended to name 'On the Great Yearning' after the Cretan princess. For in the heart of his being the stern Zarathustra is a woman.

In the course of copying out *Thus Spake Zarathustra* Nietzsche was already beginning to mystify his message. Scarcely had he revealed its meaning than he set about concealing it again. Zarathustra's secret vanished behind a smokescreen of rhetoric. The fourth part of the book turned into an Aristophanic satyric drama, and tragedy descended into farce. Perhaps, in the last analysis, Nietzsche no longer wanted to be understood. Not for nothing did he give the work the subtitle 'A Book for Everyone and No-One'. Only the privileged few were expected to be able to decipher his true meaning. Only free spirits like him, those who had undergone the same experiences, suffered the same agonies and cherished the same desires, were permitted to savour the delights of this *hortus deliciarum*.

Nietzsche's sister Elisabeth was not one of this company. After her brother had become insane, she founded a cult in the centre of which stood the figure of Zarathustra. But this strange cultic figure no longer had any connection with the secret that its creator had concealed in him. When, in 1894, bankrupt and recently widowed, Elisabeth took over responsibility for nursing her mentally sick brother in Weimar, she took possession of all his copyrights. In addition she discovered masses of unpublished texts and jottings, which she edited and published, blatantly commercialising his reputation in a manner congenial to the taste of Wilhelmine Germany. She re-issued his published works in an art nouveau edition and collected the contents of his notebooks and files to form the paean of nationalistic ideology to which she gave the title *The Will to Power*. In the First World War *Thus Spake Zarathustra* was the favourite reading of the German troops in the trenches, and following the Kaiser, Adolf Hitler too found his image reflected in the mirror of the Superman, while Zarathustra's motto 'Glory be to the man of steel' was adopted by the SS.

After the collapse of the Third Reich Nietzsche found himself in the dock in the Nuremberg war trials. Hitler's racist war, alleged the chief French prosecutor, was the product of Nietzsche's theories. Another Frenchman, however, Georges Bataille, sprang to the philosopher's defence, mounting a vigorous attack against what he considered the abuse of Nietzsche's ideas by the Nazis.

Bataille could not have known that his plea would result in the emergence of a new Nietzsche cult in post-war Europe, which would lead a succession of writers and thinkers to identify with the author of *Thus Spake Zarathustra*. Nietzsche was now a pioneer of modernism, a 'good European', an intrepid immoralist, a brilliant social critic and the herald of a liberated, democratic mankind.

But these new generations also failed to penetrate his secret. Maybe it was because the very aura of mystery that enshrouded him was what appeared to be the most interesting facet of his personality. Only in this way could he be open to endless new interpretations – an enigma susceptible to the whims of fashion, taking on a new meaning for each successive age.

How boring, in contrast, would the 'truth' turn out to be. Indeed, did he himself not maintain that there was no such thing as 'the truth'?

Truth, he said, is a woman who had good reason to keep her secret to herself.

Notes

Abbreviations

HKG   *Jugendschriften, Historisch-Kritische Gesamtausgabe*, edited by Hans Joachim Mette, Munich 1933–34

S   *Werke in 3 Bänden*, edited by Karl Schlechta, Munich 1956

KGB   *Kritische Gesamtausgabe des Briefwechsels*, edited by Giorgio Colli and Mazzino Montinari, Berlin/New York 1975

W   *Sämtliche Werke, Kritische Studienausgabe*, edited by Giorgio Colli and Mazzino Montinari, Munich/Berlin 1980

G   *Begegnungen mit Nietzsche*, edited by Sander L. Gilman and Ingeborg Reichenbach, Bonn 1981

B   *Sämtliche Briefe, Kritische Studienausgabe*, edited by Giorgio Colli and Mazzino Montinari, Munich/Berlin 1986

Preface

1. Thomas Mann, *Das essayistische Werk*, Frankfurt 1968 (8 vols), Vol. II, 37.
2. Ibid., 39.
3. W 5, 87.
4. Andreas Patzer (ed.), *Briefwechsel Franz Overbeck–Erwin Rohde*, Berlin/New York 1989, Letter 67, 1 September 1886.
5. G, 274.
6. *Protokolle der Wiener Psychoanalytischen Vereinigung*, Frankfurt 1976–81 (4 vols), Vol. II, 29.
7. Sigmund Freud – Arnold Zweig, *Briefwechsel*, edited by Ernst L. Freud, Frankfurt 1984, 96.
8. Wilhelm Stekel, *Nietzsche und Wagner, Zeitschrift für Sexualwissenschaft* 4/1917, 26.
9. Günter Schulte, '*Ich impfe euch mit dem Wahnsinn*', Frankfurt 1982, 8.
10. Georg Groddeck, *Der Mensch und sein Es*, Wiesbaden 1970, 140.
11. B 6, 531.
12. Joachim Campe (ed.), *Andere Lieben, Homosexualität in der deutschen Literatur*, Frankfurt 1988, 174.
13. W 3, 349.
14. W 10, 111.
15. W 10, 373.
16. W 6, 254.
17. B 8, 290.
18. W 10, 374.
19. W 5, 19.

20. W 4, 48.
21. H. F. Peters, *Zarathustras Schwester*, Munich 1983, 188.
22. Ibid., 230.
23. Ibid., 237.
24. Martin Heidegger, *Nietzsche*, Pfullingen 1961 (2 vols), Vol. I, 474.
25. *Nietzsche-Studien* Vol. 18, 1989, xvi.
26. Giorgio Colli, *Nach Nietzsche*, Frankfurt 1980, 210.
27. Patzer, Letter 105, 17 March 1895.
28. W 1, 15.
29. Peters, 170.
30. Ibid., 239.
31. Ibid., 236.
32. Ibid., 278.
33. Ibid., 300.
34. Ibid., 288.
35. Carl J. Burckhardt, *Briefe 1908–1974*, Frankfurt 1986, 149.

1 A Plant from the Graveyard

1. S III, 107–8.
2. S III, 13.
3. Curt Paul Janz, *Friedrich Nietzsche, Biographie* (3 vols), Vol. I, Munich 1978, 35.
4. S III, 91.
5. Werner Ross, *Der ängstliche Adler, Friedrich Nietzsches Leben*, Stuttgart 1980, 23.
6. Anacleto Verrecchia, *Zarathustras Ende*, Vienna/Cologne/Graz 1986, 333.
7. W 6, 264.
8. S III, 13.
9. B 8, 288.
10. Janz, I, 39.
11. Adalbert Oehler, *Nietzsches Mutter*, Munich 1940, 26–33.
12. Lou Andreas-Salomé, *Friedrich Nietzsche in seinen Werken*, Dresden 1924, 213.
13. Oehler, 18.
14. Janz, I, 42.
15. W 5, 241.
16. G, 1.
17. S III, 109.
18. S III, 92.
19. W 6, 326.
20. S III, 17.

21. S III, 93.
22. S III, 17.
23. B 7, 138.
24. Arno Schmidt, *Fouqué und einige seiner Zeitgenossen*, Zurich 1988, 74.
25. S III, 14.
26. S III, 94.

2 Life as a Nightmare

1. G, 4.
2. W 2, 27.
3. Adalbert Oehler, *Nietzsches Mutter*, Munich 1940, 47.
4. S III, 18.
5. Oehler, 47.
6. Oehler, 44.
7. Erich F. Podach, *Gestalten um Nietzsche*, Weimar 1931, 10.
8. G, 20.
9. Oehler, 55.
10. W 12, 15.
11. W 4, 22.
12. Oehler, 55.
13. W 11, 209.
14. W 5, 386.
15. B 4, 240.
16. G, 4.
17. Oehler, 59.
18. W 6, 283.
19. W 13, 458.
20. G, 249.
21. W 4, 218.
22. B 2, 134.
23. HKG I, 191.
24. W 14, 472.
25. W 8, 194.
26. W 8, 505.
27. G, 6.
28. HKG II, 115.
29. *Kindlers Literaturlexikon*, Vol. III, Zurich 1965, 3378.
30. B 7, 108.
31. HKG I, 412.
32. Oehler, 58.
33. HKG I, 307.
34. G, 143.
35. W 12, 474.
36. HKG I, 308.
37. Elisabeth Förster-Nietzsche, *Der werdende Nietzsche*, Munich 1924, 196.

38. S III, 15.
39. HKG I, 91.
40. W 4, 142.
41. S III, 21.
42. S III, 15.
43. HKG I, 349.
44. S III, 67.
45. W 4, 145.
46. W 14, 310.
47. 'Nightmares Linked to Creativity', *Science Times*, 23 October 1984.
48. Ernest Hartmann, *The Nightmare*, New York 1984, 5.
49. Wilhelm Heinrich Roscher, *Ephialtes, Eine pathologisch-mythologische Abhandlung über die Alpträume und Alpdämonen des klassischen Altertums*, Leipzig 1900, 10.
50. Ibid., 14.
51. Ludwig Laistner, *Das Rätsel der Sphinx, Grundzüge einer Mythologiegeschichte*, Berlin 1889 (2 vols), Vol. II, 351.
52. Ibid., I, 302.
53. Ernest Jones, *On the Nightmare*, London 1931, 76–8.
54. Hartmann, 102–4.
55. Lou Andreas-Salomé, *Friedrich Nietzsche in seinen Werken*, Dresden 1924, 243.
56. G, 690.
57. W 2, 590.

3 The Pangs of Adolescence

1. Ludwig Bechstein, *Thüringen*, Munich (n.d.), 159.
2. Curt Paul Janz, *Friedrich Nietzsche, Biographie* (3 vols), Vol. I, Munich 1978, 66.
3. Werner Ross, *Der ängstliche Adler, Friedrich Nietzsches Leben*, Stuttgart 1980, 47.
4. W 6, 107.
5. S III, 48.
6. Janz, I, 129.
7. Ibid., 113.
8. B 1, 141.
9. HKG I, 110.
10. G, 38.
11. W 8, 194.
12. S III, 151.
13. HKG I, 293.
14. HKG II, 101.
15. W 6, 399.
16. HKG II, 101.
17. HKG II, 108.
18. Bechstein, 160.
19. G, 47.
20. HKG I, 100.
21. HKG I, 102.
22. Georg Groddeck, *Der Mensch und sein Es*, Wiesbaden 1970, 139.
23. W 6, 286.
24. W 6, 286.
25. W 5, 224.
26. B 1, 228.
27. W 9, 460.
28. HKG II, 10.
29. HKG I, 247.
30. HKG II, 70.
31. Quoted in Antonio Panormita, *Hermaphroditus*, Hanau 1986, 403.
32. Quoted in Gisela Bleibtreu-Ehrenberg, *Homosexualität*, Frankfurt 1981, 347.
33. HKG II, 71.
34. B 1, 217.
35. KGB I/3, 53.
36. G, 42.
37. B 1, 232.
38. HKG II, 211.
39. B 3, 46.
40. G, 42.
41. G, 587.
42. B 1, 202.
43. HKG II, 58.
44. HKG II, 415.
45. W 7, 390.
46. B 1, 289.
47. HKG II, 415.

4 The Knight, Death and the Dominatrix

1. Curt Paul Janz, *Friedrich Nietzsche, Biographie* (3 vols), Vol. I, Munich 1978, 124.
2. B 2, 12.
3. B 2, 15.
4. S III, 119.
5. W 8, 474.
6. Janz, I, 185.

7. Ibid., 254.
8. Ibid., 266.
9. W 13, 462.
10. W 5, 379.
11. S III, 148.
12. Ingmar Bergman, *Mein Leben*, Hamburg 1987, 241.
13. Karl Jaspers, *Strindberg und van Gogh*, Munich 1977, 68.
14. Maurice Merleau-Ponty, *Phänomenologie der Wahrnehmung*, Berlin 1966, 390.
15. HKG II, 275.
16. Janz, I, 47.
17. C. A. Emge, 'Nachricht von bisher unbekannten Erfahrungen Nietzsches', *Merkur*, viii, 1949, 829.
18. B 6, 396.
19. Janz, I, 221.
20. Arthur Schopenhauer, *Sämtliche Werke*, edited by Wolfgang Frhr. von Löhneysen, Frankfurt 1986 (5 vols), Vol. IV, 343.
21. B 4, 265.
22. B 2, 88.
23. S III, 133–4.
24. B 2, 96.
25. W 6, 320.
26. W 1, 346–9.
27. W 1, 354.
28. B 5, 36.
29. W 1, 131.
30. B 4, 174.
31. Janz, I, 209.
32. B 2, 218.
33. G, 68.
34. Janz, I, 210.
35. W 15, 32.
36. KGB I/3, 213.
37. KGB I/3, 321.
38. G 2, 307.
39. KGB I/3, 340.
40. Erich F. Podach, *Gestalten um Nietzsche*, Weimar 1931, 52.
41. B 2, 121.
42. B 2, 195.
43. B 2, 356.
44. Schopenhauer, II, 682.
45. Ibid., 686, 699.
46. S III, 133.
47. Janz, I, 202.
48. G, 166.
49. B 3, 212.
50. HKG II, 329.
51. Schopenhauer, II, 744.
52. W 7, 389.
53. Schopenhauer, II, 744.
54. B 5, 187.
55. W 1, 32.
56. Leopold von Sacher-Masoch, *Venus im Pelz*, Frankfurt 1980, 12.
57. Ibid., 60.
58. Ibid., 81.
59. Ibid., 121.
60. Ibid., 136, 96.
61. W 5, 178.
62. W 3, 428.
63. W 4, 86, 84.
64. Sacher-Masoch, 74, 109.
65. W 4, 84.
66. Sacher-Masoch, 62.
67. W 4, 85.
68. Sacher-Masoch, 11.
69. W 6, 306.
70. W 4, 86.
71. Sacher-Masoch, 16.
72. Sacher-Masoch, 138.
73. W 4, 73.
74. W 7, 399.
75. W 1, 783.
76. Sacher-Masoch, 135.
77. Ibid., 133.
78. Ibid., 113–17.
79. G 323.

5 *The Redemption of the Gods*

1. W 5, 121.
2. Adapted from the translation by Benjamin Jowett, New York 1948.
3. B 5, 163.
4. W 1, 91.
5. W 1, 90.
6. W 6, 69.
7. W 6, 72.
8. W 1, 116.
9. B 3, 100.
10. W 15, 46/38.
11. Curt Paul Janz, *Friedrich Nietzsche, Biographie* (3 vols), Vol. I, Munich 1978, 474.
12. Werner Ross, *Der ängstliche Adler*,

Friedrich Nietzsches Leben, Stuttgart
1980, 300.
13. G, 180.
14. W 1, 13.
15. W 8, 388.
16. W 1, 11/14/28.
17. Arthur Schopenhauer, *Sämtliche
Werke*, edited by Wolfgang Frhr. von
Löhneysen, Frankfurt 1986 (5 vols),
Vol. I, 482.
18. W 11, 286.
19. W 1, 558.
20. W 1, 33.
21. W 1, 11.
22. B 3, 138/143.
23. W 7, 87.
24. W 1, 29.
25. W 1, 108.
26. W 6, 311.
27. W 7, 91.
28. W 1, 15.
29. W 7, 390.
30. W 2, 147.
31. W 1, 44/47.
32. W 1, 27/28.
33. W 1, 140/42.
34. W 1, 16/39.
35. W 15, 142.
36. W 8, 505.
37. W 1, 39.

6 In Klingsor's Enchanted Garden

1. B 2, 298.
2. B 2, 338.
3. W 1, 147.
4. B 2, 379.
5. B 3, 52.
6. Martin Gregor-Dellin, *Richard
Wagner*, Munich 1983, 605.
7. W 6, 401.
8. B 3, 317.
9. G, 420.
10. G, 163.
11. Thomas Mann, *Das essayistische
Werk*, Frankfurt 1968 (8 vols), Vol. II,
129.
12. G, 260.
13. W 6, 419/425.
14. W 1, 494.
15. B 2, 352.

16. W 6, 290.
17. G, 189.
18. W 1, 479.
19. W 6, 289.
20. W 6, 417.
21. W 9, 539.
22. W 5, 179.
23. W 9, 583.
24. Gregor-Dellin, 646.
25. B 4, 153.
26. W 15, 85/84/56.
27. W 15, 73.
28. B 5, 241.
29. W 15, 73.
30. Curt Paul Janz, *Friedrich Nietzsche,
Biographie* (3 vols), Vol. I, Munich
1978, 787.
31. B 5, 288.
32. G, 651.
33. Janz, I, 788, 789.
34. Gregor-Dellin, 750.
35. Dieter Schickling, *Abschied von
Walhall*, Munich 1985, 75.
36. Sigmund Freud, *Briefe an Wilhelm
Fließ*, Frankfurt 1985, 27.
37. G, 345.
38. B 6, 365. This slander is detailed in J.
Köhler, *Nietzsche and Wagner*, New
Haven and London 1998.
39. Janz, II, 175.
40. KGB II, 6/2, 844.
41. W 8, 507.
42. W 8, 505/506/507.
43. W 15, 11.
44. W 8, 507.
45. W 8, 510.
46. W 2, 406.
47. W 8, 512.
48. W 8, 528.
49. B 5, 266.
50. B 5, 287.
51. B 6, 3.
52. W 8, 504–5.
53. W 2, 530.
54. W 8, 509/508.
55. Ferdinand Gregorovius, *Die Insel
Capri*, Leipzig 1868, 51.
56. W 5, 74.
57. W 8, 506–9.
58. W 3, 52.
59. W 3, 405.

7   *A Chapter of Accidents*

1.   G, 77.
2.   G, 106.
3.   G, 197.
4.   G, 256.
5.   Curt Paul Janz, *Friedrich Nietzsche, Biographie* (3 vols), Vol. I, Munich 1978, 542, 544.
6.   G, 199.
7.   G, 201.
8.   G, 126.
9.   G, 100.
10. Janz, I, 329.
11. W 15, 17/44.
12. B 5, 113.
13. G, 133.
14. G, 104–11.
15. G, 106, 111.
16. G, 107.
17. G, 106.
18. G, 109.
19. G, 237.
20. G, 117, 116.
21. G, 105.
22. G, 93.
23. G, 95.
24. G, 79.
25. G, 203, 206, 208.
26. G, 142.
27. *Der Spiegel*, 8 June 1981.
28. G, 89.
29. G, 506.
30. G, 102.
31. W 2, 478.
32. G, 103.
33. W 13, 557.
34. W 3, 352.
35. W 1, 876/881.
36. W 1, 877.
37. W 1, 882.
38. W 1, 883.
39. W 1, 877.
40. W 1, 886.
41. W 1, 890.
42. G, 219.
43. W 1, 890.
44. W 5, 243.
45. G, 263.
46. G, 264.
47. G, 268, 269.

48. G, 248.
49. G, 270.
50. G, 271.
51. G, 271.
52. G, 272.
53. G, 273.
54. G, 274.
55. G, 81.
56. B 5, 184.
57. B 5, 176.
58. B 5, 176.
59. B 5, 176.
60. B 5, 177.
61. W 6, 357.
62. HKG II, 199.
63. Richard Wagner, *Gesammelte Schriften*, Leipzig 1897 (10 vols), Vol. IX, 92.
64. C. A. Bernoulli, *Franz Overbeck und Friedrich Nietzsche*, Jena 1908 (2 vols), Vol II, 234.
65. B 5, 409.
66. G, 102.
67. W 1, 248.
68. W 1, 251.
69. W 8, 599.
70. W 1, 249.
71. W 1, 315.
72. W 1, 331.
73. V 5, 355.
74. B 5, 360.
75. B 5, 367.
76. B 5, 410.
77. B 6, 3.
78. G, 366.
79. W 15, 96.
80. B 5, 360.
81. G, 366, 367.
82. *Süddeutsche Monatshefte*, November 1931, 102.
83. B 8, 579.
84. B 3, 30.

8   *'The Honeymoon of Our Friendship'*

1.   B 5, 251.
2.   B 5, 248.
3.   KGB II, 6/1, 587.
4.   B 5, 245.
5.   G, 337.

6. G, 342.
7. W 8, 403.
8. W 8, 402.
9. W 8, 468.
10. W 8, 396.
11. G, 343.
12. W 8, 397.
13. W 10, 599.
14. S III, 53.
15. KGB II/2, 360.
16. Adelbert von Chamisso, *Sämtliche Werke*, edited by Werner Freudel and Christel Laufer, Herrsching (n. d.), 124.
17. W 8, 395.
18. *Treffliche Wirkungen, Anekdoten von und über Goethe*, Munich 1987 (2 vols), Vol. I, 368.
19. W 8, 395.
20. B 6, 470.
21. Curt Paul Janz, *Friedrich Nietzsche, Biographie* (3 vols), Vol. I, Munich 1978, 752.
22. B 5, 246.
23. KGB II, 6/1, 596.
24. H. F. Peters, *Lou Andreas-Salomé*, Munich 1986, 248.
25. KGB II, 6/1, 248.
26. W 2, 365.
27. KGB II, 6/1, 590.
28. KGB II, 6/1, 282.
29. B 5, 139.
30. Andreas Patzer (ed.), *Briefwechsel Franz Overbeck–Erwin Rohde*, Berlin/New York 1989, note to Letter 10, 29 June 1877.
31. W 6, 323/328.
32. B 5, 193.
33. KGB II, 6/1, 404.
34. KGB II, 6/2, 983.
35. Janz, I, 743.
36. KGB II, 6/2, 717.
37. Janz, I, 741.
38. Ernst Pfeiffer, *Friedrich Nietzsche, Paul Rée and Lou Salomé*, Frankfurt 1970, 37.
39. Anacleto Verrecchia, *Zarathustras Ende*, Vienna/Cologne/Graz 1986, 268.
40. *Die Zeit*, 27 April 1979.
41. B 5, 290.
42. W 3, 523.
43. G, 434.
44. W 9, 657.
45. Hugo Daffner, *Friedrich Nietzsches Randglossen zu Bizets Carmen*, Regensburg 1912, 34.
46. Georges Bizet, *Carmen*, Act I, Scene 10.
47. W 5, 250.
48. Hans Mayer, *Außenseiter*, Frankfurt 1981, 182.
49. Gerhard Härle, *Die Gestalt des Schönen*, Königstein 1986, 71.
50. W 13, 563.

9 The New Columbus

1. W 3, 369.
2. W 3, 370.
3. W 3, 372.
4. G, 628.
5. W 11, 313.
6. Joachim Campe (ed.), *Andere Lieben, Homosexualität in der deutschen Literatur*, Frankfurt 1988, 176.
7. Mayer, op. cit., 179.
8. W 3, 641.
9. W 15, 107.
10. W 2, 15/19, W 3, 636.
11. W 5, 19.
12. W 2, 13/14/15.
13. W 2, 16.
14. W 2, 18.
15. W 2, 21.
16. W 3, 17.
17. W 3, 345.
18. KGB II, 6/1, 338.
19. W 13, 458.
20. W 14, 287.
21. B 6, 47–9.
22. W 3, 341.
23. G, 610.
24. W 6, 329.
25. B 6, 138.
26. W 12, 198.
27. B 6, 151.
28. W 3, 521.
29. W 6, 398.
30. Fabrizia Ramondino and Andreas F. Müller, *Neapel*, Zurich 1988, 64.
31. B 6, 139.
32. B 5, 324.
33. W 3, 335.

34. W 14, 229.
35. W 3, 641.
36. W 3, 335.
37. W 3, 282.
38. W 3, 641.
39. W 3, 335.
40. W 14, 229.
41. W 3, 642.
42. W 3, 352.
43. W 3, 640.
44. W 5, 228.
45. Cecile Beurdeley, *L'Amour bleu*, Cologne 1977, 16.
46. W 2, 619.
47. W 14, 193.
48. KGB III/2, 212.
49. W 3, 340.
50. *Goethes Werke*, Sophienausgabe (143 vols), Vol. 44, 211.
51. B 6, 167.
52. H. F. Peters, *Lou Andreas-Salomé*, Munich 1986, 92.
53. W 9, 663.
54. W 9, 598.
55. W 9, 652.
56. W 12, 71.
57. W 12, 47.
58. W 6, 306.
59. W 6, 400.
60. W 10, 526.
61. W 5, 121.
62. B 8, 572.

10 On the Isles of the Blest

1. W 3, 532.
2. B 6, 68.
3. KGB III/2, 142.
4. KGB III/2, 197.
5. KGB II, 6/2, 227.
6. B 6, 172.
7. KGB II, 6/2, 231.
8. H. F Peters, *Zarathustras Schwester*, Munich 1983, 189.
9. B 6, 276.
10. W 15, 147.
11. W 15, 147.
12. B 7, 87.
13. Curt Paul Janz, *Friedrich Nietzsche, Biographie* (3 vols), Vol. II, Munich 1978, 401.

14. Erich F. Podach, *Gestalten um Nietzsche*, Weimar 1931, 71.
15. Ibid., 121.
16. W 9, 51.
17. Janz, II, 94.
18. André Gide, *If It Die*, translated by Dorothy Bussy, London 1950, 256–7.
19. Lawrence Grobel and Truman Capote, *Conversations with Capote*, London 1985, 146.
20. Ulrich Pohlmann, *Wilhelm von Gloeden*, Berlin 1987, 14.
21. Ibid., 27.
22. Ibid., 33.
23. Ibid., 36.
24. Gerhard Härle, *Die Gestalt des Schönen*, Königsstein 1986, 134.
25. Dagmar Nick, *Sizilien*, Munich 1987, 236.
26. B 6, 177.
27. Wilhelm Heinse, *Ardinghello und die Glückseeligen Inseln*, Nördlingen 1986, 275.
28. Ernst Pfeiffer, *Friedrich Nietzsche, Paul Rée und Lou Salomé*, Frankfurt 1970, 463.
29. B 6, 190.
30. KGB III/2, 249.
31. B 6, 189.
32. B 6, 188.
33. B 6, 190.
34. B 6, 188.
35. Werner Ross, *Der ängstliche Adler, Friedrich Nietzsches Leben*, Stuttgart 1980, 600.
36. B 6, 142.
37. W 3, 541.
38. W 11, 302.
39. Andreas Patzer (ed.), *Briefwechsel Franz Overbeck–Erwin Rohde*, Berlin/New York 1989, Letter 40, 18 July 1882.
40. W 6, 12/15.
41. W 13, 23.
42. W 13, 24.
43. W 4, 247.
44. W 4, 248.
45. Anacleto Verrecchia, *Zarathustras Ende*, Vienna/Cologne/Graz 1986, 265.

11 *'The Bird of Prey Masquerading as a Canary'*

1. B 6, 124.
2. Ernst Pfeiffer, *Friedrich Nietzsche, Paul Rée und Lou Salomé*, Frankfurt 1970, 92.
3. B 6, 185.
4. B 6, 186.
5. Lou Andreas-Salomé, *Lebensrückblick*, edited by Ernst Pfeiffer, Frankfurt 1974, 76.
6. H. F. Peters, *Lou Andreas-Salomé*, Munich 1986, 76.
7. Andreas-Salomé, 226.
8. Peters, 51.
9. Andreas-Salomé, 223.
10. Ibid., 29.
11. Peters, 37.
12. Ibid., 29.
13. Andreas-Salomé, 75.
14. Ibid., 80.
15. Ibid.
16. Curt Paul Janz, *Friedrich Nietzsche, Biographie* (3 vols), Vol. II, Munich 1978, 123.
17. Andreas-Salomé, 80.
18. Janz, II, 128.
19. W 10, 443.
20. Andreas-Salomé, 81 *passim.*
21. Ibid., 236.
22. W 11, 311.
23. Andreas-Salomé, 83.
24. Ibid., 84.
25. Ibid.
26. Ibid., 241.
27. Peters, 149.
28. W 15, 125.
29. W 15, 126.
30. Lou Andreas-Salomé, *In der Schule bei Freud*, edited by Ernst Pfeiffer, Zurich 1958, 155.
31. Peters, 129.
32. G, 425.
33. *Süddeutsche Monatshefte*, November 1931, 107.
34. Peters, 156.
35. B 6, 297.
36. W 4, 171.
37. B 6, 310.
38. B 6, 194.
39. B 6, 195.
40. B 6, 197.
41. B 6, 224.
42. Werner Ross, *Der ängstliche Adler, Friedrich Nietzsches Leben*, Stuttgart 1980, 641.
43. Peters, 179.
44. B 6, 199.
45. B 6, 222.
46. B 6, 217.
47. B 6, 251.
48. KGB III/2, 284.
49. B 6, 275.
50. B 6, 300.
51. B 6, 290.
52. Pfeiffer, 186.
53. B 6, 316.
54. Andreas-Salomé, 200.
55. Ursula Welsch and Michaela Wiemer, *Lou Andreas-Salomé*, Munich/Vienna 1988, 96.
56. Peters, 330.
57. Ibid., 339.
58. W 2, 576.
59. W 5, 327.
60. W 5, 51.
61. W 5, 291.
62. W 5, 38.
63. Sigmund Freud, *Briefe an Wilhelm Fließ*, Frankfurt 1985, 438.
64. Sigmund Freud, *Gesammelte Werke*, Frankfurt 1968 (18 vols), Vol. 10, 151.
65. Sigmund Freud, *Studienausgabe*, Frankfurt 1982 (11 vols), Vol. II, 292.
66. *Protokolle der Wiener Psychoanalytischen Vereinigung*, Frankfurt 1976–81 (4 vols), Vol. I, 338.
67. Ibid., 337.
68. B 6, 573.
69. Sigmund Freud – Arnold Zweig, *Briefwechsel*, edited by Ernst L. Freud, Frankfurt 1984, 89.
70. Freud, *Studienausgabe*, II, 409.
71. Sigmund Freud – C. G. Jung, *Briefwechsel*, Frankfurt 1974, 544.
72. Otto Rank, *Das Trauma der Geburt*, Frankfurt 1988, 150, 151, 184.
73. Paul Roazen, *Sigmund Freud und sein Kreis*, Bergisch–Gladbach 1976, 398.
74. Freud–Zweig, *Briefwechsel*, 35, 37.
75. Ibid., 85.

76. Ibid., 87, 89.
77. Ibid., 90.
78. Ibid., 96.
79. Freud, *Studienausgabe*, III, 343.
80. Ibid., 347.
81. W 5, 322.
82. *Protokolle der Wiener Psychoanalytischen Vereinigung*, II, 27.
83. Ibid., 28.
84. Ibid.
85. W 1, 67.
86. Freud, *Studienausgabe*, IX, 428.
87. Ibid., 438.
88. Ibid., 439.
89. Isadora Duncan, *My Life*, New York 1927, 141.
90. Ibid., 151–8.
91. B 6, 318.
92. W 6, 337.
93. B 6, 288.
94. B 6, 306.
95. B 6, 307.
96. B 6, 308, 309.
97. Werner Ross, *Der ängstliche Adler, Friedrich Nietzsches Leben*, Stuttgart 1980, 651.
98. B 2, 262.
99. B 5, 226.
100. Friedrich Nietzsche, *Kritische Gesamtausgabe*, edited by Giorgio Colli and Mazzino Montinari, *Werke*, Berlin 1967–77 (30 vols), Vol. VII, 4/2, 567.
101. W 3, 643/647.
102. Elisabeth Förster-Nietzsche, *Der einsame Nietzsche*, Leipzig 1925, 533.
103. G, 678.
104. Thomas de Quincey, *Confessions of an English Opium-Eater*, London 1822, 90.
105. Förster-Nietzsche, 532.
106. B 6, 568.
107. G, 510.
108. G, 525.
109. G, 526.
110. Ibid.
111. G, 492.
112. W 10, 29.
113. G, 494.
114. G, 569.
115. Anacleto Verrecchia, *Zarathustras Ende*, Vienna/Cologne/Graz 1986, 397.

12 *Zarathustra's Secret*

1. B 8, 461, 298.
2. B 8, 286.
3. W 6, 256.
4. W 6, 259/260.
5. W 6, 335/336.
6. W 6, 337.
7. W 6, 339.
8. W 14, 495.
9. W 6, 335.
10. W 6, 336.
11. B 6, 311.
12. B 6, 324.
13. G, 609.
14. W 6, 337.
15. W 6, 344.
16. W 10, 134.
17. W 6, 345.
18. B 6, 321.
19. B 6, 348.
20. B 6, 326.
21. B 6, 321.
22. B 6, 333.
23. B 6, 324.
24. B 6, 328.
25. B 6, 356.
26. KGB III/2, 360.
27. B 6, 496.
28. B 6, 363.
29. B 6, 525.
30. Thomas Mann, *Das essayistische Werk*, Frankfurt 1968 (8 vols), Vol. III, 27.
31. B 6, 444.
32. B 6, 99.
33. B 6, 109.
34. B 6, 111.
35. B 6, 112.
36. B 6, 122.
37. W 9, 494.
38. W 9, 496.
39. W 6, 404.
40. G, 101.
41. B 8, 566.
42. W 10, 340.
43. Anacleto Verrecchia, *Zarathustras Ende*, Vienna/Cologne/Graz 1986, 335.
44. *Psychoanalytische Traumforschung,*

edited by Günter Ammon, Hamburg 1974, 64.

45. W 10, 210.
46. W 6, 341.
47. W 10, 108.
48. W 10, 107.
49. W 3, 525.
50. W 10, 150.
51. W 9, 596.
52. W 10, 157.
53. W 11, 311.
54. W 3, 649.
55. Friedrich Hölderlin, *Sämtliche Werke und Briefe*, edited by Günter Mieth, Munich 1970 (4 vols), Vol. I, 726.
56. Ibid., 727.
57. HKG II, 2.
58. HKG II, 4.
59. W 4, 142.
60. W 10, 168.
61. Hölderlin, II, 565.
62. Ibid., I, 599.
63. Ibid., 602, 603, 604.
64. Ibid., 720.
65. Ibid., 696.
66. Ibid., 617.
67. Ibid., 629.
68. Ibid., 644.
69. Ibid., 632.
70. Ibid., 705, 725, 732.
71. W 3, 493, W 7, 462.
72. W 1, 806.
73. B 6, 366.
74. W 4, 75.
75. W 10, 349.
76. W 9, 519.
77. Curt Paul Janz, *Friedrich Nietzsche, Biographie* (3 vols), Vol. II, Munich 1978, 232.
78. Gustave Flaubert, *Die Versuchung des heiligen Antonius*, Frankfurt 1979, 124.
79. W 6, 34.
80. Cosima Wagner, *Die Tagebücher*, Munich 1977, Vol. III, 60.
81. W 11, 63.
82. W 5, 153.
83. W 11, 272.
84. W 12, 202/201.
85. W 4, 11.
86. W 9, 607.
87. W 9, 600/606.
88. Fabrizia Ramondino and Andreas F. Müller, *Neapel*, Zurich 1988, 217.
89. Janz, I, 744.
90. Marcel Reich-Ranicki, *Thomas Mann und die Seinen*, Frankfurt 1987, 24.
91. W 9, 574.
92. W 9, 577.
93. W 9, 580.
94. W 9, 590.
95. W 3, 467.
96. W 14, 253.
97. W 3, 480.
98. W 3, 481.
99. S III, 16.
100. W 3, 26/27/28.
101. W 3, 481.
102. W 3, 481.
103. W 14, 256.
104. W 1, 13.
105. W 3, 570.
106. W 9, 480/614.
107. *Süddeutsche Monatshefte*, November 1931, 78.
108. G, 484.
109. W 3, 570.
110. W 12, 79.
111. W 3, 570.
112. W 14, 271.
113. W 3, 636.
114. W 6, 337.
115. W 6, 338.
116. W 14, 758.

Further Reading

Nietzsche's main works are available in English translation published by
Penguin: *The Twilight of the Idols* and *The Anti-Christ* (1968); *Thus Spoke
Zarathustra* (1969); *Ecce Homo* (1979); *Beyond Good and Evil* (1990); *The
Birth of Tragedy from the Spirit of Music* (1993); *Human, All Too Human*
(1994).
A standard reference book is *The Cambridge Campanion to Nietzsche*, edited
by B. Magnus, Cambridge 1996.

BIOGRAPHICAL, LITERARY AND PHILOSOPHICAL STUDIES

Bernoulli, C. A., *Franz Overbeck und Friedrich Nietzsche, Eine Freundschaft*,
Jena 1908
Borchmeyer, D. and Salaquada, J., *Nietzsche und Wagner, Stationen einer
epochalen Begegnung*, Frankfurt 1994
Burgard, P. (ed.), *Nietzsche and the Feminine*, Charlottesville 1994
Conway, D. W., *Nietzsche and the Political*, London/New York 1997
Coplestone, F. J., *Friedrich Nietzsche: Philosopher of Culture*, London/New
York 1975
Hayman, R., *Nietzsche: A Critical Life*, London 1980
Heller, E., *The Importance of Nietzsche*, Chicago 1988
Hoffmann, D. F., *Zur Geschichte des Nietzsche-Archivs*, Berlin 1991
Hollingdale, R. J., *Nietzsche: The Man and his Philosophy*, Baton Rouge and
London 1965
Hollingdale, R. J., *Nietzsche*, London 1973
Janz, C. P., *Friedrich Nietzsche: Biographie*, 3 vols, Munich 1978–79

Jaspers, K., *Nietzsche: An Introduction to the Understanding of His Philosophical Activity*, Chicago 1965

Kaufmann, W., *Nietzsche*, Princeton 1950

Köhler, J., *Nietzsche and Wagner: A Lesson in Subjugation*, New Haven and London, 1998

——, *Nietzsches letzter Fraum*, Munich 2000

——, *Who was Friedrich Nietzsche?*, Inter Nationes, Bonn 2000

——, *Nietzsche, Biographische Passionen*, Munich 2000

Mann, Thomas, *Nietzsches Philosophie im Lichte unserer Erfahrung*, Berlin 1948

Ottmann, H. (ed.), *Nietzsche – Handbuch*, Stuttgart/Weimar 2000

Pasley, M. (ed.), *Nietzsche: Imagery and Thought*, London 1978

Peters, H. F., *Zarathustras Schwester, Fritz und Lieschen Nietzsche – ein deutsches Trauerspiel*, Munich 1983

Pfeiffer, E. (ed.), *Friedrich Nietzsche, Paul Rée und Lou Salomé, Die Dokumente ihrer Begegnung*, Frankfurt 1970

Ross, W., *Der ängstliche Adler: Friedrich Nietzsches Leben*, Stuttgart 1980

Stern, J. P., *A Study of Nietzsche*, Cambridge 1979

Thomas, R. H., *Nietzsche in German Politics and Society 1890–1918*, Manchester 1983

Verrecchia, A., *Zarathustras Ende, Die Katastrophe Nietzsches in Turin*, Vienna/Cologne/Graz 1986

Volz, P. D., *Nietzsche im Labyrinth seiner Krankheit*, Würzburg 1990

Index